Knowing Persons

Knowing Persons

A Study in Plato

LLOYD P. GERSON

OXFORD
UNIVERSITY PRESS

Great Clarendon Street, Oxford OX2 6DP

Oxford University Press is a department of the University of Oxford.
It furthers the University's objective of excellence in research, scholarship,
and education by publishing worldwide in

Oxford New York

Auckland Cape Town Dar es Salaam Hong Kong Karachi
Kuala Lumpur Madrid Melbourne Mexico City Nairobi
New Delhi Shanghai Taipei Toronto

With offices in

Argentina Austria Brazil Chile Czech Republic France Greece
Guatemala Hungaray Italy Japan Poland Portugal Singapore
South Korea Switzerland Thailand Turkey Ukraine Vietnam

Oxford is a registered trade mark of Oxford University Press
in the UK and in certain other countries

Published in the United States
by Oxford University Press Inc., New York

British Library Cataloguing in Publication Data

Data available

Library of Congress Cataloging in Publication Data

Data available

Typeset by John Waś, Oxford
Printed in Great Britain
on acid-free paper by
Biddles Ltd.,
King's Lynn, Norfolk

ISBN 0-19-925763-9   978-0-19-925763-8
ISBN 0-19-928867-4 (Pbk.)   978-0-19-928867-0 (Pbk.)

10 9 8 7 6 5 4 3 2 1

For Aslı

Acknowledgements

It is a pleasure for me to acknowledge the personal, professional, and institutional support I have received while working on this project.

A draft of the entire script was read by Christopher Gill, Asli Gocer, and Christopher Shields. I am deeply grateful for their good-natured engagement with my efforts to understand Plato and for their unstinting criticism. I know that each of them has saved me from many ghastly errors, though I am confident that each would insist that the final product reflects their inability to save me from many others. The penultimate draft was also read by two anonymous readers for Oxford University Press, whose comments have been extremely useful to me in improving the structure and presentation of this work. I would also like to acknowledge the assistance of my graduate student Lee Churchman, who not only read a complete draft of the book and made many helpful suggestions, but has also been a lively and able interlocutor. Nicholas Smith and Christopher Rowe allowed me to assail them with some exegetical flights of fancy and responded with due scepticism. I hope I have been able to offer a reasonable response to their forceful objections and questions. For a number of years Mark McPherran has organized the delightful Arizona Colloquium on Socrates and Plato at the University of Arizona. On several occasions I have been honoured to present papers at the Colloquium, and I have benefited enormously from the criticisms of the attentive audiences. Mark McPherran himself was a lively critic, as were Julia Annas, Charles Kahn, and Terence Penner. I regret that I cannot recall the names of all those who participated in the meetings and who shared their knowledge of Plato with me.

Section 1.1 of this book is in part based on 'Socrates' Absolutist Prohibition of Wrongdoing', which was originally delivered at the Arizona Colloquium and subsequently published in *Wisdom, Ignorance and Virtue:*

New Essays in Socratic Studies (1997); section 2.3 is in part based on my colloqium presentation 'Knowledge and Being in the Recollection Argument', subsequently published in *Recognition, Remembrance, and Reality* (1999). Both of these volumes were edited by Mark McPherran. I am grateful to Academic Printing and Publishing for permission to reprint material from these essays.

In the spring of 1998 the University of Toronto awarded me a Connaught Research Fellowship that released me from teaching duties and gave me an opportunity to complete a large portion of this book.

L.P.G.

May 2002

Contents

Introduction   1

1. Souls and Persons   14
   1.1. Paradox and Selfhood   15
   1.2. Socrates and Self-Knowledge   29
   1.3. *Protagoras* and the Power of Knowledge   40

2. Immortality and Persons in *Phaedo*   50
   2.1. The Structure of the Proof of the Immortality of the Soul   52
   2.2. The Cyclical Argument   63
   2.3. The Recollection Argument   65
   2.4. The Affinity Argument   79
   2.5. The Objections of Simmias and Cebes   88
   2.6. Socrates' Reply to Cebes and the Argument from Exclusion of
        Opposites   92

3. Divided Persons: *Republic* and *Phaedrus*   99
   3.1. Tripartition and Personhood   100
   3.2. Tripartition and Immortality in *Republic* Book 10   124
   3.3. *Phaedrus*   131

4. Knowledge and Belief in *Republic*   148
   4.1. Knowledge vs. Belief   148
   4.2. The Form of the Good   173
   4.3. The Divided Line and the Allegory of the Cave   180

5. *Theaetetus*: What is Knowledge?   194

    5.1. Interpreting *Theaetetus*   194

    5.2. Knowledge is Not Sense-Perception   200

    5.3. Knowledge is Not True Belief   214

    5.4. Knowledge is Not True Belief with an Account   226

6. Personhood in the Later Dialogues   239

    6.1. *Timaeus*   239

    6.2. *Philebus*   251

    6.3. *Laws*   265

Concluding Remarks   276

Bibliography   282

Index of Texts   292

Index of Modern Authors   302

General Index   305

Introduction

This is a book principally about Plato's account of persons. No doubt some readers will be immediately sceptical of the assertion that Plato has such an account to offer, especially if it is claimed, as I shall, that for Plato persons are different from human beings.

When we see a sign in an elevator saying that this device can hold eight persons, we encounter one ordinary use of the word 'person', in which persons are no different from human beings. Perhaps this use is even the dominant one. Nevertheless, it is not terribly unusual to encounter another use of the word, as in 'I am not the person I once was' or 'a foetus is a human being, though not a person', where it is clear that a contrast is being drawn between the use of 'person' and 'human being'. Leaving ordinary usage aside, contemporary philosophers have shown a lively and growing interest in the question whether 'human being', i.e. member of the species *homo sapiens*, and 'person' can or cannot be usefully distinguished.[1] Naturally, this question is closely bound up with such issues as personal identity, moral responsibility, and, most recently, a host of issues within cognitive science broadly conceived.

[1] See e.g. the collections by Peacocke and Gillett (1987); Gill (1990); and Cockburn (1991). The essays contained in Gill's volume are especially concerned with the question of whether or not there is a concept of person distinct from the concept of human being in antiquity. See also the monographs by Braine (1992); Gill (1996); Sprague (1999); and Baker (2000). Braine, though he identifies the person with the human being, has a view of the person deeply at odds with what can loosely be termed the 'scientific image'. Gill argues that there is a concept of person or self in antiquity but that it is very different from the Cartesian 'subjectivist-individualist conception'. Sprague argues for a Wittgensteinian/Rylean conception of person against what he terms 'mindism', the Cartesian view that a person is essentially a mind. Baker argues that persons are not identical with human beings but are constituted by human bodies.

In this book I shall argue that Plato does indeed wish to distinguish between human beings and persons. Since, however, he does not have a technical or even semi-technical term for 'person' as distinct from the ordinary words for a human being, such as ἄνθρωπος, it is not an entirely straightforward matter to show exactly how the distinction is operating in a given text. We can start by distinguishing body and soul. It is not completely misleading to say first of all that, for Plato, a person is a soul and a human being is a composite of soul and body.[2] Certainly, there are many passages in the dialogues in which the body is treated as a possession of a subject and that subject is identified, implicitly or explicitly, with a soul. There are several reasons, however, why the matter is actually more complex than this. First, for Plato a 'body' (σῶμα) is different from a 'corpse' (νεκρός). A human body belongs to a live subject, a subject of, among other things, states that are naturally thought of as bodily states. Is this subject the soul or the composite soul plus body? If it is the latter, any distinction between persons and human beings will perhaps seem entirely nugatory. What then would be interesting about us is what distinguishes us from other biological kinds, not what distinguishes us as persons from the biological kind 'human being'. Plato, by contrast, divides subjecthood between body and embodied person. Whereas the body is the subject of, say, a state of depletion, the embodied soul or person is the subject of hunger. Plato, therefore, does not believe (or at least eventually came not to believe) that the subject of such bodily states as sensations, appetites, and emotions is the human being. Rather, he believed that the subject of these states is the embodied soul or person. So, the crude distinction between body and soul according to which the person is identified with soul has at least to be refined to account for the fact that persons or souls can be the subject of some bodily states.[3]

Second, Plato believed (or, again, came to believe) that we survive the death of the human being with whom we are ordinarily identified. That fact in itself makes it pretty clear that for Plato persons or at any rate 'we'

---

[2] For example, at *Phaedrus* 246 C 5–6 it is said that the composite of soul and body is named 'the whole living being' (ζῷον τὸ σύμπαν) or the human being (cf. 249 B 5). It is this composite that is called 'mortal'. If it turns out that *we* are *immortal*, the straightforward inference is that we are not human beings.

[3] Being the subject of a bodily state need only imply minimally that reference to the body or its parts is ineliminable from a description of the state. This would be true, for example, if the body were *instrumentally* necessary for the state to occur.

are not human beings.[4] But given the first point, it is deeply obscure what it would mean to hold that the person who is the subject of bodily states 'here below' is identical with the person who survives death and who may or may not have a memory of bodily existence. So, the initial crude distinction must be refined further to account for personal identity across embodied and disembodied states.

Untangling what Plato says around the above two points is a central task of this book. Plato's account of persons, however, is not usefully detachable from his metaphysics and from his epistemology. Human beings or, as we might say, embodied persons are situated within a hierarchical metaphysics by Plato. We, in so far as we are the subjects of bodily states, belong to the sensible world, which is in some way an image or copy of the really real intelligible world. And we, in so far as we are separable from our bodies, belong in some way to that really real world. A simple analogy suggests itself: sensible world : intelligible world :: embodied person : disembodied person. But, of course, this analogy limps, because the fourth term is apparently not something that exists so long as the third term does. Nevertheless, we shall discover that there are good textual grounds for insisting that Plato distinguishes between the endowment of personhood and the achievement of personhood and that our endowment—the persons we are here below— does stand to an ideal of achievement roughly as images stand to their eternal exemplars. If this is so, much of what Plato says about persons can be illuminated by bringing the metaphysics to bear on the psychology.

Plato's basic epistemology is, appropriately enough, a reflection of his hierarchical metaphysics. Indeed, we can justifiably treat his account of cognitional states of which sensibles are the objects as images of cognitional states of which intelligibles are the objects. Stated otherwise and roughly, embodied cognition images disembodied cognition. This is so because for

---

[4] One could say, of course, as does Thomas Aquinas, for instance, that our soul does survive our death but that the soul is not the person but rather some part or aspect thereof. See e.g. *Summa theologiae*, qu. 75, art. 4. Interestingly, there are no philosophical arguments in the *Summa* for this view. Aquinas' arguments for identifying person with human being are basically Aristotelian arguments for hylomorphism. But Aristotle, like Aquinas, has a good deal of difficulty in maintaining consistently the view that the human being and not the soul is the subject of all the states that we typically claim to experience. On the Thomistic conception of soul in comparison with the Platonic see Pegis (1934), 121–87.

Plato an ideal person, that which we strive to be, is a subject of an ideal cognitional state, namely, knowledge (ἐπιστήμη). The transformation or peregrination of an embodied person into an ideal person is essentially an intellectual passage. I am especially intent upon showing that for Plato personal development, as we might put it, is intellectual development, specifically, transformation into a knower. In claiming this, I mean to say something more than the commonplace that philosophical knowledge is supposed to make one 'a better person'. This transformation is situated within the framework of a hierarchical metaphysics.

For Plato, embodied persons are the only sorts of images that can reflexively recognize their own relatively inferior states as images and strive to transform themselves into their own ideal. The view of personhood which I attribute to Plato is remarkable in many respects. But as I hope to show, it is for all that thoroughly Platonic. It coheres in a satisfying manner with his metaphysics and epistemology. Such an interpretation goes against the grain. Many of those who write on Plato's psychology and who in some way take up the issue of personhood treat the psychology as autonomous. Perhaps this happens less than in the case of ethics, where, to judge from much of what is written, Plato the moral philosopher never had the slightest acquaintance with Plato the metaphysician or Plato the epistemologist. Still, scholarship on Plato's psychology is largely written in splendid isolation from Plato's revisionist views about being and knowledge. One may, I suppose, have a certain sympathy for this approach, especially if one is impressed by the shrewd insights about human motivation contained in the former and largely embarrassed by the eccentricities of the latter. I am far from maintaining that a philosopher whose general philosophical orientation is an unholy mess is incapable of expressing valuable, even brilliant, insights about this or that. Nor am I going to maintain that whatever good there is in Plato's account of personhood must be purchased at the cost of swallowing the 'whole package' of Platonism. I shall argue, however, that if we want to understand that account fully and adequately, we need to situate it within a wider framework.

For my purpose of using Plato's epistemology to illuminate his psychology, I want to make a sharp distinction between knowledge or cognitional states in general, on the one hand, and the methodology for acquiring knowledge, on the other. In this book I am principally concerned with the former and not the latter. I shall be concerned with methodology—dialectic, hypothesis, collection, and division—only in so far as they reflect on the psychology. Similarly, I believe we need to distinguish knowledge from conditions or signs of the presence of knowledge, such as the ability to give an account (λόγος) of what one knows. I suspect that a lot of unnecessary confusion has been engendered by scholars supposing that knowledge just is the ability to give an account of what it is one knows. It seems rather obvious, however, that knowledge cannot just *be* the ability to give an account of one's knowledge. And as important as the issue of λόγος is in Plato's philosophy, I do think that an interpretation of what Plato takes knowledge to be is logically prior. In any case, I shall not directly focus on those texts in which Plato speaks directly about how knowledge is acquired or displayed or communicated.

In writing about Plato's account of personhood, I am aware that I may be thought to be imputing to him anachronistically a modern concept. That Plato's account of personhood differs in many significant ways from modern accounts goes without saying. I only wish to insist that he *does* have an account of personhood and that it lies at the heart of many of his distinctive psychological and moral and epistemological doctrines. I ask the reader not to anticipate the development of my argument and assume that I am attributing views to Plato that I in fact do not. Arguing that for Plato persons are not human beings leaves almost a blank canvas to be filled in by a picture of what persons are. That is what I propose to do.

There is a cluster of issues around the modern concept of person. These include personal identity, autonomy or freedom, moral responsibility, the 'first-person perspective', and self-consciousness. Not surprisingly, Plato's account of personhood is not easily represented in these terms. At least part of the reason for this is that the manner of raising these issues in the modern setting does not typically presume a distinction between person and human being. Rather, it presumes a distinction between human being/ person and something else, say, non-human animals or machines or just 'things'. Nevertheless, Plato addresses most of these issues, albeit usually in an oblique fashion.[5]

---

[5] See Gill (1991), who argues that what he calls 'the post-Cartesian' concept of a person has two characteristic features: (1) persons have a special kind of self-consciousness and (2) persons have a 'first-person stance'. Although Gill does not consider Plato and the Platonic

In this book I have generally been able to sidestep the question of whether or not Plato's thought developed in any way.[6] With two important exceptions, in the matters with which I am dealing I have found a consistency in Plato's doctrines throughout the dialogues. So, I shall not engage anti-developmentalists generally apart from here in this introduction. The two exceptions concern the partitioning and immortality of the soul. I suppose that Plato probably did not have arguments for the immortality of the soul or, what amounts to the same thing, arguments that persons survive their own death when writing his earliest dialogues. The earliest ethical argument advanced by Plato does not assume that persons survive their own death. It does not deny it either. But that argument is quite independent. I shall claim, however, that by the time of the writing of *Phaedo*, Plato did come to believe that he could offer plausible arguments for the immortality of the soul which are at the same time arguments for the continued existence of persons and that this fact does reflect importantly on the psychology as well as on the ethics. Second, in *Republic* Plato offers a famous argument for the tripartitioning of the soul. It is on the basis of this argument that he claims, among other things, that he can account for the phenomenon of incontinence or weakness of the will or ἀκρασία. But Plato in *Protagoras* *denied* that ἀκρασία could exist, and he did so on the basis of an account of the soul or person that presumes psychic integrity or undividedness.

I am rather more inclined to believe that tripartitioning represents a genuine development in Plato's thinking than does immortality. It is possible that Socrates' profession of agnosticism about immortality in *Apology*, for instance, serves a dramatic purpose and does not represent Plato's own view at that time. And it is possible that one of the reasons the 'Laws' give to Socrates for staying in prison in *Crito*, namely, that he will probably undergo punishment in the afterworld if he violates the law, is based on a belief Plato shared. I would insist, however, that if Plato ever did believe that persons do not survive their physical death, then his account of embodied personhood would be far less cogent or sustainable. If we do not have a

tradition in his account, he does conclude that 'there is probably *not* a (post-Cartesian) concept of person in Greek philosophy' (193). I shall be arguing at some length that Gill's conclusion is at any rate mistaken in regard to Plato, and by implication, Platonists.

[6] See e.g. Nails (1995); Kahn (1996), esp. ch. 2; Cooper (1997), introduction; Annas (1999), ch. 1; and Press (2000), for various anti-developmentalist arguments.

personal identity when separated from our bodies, it is difficult, though of course not impossible, to see the grounds for holding that non-bodily entities are the subjects of bodily states. Accordingly, it would be very difficult to see the grounds for maintaining that one ought to care for the soul more than for the body. I mean that if the soul is not me but a part of me or a property of me, then whether I care for that part or property more or less than any other is not a matter that is going to be decisively determined by anyone else. If, as Plato regularly insists, one *ought* to care for the soul more than for the body because the soul identifies oneself and the body is only a possession, such a claim rests, perhaps necessarily, on the premiss that my identity is non-bodily. And that claim can only be sustained in a non-question-begging manner, or so Plato thought, if one can show that one survives bodily death. In short, I think Francis Cornford was absolutely correct in his observation that the immortality of the soul and the theory of Forms are the two pillars of Platonism.[7]

It is certainly possible to maintain a distinction between persons and human beings without implying personal survival of bodily death.[8] There is actually a wide variety of such views: in general, many of them seek to distinguish mental states from bodily states while claiming that the subjects of the former are persons and the subjects of the latter are human beings. So, roughly, for example, the person feels the pain but the human being is in a certain neurophysiological state. Naturally, one wants to know what 'person' adds to the claim. Why not simply say, according to some version of a 'dual-aspect theory', that human beings are the sorts of things that can be the subjects of both mental and bodily states? In order to maintain the position that 'person' is not just a synonym for 'human being' or just one way of referring to human beings under certain stipulated conditions, it

[7] I shall have very little to say about Plato's views on reincarnation except to point out the obvious, namely, that a whole range of possibilities open up for Plato with the establishment of the separation of person from human being. These include reincarnation of persons as a means of punishment and reincarnation of persons as living creatures other than human beings. These and related issues are posterior to the ones dealt with in this book.

[8] Baker (2000), for example, argues for a position she calls 'the constitution view of the person', according to which a human person is constituted by a certain type of organic body. This position is in many respects a version of the hylomorphism sometimes attributed to Aristotle and explained as an alternative to Plato's dualism.

would seem that one would have to argue that persons—not their states—are a type of entity different from the natural kind human being. One way of doing this would be to argue that persons belong to another natural kind different from but organically related to human beings. Another way would be to show that persons are simply non-bodily entities. Given that Plato is rather partial to the bipolarity of material/immaterial or bodily/non-bodily, it is surprising and impressive that he does not take it for granted that persons belong in the immaterial or non-bodily camp. It is true that he maintains that the soul is immortal in part because it is non-bodily. But it is false that he maintains that the embodied person is unqualifiedly identical with this non-bodily entity. To put it simply, Plato is not a Cartesian dualist. And it is for this reason that he can speak about *achieving* immortality, something that hardly makes sense if one is already that non-bodily immortal entity. In fact, it will turn out that Plato quite clearly situates his view of embodied persons somewhere between the view that they are just another natural kind and the view that they are unqualifiedly non-bodily entities.

Other scholars have understood Plato's non-Cartesian dualism differently. For example, Christopher Gill distinguishes between what he calls 'the subjective-individualist' conception of person and the 'objective-participant' conception of person.[9] He argues that the former is, roughly, a Cartesian/post-Cartesian or Kantian concept and that the latter better reflects the concept of a person in Greek thought generally. The principal features of the 'subjective-individualist' conception of a person are: (1) self-consciousness of oneself as a unified locus of thought and will; (2) ethical autonomy; (3) the capacity for disinterested moral reasoning; (4) a capacity for establishing one's ethical stance or one's own authentic selfhood; (5) a sense of personal identity. The principal features of the 'objective-participant' conception are, by contrast: (1) rational action, but not necessarily with conscious awareness that it is so; (2) interpersonal or communal interaction; (3) ethical behaviour that is capable of being formed by interpersonal or communal interaction and reflective debate; (4) capacity for rational action based upon the extent to which such interaction occurs; (5) identification of oneself as situated among other kinds of being, including animals and gods.

---

[9] See Gill (1996), 6–13; also 260–87, where Gill applies his 'objective-participant' account to Plato's *Republic* in contrast to an account by Terence Irwin, that Gill characterizes as 'subjective-individualist'.

Gill's contrast raises many interesting issues. But I do not find that it matches my own contrast between what I understand to be the difference between Platonic and Cartesian dualism. For one thing, points (1), (2), (3), and (4) of the 'subjective-individualist' conception are, as I shall argue, authentically Platonic. And though I believe that all the points in his characterization of the 'objective-participant' conception are Platonic as well, I do not believe that they appropriately characterize the *ideal* person for Plato. The fundamental contrast for Plato is between the ideal disembodied person or self we strive to become and its embodied image. The latter exhibits features of both Gill's 'subjective-individualist' and 'objective-participant' conceptions precisely because it is that image. Indeed, the reason why point (5) of the 'subjective-individualist' conception—personal identity—is not unambiguously a part of the Platonic conception is that it is the identity of ideal and image, not that of various diachronic images, that is primary. And since the ideal is a subject of universal knowledge, stripped entirely of 'personality', personal identity in, say, the Lockean sense is, as Gill rightly holds, inappropriately counted part of Plato's conception.

Locke, in chapter 27 of his *Essay concerning Human Understanding*, famously held that a person is 'a thinking intelligent being, that has reason and reflection, and can consider itself as itself, the same thinking thing, in different times and places; which it does only by that consciousness which is inseparable from thinking, and, it seems to me, essential to it: it being impossible for any one to perceive without perceiving that he does perceive'. Locke here and in the remainder of his discussion ties personal identity to memory.[10] Gill is, I think, right to exclude personal identity thus understood from his account of the Greek conception of a person.[11] One of

---

[10] 'For, since consciousness always accompanies thinking, and it is that which makes every one to be what he calls self, and thereby distinguishes himself from all other thinking things: in this alone consists personal identity, i.e., the sameness of a rational being; and as far as this consciousness can be extended backwards to any past action or thought, so far reaches the identity of that person; it is the same self now as it was then; and it is by the same self with this present one that now reflects on it, that that action was done.' Both quotations are from § 9 of chapter 27 of the second edition of Locke's *Essay* (1694). Leaving aside memory, Locke's view of the person as a locus of self-conscious awareness is, as we shall see, very much in line with Plato's.

[11] Most interestingly, Plotinus in his *Enneads* (4. 3. 31–2) considers at some length the question of whether memory is necessary for personal identity of the self that is at one time embodied and then disembodied. His rather nuanced and qualified conclusion is

my main contentions is that Plato's account of personhood or the self has to be understood from the 'top down', i.e. within the context of his hierarchical metaphysics. Therefore, Gill's contrast is not so much mistaken as it is only obliquely related to the primary contrast. All of the features of the 'objective-participant' conception do indeed belong, as Gill in fact implicitly recognizes, to the developmental stages of the embodied person towards his or her ideal. That ideal has many features of the 'subjective-individualist' conception, though not exactly as Descartes or Locke or Kant would have it. The embodied person imperfectly or derivatively represents the ideal. Just as the sensible world, midway between the really real and nothing, will appear in contrary ways, so the embodied person will, to use Gill's contrast, manifest both subjective-individualist and objective-participant features.

Treating memory as a criterion of personal identity is perhaps the underlying reason for the modern tendency to include idiosyncratic content in the notion of subjectivity. Gill is, I suspect, also right to be sceptical about the antiquity of a concept of subjectivity, but only in so far as that is thought to contain idiosyncratic content. Plato's notion, as I shall try to show, is more subtle because though idiosyncratic subjective content does appear in his treatment of embodied subjectivity, it does not belong in the disembodied ideal. But then we must naturally ask in what sense there is truly identity between the embodied person and that person's disembodied ideal state. Once again, Plato's answer is to be found in his account of knowledge as constitutive of that ideal state.

The first chapter of this book develops the account of persons in the early dialogues underlying what can be most simply termed 'the Socratic paradoxes'. Just as I do not make any strong assumptions about development, so I do not make strong assumptions about the distinction between Socratic and Platonic philosophy. The only assumption that I do make that is relevant to my argument in this chapter is that Plato himself adopted these paradoxes as representing genuine insights into reality, even if they were also held to be true by Socrates. I would even be prepared to admit that Socrates as well as Plato held more or less to the account of persons

---

that in the ideal disembodied state one does have memory of embodied experiences. In this matter, as in all others, Plotinus wishes to be true to Plato, though his struggle with the question of memory as a necessary condition for personal identity is, I suppose, evidence of his philosophical honesty.

underlying them. The only view I am committed to opposing here is that according to which Plato did not endorse the truth of the paradoxes. I reject, but I do not in this book argue against, those who attribute these paradoxes to Socrates and not Plato, or those who refuse to attribute them to anyone in particular.

The second chapter is devoted to *Phaedo*. I try to explicate the account of the person that is developed there along with the proofs for the immortality of the soul. In this dialogue, along with the claim for the immortality of the soul is to be found the separation of Forms and the consequent demotion of the reality of the sensible world. It is within this context that the relation between embodied and disembodied persons is to be properly situated. This relation is to be understood as one between endowed and achieved personhood or selfhood. As I show, for Plato the ideal person is a knower, the subject of the highest form of cognition. That this form of cognition is apparently attributable only to disembodied persons is of the utmost importance. For from this it follows that the achievement of any embodied person is bound to fall short of the ideal.

The third chapter takes up the argument for the tripartition of the soul in *Republic* and the consequent deepening of the account of personhood. An embodied tripartite soul is a disunited person or self. Selfhood for the embodied person is chronically episodic and plastic. Self-transformation can now be articulated in terms of the unifying of the person into one part, the rational faculty. Again, with tripartitioning Plato can deal more perspicuously with the relation of person to human being and body. The embodied person is an entity capable of self-reflexively identifying itself as the subject of one or another of its psychic capacities. The *successful* embodied person strives for and ultimately achieves a permanent identification with a subject of rational activity.

The next two chapters are devoted to the accounts of knowledge in *Republic* and *Theaetetus*. Here I aim to show (1) that, contrary to some recent commentators, *Theaetetus* does not alter the account of knowledge in *Republic*—indeed, it is intended to support that account with a *reductio ad absurdum* argument; and (2) that Plato's account of knowledge in both dialogues reflects crucially on his account of personhood. In fact, since the person is essentially and ideally a knower, the concepts of knowledge and person are inseparable. In addition, as I try to show, modes of cognition other than 'knowledge' (ἐπιστήμη) itself are understood by Plato to be images of their paradigm with respect to both content and state. Thus, both the contents of 'belief' (δόξα) and belief states themselves are images of their ideals. The intimate connection between belief states and their contents reflects in a diminished way the intimate connection between the state of knowing and *its* objects. The daily bread of embodied persons is belief. Their identity is in part constituted by their beliefs. Thus, transformation of belief brings about self-transformation.

The last chapter tries to show that in *Timaeus, Philebus,* and *Laws* all the essentials of the account hitherto developed are maintained. The first-mentioned dialogue offers a cosmology in which persons are clearly situated. In the section on *Philebus* I offer an interpretation of the defeat of hedonism that shows persons to be ideally knowers. The defender of hedonism is undone by the presuppositions of his own defence. Self-transformation is preceded by self-recognition. *Philebus* offers an account of ideal embodied life, but does not abandon Plato's previous account of ideal disembodied life. In the section on *Laws* I am especially concerned to show that Plato did not abandon tripartitioning of the soul, as some have maintained. Rather, in all essentials the account of personhood remains the same.

This book aims at elucidating a set of themes in Plato rather than at a comprehensive interpretation of any of the dialogues. I have perhaps come closest to offering such an interpretation of *Phaedo* and *Theaetetus,* but even in these cases I am aware of having left out of account many issues. Naturally, I hope to have avoided misinterpretations owing to a failure to have considered arguments in the larger context of the dialogues within which they are found. That remains for others to judge. I am, however, operating on the assumption that it is after all possible—while exercising due diligence and respecting Plato the literary artist—to extract arguments from the dialogues and even to arrive at reasonably plausible conclusions regarding the philosophical positions constituted by these arguments. I think the majority of those writing on Plato share this assumption, though I know that many do not. To the latter, I would only say that the Plato who emerges from this book is not in my opinion at odds with the elusive, paradoxical, ironic artist they identify as the author of the dialogues.

I have not hesitated to cite many excellent existing translations of Plato. When no name of a translator is noted, the reader may assume that the translation is my own. I have with regret maintained a consistent gender bias in the use of pronouns, principally in order to avoid mistranslating Plato and importing confusion into the necessarily complicated account of his arguments.

CHAPTER I

Souls and Persons

In this chapter I am going to explore the roots of the Platonic notion of the person or self. I shall use the terms 'person' and 'self' interchangeably and I shall argue that persons or selves are treated by Plato as distinct from the natural kind human being. In Plato's ordinary use of the Greek language the word ἄνθρωπος refers to an individual member of this natural kind. As we shall see, there are various circumlocutions used by Plato to refer to persons or selves. Sometimes the claim that Plato is speaking about a person and not a human being is an inference from an argument. Clearly, such inferences need to be carefully scrutinized. We must acknowledge the possibility that the inference is ours and not Plato's.

When in this book generally I speak of Socrates, I mean to refer to the thought of the author of the dialogues in so far as this can be known. I do not think we can have any significant knowledge about the thought of the historical Socrates. Even if we had such knowledge, I would not expect to find it in the dialogues, for there what we encounter is Plato's literary construct. By the 'early dialogues' I mean: *Apology, Crito, Euthyphro, Ion, Hippias Minor, Laches, Lysis, Charmides, Theages,* and *Alcibiades I.*[1] In these dialogues there is a nascent concept of the person or self. That concept is presupposed in a number of ethical arguments. And, as we shall see presently, it is connected to a number of considerations regarding cognition generally and knowledge in particular. This is evident in the idea of self-

---

[1] I take no strong position on the authenticity of these last two works. I tend to accept their authenticity, but nothing I shall say in this chapter depends on that.

knowledge, although, as we shall see, it is far from clear that self-knowledge is equivalent to knowledge of a self.

1.1 Paradox and Selfhood

The so-called 'Socratic paradoxes' are paradoxical because they fly in the face of conventional beliefs regarding our interests.[2] For example, the paradoxical claim that 'it is better to suffer than to do evil' directly confronts the ordinary and deeply held belief that doing evil does not harm one at all whereas suffering evil or having evil done to one harms one almost by definition. The paradox that 'no one does wrong willingly' seems to reject the common belief that doing wrong is at least sometimes in one's interest and that people normally act willingly in their own interest. The paradox that 'a worse man cannot harm a better man' just sounds like philosophical madness. Surely, this happens all the time. Similarly for the claim that 'the greatest harm for a wrongdoer is to go unpunished'. The dispute between a Socrates who makes such wild assertions and a typical Athenian gentleman is not, for example, over whether suffering evil—say, receiving an unjust blow—is more painful than delivering one. *Of course* it is. Rather, the underlying dispute is over whether one's interests are always better served by doing that which produces on balance less pain. If my only choice is between inflicting pain unjustly and having pain unjustly inflicted on me—between being the hammer or the nail—could it ever be in my interest to choose the latter? Socrates thinks not just that it is sometimes in my interest to choose the latter but that it is always and necessarily so. Clearly, there is a problem here concerning what exactly constitutes our interests.

If we state the matter of the dispute in this way, one might reasonably respond that different people have different interests and Socrates is hardly in a position to privilege his own. Perhaps it is in *his* interest as he conceives it to suffer rather than to do evil because, say, the shame he would feel in doing the latter would trouble him more than the pain he would experience

---

[2] There is no canonical list of the paradoxes—indeed, no universal agreement on what a 'Socratic paradox' is. The claims I am focusing on reveal most effectively the presumptions about personhood that I wish to explore. See especially M. J. O'Brien (1967), ch. 1, and Santas (1979), ch. 6, for useful introductions to the paradoxes.

in suffering the former. Someone else, however, perhaps unencumbered by shame, may conceive his own interest differently.[3] The point is seemingly a powerful one. It presumes that each of us is authoritative in determining his or her own interests: that if, for instance, I hold that my interest is served better by doing evil than suffering it, then no one can legitimately gainsay my claim. Interests are like matters of taste: each person is their ultimate arbiter. It is, nevertheless, fairly obvious that we are not always infallible assessors of our own interests. It is even fair to assume that at times someone else might actually make a better judgement regarding another's interests than that person. But Socrates' position would be uninteresting and unpersuasive if he were merely claiming that the one who prefers to do rather than to suffer evil might some day reassess his priorities and decide that, on balance, yes, it is better for him to suffer than to do evil. This simply cannot be Socrates' position because he holds that even if you go to your death believing that it is better to do than to suffer evil, you are tragically wrong about your own interests. That is, an evildoer has not served his own interests, whatever he may think, right up to the end of his life.

Why is Socrates convinced that people habitually and perversely miscon-strue their own interests? The short answer is that apparently he believes that our interests are primarily or even exclusively psychical interests. He believes that a person, the subject of interests, is not a human being but rather a soul, an entity distinct from that human being. If Socrates were simply maintaining that psychical interests are more important than bodily interests, it would be open to anyone to object that they may be more important to *him* but that does not make them necessarily more important to anyone else. In that case, he would be like someone who argues that you ought to like ballet more than football because *he* does. No, Socrates must be presuming that everyone's interests are exclusively or especially psychical because a soul is what a person is. If a person is a soul, then it would seem to follow that what is other than the soul, in particular, one's body, is something like a possession and that the composite of soul and body is the composite that is oneself plus a possession. Then the argument goes: if you care for yourself more than for your possessions, you ought to

---

[3] This is the implication of the objection in *Gorgias* that Callicles makes to Socrates' refutation of Polus' stubborn assertion that doing evil is better than having evil done to you. See 482 C 4–483 C 6.

care for your soul above all else. Since most people evidently have a hard
time distinguishing themselves from one of their possessions, their bodies,
they mistakenly believe that their interests are the interests of bodies. When
someone says, for example, that it is in his interest to avoid pain whatever
the cost to his soul, he is assuming that he is a body, or a living body, not
a soul. At least, he is assuming that bodily interests, as we may call them,
are closer to *his* interests than are psychical interests. He would typically
express this by saying that looking after his body is more in his interests
than looking after his soul.

A moment's reflection, though, shows the puzzling nature of the view
that the person is the soul and the body is a possession. If this is the case,
then surely the body is a strange sort of possession.[4] It is especially odd to
speak of one's interests over against those of one's body as if the body were
a *mere* possession. This is so because 'body' is, too, ambiguous. Evidently,
the body includes its states—bodily states—but these are in part states the
subject of which is a person. My pleasures and pains, for example, are states
of me, unlike ordinary possessions which straightforwardly belong to me
but are in no sense me. Granting these points, Socrates would seem to
risk a reversion to the previous objection, namely, that *he* might prefer one
sort of state whereas other people prefer other sorts. In other words, his
interlocutors do not have to base their rejection of the 'paradoxes' on the
absurd notion that it makes any sense at all to choose the interest of an
ordinary possession over the interest of oneself. Rather, they can claim, for
example, that they prefer to be in whatever state one is in when one does
evil to whatever state one is in when suffering evil, all things considered.
And this would mean that again, the admonition that it is better to suffer
than to do evil is nothing more than an expression of Socrates' personal
preference.

At this point, one might object that if Socrates can show that care for
the soul is, from a disinterested perspective, more desirable than care for
the body (or even any other lesser possession), he has shown all he needs
to show. His success or lack of success in convincing his interlocutors that

---

[4] John Locke, in *The Second Treatise on Government*, ch. 5, § 27, asserts that 'every man
has a property in his own person', meaning 'his own body'. But this is, of course, not
equivalent to a claim that the person is a soul. For Locke, unlike Plato, the body is not
exclusively a possession.

they ought to do what is in fact best for themselves is, as it were, an extra-philosophical matter.[5] There is much to be said for this objection. One might hold generally that in this regard Plato is like Aristotle, who, in his *Nicomachean Ethics*, offers a scientific analysis of happiness. Such an analysis prescinds entirely from the question of whether people think they are happy when in fact they are not and whether people can be persuaded to pursue genuine happiness. Aristotle, as a scientist, just tells us what happiness really is, analogous to a doctor who just tells us when we are ill, whatever we might choose to believe.

I do not think that, finally, this will do. Plato's *Apology* illuminates the underlying problem particularly well. Socrates proclaims, 'For I go around doing nothing but persuading both young and old among you not to care for your body or your wealth in preference to or as strongly as for the best possible state of your soul' (30 A 7–B 2).[6] This text and others like it are interesting because they are so obviously question-begging. Why, we may ask, should anyone be persuaded to alter their interests, say, to put their soul before their body? The question is an instance of a general question, 'why should anyone prefer one thing to another?' If the question is about alternative means to an end, it is quite a good question. At least, one might claim that, from a disinterested perspective, it is possible to show why one thing is more likely to achieve an end than another. But if the question is about ends themselves, say, the state of one's body and the state of one's soul, then it is far from obvious that one can provide a cogent argument (as opposed to mere affirmation) that the latter should be preferred to the former. Why, after all, *should* one prefer ballet to football? No wonder that Socrates' benighted interlocutors will not bear being told what they ought to do on the assumption that they are something other than what they manifestly think they are.

The concept of 'interests' is ambiguous in a way that, say, the concept of 'health' typically is not. There is nothing even faintly paradoxical in claiming that someone is unhealthy though he believes otherwise. Sometimes 'interests' is used in a similar way, such that we can say fairly confidently that one is acting against one's own interests, despite having a belief to the contrary. But here is where the ambiguity arises. My interests seem to

<hr/>

[5] I owe this objection to Nicholas Smith.
[6] Cf. 29 E 7–D 3; *Crito* 47 C 1–48 A 4; *Gorg.* 477 A 5–E 6, 511 C 9–512 B 2.

include an ineluctable subjective element. That is why the very idea of a 'disinterested perspective' on my interests is dubious. It would certainly be odd for me to hold that I have no interest in my own health, though it is not absurd or self-contradictory. So, though I could be unhealthy when I think I am not, it is not the case necessarily that being unhealthy is counter to my interests. Accordingly, when Socrates holds that it is never in one's interests to be an evildoer or unjust person, he is trading on an ambiguity. In one sense, his claim depends on his confidence that what is in a person's interests can be determined independently of what that person thinks. But in so far as that person's acknowledgement that something is in his interests is essential to it being so, his claim is in fact rather hollow.

If the exhortation to prefer care of the soul to care of the body is, however, an exhortation to prefer care of oneself to care of one's possessions, then the argumentative possibilities only seem more promising so long as we do not fix our attention on the kind of possession the body is. Assume it is true at least that all parties can agree that possessions without possessors make no sense. Let us suppose, in other words, that the concepts of 'possessor' and 'possession' are analytically connected. So, if preferring one's possessions over oneself means preferring one's possessions to the *loss* of oneself, it is easy to see that this makes no sense because there can be no possessions without possessors. Nevertheless, if, for instance, pleasure can be legitimately construed as an interest *I* have and not the interest of my possession, then we are back to the problem of why one should prefer Socrates' ordering of *his* interests to one's own.

If the person or self is just a soul without any bodily states whatsoever, the Socratic paradoxes can be provided with stronger arguments. Unfortunately, the fact that bodily states seem to be states of the person and only in a weird sense states of a possession undercuts these arguments for the reason given above. The problem is evident if one considers, for example, Socrates' absolutist prohibition of wrongdoing in *Crito*: 'one ought then never to do wrong [οὐδαμῶς ἄρα δεῖ ἀδικεῖν]' (49 A 6–7).[7] This prohibition, which I have termed 'absolutist' since it allows no qualification, sums up in a way Socrates' philosophy. It is a prohibition that has not received much perspicuous defence. Gregory Vlastos's work in this area is instructive. He

---

[7] Cf. *Ap.* 29 B 6–7; *Gorg.* 469 B 12, 508 C, etc., and see Gerson (1997b) on this absolutist argument.

argues that the absolutist prohibition rests upon a principle he calls 'the sovereignty of virtue'.[8] The closest Vlastos comes to a definite expression of this principle is in his later work *Socrates, Ironist and Moral Philosopher*.[9] Vlastos there explains, 'Virtue being the sovereign good in our domain of value, its claim upon us is always final.' I think it is plain that this is not so much a defence of moral absolutism as an expression of it. Accordingly, the mere assertion of the sovereignty of virtue or of moral absolutism does not suffice as the basis for the paradoxes. Granted that the soul is harmed more than the body by doing injustice, why should one be concerned about this if one is not already? One might reasonably insist that, say, harming one's own soul is much like harming one's own reputation, something that, on balance, is at least bearable considering other gains.

In a passage shortly before the statement of the absolutist position, Socrates asks, 'And is life worth living for us with that part of us corrupted [μετ' ἐκείνου ἄρ' ἡμῖν βιωτὸν διεφθαρμένου] that unjust action harms and just action benefits? Or do we think that part of what is ours, whatever it is [ὅτι ποτ' ἐστι τῶν ἡμετέρων], that is concerned with justice and injustice is inferior to the body?' 'Not at all,' replies Crito. 'Is it more valuable [τιμιώτερον]?' 'Much more' (47 E 6–48 A 1).[10] Despite the studied avoidance of the use of the word ψυχή here, there is little doubt that 'the part of what is ours' refers to the soul.[11] The claim that the soul is more valuable than the body, construed as the superiority of the interests of the soul to those of the body, gets us no further, at least so long as we can variously attach importance to psychical or bodily interests. Neither does the claim that life is not worth living with a corrupted soul, at least on the most obvious

---

[8] See Vlastos (1971), 5–7, 'The Paradox of Socrates', where the idea of the sovereignty of virtue is eloquently described, though the phrase is not used.

[9] See Vlastos (1991), 210–11. Vlastos later (216–17) somewhat qualifies his account of the sovereignty of virtue. According to him, though virtue is necessary and sufficient for happiness, there are other goods which could, with and only with the presence of virtue, provide 'small, but not negligible, enhancement of happiness'. I do not think this qualification affects my argument.

[10] Cf. *Gorg.* 479 B–C, 512 A–B; *Rep.* 445 A–B, where a similar contrast between body and soul is made.

[11] See Burnet (1924), ad loc., who suggests that the circumlocution is owing to the fact that in the 5th cent. BC the idea that the soul was the seat of goodness and badness was novel. This seems implausible, but Burnet is assuming that the views of the historical Socrates are here being represented.

interpretation. For one might wish to argue, say, that a corrupted soul is less of a burden than a broken body. In fact, that is very much like the argument of one who wants to claim that doing evil is better than suffering it.

One might conceivably argue that it is incoherent to value bodily states more than psychical states because the latter identify us whereas the former do not. If this were so, then someone who preferred bodily states to psychical states would be making a blunder analogous to one who preferred the well-being of his possessions to his own well-being. But as we have seen, it is far from obvious, especially on empirical grounds, how to make the case that bodily states are not states of me whereas psychical states are.

In *Charmides* Socrates reports a view about health that he claims to have learnt from a Thracian doctor.

> He said that just as you ought not to try to cure the eyes without the head, or the head without the body, so neither ought you to try to cure the body without the soul. And this is the reason why the cure of many diseases is unknown to the doctors of Hellas, because they disregard the whole, which ought to be studied as well, for the part cannot be well unless the whole is well. For all good and evil, whether in the body or in the whole human being [παντὶ τῷ ἀνθρώπῳ], originates, as he said, in the soul, and overflows from there, as if from the head into the eyes. And therefore if the head and body are to be well, you must begin by curing the soul. That is the first thing and the main thing. (156 D 8–157 A 3, trans. Sprague, slightly modified)

The distinction between body, soul, and 'whole human being' is not entirely clear here. Straightforwardly, what seems to be implied is that soul is to body as head to eye and body to head. And this would make 'soul' evidently equivalent to the 'whole human being'.[12] But this cannot be correct, for well-being in the 'whole human being' *originates* in the soul; it is not equivalent to well-being in the soul. Socrates is here, in fact, making a rather commonsensical claim that a pain, namely, Charmides' headache, ought to be dealt with first by treating the soul. In addition, he is making the somewhat less commonsensical claim—at least not so well known to Greek physicians—that one should *start* with the soul in treating the whole man. The disregard of these physicians for the whole human being is indeed disregard for the soul—not, however, because the soul is the whole human

---

[12] Robinson (1995), 5, takes 'soul' and 'whole' man as indistinguishable. But I do not think this follows from the preceding analogy of soul to body as head to eye.

being but because in disregarding the most important part, they disregard the whole human being.

The claim that the soul is the most important part of a human being because if it is unwell the whole man will be unwell might seem to provide a basis for the paradoxes. In fact, it does not. First, a generalization from the claim that headaches originate in some psychical disturbance is dubious. It might well be both that some bodily diseases have no psychical origin and that some psychical disturbances have no bodily sequelae. Second, and more importantly, someone might prefer, all things considered, a state in which the soul has adversely affected the body to one in which the soul has not. For example, one might prefer some unspecified adverse bodily effects one experiences by being an unjust individual to the adverse bodily effects of being the just individual upon whom injustice was visited. The problem here is the subjectivity of the assertion that care for the soul should be paramount just because it is the origin of (some) bodily ailments. What is needed is a better defence of the strange claim that one cares for oneself *only* by caring for one's soul. And that depends on showing that one is identified in some strong sense with one's soul.

The identification of the person or self with the soul is made explicitly in *Alcibiades I* 130 C 1–3: 'Since a human being is neither his body, nor his body and soul together, what remains, I think, is either that he's nothing, or else, if he is something, he's nothing other than his soul.' And, two lines later: 'Do we need any clearer proof that the soul is the human being [τὸν ἄνθρωπον ψυχήν]?' 'No, by Zeus, I think you've given ample proof.' Many scholars have questioned the authenticity of this dialogue for many reasons, including this explicit identification of soul and human being.[13] Indeed, there is no other dialogue among those recognized as 'early' in which the identification is made so explicitly. Nevertheless, I think we can be reasonably confident that at some point Plato did at least identify the moral and intellectual subject with the soul.[14] But even if *Alcibiades I* is authentic, it does not help all that much. Let the soul be the human being,

[13] See Pradeau (1999), 219–20, for a convenient table listing the opinions of scholars on the authenticity of the dialogue. Pradeau, 24–9, and Annas (1985), 131–2, argue persuasively for authenticity. See also Pépin (1971), pt. I.

[14] See esp. *Laws* 959 B 3–4, but also 721 B 7–8, 773 E 5 ff.; *Phaedo* 76 C 11, 92 B 5, 95 C 6; *Tim.* 90 C 2–3. In the course of the *Alcibiades I* passage (129 B 1–130 A 1) Socrates asks, 'in what way might the self itself [αὐτὸ ταὐτό] be discovered?' Goldin (1993) argues that this

as the text says, or, more accurately the 'real' or 'true' human being, since this text is not denying that the body–soul composite is a human being. This fact in itself does not entail that 'care for the soul' is to be construed as Socrates would have it. For many so-called 'bodily states' need not be supposed to be states of the body but rather states of the soul for which the body is instrumental. In that case, care for the soul may be exercised equally by one who nurtures those of his psychical states that are tied to a body and one who, say, nurtures his moral virtue.[15] One who is pursuing food or sex may be said to be no less solicitous for his own well-being than one who is pursuing philosophical wisdom. The former need not be supposed to be preferring his body over himself, but rather certain of his states that require a body to certain others that, for all we know, do not.

I suppose that a rather commonsensical defence of Socrates would hold that being in a virtuous state is more important than being in a pleasurable state because somehow the former identifies us more closely than the latter. But surely without any supporting evidence, this is mere bluff. Gregory Vlastos immortalized the rhetoric of this position long ago when he offered this commentary on Socratic absolutism. 'If you have only one more day to live it makes no sense to spend it in any way other than that which makes you a better person.'[16] With all due respect for one of the greatest of all Plato scholars, 'it makes no sense' is mere rhetoric. Indeed, prima facie it makes perfect sense to pursue bodily pleasures right up to the end if you find the state you are in when you experience these more satisfying than any other.[17]

is a reference to the Form of Self, or a Form of the Same, not, as Annas (1985: 131) and others hold, a reference to the real, i.e. impersonal, part of the soul.

[15] *Euthyd.* 279 A 1–281 E 2 argues that all human goods depend upon the possession of the virtue of wisdom for their goodness. But this argument for the indispensable instrumentality of wisdom actually undercuts any claim that care for the soul is absolutely preferable to care for the body.   [16] Vlastos (1971), 5–6.

[17] A related critique of 'impersonal' moral principles has been powerfully advanced in various publications by Bernard Williams. See e.g. Williams (1990), 'Persons, Character and Morality', 1–19, and (1985), 111. Williams finds inadequate what he variously calls the 'Kantian or Platonic account of the individual' according to which idiosyncratic or individual commitments and interests—'ground projects'—are excluded from moral calculation. He is careful to insist that ground projects do not have to be self-centred or selfish. Someone holding what I take to be the Platonic position needs to show that the idiosyncratic flows not from the ideal or normative but from an inferior image of the

Conceptually, what Socrates needs is an argument that more firmly identifies the self or person exclusively with the subject of psychical states. An argument for the immortality of the soul presumably serves this purpose, so long as the immortal soul is the person and is disembodied. If the permanent or ultimate state of the self is disembodied, then at least there is some reason to hold that states of the self that require a body are somehow less truly identifying. It should be evident by now that this will not, finally, do unless it can be shown that one who prefers the states requiring a body to the states which do not require a body is making a mistake, a mistake he would not want to make if he had understood what he was doing.

In *Apology* (40 C–41 D) Socrates expresses a type of agnosticism about the immortality of the soul.[18] This agnosticism prevents him from offering a non-question-begging argument on behalf of moral absolutism. The first dialogue (on the traditional chronology) in which the immortality of the soul is proclaimed by Socrates is *Meno* (81 A, 86 A 8–B 2); and the first dialogue in which the moral consequences of immortality are discussed is *Gorgias* (493 A ff., 523 A ff.), albeit in a myth. It might appear at first that if the entirety of the argument for moral absolutism is prudential—that is, the only reason for preferring virtue over vice in this life is fear of punishment in the next— then Socrates' moral absolutism is misnamed if not misconceived. As we

person. It is true that according to the inferior image persons will typically introduce considerations into moral calculation that are at odds with the objective or 'impersonal'. But judging the latter as therefore inadequate depends upon a view of the person which holds the idiosyncratic to be ineliminable from the concept of the person. This is what Williams and others do. Socrates' absolutism is, I believe, ultimately based on the assumption that the idiosyncratic may be ineliminable from the ordinary lives of embodied persons but that it is no part of an ideal life.

[18] See Brickhouse and Smith (1989), 257–62, on the status of Socrates' claims about the afterlife. What I am calling Socrates' agnosticism is his advancement of two alternatives: death is either like a dreamless sleep or like a change to another place. One might maintain that the latter alternative, since it includes the suggestion that there are judges in Hades, implies that there may be negative judgements—that is, that an afterlife might not be such a good idea for the wicked. Nevertheless, Socrates does in this passage twice say that death is a blessing and does not offer divine punishment in the afterlife as a reason for refraining from wrongdoing. Perhaps the most that we can infer from this passage is something like a Pascalian wager to the effect that a bet on immortality is a safer bet than a bet on extinction. But this will certainly be inadequate for supporting the absolutist claim.

shall see, however, what follows for the self from the immortality of the soul makes matters far more complicated than this.

The first passage in *Gorgias* relevant to my theme contains the myth of the water-carriers:

Once I even heard one of the wise men say that we are now dead and that our bodies are our tombs, and that the part of our soul in which our appetites reside is actually the sort of thing to be open to persuasion and to shift back and forth. And hence some clever man, a teller of stories, a Sicilian, perhaps, or an Italian, named this part a jar [πίθος], on account of its being a persuadable [πιθανός] and suggestible thing, thus slightly changing the name. And fools [ἀνόητοι] he named uninitiated [ἀμύητοι], suggesting that that part of the souls of fools where their appetites are located is their undisciplined part, one not tightly closed, a leaking jar, as it were. He based the image on its insatiability. Now this man, Callicles, quite to the contrary of your view, shows that of the people in Hades [Ἅιδου]—meaning the unseen [ἀιδές]—these, the uninitiated ones, would be the most miserable. They would carry water into the leaking jar using another leaky thing, a sieve. That's why by the sieve he means the soul (as the man who talked with me claimed). And because they leak, he likened the souls of fools to sieves; for their untrustworthiness and forgetfulness makes them unable to retain anything. (493 A 1–c 3, trans. Zeyl)

There is a good deal that is obscure in this story and perhaps we cannot rely too heavily on its implications. Still, several important points seem to emerge. First, it is clear that the identity of the person is with the soul and the body is something alien to it, namely, a tomb. Second, whatever may be the exact comparison that is being made, it does seem that Socrates is referring to the consequences for the disembodied part of the human being of one's sojourn here below in the 'tomb'. The souls of fools differ from the souls of the 'initiated ones' in that the former suffer in Hades. They suffer owing to defects in their souls. That they are in a miserable state overall is evidently not in their control. That is, an individual might opt for a life of wickedness or dissoluteness gauging full well the pluses and minuses of such a life. But such an individual, so this story goes, does not have a choice of *not* being miserable in Hades. At the very least, this fact makes the claim that one ought to care for one's soul at all costs slightly less opaque.

Towards the end of *Gorgias* the prudential argument for the superiority of the virtuous life over the vicious life is made in the most unambiguous terms: 'For no one who isn't totally bereft of reason and courage is afraid to die; doing what's unjust is what he's afraid of. For of all evils, the ultimate is that of arriving in Hades with one's soul stuffed full of unjust actions' (522 E 1–4). Socrates proceeds to elaborate on an eschatological myth in which at death judgement occurs and the virtuous are sent to the Isle of the Blessed and the wicked to Tartarus. The separation of body and soul and the identification of the person with the latter are clear from the story, for it is the state of the latter that is judged by the gods. Nevertheless, it is also clear that embodied acts are attributed to persons so conceived.[19]

The crassly prudential argument for virtuous living contains some important hints about the concept of person being employed here.[20] When persons arrive for divine judgement, their bodies are stripped from them so that their naked souls can be inspected. The judges are able to determine from this inspection which souls have been virtuous and which have been vicious. Wicked souls bear the marks of their embodied wickedness. Evidently, if we are supposed to fear punishment in the disembodied state, this is because we are just souls or at least that we are somehow identified by our souls. This punishment is, fittingly, we are told, either remedial or exemplary.[21] I think it is a mistake to suppose that this excludes retribution

---

[19] See 526 C 1–2, where the soul of a just man is judged after being deemed to have lived a good life. I take it that this is meant to imply the identification of the person with the soul. See also 525 A 1–6, where the soul is judged for its wicked actions here below.

[20] See 7th Letter 335 A 2–7: 'Truly, we should always be persuaded of the ancient and holy doctrines which reveal to us the immortality of the soul and the fact that there are judges and the greatest punishments awaiting us when our souls are separated from our bodies. Therefore, suffering the greatest sins and acts of injustice ought to be held to be a smaller matter than to do them.' Dodds (1959), 385, in his comment on 527 A 7, says that 'acceptance of the myth is similarly [viz. Phaedo 85 C–D] recommended here, faute de mieux: but Socrates really bases his appeal on the preceding ethical arguments, which are independent of the myth, though they lead to the same rule of life'. I think the matter is not so simple and that the ethical arguments are, for reasons already alluded to, inseparable from arguments about the separability of the soul. It is no doubt possible to mitigate the crassness of the prudential argument. See e.g. Geach (1969), 'The Moral Law and the Law of God', 117–29, who argues that the question 'why should I obey God's law?' is 'really an insane question'. But Geach has in mind a conception of a deity very different from that held by Plato in Gorgias. The 'insanity' of the question presumably depends upon divine omnipotence.

[21] See 525 B 1–3. Dodds (1959), 380–1, ad loc., worries that exemplary punishment is useless for those who have arrived in Hades, having presumably already lived their lives,

as a justification for punishment. It seems, in fact, to be a necessary condition for any just punishment. What is not clear, however, is whether the punishment for wickedness and the corruption of the soul that earns such punishment are different. The latter question is relevant to deciding how the myth of divine punishment and rewards can contribute to the philosophical argument supporting the paradoxes. Perhaps in a mythical context it makes no sense to ask how exactly souls are punished. But it is certainly important to understand how wickedness damages a soul. It seems implausible that the *only* downside to a life of unjust behaviour is that the gods will somehow punish you when you die. Plato does not seem to have ever altered his view that wrongdoing is itself harmful to the wrongdoer notwithstanding any adverse 'external' consequences. If, it seems, injustice does not itself harm the soul but, like a lamb destined for slaughter, merely 'marks' it so that a divine judge is able to punish wickedness, then the *only* argument Socrates has is the prudential one. I do not suppose that this cannot be the case, but I think it is worth asking if Plato was in fact satisfied with basing his entire ethics on an argument that in turn rests on a myth. That is why it is perhaps reasonable to take the mythical punishment as just a vivid representation of the real adverse 'internal' consequences. At least, this would enable us to see that they are necessary or unavoidable. If that is so, we need to ask exactly how wrongdoing or bad soul care harms one.

The refutation by Socrates of Callicles' argument for hedonism may seem to provide an answer to the above question. For Socrates argues inductively that the good aimed at in any art consists in a product that is well ordered. This includes the art of medicine, which aims at a well-ordered and harmonious body. So, too, it seems that a well-ordered and harmonious soul is the good aimed at in any art concerned with the soul (504 B 4–5). Apart from the fact that this conclusion is arrived at by a perhaps dubious inductive comparison with arts, let it be granted that a well-ordered and harmonious soul is, as Socrates goes on to say, one in which justice and temperance and the other virtues have been implanted (504 D 9–E 4). Nevertheless,

and inaccessible for those who have not yet arrived there. Dodds therefore concludes that Plato must be suppressing his belief in reincarnation. But I do not see how reincarnation helps, since it is no more evident to us that a creature we encounter here below is suffering punishment for a previous life. In addition, surely we can be impressed and even frightened by eternal damnation owing to the very myth we are reading.

the honorific terms 'order' ($\tau\acute{\alpha}\xi\iota\varsigma$) and 'harmonious' ($\kappa\acute{o}\sigma\mu\iota o\varsigma$) have little relevance to the issue at hand. For it is obviously open to a Callicles to reply that a well-ordered and harmonious soul is *not* of paramount interest to him, even allowing that psychical well-orderedness is just what virtue is. Even if it is the case that wrongdoing necessarily produces a disordered soul, it is not obvious why this fact alone should concern anyone. The analogy with physical health is seductive but unsatisfactory. It really does seem preposterous that, all things being equal, one would prefer being physically unhealthy to being physically healthy. Good health is something that all human beings seem to enjoy when they have it. But without argument this cannot be taken simply to be the case for psychical health. For one thing, it does not seem to be empirically true. For another, even if psychical ill health is recognized by someone to be, all things considered, undesirable, it may also be not unreasonably held by the same person that, on balance, a healthy body and an unhealthy soul is a better state than the opposite.

Gorgias makes substantial use of the analogy between bodily and psychical health. It presumes what *Republic* will later argue, namely, that psychical health is as intrinsically desirable as bodily health. But as I have just claimed, this really amounts to saying that psychical health is intrinsically desirable if you find it intrinsically desirable. That malefactors are punished by the gods when they die is one thing. It is quite another thing to hold that one *ought* to find psychical health intrinsically desirable, not just prudentially desirable under threat of perdition.

Presumably, wrongdoing must be shown to operate on the soul in a way similar to the action of some toxic concoction on the body, and once you recognize this, you will immediately concede that such a state is unequivocally undesirable. There must be no escape. Socrates must be able to say to his interlocutors, like the inscription over the gate of Dante's Inferno, 'Abandon all hope you who enter here.' Wondering how Plato solves this problem, we realize that the solution is at the same time going to amount to an account of the person or self. The soul must be understood such that injustice somehow entails the deconstruction or dissolution of the person. In short, it must entail a loss of what no person could accept losing when in full recognition of the facts. Yet it is manifestly false that wrongdoing necessarily results in the loss of personal identity. After all, one supposes that it is the same wrongdoer who arrives naked before the gods for judgement and who engages in embodied wrongdoing. In addition, if the same person has both bodily states and psychical states, then one who favours one of the former—say, pleasure—over one of the latter—say, being just—is hardly going to be the worse for it, where 'worse' is to be understood as 'less' of a self or person. Either 'less' here is being used by the wrongdoer's opponent metaphorically, in which case it is irrelevant to what needs to be shown, or its use just begs the question. Finally, the very claim that the soul is immortal—whether made in a myth or made on the basis of argument— seems to undercut a strategy intended to show that wrongdoing entails a non-metaphorical loss of self. Much of what Plato has to say on this matter is contained in *Phaedo* and *Republic*. The analysis in these dialogues provides him with a way of explaining the corruptive effects of wrongdoing and also of dealing with the ambiguities of an identical self being the subject of both bodily and psychical states. Before we turn to that analysis, we should look at the idea of self-knowledge as it is presented in the early dialogues. For it is in Socrates' evident attention to the Delphic oracle's pronouncement 'Know thyself' that the beginnings of an answer are to be found. And in the last section of this chapter we shall look at the important model of personhood presumed in the argument in *Protagoras* that weakness of the will is not possible.

1.2 Socrates and Self-Knowledge

The ideas of self-knowledge and of introspection as a method of acquiring self-knowledge have a venerable history. The typically cryptic remark of Heraclitus, 'I searched out myself' (ἐδιζησάμην ἐμεωυτόν), seems to indicate a form of investigation or exploration different from that which is evident generally in the cosmological speculations of the Ionian philosophers. For one does not search out oneself in the way that one searches out explanations for the marvels of nature. A quest for self-knowledge can evidently be understood in a variety of ways. First of all, it can constitute an effort to understand one's own desires, beliefs, and so on. It can also amount to an effort to discover an individual self or substance, a species or type to which the individual belongs, or a source, origin, or cause of the individual.

Two questions naturally arise regarding the fragments of Heraclitus.

What is it that he supposed he discovered when he 'searched out himself' and how does this sort of exploration differ from any other? Presumably, the results of his search are contained in such fragmentary sayings as 'a human being's character is his fate [ἦθος ἀνθρώπῳ δαίμων]', 'you would not find out the limits of the soul even travelling along every road; so deep an explanation does it have [ψυχῆς πείρατα ἰὼν οὐκ ἂν ἐξεύροιο πᾶσαν ἐπιπορευόμενος ὁδόν· οὕτω βαθὺν λόγον ἔχει]', and even 'nature loves to hide itself [φύσις κρύπτεσθαι φιλεῖ]'. It is not unreasonable to characterize Heraclitus' 'method' here as in some way introspective and to surmise that he thought that with it he could learn truths about himself as well as other human beings, and more generally truths about the cosmos. In time, introspection came to be recognized as a means of arriving at knowledge of god or gods.[22] More precisely, the knowledge acquired through introspection was either identical with knowledge of the divine or somehow an inferential basis for that knowledge. For Heraclitus in particular, self-examination was a means to wider knowledge because we have a λόγος or rational account in common with the cosmos.

If introspection is a distinctive method—different from, say, the empirical method of carefully dissecting an animal in order to discover its anatomy and physiology—it is because in introspection one does something different from any sort of 'looking outward'. One examines one's own beliefs or desires or feelings. Perhaps Heraclitus came to the conclusion that character is fate because he somehow examined his own array of mental furniture and discovered there the explanation for his own fate in some respect. Naturally, it is possible to examine the beliefs, desires, and feelings of others, but one can do so only indirectly, via behaviour of various sorts, including linguistic. By contrast, it seems at least prima facie that our access to our own states is generally direct or at any rate private. Yet Heraclitus might not have been the best judge of his own character, and even if he were in a better position to judge it than others because, say, he had a more comprehensive and honest view of his own life than any other person did, he is certainly not an infallible judge. After all, people do sometimes exhibit what others would

---

[22] See *Alc. I* 132 D–133 C. See Kremer (1981), who provides many examples of ancient philosophers and theologians who variously viewed 'Selbsterkenntnis' as identical with 'Gotteserkenntnis' and as a means to it.

characterize as a woeful lack of self-knowledge despite their claims to have sought it out and actually to possess it.

Introspection in the Heraclitean manner is both historically and theoretically tangled up with another form of cognition, namely, self-reflexivity.[23] I shall here briefly introduce the idea of self-reflexivity, a concept that will later concern us at some length. By this term I mean awareness or cognition of one's own occurrent psychical states.[24] The term 'self-reflexivity', as I use it, is roughly equivalent to 'self-consciousness' as it is sometimes used by philosophers today. Introspection presupposes self-reflexivity, but not vice versa. One can be aware of one's own mental states without examining them in any way or without drawing conclusions about their implications, as does Heraclitus. But what makes introspection or self-examination supposedly unique or uniquely fruitful is that it requires self-reflexivity. That is, it requires that the subject who introspects be identical with the intentional object introspected or at least with the subject of that intentional object.

Generally, when self-reflexivity obtains, if a subject is (1) in a mental state and (2) is aware that he is in that mental state, then the subject in (1) and (2) is identical. For example, if I feel angry and I am aware that I feel angry, the 'I' who is aware is identical with the 'I' who feels angry. Although it is true that 'anger' does not stand for an intentional object, it does not follow from this that 'my being in a state of feeling angry' cannot be an intentional object for me. The answer to the question of whether 'my being in a state of feeling angry' can or cannot be an intentional object depends on whether my awareness of myself in this state is *cognitional* awareness. If it is not, then there does not seem to be a difference between 'feeling angry' and 'being aware that I feel angry', in which case no intentional object is present. If it is, then my being aware that I feel angry seems to be intimately connected to the *belief* that I am angry, the belief whose intentional object is 'my being in a state of feeling angry'. What is unusual about self-reflexivity is that

---

[23] See Tugendhat (1986), who is largely concerned with the distinction between self-reflexivity and introspection, although he generally uses the term 'self-consciousness' for the former and 'self-determination' for the latter.

[24] What I call 'self-reflexivity' is what in the Latin version of the 15th proposition of the *Liber de causis* was rendered as *reditio completa*. The *Liber de causis* is a work largely excerpted from Proclus' *Elements of Theology*. Both the Latin terms *reditio* and *reflexio* are used in medieval philosophy and afterwards to indicate the mind's access to its own states.

the subject of the intentional object, the mental state, is identical with the subject of the belief.

Paradigmatic examples of self-reflexivity are cognitive, and are typically interpreted as cases in which one knows that one knows. Thus, the evidence that I know that $1 + 1 = 2$ is just that I know that I know that $1 + 1 = 2$ and vice versa. In other words, it is self-evident to me. The evidence that I know that I feel tired is that I know that I know it. But these two examples seem importantly different, for one might well want to claim that I can know that $1 + 1 = 2$ (or anything else for that matter) without knowing that I know it, while it is not so obviously the case that I can feel tired without knowing that I feel tired.[25] The difference is thought to reside principally in the fact that the objects of cognition are intentional, whereas the objects of affective states are not. The knowledge can be 'there' waiting for me to become aware of it, whereas the tiredness is not 'there' waiting for it to be felt. It is only 'there' *when* it is felt. When we come to face Plato's account of knowledge, we shall need to explore in greater detail the distinction between dispositional and occurrent mental states and the comparison of the cognitive with the affective.

It is important to realize that, although paradigmatic examples of self-reflexivity are cases in which one knows *that* one knows, it does not necessarily follow from this that knowledge is paradigmatically propositional. The main reason why someone might suppose that knowledge is propositional is that it is assumed that knowledge is a form of belief and all beliefs have propositions as their intentional objects. But if knowledge is not a form of belief, then it is an open question whether the paradigmatic examples of self-reflexivity, i.e. cases of knowledge, are propositional. At least one reason for thinking that if knowledge is self-reflexive it is *not* propositional is that the mental state of the subject that self-reflexively knows is not accurately described as a relation between a subject and a proposition. Thus, if I am in the type of mental state that is knowledge, where knowledge is in some way an attribute of me, it is far from obvious that this is equivalent

---

[25] Of course, I and anyone else may appeal to all sorts of behavioural evidence to support the claim that I am tired. Whether one can feel tired without being tired, however, depends entirely on whether 'tired' is or is not defined with reference to self-reflexive awareness. See Lloyd (1964) for an important study of the distinction between introspection and self-reflexivity in the Platonic tradition.

to saying that I am related to a proposition. Even if it is true that in virtue of being in that mental state I may be related to a proposition, it does not follow that being in that mental state is equivalent to being related to that proposition.

Neither introspection nor self-reflexivity ought to be confused with direct knowledge of an entity called 'the self', if there be such. Introspection is notoriously unreliable. Being aware of my mental states is no more a sure path to knowledge of the self than reading the writing on a blackboard is a sure path to knowledge about the nature of blackboards. Nevertheless, both introspection and self-reflexivity might yield evidence that would indirectly support conclusions about the subject that introspects and the subject that is self-reflexively aware of its own states. If self-reflexivity does not reveal knowledge about one's self or about a person, nevertheless, it might be the basis for conclusions regarding the sort of entity capable of self-reflexivity.

The Platonic texts in which discussions of self-knowledge are to be found contain references both to introspection and to self-reflexivity. Self-knowledge in these texts is variously treated. Socrates' bold claim in *Apology* that 'the unexamined life is not worth living [ὁ ἀνεξέταστος βίος οὐ βιωτὸς ἀνθρώπῳ]' (38 A 5–6) may well be a ringing endorsement of Heraclitean introspection. But it may also have nothing to do either with introspection or with self-reflexivity, if the 'unexamined life' is just the life in which philosophical scrutiny of any sort has no part.

There are, however, texts that are clearly concerned with the complexities of self-knowledge, including both introspection and self-reflexivity. In *Alcibiades I* and in *Charmides* one who aims for self-knowledge must know the soul's virtue, namely, 'temperance' or perhaps more accurately 'soundness of mind' (σωφροσύνη)[26] In these texts self-knowledge understood as soundness of mind consists roughly in understanding one's place within the moral universe.[27] It is not so clear, however, how the claim made earlier in *Alcibiades I*, that the person is the soul and self-knowledge is knowledge of

[26] *Alc. I* 131 B 4–5, 133 C 18–19; *Charm.* 164 D 4. See Annas (1985), esp. 118–20, on the translation of σωφροσύνη as 'soundness of mind' and some of the implications of the identification of self-knowledge with σωφροσύνη so construed.

[27] See Annas (1985), 121: 'What is relevant is knowing myself in the sense of knowing my place in society, knowing who I am and where I stand in relation to others. The self-knowledge that is σωφροσύνη has nothing to do with my subconscious and everything to do with what F. H. Bradley called "my station and its duties".'

this fact, is to be connected with the claim that self-knowledge is equivalent to soundness of mind . Perhaps the most obvious way of connecting the two claims is as follows. To know something is more or less to know its peculiar excellence or virtue. So, if persons are souls, knowing oneself amounts to knowing both that fact and the excellence of soul, namely, its soundness of mind.[28]

Much depends on how we understand this soundness of mind. In *Alcibiades I* it seems that it extends far beyond having an accurate assessment of one's social standing. In fact, it seems to consist primarily in being able to distinguish oneself from one's possession, the body, and the possessions of one's possession.[29] The most profound effect of failing to have soundness of mind is to mistake oneself for one's possessions and thereby to fail to appreciate what is good for oneself. But then what is good for the soul is more than just knowing, formally, so to speak, that what is good for it are psychical goods. One must know concretely what these goods actually are.[30] Self-knowledge thus conceived is acquired indirectly, via the knowledge of another soul. That self-knowledge is, first, knowledge of the soul and then knowledge of its virtue, soundness of mind. In a way this encapsulates the essence of Socrates' philosophy, as the ancients believed.

The recognition that one is different from either the body or the composite of the body and the soul and that one's body is in fact a possession of oneself is, as we have already seen, problematic even on Plato's own terms. Nevertheless, the core idea that virtue consists in a type of knowledge, specifically, self-knowledge, stands as an important and far-reaching insight. It is, as we shall see, the basis for the claim that knowledge transforms the knower. In order to see precisely how this is so, we shall need to have a deeper understanding of Plato's conception of knowledge.[31]

In *Charmides* we find the dialectical equation of wisdom and soundness of mind and their characterization both as a kind of self-knowledge and as involving a kind of self-reflexivity (167 A 1–7; cf. 169 E 4–5). Since the

[28] At 133 B 9–10 the ἀρετή of soul is said to be σοφία. It is not too difficult to see that wisdom could here be understood as knowledge of one's 'place'.

[29] The entire passage 131 A–E aims to show this.

[30] So 133 C 21–3, where Socrates says that σωφροσύνη is a condition for knowing what is good for oneself.

[31] On Plato's claim that virtue is knowledge, a claim which I do not treat as a paradox, see Penner (1973); Santas (1979), chs. 6 and 7; Irwin (1995), ch. 3.

dialogue ends in ἀπορία and since the proposed definition is offered not by Socrates but by his interlocutor Critias, it is difficult to draw positive conclusions from the complex examination. Critias has interposed himself between the young Charmides and Socrates after the boy has failed in two attempts to define σωφροσύνη. Critias himself defines it as 'doing one's own' (161 B 6). In response to Socrates' criticism that 'doing one's own' must involve knowledge of what it is that is being done, Critias emends his definition to 'knowing oneself' (τὸ γιγνώσκειν ἑαυτόν, 164 D 4). It is this emended definition that is to be the subject of analysis for the remainder of the dialogue.[32]

Socrates begins by asking Critias what self-knowledge is 'of' (τινός, 165 C 5–6) and what is its 'task or product' (ἔργον, 165 D 5). Socrates adduces the examples of medicine and housebuilding, where the knowable object and the product of the applied knowledge is straightforward. Critias reasonably objects that self-knowledge is not like medicine and housebuilding, for though self-knowledge is knowledge of something, it does not have a product.[33] In this respect, it is like calculation and geometry. Soundness of mind is in fact the only 'knowledge' (ἐπιστήμη) that is both knowledge of 'other types of knowledge' (ἄλλων ἐπιστημῶν) and of itself (166 C 2–3).[34] This rather cryptic explanation opens the door for Socrates to ask whether, if soundness of mind is knowledge of other types of knowledge,

---

[32] See esp. Tuckey (1951), 27–73; Wellman (1964); Martens (1973), 39–91; Ebert (1974), 55–82; Gloy (1986); and Liske (1988) on the relation between self-knowledge and self-reflexivity in *Charmides*. Although these scholars offer differing analyses of the nature of self-reflexivity, they all recognize the distinction between this technical epistemological concept and the traditional meaning of 'self-knowledge'.

[33] Critias' reply, implicitly accepted by Socrates, turns upon the important distinction between theoretical and productive knowledge. In Socrates' defence, however, it might be said that since it is the virtue of soundness of mind that is being defined as self-knowledge, it is reasonable to expect that self-knowledge will have some practical or concrete benefit. The putative benefit of soundness of mind so defined will be taken up later at 171 D–175 E.

[34] Critias here makes the shift from 165 D 7, where Socrates has taken him to be claiming that soundness of mind is (1) 'self-knowledge' (ἐπιστήμη ἑαυτοῦ) to 166 C 2–3, where he claims that it is (2) 'self-reflexive knowledge' (ἐπιστήμη ἑαυτῆς). Some scholars take this as a fallacy of equivocation, whether intentional or not, on Plato's part. I doubt this. In fact, I believe that Plato is moving towards the claim that genuine knowledge, whether it be of one's self or not, must be self-reflexive. That is, he is dialectically advancing the hypothesis that (1) entails (2).

it is also knowledge of the 'absence of knowledge' (ἀνεπιστημοσύνης, 166 E 7). Critias readily agrees and Socrates then says:

Then only the one who is sound of mind will know himself and will be able to examine what he knows and does not know, and in the same way he will be able to inspect other people to see when someone in fact knows what he knows and thinks he knows, and no one else will be able to do this. And being of sound mind and soundness of mind and knowing oneself amount to this, to knowing what one knows and does not know. (167 A 1–7, trans. Sprague, slightly modified)

Socrates thus interprets Critias' explanation of self-knowledge as the knowledge of what one knows and what one does not know and what someone else knows and does not know. At first glance, we do not see why one's self-knowledge, understood as knowledge of types of knowledge, should extend to the knowledge of what others know. But as it will turn out, this is exactly right. For it is only if one has knowledge of what one knows that one is conceivably in a position to have knowledge *that* someone else knows and what it is that is known.

Socrates next undertakes an inductive examination of whether knowledge of knowledge is a coherent notion. He attempts to show that, at least in numerous cases of perceptual, affective, and cognitive powers—vision, hearing, appetite, wish, love, fear, opinion, and so on—objects of these must be different from the power itself. Similarly, if knowledge is related to what it is knowledge of in the same way, for example, that the greater is related to the smaller, then knowledge of knowledge would be like something being greater than itself (167 C–169 C). The question of whether there can be knowledge of knowledge is left unanswered. Instead, says Socrates, assuming that it is possible for there to be such knowledge, is it also possible that one can know what one knows and what one does not (169 D 3)?[35] In addition, if the latter is possible, it remains to be shown whether it is equivalent to self-knowledge (170 A 2–4). And indeed, it remains to be shown whether it is in fact soundness of mind.

The upshot of the investigation of whether one can know what one

---

[35] Kahn (1996), 196, notes the conditional nature of the ensuing investigation. *If* knowledge of knowledge is possible, we can examine whether one can know what one knows. But even if it should turn out that one can know what one knows and does not know, it does not follow either that this is what self-knowledge is or that self-knowledge is soundness of mind.

knows and what one does not know is that knowledge of what one knows and does not know is not knowledge with an additional content. This is important if it is held that soundness of mind is a distinct and beneficial type of knowledge. Someone who *only* had soundness of mind thus conceived would know that he had certain types of knowledge and lacked others, but would not have these types of knowledge themselves (170 C 9–D 2). His soundness of mind alone could not access this knowledge, as we might say. Similarly, in the case of others, the man of putatively sound mind will recognize that others have claimed some types of knowledge, but he will not know what knowledge they actually possess (170 D 5–9).[36]

That one person cannot know that another person knows something unless the former knows that very thing is a profound claim about the nature of knowledge. It is the claim that first-person knowledge is prior to a claim to know that another person has knowledge. It is a claim that begins to reveal the strictness of the requirements for knowing. Indeed, we shall see in later chapters that the argument for the priority of first-person knowledge is really an argument that there is no such thing as third-person knowledge. That is, there is no knowledge of the sort that consists in my knowing that someone else knows something. Part of the reason for this is that third-person knowledge would be propositional ('A knows that B knows X'), whereas in fact there is no such thing as propositional knowledge or, to be more precise, propositional ἐπιστήμη, according to Plato. That there is no such thing as third-person knowledge, however, should not lead us to suppose that first-person knowledge is to be identified with knowledge of the idiosyncratic states of the person. It is precisely because knowledge for Plato is unqualifiedly universal and persons are primarily knowers that subjectivity in the modern sense is not an integral part of Plato's account of persons.

[36] The text actually says that the man of putatively sound mind will know *that* the other has some knowledge (D 7–8) but this contradicts the claim made immediately prior to this that he will not know whether the other knows or does not know what he claims to know (D 5–6). If I do not know that you know what you claim to know, how can I claim to know that you know *anything*? So, I am inclined to interpret the words in D 7–8 loosely. All the sound-minded man knows of the other is that he claims to know something, not that he actually does know. Similarly, if I only know that I know without knowing what I know, this is equivalent to my belief that I know something, though I do not know what it is.

Charles Kahn has pointed out that the priority of first-person knowing has important consequences for Socrates' efforts to test the knowledge claims of others.[37] For one thing, if Socrates' interlocutors cannot know that Socrates knows unless they themselves know, then Socrates is for them as if he were ignorant. Even if he knows, that knowledge is useless to others. And we are all, I take it, as readers of Plato, Socrates' interlocutors. For another, communicating knowledge in the ordinary way, by speech, becomes entirely problematic if one who knows tries to communicate knowledge to one who does not. For the latter is in no position to make the claim that what is being communicated to him is knowledge. Why should any of Socrates' interlocutors accept what he says as true?

The priority of first-person knowledge over third-person knowledge claims is conceptually tied to self-reflexivity. A simple way to see this is to consider that it is *never* self-evident to the first person that the third person knows, whereas the first person knows if and only if that person is aware of his knowing. That is why whatever claim the knower makes about another person, it is not knowledge. Another way to see the connection between first-person knowledge and self-reflexivity is to make a distinction between potential knowledge and actual knowledge. Obviously, the doctrine of recollection, first introduced in *Meno* and later developed in *Phaedo*, depends upon such a distinction. As we shall see, *Theaetetus* also explicitly makes this distinction. There are, however, two crucial points in this regard. First, actual knowledge is logically prior to potential knowledge. That is, the latter is defined in terms of the former. Second, actual knowledge is distinct from potential knowledge only if it is essentially self-reflexive. Since actual knowledge does not have a content different from the content of potential knowledge, the only way they can be different is by self-reflexivity. This is just the difference between the presence of the content and the awareness of the presence. And that is why it is a mistake to suppose that knowledge must be propositional. If knowledge were propositional, then

---

[37] Kahn (1996), 201, thinks that the main consequence is that Socrates' profession of ignorance of the things he tests for in others cannot be taken at face value. This would be true, I think, if knowledge were required to show that someone else does not know. But Socrates' refutative method does not necessarily require this. From the fact that I cannot know that you do not know unless I know, it does not follow that I cannot show that you could not know what you claim to know because, for example, that which you claim to know is not logically possible.

the content of what I know when I am aware of the content in me would be different from the content of what I know in the first place, or potentially. Thus, the proposition '*p*' is different from the proposition '*s* knows *p*'. As Socrates has argued, knowledge of knowledge is not knowledge with an additional content. These two points make it clearer why knowing what one knows and what one does not know can be reasonably taken as self-knowledge. That is, in knowing what one knows and does not know, one knows the content of one's own psychical state. In addition, they explain why self-knowledge so understood is entirely different from some putative introspective knowledge of a self or of one's own character.

The outline of the connection between personhood and knowledge is just barely visible here. As I shall try to show in due course, an immaterial person is the only sort of thing capable of knowledge as Plato understands it. This is because an immaterial person is the only thing capable of self-reflexivity. It is the only sort of thing wherein that which knows is identical with the subject of the state that is known. Further, the ideal for a person is to be exclusively in such a state of knowing. In this way, achieving knowledge can be seen as the core result and meaning of authentic self-transformation. Finally, in so far as knowledge is the ideal cognitive state, the *ne plus ultra* of cognition, all other cognitive states have to be understood as defective or at least derivative versions of the ideal. The possibility thus presents itself that for embodied persons, unqualified—i.e. actual and self-reflexive—knowledge is not available.

The claim of *Charmides* that the virtue of σωφροσύνη is self-knowledge of a special sort is only one version of the more common general claim made by Plato that virtue is knowledge. Superficially, it is not especially paradoxical to assert that human excellence consists entirely or in part in having a certain type of knowledge. One obvious objection that might be raised against such an assertion, however, is that it is difficult to see why one could not have knowledge and still not be excellent or virtuous. Plato offers an answer to this question in *Protagoras*, which I discuss below. It is the answer to the question—that no one does wrong willingly—that is truly paradoxical.

1.3 *Protagoras* and the Power of Knowledge

In *Protagoras* we find the much-studied argument for the impossibility of ἀκρασία or incontinence or weakness of the will.[38] I do not intend here to explore all the subtleties of this argument. Rather, my aim is to show how the rejection by Socrates of the possibility of ἀκρασία depends upon a certain concept of the person and of knowledge, a concept that is consistent with those features of personhood outlined earlier.

Socrates offers the following question to Protagoras:

Come, now, Protagoras, reveal to me this part of your thinking too. How do you regard knowledge? Do you agree with the majority on this score, too, or do you think otherwise? To the majority, knowledge seems to be something neither strong nor ruling nor in charge in us. They don't think about it this way at all; rather they believe that on many occasions, though knowledge be present in a man, it is not knowledge that is in charge in him but something else, sometimes passion, sometimes pleasure, sometimes pain, sometimes love, and many times fear. Very simply, they think knowledge is like a slave dragged about by all these other things. Does it seem to you to be like this or do you think that knowledge is something noble and the sort of thing to be in charge in a man and that if someone knows what is good and bad, he would not be overpowered by anything so as to do anything but what knowledge commands? Or rather, is wisdom sufficient to assist a man? (352 A 8–C 7)

Protagoras agrees with the claims by Socrates implicit in these questions, though he does so undoubtedly without being entirely aware of the consequences of his agreement. For at the end of the argument against the possibility of ἀκρασία, Socrates will apply the conclusion to refute Protagoras' contention that one can be courageous without having knowledge.

Socrates argues against the many that what is commonly called 'being overcome by pleasure though one knows the right thing to do' is really 'ignorance' (ἀμαθία) or absence of knowledge.[39] The understanding of this argument seems to me to have been bedevilled by two irrelevancies. First, it is assumed that the hedonism that functions in a premiss of the argument

---

[38] 352 A 1–C 7. On this most complex argument see esp. Taylor (1976), 170–200; Penner (1991); Irwin (1995), 81–94; Price (1995), 14–27; Kahn (1996), 226–57.

[39] 357 D 1 provides the correct name for what at 352 E 8–353 A 2 is the ordinary description.

is essential to the argument.⁴⁰ But, the claim continues, since Plato (or Socrates) is not a hedonist, then the argument fails or ought to fail. Second, it is assumed that 'knowledge' (ἐπιστήμη) in the argument is to be understood in the technical sense developed in *Republic* so as to exclude mere belief.⁴¹ If that were so, then the scope of the argument would be severely limited. I shall address both of these points in the course of my analysis.

The basic argument offered by Socrates is as follows: (1) Assume, with those who believe that being overcome by pleasure is a fact of life, that someone chooses X over Y, knowing that Y is better but being overcome by the pleasurableness of X (355 A 5–B 2). (2) 'Pleasurable' and 'good' are two names for the same thing (355 B 3–C 1). (3) So, then, someone chooses X over Y, knowing that Y is better because he is overcome by the goodness of X (355 C 3–8). This conclusion is taken to be absurd and therefore to reveal the falsity of (1) (355 D 1–3). That is, assuming that 'pleasure' and 'good' mean the same thing, it makes no sense to say that someone does what he knows to be not good because he is overcome by pleasure. The only thing missing from this basic argument is a motivational assumption, namely, that the achievement of 'good' (here said to be equivalent to 'pleasure') is the reason why anyone chooses to do anything. This assumption is, I take it, uncontroversially present throughout the argument, as one would expect from the ordinary meaning of 'good' in Greek.⁴²

⁴⁰ See e.g. Irwin (1995), 92. Penner (1997), 128–30, argues against the relevance of hedonism to Socrates' argument.

⁴¹ See Penner (1996), with references. Penner's view is that ἀκρασία (or what he calls 'synchronic belief-ἀκρασία') is impossible. That is, it is impossible that at the critical moment one should act counter to what one believes to be best at that moment. He also believes that 'diachronic knowledge-ἀκρασία' is possible and that that is what is being argued against in the *Protagoras* passage. But 'diachronic belief-ἀκρασία' is possible because at the crucial moment one could forget or otherwise have an ineffective belief. This is counter to the way both Aristotle and Plato (in *Republic*) understand ἀκρασία. See also Penner (1997), 45–8.

⁴² See e.g. *Meno* 77 C 1–2, where it is said that 'everyone desires good things' and it is just assumed that everyone acts to achieve these in so far as it is possible. At *Gorg.* 467 B 3–6 Socrates agrees with Polus that tyrants do 'what seems best to them [ἃ δοκεῖ αὐτοῖς βέλτιστα]' but not 'what they want [ἃ βούλονται]'. It is here assumed that everyone acts to achieve what they think best. Socrates is objecting that there is a difference between what people think is best for them and what is in fact best. And it is only the latter that they truly want. This distinction is irrelevant to the psychological impossibility of incontinence as it is described in *Protagoras*.

On the one hand, since this argument is intended to show that what is called 'being overcome by pleasure' is not *that*, it can hardly be said that hedonism is not germane to the argument. For present purposes, I understand hedonism minimally as what is held in premiss (2) above. On the other hand, it seems clear enough that 'pleasure' is just a place-holder in the argument and that whatever we say is identical with the good and at the same time declare that by which we are 'overcome' is going to yield the same absurdity. That is, one cannot be overcome by *X* when one knows that not-*X* is what one desires, whatever *X* is supposed to be. The reason is simply that it is here supposed that one desires and acts to achieve one's own good. If someone knows that something is not one's own good, he cannot at the same time be overcome by his thought that it is.[43] So, even a non-hedonist has to face the putative incoherence of the phenomenon of incontinence.[44] Further, knowledge, understood as opposed to or superior to mere belief, is equally irrelevant to the argument. For it is enough if I believe that something is not good for me that I cannot be overcome by what I think is good for me. That is, the motivational force of belief is equivalent to that of knowledge.[45] Indeed, once Plato in *Republic* distinguishes a technical and narrow sense for ἐπιστήμη, he can develop its unique psychological properties. But for present purposes the differences between knowledge and belief are not relevant.

[43] One might object that one can have 'mixed feelings' about something, thinking it both good and not good for oneself. Indeed, in the course of evaluating an action or a proposed goal, one might have such ambivalence and nothing in the argument gainsays its relevance to the description of the mental state of the agent. But what is essential for the argument is one's decision about whether something is good or not good, all things considered. It is this decision and consequent belief that is the starting point for action. The problem about incontinence is, after all, a problem about action and not about the vagaries of decision-making. The simple way, and indeed, according to the argument, the *only* way to determine whether someone thinks that something is good for himself or not is whether he acts to obtain it.

[44] Socrates says in a number of places throughout the argument that hedonism is the assumption of the many and that they are unable to offer any alternative. The only place where he himself seems to endorse hedonism is at 353 E 6–354 A 1, where he says that this is the view of Protagoras and himself. But Protagoras has already baulked at hedonism (351 B–E). And the view that Socrates advances prior to the main argument is that pleasurable things are good in so far as they are pleasurable (351 E 2–3). That is, Socrates holds that pleasure is good, not that pleasure is the good.

[45] See on this point Penner (1996).

There is another important assumption in the argument which I have hitherto glossed over. It is that the desire for, in this case, pleasure is informed by what one believes. That is, the argument is claiming that we cannot be overcome by pleasure because what we are overcome by is a desire which in turn is based on a belief. But the only belief that is relevant to the sort of case at issue is the belief that good (or more good) is to be had by resisting than by allowing oneself to be overcome. There is no conceptual room for any other belief. Two possible alternative models of action are thereby excluded: (1) desire as a principle of action independent of belief; and (2) desire as a principle of action informed by a belief that contradicts a simultaneously occurring belief. An agent, it is supposed, is a unified principle of action. That is, he acts on desire informed by belief. So, if one believes that something is bad, then one cannot act to achieve its contradictory where acting is entailed by desire. True, one could desire the bad under all sorts of counterfactual conditions, but the desire would not in itself be a principle of action. Thus, one could wish that eating the poisoned food would produce pleasure, but on the assumption that one believed that it would not, one could not be overcome by that desire—that is, one could not act on it.

I believe, as did both Plato and Aristotle, that on the model of action assumed in this argument ἀκρασία is impossible.[46] This model holds that persons are rational agents, i.e. that reasons are causes of action, where action includes refraining from acting. In addition, it holds that the reasoning that causes an action is a unified or coherent process. I mean that if the reason for doing something is a belief that p, then it is necessarily the case that one does not simultaneously believe that not-p. Alternatively, we might put this by saying that the only reasons for acting are effective beliefs, beliefs that, all things considered, doing such-and-such is the way to obtain what one desires. If I believe that refraining in this instance is good for me, I cannot be overcome in the relevant sense, for being overcome implies that the action contradicts what I believe is good for me. If I do 'go for' the pleasure, it is

---

[46] See *NE H* 5, 1147^{b}15–19. Kahn (1996), 243, holds that the argument of *Protagoras* does not show that ἀκρασία is impossible, but that it is intended to get Socrates' interlocutors to agree that no one does wrong willingly. I would maintain, however, that the impossibility of ἀκρασία and the claim that no one does wrong willingly are independent, and that whereas Plato consistently held the latter, he changed his mind about the former.

because I have a belief that is effective for acting.[47] And that is not ἀκρασία. I might, of course, at the same time that I believe something is bad for me believe all sorts of things that in fact contradict this belief. Such opacity of belief states is irrelevant here. What the argument rejects is the possibility that I should have a belief that something is bad for me and at the same time act to achieve it, where action is based solely on effective belief.[48] Stated otherwise, the only objective measure of what I believe, all things considered, is good for me to do is what I act to obtain. The after-the-fact attribution of belief to the agent guarantees that the agent acted to obtain what he thought best for himself all things considered. The claim that an agent acted incontinently would directly contradict this.

The reason why knowledge cannot be overcome is exactly the same as the reason why effective belief cannot be overcome.[49] However, knowledge does have an advantage over belief, as *Meno* (97 E–98 B) explains. Knowledge is stable, whereas true belief is unstable. The stability of knowledge is owing to its being tied down by an 'explanation' (αἰτίας λογισμῷ). I shall not now

---

[47] What I mean by 'effective belief' is close to what is implied in Plato's use of the term 'willing(ly)' (ἑκών). 'No one does wrong willingly', as it is usually understood, is taken to imply and be implied by the claim that everyone acts to achieve what he thinks is good for himself whether or not this be in fact so. An action performed to achieve this is done 'willingly'. An effective belief adds explicitly to the notion of 'willingly' the content of what one thinks is good for oneself. The idea of an effective belief is also close to the Aristotelian notion of 'choice' or 'intention' (προαίρεσις). See esp. NE Γ 6, 1113ᵃ2–7.

[48] Penner (1997), 121–3, thinks that the strength of knowledge (and hence the relative weakness of belief) resides in its stability through the deliberative process. But if at t_1 I believe that, though I want X, X is not in my interests to do and at t_2 I 'go for' X because my belief has 'wavered' or been occluded, I am not acting acratically. Penner must allow that non-occurrent beliefs are the beliefs that are 'overcome' by the desire for pleasure. If, however, this is the case, then I do not see the difference between an occurrent belief and knowledge with respect to effectiveness in action. Indeed, Penner seems to concede this when he says that 'synchronic belief-ἀκρασία is *not* what is overcome by pleasure, but rather diachronic belief-ἀκρασία' (124).

[49] As 358 B 7–C 1 says, 'No one who either knows [εἰδώς] or believes [οἰόμενος] that something else is better than what he is doing, and is in his power to do, subsequently does the other, when he can do what is better.' See *Meno* 97 B–98 A, where Socrates argues that true belief is as valuable as knowledge when it comes to action. It would seem, however, that as a principle of the psychology of action, false belief can be just as effective as either knowledge or true belief. The reason for this is simply that all our beliefs are held by us as true. If they are false, *we* are not aware of that. It does not seem to be psychologically possible for someone to act on a false belief, believing it to be false.

pursue the explanation of why having the reason why a belief is true puts one in a state more stable than one wherein one does not have the reason why the belief is true. On the face of it, it is hard to see why one's stubborn belief that p cannot be every bit as stable as someone else's knowledge that p. If, however, knowledge alone is non-propositional, the psychological difference between being in a state of knowing and being in a state of belief may turn out to be considerable.

The point I wish to make now is that knowledge (or belief) is held by Plato to be effective in action because embodied persons are taken in *Protagoras* to be primarily unified rational agents. The reason why I cannot act contrary to what I believe is, all things considered, in my best interests is that what I act to obtain is determined exclusively by what I believe. That persons are rational means that their identity is determined at least in part by their cognitive states. Thus, even the person who believed that acting viciously was the high road to happiness would be identified as the subject of this belief. It would be misleading at this point to try to fix this definition more firmly. A modicum of vagueness is not out of keeping with the level of analysis attained in the text. As rational agents, persons act owing to the cognitive states they are in, especially their effective beliefs at the moment of acting. Accordingly, beliefs generally and quite literally *transform* persons. And if it is indeed true that knowledge is something more permanent than belief, then the transformation is all the more portentous when knowledge arrives.

It seems odd to hold that persons are identified by their beliefs if one supposes that persons *have* beliefs. For if persons have beliefs, then they should be identified independently of these possessions. Indeed, as we have seen in *Alcibiades I*, Plato makes much of the distinction between a person and his possessions, including his body. Why are not beliefs possessions as well, albeit peculiarly intimate ones? The basic answer to this question, which I shall work out in some detail in subsequent chapters, is that for Plato, embodied persons are partly constructed as subjects of belief states.[50]

---

[50] Stating the point this way suggests that persons are aggregates and not substantial unities. This is not entirely false. Still, for Plato there is a unity in a way controlling the embodied aggregate, namely, the disembodied ideal. That is presumably why I cannot escape my disembodied fate by acquiring new beliefs and thereby becoming a different person.

We are no more endowed with complete personhood at conception than we are endowed with complete humanity. The construction of personhood is done in fits and starts and is fraught with all sorts of conflicts throughout one's life. In addition, effective beliefs, at any rate, are occurrent beliefs.[51] Having a belief occurrently just means being in a mental state and reflexively cognizing that you are in that state. Putting the matter thus makes it clearer that identity really is delimited by cognitive states.

Identifying human beings is different from identifying persons. Socrates the human being is identified, say, by deme and family. Socrates the person is identified in part by his beliefs, including such beliefs as, say, care for the soul is of the utmost importance, the unexamined life is not liveable, and the belief that at death his friends will have on their hands a corpse but not him. Presumably, at one time he did not have these beliefs. If we say that a person is identified by all the beliefs that he has at one time, we shall have to say that every time a belief is acquired or discarded, the person changes. This is not necessarily absurd. Indeed, in so far as embodied persons share the instability of the sensible world, their changeability seems inevitable. But since embodied persons, like the sensible world generally, are images of ideals, it would be a mistake to fail to bring in those ideals in fixing their identity. The reason why knowledge is superior to belief in *Meno* and *Protagoras* is that it serves the stability or fixity of personhood.

The primacy of self-reflexivity in belief states as well as in knowledge contributes to understanding why or in what sense persons are constituted as subjects of beliefs. It is perfectly natural to speak of the beliefs someone else has or the beliefs one has oneself, speaking as it were in the third person. But the view that the person is distinct from these or other such 'possessions' apart from the way the subject of a belief is distinct from the belief is utterly obscure and problematic. For example, if we ask about someone's beliefs and we decide that the person holding those beliefs is a racist, we might well be puzzled over what it is we are attributing the term 'racist' to other than the subject of these beliefs. Perhaps we would say that the person is a racist if he behaves in a racist manner. But surely he behaves in a racist manner because he has racist beliefs. That is why he is a racist. By contrast, to say

---

[51] I leave out of this sketch any discussion of unconscious beliefs or beliefs of which we are not presently aware. These are, of course, of the utmost importance, on many theories.

that he is not a racist, although his beliefs are, is quite opaque. I suspect part of the oddness felt in the claim that personhood is in part determined by beliefs is that beliefs are supposed to be dispositions. But if they are, as Plato holds, mental states, it is easier to see why personhood should be held to be constituted by beliefs. On the concept of the person in *Protagoras*, according to which incontinence is impossible, there is nothing else for the person to be the subject of besides his beliefs. At the same time as we come to realize that a belief is paradigmatically a self-reflexive, occurrent state, albeit not equivalent to knowledge, we can perhaps realize why Plato would want to say that a person is constituted as the subject of that state.

Many scholars have argued for the poverty of the models of person-hood and of action in *Protagoras*.[52] In assuming that action is determined solely by effective beliefs, Plato does not seem to allow that some sort of desire, independent of belief, could initiate an action even counter to a belief. In short, why should all beliefs be effective beliefs? But since the desire quite obviously belongs to the person who acts, if that person is a rational agent, how *could* the desire initiate the action unless it were based on an effective belief? In *Protagoras* it is supposed that rational agents or persons act to achieve what they believe to be their own good. Be-ing overcome by what is believed to be contrary to one's own good is impossible. Certainly, an agent can act to achieve what is in fact bad for himself, but he cannot act to achieve what is thought by him to be so. This seems immensely implausible. People seem to act contrary to their own interests *as they conceive them* all the time. Accordingly, a more re-fined notion of what a person is seems to be required. Nevertheless, we should not underestimate the difficulty in doing this. For unless desires are cut off entirely from the putative acratic, so that they are virtually the desires of a different person, then there seems to be little difference be-tween the person who is overcome with desire and the person who gives in to desire. But for the person to give in to desire is to act as a subject of belief, albeit a fallible one. And that is precisely the problem. For giv-ing in to desire is hard to distinguish from acting on an effective belief,

---

[52] See e.g. Taylor (1980), 518. Taylor argues that in Plato there is a 'failure to appreciate the complexities of the concept of desire and of its relations with judgments on the one hand and action on the other'.

namely, the belief that, all things considered, this is the best thing for the person to do.

It is easy to confuse the denial of the possibility of ἀκρασία with the claim that no one does wrong willingly. The latter is a claim made before *Protagoras*, in *Protagoras*, and after *Protagoras*, even after the possibility of ἀκρασία is recognized.[53] If ἀκρασία is impossible, then no one does wrong willingly, given the above assumptions about action. But if no one does wrong willingly, it does not follow that ἀκρασία is impossible.[54] Indeed, unwilling wrongdoing is precisely what ἀκρασία is. Unwilling wrongdoing is excluded by the impossibility of ἀκρασία. So, showing that ἀκρασία is possible amounts to the basis for understanding how all wrongdoing is unwilling. One *could* admit that all wrongdoing is unwilling and continue to maintain that ἀκρασία is impossible, but one would then have to identify the agent of wrongdoing as other than the agent who was unwilling. Paradigmatically, such would be the case if one is forced by someone else to do something against one's will. With this paradigm in mind, it is relatively clear that if one can be said to do wrong willingly without the interference of an outside force, it is because somehow a division of agency has been determined to exist *within*. Speaking quite generally, a division of agency within the one person between agent *A* and agent *B* would explain how *A* is unwilling but *B* is the agent of the wrongdoing. At the same time, of course, *A* and *B* cannot be agents exactly like the agents in the paradigmatic case. For if they were, first, there would be nothing that could be called ἀκρασία and second, it would be arbitrary to assign the action to the agent who is unwilling rather than the agent who is willing. And if this is the case, what would it even mean to say that the agent who did wrong was unwilling?

What is in fact required, again speaking quite generally, is a duality of agency within one person. In order to maintain both that ἀκρασία is possible and that no one does wrong willingly, Plato must show that phrases like 'I want it and I don't want it' or 'I am acting against what I will' or 'I am giving in to desire' can be assigned a literal meaning, that is, a meaning where 'I'

[53] See *Gorg.* 488 A 3; *Prot.* 345 D 8, 358 C 7, 358 E 2–359 A 1; *Rep.* 589 C 6; *Tim.* 85 D 2, E 1; *Laws* 731 C 2.

[54] Penner (1997) holds that the impossibility of what he calls 'knowledge-ἀκρασία' entails and is entailed by 'no one does wrong willingly', but the impossibility of 'belief-ἀκρασία' is not. Penner denies that in *Protagoras* Plato is defending the impossibility of belief-ἀκρασία.

is not used equivocally. As I shall argue in subsequent chapters, Plato does offer an account of personhood that enables him to show precisely this. Only of persons, as Plato conceives of them, can it be said that they act incontinently and that they never do wrong willingly.

The problem so forcefully posed by *Protagoras* just underscores this difficulty for the moral position advanced in the early dialogues. As I have suggested, Socrates is not a hedonist in *Protagoras*, but he has not shown that hedonism is a bad option. In fact, he has provided a model of action that serves hedonism quite well. What is required is an account of embodied personhood that is more plausible than that entertained in this dialogue. That account will allow us to see not only how knowledge is self-transforming but how rational agency is compatible with acratic action.

In the next chapter I turn to Plato's *Phaedo*, where I aim to show that we can find an understanding of embodied personhood more capacious and complex than that found in *Protagoras*. There we find the beginning of an account that is more fully developed in *Republic*. In part, this account is based on the arguments for the immortality of the soul and the consequent need to consider the embodied person in relation to the disembodied ideal. The argument for the immortality of the soul inevitably raises the question of the identity of the person. As we shall see, this identity is determined largely via an extended epistemological argument. In the light of this argument, we can better explain the idea that persons are subjects of cognition, including belief states. In addition, we shall find the material for an answer to the question of how a rational agent can be the subject of arational desires.

CHAPTER 2

Immortality and Persons
in Phaedo

Plato's *Phaedo* includes the first arguments for what Francis Cornford aptly called 'the twin pillars of Platonism', namely, the existence of separate Forms and the immortality of the soul. In this chapter I am especially interested in what *Phaedo* tells us about persons, both embodied and disembodied. The proofs for the soul's immortality provide the context and the justification for distinguishing persons and human beings. *Phaedo*, more than any other dialogue, brings together in argument the two notions of personhood and knowledge. In fact, as we shall see, at least one of the actual proofs for the existence of separate Forms is closely connected to the proof that persons are, ideally, disembodied knowers.

Attempting actually to prove the immortality of the soul (as opposed merely to asserting it, say, on religious grounds) is an odd project, as evidenced by the fact that rarely have philosophers outside of the Platonic tradition tried to accomplish the feat.[1] Even within that tradition, all the proofs to be found are variations on those employed in the *Phaedo*, *Republic*, *Phaedrus*, and *Laws*. Apart from anecdotal reports adduced as evidence of reincarnation and personal religious revelation, it is difficult to understand how a proof of immortality is supposed to work. In a very general Platonic sense, we can reasonably interpret the question 'Is the soul immortal?' as

---

[1] The origin of Plato's belief in the immortality of the soul may well be in his association with contemporary Pythagoreans. See Kahn (2001), 13–15, 48–62, for a concise summary of the evidence for Plato's Pythagoreanism.

similar to the question 'Is piety what is dear to the gods?' or 'Is virtue teachable?'—questions from the *Euthyphro* and *Meno* which ask about a property or πάθος of a Form or an εἶδος. And just as in the case of those dialogues it gradually dawns on the interlocutors that one cannot know whether something is a πάθος of an εἶδος until one knows what the εἶδος is, so we may suppose that one cannot know whether immortality belongs necessarily to the soul until one knows what the soul is. So much is fairly straightforward. But there are complications.

First, as in the case of the definitions of piety or virtue, Socrates' principal data for dialectical analysis are common conceptions or references of the words 'piety' and 'virtue'. In the case of ψυχή, the commonest of common conceptions is that soul is whatever it may be that differentiates a living being from a dead one.

Whatever *that* may be is deeply obscure. The interest of the worried interlocutors in *Phaedo* in the immortality of the soul is focused on personal immortality. And the connection between whatever it is that differentiates a living being from a corpse and personal immortality is far from perspicuous. In fact, the notions of soul and immortal person are at least in part in tension in so far as soul is taken to be just life and life is no more when there is a corpse.

Second and relatedly, the sort of evidence that might be adduced to discover exactly what the soul is and the sort of evidence for personal immortality seem diverse. What was true in the middle of the fourth century is equally true now, when learned discussions regarding the definition of death obviously have absolutely nothing to do with philosophical speculation about personal immortality. Indeed, it is not obvious why the question of personal immortality should have anything to do whatsoever with the question of the nature of soul. *Phaedo* is deeply involved with evidentiary strategies that unite the two questions. As we shall see, the union of the two is found in a claim that soul is life and life is paradigmatically or ideally self-reflexive cognition. So, if my soul can be shown to survive the demise of my body, then this is equivalent to showing the survival of a self-reflexive cognizer. It will turn out that this is just the self or the person one ideally is. The embodied person is an image of that ideal.

The principal divisions of the arguments for immortality in *Phaedo* are: (1) the Cyclical Argument (CA) (69 E 6–72 E 1); (2) the Recollection Argument (RA) (72 E 3–78 B 3); (3) the Affinity Argument (AA) (78 B 4–84 B 4); and (4) the Exclusion of Opposites Argument (EA) (102 A 10–107 B 10). To this *divisio textus* must be added (5) the objections of Simmias and Cebes (84 C 1–88 B 8); (6) the reply to Simmias' objection (88 C 1–95 A 3); and (7) Socrates' autobiography and method of hypothesis (95 A 4–102 A), which is in effect the prelude to (4), which is the reply to Cebes' objection. Part of the problem with this division is that it encourages us to treat the arguments independently. If done this way, it is not difficult to show that the arguments are invalid or unsound, sometimes bizarrely so. I want to try to show that the putatively independent arguments are all elements of one large argument. Therefore, they are not independent. This large argument does not, finally, amount to an unassailably valid argument for the immortality of one's own soul, but it does reveal a great deal about how Plato viewed the connection between the nexus of concepts with which this book is concerned.

2.1 The Structure of the Proof of the Immortality of the Soul

Against the background that the soul is simply whatever it is that differentiates a living thing from a corpse, a proof of the personal immortality of the soul must essentially do four things: (1) it must show that the soul is more than a property that differentiates the living from the dead—rather, it must show that the soul is an entity; (2) it must show that the soul is an entity that can exist on its own or independently, that is, an entity that can exist when the body or the human being does not; (3) it must show that this entity is identical with the person; (4) it must show that this entity, identical with the person, is everlasting or indestructible. The CA argues for (1) and (2) on the assumption that dying and being born are opposite processes in a specific way (70 D 2–5). The RA is taken as establishing (3) on the assumption of the existence of Forms (76 D 5–E 7). The AA argues for (4) on the assumption that knowledge of Forms is possible (79 D 1–8). The objection of Simmias is an objection to the CA and the RA, and its rebuttal is taken as establishing (1), (2), and (3) independently of the unargued assumptions of the CA and the RA. The objection of Cebes is an objection to the AA, and its rebuttal, EA, is taken as establishing (4) on the assumptions held in both the RA and the AA. Thus, the arguments CA, RA,

AA, and EA are fragments of the entire proof: no one of them is intended to stand on its own. The strategy of the entire proof is aimed at showing that each person can come to understand that he is, counter to appearances, really identical with an immaterial entity whose existence is not threatened by the death of any human beings including the one that others recognize him to be.

It is sufficiently clear that the interlocutors in this dialogue are interested in their own survival of death or personal immortality, but it is far from clear what personal immortality means. Presumably, a proof that we survive the destruction of our bodies means that our bodies are not us. Or, stated more accurately, if we are immortal, then nothing that requires a body can be part of who we are or, to put it Platonically, who we *really* are.[2] Strictly speaking, a proof of personal immortality should be preceded by a definition or at least a working hypothesis regarding what a person is supposed to be. Nothing of the sort is provided in the dialogue. If we recur to *Alcibiades I* or to the underlying assumption of the Socratic paradoxes, we might suppose that the person is taken to be the soul, and so the immortality of the soul is the immortality of the person. Not exactly.

As we saw in the first chapter, the soul or the person is the subject of pleasures and pains and, generally, countless bodily states and emotions, as well as the subject of thoughts. One might anticipate that a proof of the immortality of the soul that is going to be a proof of personal immortality either amounts to a proof of the survival of the subject of all the activities and states that a soul or person is capable of or else must include an argument that some of these are dispensable for personal identity. But this is a false dichotomy. For not all that we are capable of under certain circumstances is necessary for our personal identity under all circumstances. For example, even if we need a body to feel pleasure, our identity is not necessarily obliterated if we are no longer capable of feeling pleasure. Similar remarks may be made about the loss of bodily parts or emotions and even memory. It is hardly surprising to learn that the argument in *Phaedo* takes thought as the *conditio sine qua non* of personal identity. What we should find most

---

[2] Gallop (1975), 90, rightly observes that 'if such features as memory or emotion are required for personal immortality, but are, at least implicitly, excluded from survival by the philosophical arguments, then personal survival not only goes unproven in the *Phaedo* but is actually ruled out'.

deserving of close inspection, however, is how a disembodied subject of thought and an embodied subject of a broad range of psychic and bodily states are taken by Plato even to be related, much less identical.

The connection between personal immortality and personal identity is itself obscure. For it is not evident that whatever criteria are adduced to identify a person through time will be the same as those adduced to identify a person with that which remains when that person's body is destroyed. If these criteria are not the same—as they surely are not if *embodiment* is included in the former—then the term 'person' is equivocal when, for example, used of that strange-looking individual found at one time walking in the streets of Athens, at another fighting at Potidea, and now residing in Platonic heaven. The proof of the immortality of the soul looks to be logically detached from anything like a proof that I can expect to reidentify myself when my body is destroyed.[3]

In the passage immediately preceding the CA Socrates introduces his proof of the immortality of the soul with an apologia for philosophy. Here he makes one of his most arresting pronouncements: 'philosophy is nothing but the practice for dying and being dead [ἀποθνῄσκειν τε καὶ τεθνάναι]' (64 A 5–6; cf. 67 D 7–10). On the basis of the agnosticism about the afterlife that Socrates evinces in *Apology*, this pronouncement, or at least the last conjunct of it, is nonsense.[4] Since *Apology* also represents Socrates as devoted to philosophy, we can either say that the Socrates of *Phaedo* is Plato and the Socrates of *Apology* is the historical Socrates or else we can say that Plato changed his view about philosophy during the interval between writing the two dialogues. In either case, philosophy is here conceived of in a remarkably new manner. In the absence of any compelling reason to limit the meaning of the phrase, we might take 'dying and being dead' to refer

---

[3] At the end of the dialogue, 115 C 4–D 1, Socrates playfully chides his friends for thinking that 'he' will be left to bury after his death, when in fact 'he' will be gone to be among the blessed. The confusion in the assumed criteria for personal identity in the interlocutors is clearly the point of this. If they recognize that Socrates is other than his body, then they should not think that they will bury him when he is gone from his body.

[4] At 64 B 9 the words οἵου θανάτου ('what kind of death') suggest that the death philosophers seek is a metaphorical death. But since the theme pronounced here is obviously the literal survival of the person in physical death, it is best to take the conjunction 'dying and being dead' to include both metaphorical and literal dying. The ambiguity between metaphorical and literal dying is consistently reinforced throughout the entire passage up to the introduction of the theory of Forms at 65 D 4.

both to the metaphorical 'dying and being dead to bodily desires' that the true philosopher pursues and to the actual physical process of dying and death when the soul is finally released from the body. Before Socrates has offered a proof of the immortality of the soul, he is represented here as staking his life on this claim about what philosophy is.

One plausible inference from the claim is that the death of the body is not the death of the person, and embodied existence is only a prelude to disembodied existence. Therefore, the living human being is not equivalent to the person. The relation between the disembodied person and the embodied version is obscure, but it would be a serious mistake to assume without further argument that the possibility of disembodied existence for a person entails a particular sort of theory about how the person and the body or the human being are connected. It would be a mistake principally because the relation between the disembodied person and the embodied person does not entail anything in particular about the relation between the embodied person and the living human being or the human body. For this reason, it is best to put aside, at least for the moment, the standard arguments against dualism.

There are two fundamental points to be made in this regard, one stemming from the discussion in the first chapter and one that arises from the metaphysics of *Phaedo*. First, Plato, as we have seen, tends to treat the relation between the soul and the body as that between a person and his possession. More particularly, as we have also seen, this possession is treated as an instrument of subjectivity and agency such that Plato can say that the same person who thinks also feels pain. This we saw produced a stubborn problem for a claim that one ought to abandon care of the body for care of oneself. Second, in wondering about the relation between the disembodied person and his embodied predecessor (or successor), the Platonic comparison that most naturally comes to mind is the relation between an immaterial and separate Form and its sensible instances. If it should in fact turn out that Plato views embodiment as somehow analogous to instantiation, then we should not be surprised to see many of the puzzling things Plato has to say about the sensible world reflected in his account of embodied personhood.

The puzzle regarding the identity of a disembodied and an embodied person is analogous to a puzzle regarding the identity of a Form and an instance of it. To take an example that turns up later in *Phaedo*, neither the Form of Largeness nor the 'largeness in us' can ever accept their opposites (102 D 6–E 2; cf. 103 B 5).[5] There are two salient features of the distinction between the Form of Largeness and the 'largeness in us' that are here relevant. First, the Form of Largeness is that in virtue of which there is largeness in us (cf. 100 D 7–8). Owing to its instrumental causal role, the two must be identified in some way. Second, an account of the largeness in us would be identical to an account of the smallness in us. It is the same quantity, say, six feet, that makes someone larger than one person and smaller than another. No such limitation applies to the account of the Form of Largeness. The two points together comprise the core of Plato's image metaphysics. I am not here arguing for the cogency of this view. I only wish to indicate that Plato has the metaphysical apparatus for thinking about embodied persons as images of disembodied ideals roughly in this way. Thus, the account of embodied personhood necessarily includes features that are necessarily excluded from disembodied personhood. Yet, this fact does not destroy their identity.[6]

That philosophers long to die suggests that, as Socrates says (64 C 4–8), death is nothing but the 'separation' (ἀπαλλαγήν) of the soul from the body. This separation borrows the ambiguity of the phrase 'dying and being dead'. On the one hand, if 'death' is stipulated to be just the result of renouncing worldly concerns, this hardly requires an argument. On the other hand, if Socrates means literal separation, then he has already assumed by definition the truth of (1) above, namely, that the soul is an entity. The ambiguity, however, is not gratuitous. To the extent that one finds it both possible and desirable to separate oneself metaphorically from

---

[5] See Gallop (1975), 194–6, with references, on the two main interpretative problems with this claim: (1) is the claim meant to be generalized so as to include Forms of substantives, like snow or fire? (2) is the claim postulating 'immanent Forms'? Our understanding of the theory of Forms is closely tied to the answers to these questions. Bostock (1986), 179–83, argues that 'largeness in us' is to be understood as indicating 'some chunk' of the Form. Bostock thinks that this manifest absurdity is revealed as such in *Parm.* 131 A–E. This seems implausible, especially given the centrality of the theory of Forms (which includes the manner in which Forms are participated in) for the proof of the immortality of the soul.

[6] Although the embodied person is not an instance of his disembodied self, he is presumably an instance of a Form of Soul, if there be such, and he stands in relation to his ideal self roughly the way an instance of a Form stands in relation to the Form.

the body, the establishment of (1) is supported. A philosopher is best able
to appreciate the proof of personal immortality because a philosopher is
most likely to appreciate the truth of the premiss that the soul is an entity
literally separable from the body. And literal separation is supported by
metaphorical separation, which again the philosopher is most likely to
experience. In addition, since *Phaedo* is a work of philosophy addressed to
the reader, as the reader *does* philosophy by studying the arguments in the
dialogue, he is engaged in the act of supporting the truth of the premiss of
literal separation by means of metaphorical separation. That is, the more
one engages in what Plato considers to be non-bodily activity, the more one
is inclined to recognize that one is an entity other than a body.

The following description of the philosopher who longs for detachment
from bodily concerns is, I would suggest, an actual constituent of the
argument for immortality. It is not, as is sometimes supposed, one of Plato's
typical diversionary perorations on philosophy. The philosopher's soul,
Plato says, 'attains truth' by 'reasoning [τῷ λογίζεσθαι]' (65 B 9, C 2). And
it reasons best when it has the 'least possible association with the body' (C
5–9). The soul of the philosopher utterly disdains the body and flees from
it and seeks rather to be 'alone by itself [αὐτὴ καθ᾽ αὑτήν]' (C 11–D 2).[7]
I believe that the superficial interpretation of these words is that Plato is
urging that bodily concerns distract the philosopher from doing his work.
If you are worried about your clothes or your food, your mind will not be
fully engaged in philosophy. This is undoubtedly true enough so far as it
goes, and indeed is supported by the long speech at 66 B 1–67 B 5, where the
distractions of embodiment for the philosopher are adduced. But the subject
of this work is the immortality of the soul. In order to prove this, part of what
must be shown is that the soul can exist 'alone by itself'. This is what the
philosopher habitually shows, as does the engaged reader of this dialogue.

I have referred to the renunciation of worldly concerns as 'metaphorical
dying'. But for Plato, who views the entire sensible world as an image of
what is really real, 'metaphor' is an ontological concept. Paradoxically, re-

---

[7] The use of the phrase 'alone by itself' for the disembodied soul puts us in mind of the
same phrase in its typical use by Plato to refer to Forms, especially later in this dialogue.
Cf. 78 D 5, 83 B 1, 100 B 5. As we shall see, the AA depends on the general similarity
of soul to Forms, but that argument obviously does not presume the similarity of the
disembodied soul to Forms.

nunciation of worldly concerns—the practice and the goal of philosophy—is *literally* metaphorical dying. It will turn out that what differentiates embodied persons from other images is that they are able to be self-conscious of their status as images. As one 'dies to the body', one comes to recognize oneself as a living metaphor for what is really real. The recognition is identical to the construction of an ideal self in so far as that is possible for the embodied person.

Abruptly and portentously Plato introduces the Forms—Justice, Beauty, Good, and so on (65 D 4–7). The philosopher, 'using his intellect alone by itself and pure, tries to hunt for each of the things that are [i.e. Forms], each alone by itself and pure' (66 A 1–3; cf. 79 D 5–6). Thus, a parallel of some sort between soul and Forms begins to be entertained. The soul, like Forms, can be alone by itself. According to the ambiguity that infects this passage, the soul is alone by itself either metaphorically when it thinks without reference to the body or alone by itself literally when the human being dies. That there is a critical difference between the two possibilities is evident in the following passage:

Well now, it really has been shown us that if we're ever going to know anything purely, we must be rid of it (the body), and must view the objects themselves with the soul by itself; it is then, apparently, that the thing we desire and whose lovers we claim to be, wisdom, will be ours—when we have died, as the argument indicates, though not while we live. Because, if we can know nothing purely in the body's company, then one of two things must be true: either knowledge is nowhere to be gained, or else it is for the dead; since then, but no sooner, will the soul be alone by itself apart from the body. And therefore while we live, it would seem that we shall be closest to knowledge in this way—if we consort with the body as little as possible, and do not commune with it, except in so far as we must, and do not infect ourselves with its nature, but remain pure from it, until God himself shall release us; and being thus pure, through separation from the body's folly, we shall probably be in like company, and shall know through our own selves all that is unsullied—and that, I dare say, is what the truth is; because never will it be permissible for impure to touch pure. (66 E 4–67 B 2, trans. Gallop)

The ambiguity between literal and metaphorical separation is evident in this passage. The soul is alone in the primary sense when the human being has died. It is alone metaphorically when it is not 'infected' with bodily nature. In the former state knowledge is attainable; in the latter we are as close to it as we may be when we consort with the body as little as possible. One would think that the plain sense of this text is that unqualified knowledge is not possible for embodied persons.[8] There are, however, several reasons for wondering if this can be so. For one thing, the vocabulary used for knowledge in this passage is rather loose. The two terms used, γνῶναι and εἰδέναι, are very general. Taken in this most general sense, Plato would seem to be committing himself to an extreme sceptical position. More importantly, both the RA and the AA seem to assume that knowledge of Forms is possible for the embodied individual. If this is indeed the case, then the contrast between knowledge and 'close to knowledge' is not a contrast between states possessed by disembodied and embodied agents. In fact, it is not so clear that either the RA or the AA assume that knowledge is possible for embodied individuals as opposed to being possible for us *in some condition*. I deal with these arguments below. And, as for the cognitive vocabulary, the context of the passage which includes the introduction of Forms makes it clear that the objects of cognition here are the Forms themselves. If that is the case, then in denying that the embodied person has cognition of Forms, Plato is not denying that there is cognition in some sense of other things.

Let us hypothesize for the moment that this passage contrasts the knowledge that is possible in the disembodied state with something else. Even more generally, suppose that disembodied existence enables *some* type of cognition (whatever we choose to call it) that is not available to anyone currently inhabiting a body. The resulting parallel to the relation between Forms and sensible images or instances is striking. Embodied cognition is to disembodied cognition as sensible instances or images of Forms are to the Forms themselves. Only when the soul is 'alone by itself' is it capable of cognizing the Forms, which are also 'alone by themselves'.

Of immediate interest in this hypothetical isomorphic structure is how it provides an insight into the strategy for the proof of the immortality of the soul. A sort of transcendental strategy immediately suggests itself. This would aim to show that embodied cognition depends somehow on disembodied cognition. The dependence is not general, but particular. The embodied cognitive states or acts of *this* embodied person depend on the dis-

---

[8] Cf. Simmias' words at 85 c 3–4: 'I think, Socrates, as perhaps you do, too, that in these matters certain knowledge is either impossible or very hard to come by in this life.'

embodied cognition of the identical person having occurred. This strategy is most evident in the RA, which assumes that such disembodied cognition must have already existed as a condition for the possibility of learning. But it is also used elsewhere, as we shall see.

The characterization of the philosopher as striving to disengage from bodily concerns in order to approach knowledge of Forms implicitly contains a moral claim as well as a psychological and epistemological one. Engaging in philosophy supposedly prepares one for being dead in a way that nothing else does. The cognition that the philosopher strives for is supposed to be morally transforming. One does not have to be a philosopher in order to be an immortal soul. One has to be a philosopher in order to be a happy person. Or, at least, philosophy is required for the excellence that is rewarded with happiness. I addressed the matter of the apparently necessary connection between knowledge and virtue in the last chapter. Here the connection is surely starker. One who has while embodied sought knowledge has been transformed into something godlike. How exactly does this transformation work?

Philosophy is the vehicle of transformation because, as the above passage indicates, one engaged in philosophy detaches oneself from the body. This detachment, as Socrates will explain in vivid terms later on, is an increasing unwillingness to 'share the body's opinions and pleasures' and thereby become contaminated (cf. 86 D–E). But as I have already indicated, and as I shall argue at some length in the next chapter, those opinions and pleasures belong to the same person who aims to renounce them. The renunciation or detachment consists in distancing oneself from an embodied subject and identifying oneself with an ideal disembodied subject, the knower. Engaging in philosophy is a two-sided activity: identifying oneself with the subject of knowing and alienating oneself from the subject of embodied states. The 'anti-philosopher' would do the opposite. Prior to literal death, the identification is never perfect or complete. Even the philosopher is residually attached to the body in the sense of being the subject of bodily desires right up to the moment of death. The proof of the immortality of the soul and the identification of it with a subject of knowing are meant to establish the ideal against which success or failure in this life can be measured.

Ideally, a disembodied person engages in contemplation of Forms. That person is a subject of thought completely taken up with that thought. At 79 D 6, for example, 'wisdom' ($\phi\rho\acute{o}\nu\eta\sigma\iota\varsigma$) is the 'state' ($\pi\acute{a}\theta\eta\mu a$) of a soul that has come to be 'alone by itself' ($a\mathring{v}\tau\grave{\eta}\ \kappa a\theta$' $a\mathring{v}\tau\acute{\eta}\nu$) with Forms. The mere lover of wisdom, the philosopher, is transformed in his identity by a transformation in his beliefs. The critical belief is not that 'philosophy is a good thing' or even that 'the philosophical life is the best life'. An Alcibiades could believe these things and act otherwise, though *Protagoras* does not contain the conceptual resources to explain how. The critical belief pertains to one's self-identity.[9] Like the fairy-tale prince, switched at birth, who must first be persuaded of his true identity in order to bc persuaded to reclaim his royal destiny, one must be made to believe what the proof of immortality tries to show.

As we shall see shortly in the AA, Plato views knowing as a state of cognitive identification with Forms. It is not a representational state. In knowing, the knower becomes what he knows. Thus, we cannot imagine the ideal person reading about or thinking about the truth, where 'about' is a marker for the gap between thinker and truth. More particularly, the ideal disembodied thinker's intentional objects are the Forms with which it is self-reflexively identical. That is, the thinker is aware that it is in a mental state consisting of identity with Forms. On this basis, it is not difficult to see that wisdom would be self-transforming. There is nothing for the disembodied ideal person to be other than a thinker. If the ideal is to be eternally identical with Forms by knowing them, embodied cognition is self-transforming because or in so far as it approaches the disembodied ideal.

Whereas disembodied cognition is non-representational, embodied cognition is entirely so. The representations the embodied person typically trades in are beliefs. These representations are in a way images of Forms, just as the embodied person is in a way an image of the disembodied person. Even the critical belief that one's true identity is as a subject of the state of knowing is itself an image of that state. This is so because the one who holds this belief—say, Socrates in the present dialogue—is residually distanced from that ideal. Just by articulating or defending or even acting on that belief, he implicitly acknowledges that, as an embodied person, he is something other than simply a knower. He is literally an image of a knower.

---

[9] At *Theaet.* 176 B–D the critical belief about our identity is expressed as a belief that our ideal is to 'become like god' as much as is possible.

The beliefs that are referred to as the 'Socratic paradoxes' are generally held to be preposterous by Socrates' interlocutors because they do not share his belief that a person is a soul. For example, Callicles in *Gorgias* disdains and rejects the personal implications of assenting to the outrageous claims made by Socrates (481 c). In *Phaedo* the view underlying the paradoxes is deepened because of the proof of the immortality of the soul. The disembodied person is not simply a soul but rather more precisely a subject of knowing. Persuading someone that the embodied person is an image of *that* is perhaps rather more daunting than persuading someone to care for his soul. And yet, as we have seen, why would anyone want to care for his soul if he did not believe that he was thereby caring for himself?

According to the model of personhood in *Protagoras*, if a person could know what was in his best interests, he could not but act to achieve that. Even if he only believed that something was in his best interests, he could not at that moment act contrary to that belief. But it will turn out that embodied persons *can* act contrary to what they believe to be in their best interests. Accordingly, a new model of personhood will be required. The possibility of incontinence also raises the question of whether one can act contrary to one's *knowledge* of what is in one's best interests. If, as *Phaedo* seems to suggest, knowledge is not available to an embodied person, then the question would not arise. But there is another excellent reason why an embodied person could not know that he is a knower, and that is that while embodied, he is not. Even if he could know that a person is *ideally* or in a disembodied state a knower, he would still be left with the problem of whether it would even be true to believe that he was identical with that. One of the very remarkable things about *Phaedo* is that Plato's strategy is aimed at showing that an embodied person is ideally a knower even if he cannot know that.

The self-identification that transforms the person in the direction of the ideal state is characterized by Socrates as a sort of purification (67 c 3). This purification is probably to be identified with the practice of philosophy at 64 A 5–6.[10] Philosophical purification is specifically the removal of false beliefs that are a condition of being born into and raised in a corrupt society. As false beliefs are replaced by true ones, an inferior image of the ideal person

---

[10] With Gallop (1975), 227–8, and against Burnet (1911), 38, I believe that the backward reference is to the previous discussion, not to some ancient doctrine of purification.

is replaced by a superior one. That is no doubt why Socrates declares at 89 D 2–3 that there is no greater evil that can befall anyone than μισολογία, hatred of λόγος. To renounce λόγος in the sense of rational discourse is to sentence oneself to whatever false beliefs happen one's way. The misologist does not renounce beliefs, of course, because beliefs are constitutive of the person he is; he renounces his best chance for the acquisition of true beliefs.

Plato recognizes a kind of embodied person who acts in way a philosopher acts without being virtuous. The practice of virtue by non-philosophers is a kind of 'shadowy image' (σκιαγραφία) of the real thing (69 B 6–7). This is later described as 'popular and civic virtue' (δημοτικὴν καὶ πολιτικὴν ἀρετήν, 82 A 10–B 1).[11] The illusion of virtue is produced by behaving virtuously without being genuinely virtuous. This occurs when virtuous deeds are done exclusively for prudential reasons. It follows that the person who has become truly virtuous as opposed to merely acting virtuously is transformed internally, not externally. But it is still not sufficient to say that the transformation consists in his now doing virtuous deeds for the right reason rather than for the wrong reason. True enough. But 'right reason' is an empty phrase when it at once seems to suggest an ulterior motive and no motive at all. The genuinely virtuous person performs virtuous deeds because he is virtuous, just as water flows downhill because it is water. Becoming virtuous is thus a transformation of the self and by the self in the direction of the disembodied ideal. The ideal self or person is a cognitive agent, and so we should expect that the transformation is primarily cognitive in nature. In Platonic terms, the transformation consists not in becoming what one is not, but in becoming what one really is. It is a transformation from image to reality. How exactly this transformation is supposed by Plato to occur will be at the forefront of my account henceforth.

2.2 The Cyclical Argument

The CA, taken on its own, is an argument unlikely to persuade anyone who gives it a moment's thought. The argument asserts two general principles: (1) all things come to be one way: opposite things come from opposites (71 A

---

[11] Cf. *Rep.* 365 C 3–4. In the myth at the end of *Phaedo*, 114 B 6–C 8, the difference is reflected in differing rewards in the afterlife.

9–10); and (2) between opposites there are two processes of coming-to-be, from one to the other (71 A 12–B 2). For example, between two opposites, the larger and the smaller, there is a process of getting larger which comes from the smaller one and getting smaller which comes from the larger one. These principles are then applied to the opposites living and being dead (71 C 1–5). Accordingly, there must be two processes between these (71 C 6–7). One of the processes is obvious, 'dying' (τὸ ἀποθνῄσκειν, 71 E 5). The opposite process must be 'coming-to-life again' (τὸ ἀναβιώσκεσθαι, 71 E 13). If indeed there is such a process, it must be a process of living people being born from the dead (71 E 14–72 A 2). If this is the case, it is sufficient evidence that the souls of the dead must exist somewhere and it is from this place that they come to life again (72 A 6–8).

It is easy enough to adduce counter-examples to (1), like odd and even or married and divorced, or ripe and unripe, though as a principle drawn from a theory of biological change it obviously depends on how the processes of change are designated. The real flaw in the argument is in the assumption that dying and coming to life are opposites in the relevant way—that is, in assuming a tendentious definition of the relevant terms. On the one hand, if we assume that dying and coming to life are opposites in the way that combining and separating are opposites—that is, the combining and separating of two entities, a soul and body—then, of course, it would follow that the soul would have to exist apart from the body, prior to and subsequent to their having been combined and divided. On the other hand, if dying and coming to life are opposite properties of one body, something like animation and deanimation, then it *does not* follow that the soul has to exist apart from the body any more than the fact that something that becomes larger has to have been smaller and something that has become smaller has to have been larger implies that the large has to exist apart from the small. So, the fact that dying and coming to life admit of an interpretation according to which the argument does not work means that the interpretation according to which it does has to be defended and not simply assumed.

We have already seen that Plato is manipulating the ambiguity between metaphorical dying and literal dying. How would someone come to be persuaded that literal dying is the separation of the soul and the body in the way that the argument assumes? Perhaps by the discovery of the identity of the soul and person that is metaphorical dying to the body. Even if it is not Plato's main intention that the λόγος being presented to the reader serves that discovery by leading him to reflect on his own identity, it does function in that way. For the belief that the death of my body is not the death of me is substantially the same as the belief that my body, though it be mine, is not me either.

In support of this interpretation, let us recall that Plato has Simmias raise an objection that puts into question precisely the tendentious definition of death (85 E 3–86 E 5). If the soul is an 'attunement' (ἁρμονία), then death is not a case of the separation of two entities that were combined. That the objection requires a lengthy reply (88 C 1–95 A 3) suggests that Plato takes it seriously. Rather than take the CA as a self-standing argument, it seems more appropriate to take it as a display of the need to establish one of the premises of the main proof, namely, that the soul is an entity.[12]

2.3 The Recollection Argument

The RA has deservedly garnered much more intense scrutiny than its predecessor. It raises a host of central philosophical issues. The basic argument is simple, which certainly cannot be said about the details: it is that our manifest capacity for *recognition* requires a previous cognition (73 C 1–2). But since there is no evidence that the relevant cognition occurred while we were embodied, we must have existed in a disembodied state. It was in this disembodied state that we had the original cognition. The argument is encapsulated in the claim that Cebes says Socrates habitually makes, namely, that 'learning is nothing but recollection' (μάθησις οὐκ ἄλλο τι ἢ ἀνάμνησις τυγχάνει οὖσα, 72 E 5–6). As Cebes takes this claim, it would not be true unless our souls existed before embodiment. Let us note, however, that the claim that learning is nothing but recollection is also a claim that *we* existed prior to embodiment. It is a claim about the person, the identical agent of disembodied cognition and embodied recognition. This agent is here implicitly identified with the soul.

---

[12] See Williams (1969), who thinks that in this argument Plato has produced a sophism according to which one can exist before one exists. But the distinction between person and human being and the exigencies of the proof of personal immortality seem to me to make this charge beside the point.

The key operative cognitive term in this argument is 'knowledge' (ἐπι-στήμη), but it appears to be used so loosely that it is virtually equivalent to 'cognition'. For example, it is used for objects of sense-perception as well as for Forms (cf. 73 C 8, D 3, 74 B 2). A self-conscious technical restriction in the use of the term ἐπιστήμη such as we shall find in *Republic* is not in evidence here. That is why it seems to me that focusing on a priori knowledge in this argument is somewhat misleading. It is no doubt true, as has often been pointed out, that many kinds of learning—factual learning, skills learning, and so on—do not involve recollection. All that needs to be shown for the argument to succeed is that there are examples of what can be loosely called 'cognition' that probably could not have occurred if we had not had certain other disembodied cognitive experiences.

The first condition for recollection Socrates lays down is that if someone recollects or recognizes something, he must have previously known it (73 C 1–2). The second condition is that if someone, on perceiving something, 'recognizes' (γνῷ) that thing, he also must 'think of' (ἐννοήσῃ) something else (C 6–8); third, that something else is the object not of 'the same knowledge' (ἡ αὐτὴ ἐπιστήμη), but of another (C 8). Two general sorts of cases of recollection are proposed: from things that are 'like' (ὁμοίων) and from things that are 'unlike' (ἀνομοίων, 74 A 2–3). An example of the first is seeing a picture of Simmias and being reminded of him. Examples of the second are seeing a lyre and being reminded of a man or seeing a picture of Simmias and being reminded of Cebes. Presumably, both sorts of cases meet the three conditions for recollection generally, although it will turn out that the case of recollection that supposedly proves immortality is one from things that are 'like'.

The first problem turns upon the understanding of the terms ὅμοιος and ἀνόμοιος. These are usually taken to mean 'similar' and 'dissimilar' but I believe this is somewhat misleading. Our understanding of the terms here must be capable of being applied to the relation of sensible instances of Forms to Forms, since that is, of course, the point of the examples of ὅμοιος and ἀνόμοιος. Two things can be similar if one is an approximation of the other. But as a number of scholars have forcefully argued, instances of Forms cannot be approximations of them.[13] Two things can also be similar if they

---

[13] See Vlastos (1973c), 58–75; Nehamas (1975), 105–17; Pritchard (1995), 127–49; and n. 19 below.

are the same in some respect. I submit that it makes no sense to suppose that Socrates is claiming that a picture of Simmias is the same as Simmias in some respect(s) but different in others, whereas a picture of Simmias is not the same as Cebes in any respect. For example, a picture of Simmias could just as easily be similar to Cebes because the picture is of a man and Cebes is a man, or made in the same colours, etc. Similarity is a hopelessly vague criterion to use here. I do not think we shall get any further if we suppose that two things are similar if they are the same in a *majority* of respects, whatever that might mean.[14]

A hint of the correct understanding of 'like' and 'unlike' comes from the argument in *Parmenides* where the young Socrates suggests that Forms are paradigms in nature and things made in their image are their 'likenesses' (ὁμοιώματα, 132 D 3).[15] Parmenides immediately counters that if the images are like these paradigms, then the paradigms must be like their images. This 'symmetrical likeness' is, I take it, nothing but sameness. It is just the sameness in many cases of 'largeness' in virtue of which a Form of Largeness is posited (cf. 132 A 1–4). One reason why some have resisted interpreting ὅμοιος and ἀνόμοιος as 'same' and 'not same' is, I believe, based on the supposition that if two things are the same, then one cannot be deficient with respect to the other. But as we shall see presently, the entire argument turns upon 'deficient sameness'. Another reason is that it is assumed that two things simply cannot be the same; if they were the same, they would be one. Thus, 'the same' as used of knowledge above or as used of the Form in *Parmenides* is the only sort of sameness. But even if philosophically we should decide that it is correct only to say that A can be the same as A, whereas B can never be the same as A, to do so would, I believe, pre-empt even an accurate exposition of the theory of Forms, much less a defence of it. In fact, Plato needs a distinction between 'same' and 'selfsame' or 'self-identical' just to be able to state what a Form is.

The second problem turns upon the meaning of 'the (self)same knowledge'. Some scholars have questioned the cogency of the third condition,

---

[14] This is the view of Gosling (1965), for example, who argues that 'likeness' is similarity or resemblance in a given number of respects. He cites *Crat.* 431–3 as expressing the same view.

[15] There is a good case to be made for the claim that the theory of Forms that is examined in the first part of *Parmenides* is taken in large part from *Phaedo*.

wondering why the cognition of a picture of Simmias is not the 'same knowledge' as that of Simmias himself.[16] I believe the confusion is caused by the loose translation of the cognitive vocabulary. The cognition of a picture of Simmias is not necessarily the recognition that it is a picture of him, and so it is not the '(self)same knowledge' because there are various ways of cognizing a picture without recognizing who is being pictured. Even if in cognizing the picture one does recognize that it is a picture of someone, the knowledge of the person who is being pictured is different from the knowledge of the picture. Against Gallop, I think the point is of considerable importance both in *Phaedo* and later in *Republic*. As we shall see, Plato is committed to holding that *no* cognition of any image as such is identical with the cognition of that of which it is an image. Indeed, cognizing an image or instance of a Form as such must be a different cognition from cognizing the Form itself, otherwise the present argument has not a chance of working. For the argument turns on the claim that the cognition of the instance depends on a *different* cognitional experience having previously occurred.

The crucial case is recollection from something that is the same, and for these a fourth condition is added: one must consider whether or not the same thing is 'lacking something' ($\tau\iota\ \dot{\epsilon}\lambda\lambda\epsilon\acute{\iota}\pi\epsilon\iota$) 'with respect to sameness' ($\kappa\alpha\tau\grave{\alpha}\ \tau\grave{\eta}\nu\ \dot{o}\mu oi\acute{o}\tau\eta\tau\alpha$, 74 A 5–7). It can hardly be said that the meaning of 'lacking something with respect to sameness' is self-evident. Plato needs to show that in certain cases where, say, A is the same as B, A is somehow lacking something with respect to its sameness to B. Although 'lacking' may suggest some sort of derivation, it is not clear that it is lacking *because* it is derived from B. The causal connection is important if it is to be shown that one could not know that A was lacking something if one did not know that with respect to which it was lacking.

How do we parse 'lacking something with respect to sameness'? Presumably, 'lacking something with respect to sameness' is to be contrasted with 'lacking nothing with respect to sameness'—in other words, a case of 'symmetrical sameness'. But Plato appears to want to assert that something can *both* be the same as that which, once known, makes recollection possible *and* be 'deficient' or, one supposes, not the *same*. Does 'non-reciprocal

[16] See Gallop (1975), 117–18, who, along with Ackrill, worries that 'one cannot recognize a picture of Simmias without *eo ipso* thinking of Simmias himself'.

sameness' even make sense? Let us first examine the passage in which the key argument occurs.

The particular example of non-symmetrical sameness given by Plato is that of equal logs or stones (74 A 9 ff.). It is agreed by the interlocutors that:

(1) there is something that is just equal and this is different from equal logs or stones (A 9–13);

(2) we know this something that is just equal (B 3);[17]

(3) we got knowledge of it from the things that are equal, namely, the logs and stones (B 4–6);

(4) whereas the equal things sometimes seen unequal, that which is just equal never seems unequal (B 7–C 2);

(5) the knowledge of the equal we get from seeing equal things is recollection (C 13–D 2);

(6) the equal logs and stones are not equal in the same way as the equal; they fall short of it (D 4–7);

(7) the judgement that the equals fall short of or are inferior to the equal necessitates that he who makes the judgement must have previously known that which the equals are the same as but inferior to (D 9–E 4);

(8) we recollect the equal from sense-perception; but the knowledge that the equals are inferior to the equal could not have come from sense-perception (75 A 5–B 2);

(9) then it was before we began to use our senses that we knew the equal itself.

The argument is then generalized for all things to which we affix the seal 'what it itself is' (αὐτὸ ὃ ἔστι, D 3). These are, of course, the Forms first mentioned at 65 D.

---

[17] This line is often taken to be an unargued claim that we know what the Form of Equality is. Against this, 76 B 8–9 says that if one knows a Form one can give an account of it. But the knowledge that Simmias agrees that he has at 74 B 2–3 surely does not yield that. The knowledge that is at issue here is knowledge that is obtained from sense-perception. The words are ἐπιστάμεθα αὐτὸ ὃ ἔστιν. Bostock (1986), 67–8, recognizes that the knowledge is not philosophical knowledge of a Form, but concludes that it must then be 'humdrum knowledge' of a Form. He explains this as knowledge of the meaning of the world 'equal'. There is, however, no justification at all that I can see for positing such knowledge. It is safer to take the words as indicating minimally the presumption of the entire argument, namely, that there exists such a thing as the Form of Equality (65 D).

The argument very explicitly puts all the Forms on the same footing as the Form of Equality and, by implication, all instances or images of Forms on the same footing as the equal logs and stones or at least their equality. Nevertheless, it is true that if there were a sort of inferiority present in equals that was not present in any other instance of a Form, the necessity of prior knowledge of the Form in order to judge the inferiority would be sufficient to make the case for pre-existence of the soul. There are sufficient reasons independent of this fact to hold that however we understand the inferiority of the equals, it must be generalizable for all instances of Forms.

Unfortunately, there is a notorious textual problem which clouds the issue. It is not certain what exactly the inferiority is supposed to consist in. The text reads: ἆρ' οὐ λίθοι μὲν ἴσοι καὶ ξύλα ἐνίοτε ταὐτὰ ὄντα τῷ μὲν ἴσα φαίνεται, τῷ δ' οὔ; (74 B 8–9). Does this mean that the equal logs and stones, while remaining the same, (1) seem equal to one thing but not to another; (2) seem equal to one person but not to another; (3) seem equal sometimes and seem unequal at other times?[18] The problem with (2) and (3) and even (1) on one interpretation is that they make the inferiority of the equals relative. But that equals should appear unequal to someone or at some time hardly warrants the claim that those who so judge them are judging them over against or in comparison with the Form of Equality. For if they merely appear unequal they are not thereby in any sense deficient in equality with respect to their sameness.

There are those who hold that Plato is thinking of cases where A is lacking something with respect to B because A is an approximation of B.[19] The examples which seem to work best on this interpretation are mathematical figures. When I draw a circle on paper it seems that it can only be an approximation of what mathematicians call a circle. Approximation is on this view the correct way to understand 'lacking something with respect to sameness'. But if equals appear unequal, they are no more lacking something with respect to equality than odd things are lacking something with respect to evenness. Indeed, the example in the text does not even exclude the

---

[18] See Bostock (1986), 73–8, and Gallop (1975), 121–5, on the various possibilities of interpreting this line.

[19] e.g. Gallop (1975), 95–6. Nehamas (1975), 105–6, gives references to others who hold this view. Bostock (1986), 86–7, decisively refutes the approximation interpretation in my opinion. See also Pritchard (1995), 128 ff.

possibility that the equal logs and stones are equal in number rather than in length or width. And in that case, their apparent inequality is certainly not a deficiency with respect to equality.

The deficiency in equality has to be a deficiency in principle in equal things. One contribution to the solution of the problem is the recognition that for Plato equality is not a two-term relation but a property of each of two things.[20] And the judgement that one thing has equality to another is a judgement based on sense-perception inseparable from the judgement that its equality is constituted by the size or width or number etc. that it has. But the opposite of that property, namely, inequality, is constituted by the same size or width or number etc. To judge two things equal, on this argument, requires the judgement that, though equal, the equal things are deficient with respect to equality. They are deficient because their equality is constituted by that by which inequality is constituted as well. By contrast, things that are equal, in so far as they are equal and the Form of Equality, 'never appear unequal' (74 C 1–2).[21] On this interpretation, I gloss the text thus: the very same logs or stones that have equality to other logs or stones also have inequality to other logs or stones. This reading, it seems to me, fits the argument best and gives good sense for 'lacking something with respect to sameness'. The sensible equals lack something with respect to the Form of Equality because whereas in the latter what makes the Form equal is nothing but equality, what makes a sensible equal also makes it unequal.

It will not be doubted that it makes sense, perhaps childish sense, to insist that while being one foot long is enough to have equality to something else one foot long, it is also at the same time sufficient for having inequality to something that is, say, thirteen inches long. Reasonably enough, however, it will be rather more strenuously doubted whether this fact is sufficient to demonstrate that a Form of Equality exists, much less that the soul is immortal. Leaving aside this very large issue for the moment, I now want to

---

[20] *Contra* Bostock (1986), 75, who nevertheless understands the Greek as I do.

[21] The text αὐτὰ τὰ ἴσα ἔστιν ὅτε ἄνισά σοι ἐφάνη ἢ ἡ ἰσότης ἀνισότης; is generally taken as indicating two different ways of referring to the Form of Equality. See Gallop (1975), 123–5. It is not essential to determine whether or not this is so for the purpose of this argument, even though later (102 D 6–103 B 5) the distinction that I am making here is made explicitly.

focus on the type of knowledge that the knowledge of the Form of Equality is supposed to be.

As (8) above tells us, the knowledge in virtue of which we judge the sensible equals to be inferior is different in some way from the knowledge we acquire from perceiving these. One might suppose that the distinction that is being drawn here is one that appears explicitly in *Theaetetus*, namely, the difference between 'possessing' and 'having' knowledge (197 B 8 ff.). If, however, this is the distinction being made here, Plato undercuts his own argument because the difference between possessing and having knowledge is not a difference in the content of what is known. But if the content of the recollection is the same as the content of what is putatively known in the disembodied state, why do we need the latter? Why, that is, could one not know from sense-perception alone that the equal logs and stones are not identical with—that is, are deficient with respect to—the Form of Equality? Indeed, this is exactly what someone who wanted to defend the theory of Forms without tying it to an argument for the immortality of the soul might very well want to maintain. Whether or not one agrees that the theory of Forms and the immortality of the soul stand or fall together, there is little doubt that the present argument holds this view and is also committed to the view that there is some knowledge which we must have acquired before birth (cf. 75 C 1–5, 76 E 5–7).

There is one passage within this argument where the two sorts of knowledge—the knowledge acquired before birth and the knowledge acquired through sense-perception—appear to be identical. At 75 E 1–6 the knowledge we regain in recollection seems to be the same knowledge we have before birth.[22] And yet it is not obvious that recollecting a previous occurrence of knowledge is equivalent to the original knowledge. I might, for example, recollect a trip to a foreign land from a photograph in a magazine, but what I recollect need not be and probably is not equivalent to what I knew—that is, what I experienced—even though I could not have recollected if I had not experienced the land in the first place.

Even more significant is Socrates' claim that if someone knows some-

---

[22] 'If, having got them [i.e. pieces of knowledge] before birth, we lost them on being born, and later on, using the senses about those very things, we regain those pieces of knowledge that we possessed at some former time, in that case would not what we call learning be the regaining of our own [οἰκείαν] knowledge'?

thing, he can give an account of what he knows (76 B 5–6). If the knowledge that one acquires from recollection is the same as the knowledge in virtue of which one can give an account, then upon recollecting equality from sensible equals and getting knowledge of it (74 C 8–9), one could, presumably, give an account of equality. And since the argument is, as we have seen, explicitly generalized for all Forms, anyone who recollects the Form from sensibles has the knowledge that enables one to give an account. But this is certainly not what the interlocutors think in this dialogue. Simmias says plaintively that after Socrates' death there will not be *anyone* who can do this. Socrates in reply confirms that hardly anyone seems to know Forms, although they are reminded of what they once learnt (76 C 1–4). What hardly anyone knows cannot be identical with what everyone knows as a result of their disembodied experience. Nor can it refer to what they know when they recollect, as the text implies. Unless we wish to say either that no one recollects or that everyone can give an account, in some attenuated sense of 'can', we seem forced to recognize that the knowledge obtained from sense-perception is not the knowledge obtained in the disembodied state and that it is in virtue of the latter when *it* is actualized that an account can be given, if at all.

That the two 'knowledges' are different does not mean and cannot mean for the argument that the embodied version can be had without the disembodied somehow being present. On the contrary, that is the crux of the argument. What we seem to know (recollect) while embodied on the basis of sense-perception is that which enables us to identify sensibles as equal. We could not know that they are deficiently equal unless we had some *other* knowledge, namely, disembodied knowledge of the Form of Equality. Having known the Form in a disembodied state obviously does not entail that one can give an account of it now. Clearly, something more than recognizing the sensible equals as being deficiently so is required for being able to give an account. Since knowing the Form is normally sufficient for being able to give an account, what we acquire on the basis of sense-perception is not equivalent to that knowledge. If this is so, then the question we are faced with is why the ability to judge sensibles inferior in the relevant manner depends upon the disembodied knowledge.

One might conceive of the perfection of Forms as notional and the deficiency of sensibles as deficiency with respect to notional perfection. For example, on the basis of one's sense-experience, one can conceive of an ideal spouse and then claim that all the persons one has met are deficient with respect to that ideal. But this judgement of deficiency certainly does not entail that one cognized the ideal in a disembodied state or even that the ideal exists in reality. The cases Plato has in mind are, I think, different. They depend on analysis of the phrase 'lacking something with respect to sameness'. The failed candidate for spouse is not so lacking. He or she is not at all the same as the ideal, though that person is deficient with respect to the ideal. Those who take the approximation view of the deficiency are, I believe, implicitly thinking of the ideal as a notional one. For Plato, Forms do not play the role of notional ideals, though it is in *Parmenides* that this is stated explicitly.[23] So, if we recognize that Forms are not notional ideals but real ideals, and that the deficiency of sensibles is with respect to these real ideals, we may well wonder if our ability to judge sensibles deficient could be possible without having had cognition of the ideal. Thus, my judgement that the equal logs and stones are deficient with respect to equality is not a judgement that they imperfectly instantiate a concept of equality, imperfect either by approximation or by limitation or incompleteness. It is a judgement that the equals, though they be equal, are really deficient in comparison with something real with respect to sameness. A judgement of deficiency alone is available notionally. A judgement of deficiency with respect to sameness is available only by cognizing the two real things which are judged to be the same.[24]

Perhaps I can explain this point another way. Consider the following judgement: this is (*read*: is the same as) the colour I was thinking of. In this case, the sameness pertains to a colour I have perceived. If it is the same colour, it is hard to see what its deficiency consists of. Or, I could say of

[23] See *Parm.* 132 B 4 ff., where Socrates suggests that the regress arguments adduced by Parmenides may be avoided if Forms are 'concepts' (νοήματα) in the mind. Parmenides immediately and decisively replies that Forms, in order to do what Forms do, must be that of which one has concepts, not concepts themselves.

[24] Bostock (1986), 103–10, thinks that our ability to abstract conceptual knowledge from sensibles undermines Plato's argument. This seems to me confused. Plato agrees that we get knowledge from sensibles, but this knowledge, as Bostock recognizes, is not the knowledge that we supposedly have before birth. Without this latter knowledge, we could not judge the sensibles deficient. The possibility of abstraction and conceptualization is irrelevant to the argument that prior knowledge of Forms in a disembodied state is necessary for judging deficiencies in the sensible world.

the colour: this is not quite (*read*: is deficient with respect to) what I had in mind. But then there would be no reason to hold that it is the same. One could say that it is an approximation or generically the same (say, in the red family), but not the same. The unique judgement that something is the same as something else though deficient cannot be made by comparing something to a concept. So, if the judgement can be made—and that now appears to be the critical issue—it requires independent cognition of the two things judged to be the same and a further judgement based on this that one is deficient with respect to the other.

Plato would no doubt be confident in claiming that sensibles can be judged deficient in the relevant sense. He would insist that (1) two logs or stones can be equal and (2) the account of what this equality consists of is *not* an account of the Form of Equality. Indeed, it is an account of what is deficient with respect to equality because it is necessarily also an account of inequality, whereas the account of the Form of Equality, whatever that may be, is never an account of the Form of Inequality. Let us assume that no one would question (1).[25] Someone might, however, reply to (2) by claiming that the account of the equality of the equal logs or stones is exactly the same as the account of the Form of Equality. But this is difficult to maintain since the account of the equality of *this* log to *that* one-foot-long log will at least have to include the fact that the first log is one foot long. And though the log does not have to be one foot long in order to be unequal to a log two feet long, being one foot long is sufficient for this to be so. The account of the equality of the logs must include that which constitutes the equality. But that constitution is part of the account of its inequality.[26] An account of the equality of the logs which ignored that which constitutes their equality would just be an account of the Form of Equality. In that case, we would not be accounting for what is deficient in them.

This interpretation may be resisted as being insufficiently broad to cover cases of instances of Forms that are not relational like equality. On the

[25] Later, at 102 D 6–8, Socrates insists that not only is Largeness never small, but the largeness in us is never small. I shall return to this passage. Here I only wish to insist that this claim serves as a guarantor of sameness in instance and Form.

[26] The interpretation here can be applied to the corresponding *Republic* passages, 523 C ff., where the example is three fingers, the middle one being taller than one and shorter than the other, and 479 A–C, where Socrates avers that beautiful things seem ugly, just things seem unjust, or pious things impious.

contrary, I think that this interpretation is the only one broad enough to sustain the universality required by a theory of Forms that aims to explain sameness in difference as well as the inferiority of the sensible world. It is only, I think, because of an inadequate conception of this inferiority that one would be reluctant to admit that there are, for example, Forms of substantives or non-relational properties.[27] An account of sensible beauty or of the humanity of a person will necessarily include constituents that are not merely irrelevant to the account of the Form of Beauty and the Form of Humanity but actually constitutive of the account of something else. I take it that just as the Form of Equality never appeared to be unequal, the Form of Humanity never appeared to be feline either. But the account of Socrates' humanity will at some level inevitably include in it constituents that are part of the account of, say, a cat.

It is crucial for this interpretation that the account of a Form cannot be obtained from sensibles. If it could, the nerve of the argument for immortality would be cut. The judgement that sensibles are inferior or deficient cannot be obtained from sensibles either. This is evident from consideration of a realistic theory of universals. It is precisely because these universals are what their many instances have in common that the instances are not deficient with respect to these. There is, as it were, no conceptual space for deficiency if one considers universally exactly what many things have in common. The judgement of deficiency requires independent cognition of Forms. But the recollection that the cognition must have occurred is not equivalent to that cognition occurring again.

This is the argument for the immortality of the soul based on recollection as I understand it. More particularly, and certainly more troublesome, it is an argument for the existence of the soul or person prior to embodiment, an idea that makes even most friends of personal immortality blench. It can hardly be a conclusive argument, since it does not make a serious effort to exclude the possibility, whether this be implausible or not, of the knowledge of Forms being somehow infused in us some time after conception.[28] Nevertheless, we must not lose the insights to be gained from

---

[27] See Penner (1987), 57–62, 181–90, for an account of the recollection argument somewhat similar to mine. I cannot here do justice to the richness of Penner's overall account of the theory of Forms in the so-called 'middle' dialogues.

[28] Although, if only an immaterial entity can know Forms, in so far as embodied persons

the fact that the impossibility of acquiring the relevant knowledge while embodied is precisely what is being claimed here. A person who pre-exists embodiment in a particular body and then experiences such embodiment evidently does not require the accoutrements of such a life in order to ensure personal identity. This fact gives a distinctive meaning to 'personal' immortality. It does not seem to require the idiosyncrasies that attach to embodiment.

Although, as we have seen, it is not mere immortality of the soul but personal immortality that is at stake in this dialogue, it is obscure how personal immortality is to be understood if it does not include necessarily a continuation of the consequences of embodiment. One way of framing the problem is to ask what I could count as me if I had to exclude everything I have experienced in this body. The implausibility, indeed perhaps the impossibility, of my imagining what would be left of me after I cut out everything that belongs to this embodied existence is addressed simply and eloquently by Plato in the words 'philosophy is practice for dying and being dead'. For in philosophy, Plato thinks, one gradually detaches oneself from what one thinks inessential to one's identity. The more one gives oneself over to philosophy, the more attachment to embodied life seems delusory and childish. The argument that one had an identity prior to embodiment at least suggests that embodiment itself is not essential to one's identity.

If the remnants of embodied life are to be excluded from the essential self, the identity of the person as a knower comes more sharply into focus. The sole connecting link between the pre-embodied person and the embodied person is the knowledge acquired in the former state. At least part of my present identity is constituted by the knowledge which I must have acquired in order for me to make the relevant judgements of the inferiority of sensibles. Just because I have that knowledge, even though I cannot, it seems, access it directly, it can be considered to be 'hard-wired' into what I am.

Still, if rewards and punishments for embodied deeds are to make any sense, there must be something more to disembodied life than what would be had without embodiment. Exactly how embodiment is supposed to af-

are not immaterial entities, their knowledge of Forms would seem to be excluded. We are not, however, told why embodiment as such should make it impossible for the embodied immaterial entity to attain knowledge.

fect a subject of disembodied contemplation is not obvious. For example, at the end of the AA Socrates compares the completely disembodied existence of the 'purified' philosophers with the wraith-like post-mortem existence of those who are not purified (81 A ff.). If for no other reason, the claim that there can be a state of a person that is neither a state of embodiment nor a state of disembodiment should lead us to conclude that Plato is not a Cartesian dualist. But this still leaves Plato with the task of explaining the coherence of his own position.

I take it that the RA is at least beginning to respond to the question of the identity of the disembodied and embodied person by arguing that here below we must have knowledge that we probably or necessarily could only have acquired in a disembodied state. If the disembodied state is the ideal, then even if idiosyncratic experiences and the resulting psychological formations are an essential feature of embodied personal identity, it does not follow that they belong to that ideal. But if one's embodied life is to make any difference to whether or not that ideal is achieved or to the manner in which it is achieved, Plato owes us an account of how that is so.

If the RA could at best show pre-existence, it certainly says nothing about post-existence. When this point is raised by Simmias and Cebes (77 B 1–C 5), Socrates says that the desired result follows if we combine the RA with the CA (77 C 6–9). Superficially, this would mean that the CA supplies the post-existence and the RA supplies the pre-existence. But if the CA works at all on its own, it proves both pre- and post-existence. So, the appropriate combination is probably not of this sort. I am more inclined to believe that the combination is of the CA with the RA where the latter is construed as supporting the premiss that the soul is an entity separate from the body. If we possessed knowledge of Forms prior to embodiment, then being born or coming-to-be is a case that could perhaps with some plausibility be represented as the combining of two entities and death their separation. Of course, even if coming-to-be is the combining of two entities, it does not follow that death is their separation. The soul might be the sort of entity that is capable of one and only one combination because in combining with the body it is altered so as no longer to be able to exist on its own. So, combining the RA with the CA does not provide a conclusive case, but it advances matters by focusing on the nature of the soul and, particularly, the question of whether it is the sort of thing that is imperishable. This is the question that the AA seeks to answer.

2.4 The Affinity Argument

The AA (78 B 4–84 B 4) has not been treated kindly in the literature. In fact, it is frequently dismissed as an embarrassment for Plato.[29] In so far as the argument relies on an analogy or in so far as it is merely probabilistic, it certainly does not stand on its own as a demonstration of the immortality of the soul. But this argument, like the others, is not supposed to stand on its own. And at its core there is an argument which, far from being inconsequential, is the origin of a family of immensely influential arguments for the immateriality of the person. These arguments are refined and elaborated upon by countless later Platonically inspired philosophers. They are still, in my view, worthy of interest.

The basic argument is this:

(1) Forms are invisible entities (79 A 6–7, cf. 65 D 8–11).[30]
(2) Whatever is an invisible entity is 'invariant' (ἀεὶ ταὐτὰ ἔχον, 79 A 9–10).
(3) Whatever is invariant is most likely to be 'incomposite' (ἀσύνθετον, 78 C 6–7).[31]
(4) Whatever is incomposite is 'indissoluble' (ἀδιάλυτον, 78 C 1–4; cf. 80 B 2).
(5) Whatever is indissoluble is immortal (cf. 80 B 1–10).
(6) Souls are more like invisible entities than visible entities (79 B 16–17).
(7) Therefore, souls are likely to be invariant, incomposite, indissoluble, and immortal (80 B 1–3).

[29] See e.g. Elton (1997), who claims that the argument is so bad that it must be intended by Plato as an illustration of 'how not to argue the case for immortality, and, more generally, how not to argue the case for any thesis' (313). The argument's validity is defended by Apolloni (1996), though his analysis is significantly different from mine.

[30] It seems clear enough that by 'invisible' Plato means 'immaterial', especially if we read 79 B 16–17 as saying that the soul is like the sort of invisible entity that the Form is. And this seems the right reading for the most economical and straightforward formulation of the argument.

[31] Insinuating 'most likely' (μάλιστα) into the chain of attributes of Forms obviously alters the modality of the argument from necessity to probability. I do not think this changes much since all dialectical arguments are in a sense probabilistic.

Clearly, the crux of the argument, and the reason why it is so readily dismissed, is the assumption that souls are like the invisible entities that are the Forms. Such an assumption appears to beg the question. It seems fairly obvious that one may deny either that the soul is an invisible entity or that it is an invisible entity in the way a Form is. In the former case the argument does not seem even to get off the ground, and in the latter case it rests upon a false analogy. Simmias, as we shall see, will take the latter alternative in suggesting that the soul is a ἁρμονία. So we need to ask if there is anything in the argument that supports premiss (6).

The property of soul that is supposed to get us to agree that soul is like the Forms is its capacity for cognizing Forms. The RA has already established the fact that we must have known Forms in a disembodied state prior to embodiment. The question then becomes: why should we believe that *only* a disembodied or immaterial entity is capable of cognizing an immaterial entity? Granted that a disembodied person must have acquired knowledge of Forms, is that same person, when embodied, also capable of such knowledge? There is a passage near the beginning of the AA that evinces the same ambiguity regarding the possibility of embodied knowledge that we saw earlier:

Whenever it [the soul] investigates [σκοπῇ] alone by itself, it departs yonder towards that which is pure and always existent and immortal and unvarying, and in virtue of its kinship with it, is always with it, whenever it is alone by itself and whenever it may do so; then it has ceased from wandering and, when it is around those objects, it is always constant and unvarying, owing to its being in contact [ἐφαπτομένη] with such objects. And this state of it is called wisdom, isn't it? (79 D 1–7, trans. Gallop)[32]

It is unclear from this passage whether it is presumed that it is possible to acquire knowledge of Forms while embodied, as opposed merely to 'investigating' them. On the one hand, if the soul's immateriality is sufficient for it to be able to cognize Forms, then it is unclear why such cognition might be thought unavailable to the soul in its embodied state. On the other hand, embodiment is not inconsequential to the state of the

---

[32] See 82 D 9–83 B 4, the parallel passage at the end of the argument. Here, too, when the soul is 'alone by itself' it is able to see that which is intelligible (as opposed to that which is sensible) and invisible. But the question is precisely whether the embodied soul is ever 'alone by itself'.

person, as we have seen. Owing to embodiment, the person acquires states that are like images of the ideal disembodied state. In addition, it is owing to embodiment that cognition of Forms is, minimally, exceedingly difficult. In any case, the soul's 'kinship' (ὡς συγγενὴς οὖσα) with the Forms is the condition in virtue of which it is able to have some sort of cognitive contact with them.[33] And its kinship provides the justification for claiming that the soul is like that which is invariant, incomposite, indissoluble, and immortal. The question we are concerned with, then, is why kinship with the immaterial is necessary for cognition of it. This question amounts to nothing less than the question of what exactly knowledge is supposed by Plato to be. Since knowledge is not thematized until *Republic* and then *Theaetetus*, we cannot expect an entirely satisfactory answer to our question here. Nevertheless, there is quite a bit that can be gleaned from *Phaedo* itself.

First, let us observe a small point from the RA. It is that the ability to give an account of the objects of knowledge, that which Simmias thinks no one but Socrates can do, must be distinct from knowledge itself, which all agree everyone has to have had in the disembodied state.[34] If knowledge is distinct from an account of what is known or even the ability to give such an account, this fact tends to indicate that knowledge for Plato is a state that does not simply consist in expressing or thinking of representations of the knowable. Saying the words 'Equality is a dyadic relation of such and such a sort' or 'Justice is the proper operation of the parts of the soul' or any other real or putative account of a Form is not equivalent to having knowledge of it. For this reason, even if for no other, it is difficult to see how knowledge of Forms could be propositional, if this means that knowledge is expressing or thinking or 'having' some representation or description of an immaterial entity.

I want to suggest that underlying the AA is the idea that knowledge is for Plato a state of the soul or person that is not representational. But that is a very difficult idea for anyone to understand who comes to the question

[33] The kinship with Forms is evidently a version of the principle 'like knows like' attributed by Aristotle, *De anima* 405ᵇ10–17, 427ᵃ28, to Empedocles, Homer, and unnamed 'others'. See also *Rep* 490 B 4, 611 E 1 ff.; *Tim.* 90 D; *Laws* 899 D 7.

[34] See *Phileb.* 62 A 2–3: 'Let us consider a man who knows what justice itself is and who has the account that follows upon thinking.' *7th Letter* 342 A–E sharply distinguishes knowledge and an account. A correct account could presumably be given by someone who heard it, but that person would not thereby know that it was a correct account.

of Plato's view of knowledge from a background of modern epistemology. For virtually all accounts of knowledge in at least the analytic tradition of modern epistemology are representationalist. Plato does not consider a representationalist account of knowledge seriously until *Theaetetus*, where he rejects it, or so I shall argue. That he does so in *Theaetetus* opens up the possibility that he had already considered and rejected such an account in *Phaedo*. I am sympathetic to this possibility, especially if it makes the AA a more respectable argument. But whether by the time of writing *Phaedo* Plato had already considered and rejected a representationalist account of knowledge, some of the elements of a non-representationalist account may be assumed, with only a modicum of charity, to be present.[35]

Roughly, a non-representationalist account of knowledge holds that knowledge is a state in part constituted by the knowable, not merely caused by it. The presence of knowledge is materially equivalent to the presence of the knowable. The word 'presence' here must be understood literally, although the presence of an immaterial entity is not the same thing as the presence of a material entity. One excellent reason for holding that knowledge is non-representational is that knowledge is an infallible state and that 'I know but I may be mistaken' misconstrues the nature of knowledge altogether. If knowledge were representational, infallibility could in principle not be preserved because there would be no way of inferring from a representational state any objective state of affairs. There is no mental state that entails truth so long as that mental state is representationalist. If knowledge is a non-representational state, then knowledge is non-propositional since a proposition is a representation. This leaves entirely open the very large

---

[35] Speaking broadly, what differentiates representational from non-representational human states or activities is epistemic assessability. For example, a belief can be assessed as true or false, whereas a feverish state, for example, cannot be so assessed. So the assumption that knowledge is a representational state includes its epistemic assessability. But epistemic assessability is essentially a third-person procedure. It supposes that *A* can know whether *B* knows something. According to my interpretation of Plato's concept of knowledge, third-person assessment is parasitic on first-person assessment. Thus, *A* cannot know that *B* knows unless *A* knows. Indeed, it can be argued that on Plato's view third-person assessment of knowledge is an altogether incoherent idea. That is, *A* can *only* know that *A* knows and can never know that *B* knows. The non-representational view of knowledge for Plato is to be contrasted with the representational nature of other forms of cognition. The account of that contrast is, as we shall see, located within the context of Plato's hierarchical metaphysics.

question of how propositions can in fact represent the knowable. It also leaves open the question of whether insisting on an infallibility criterion for knowledge does not force Plato to insinuate propositions into his account of knowledge. The first question will receive attention in Chapter 4; the second in Chapter 5.

Assuming that Plato does hold that knowledge is a non-representational state, why should we suppose that only an immaterial entity can know an immaterial entity? A moment's reflection should lead us to object that Plato himself, in so far as he holds that immaterial Forms are present to their instances, is committed to denying that an immaterial entity can only be present to an immaterial entity. As Socrates says later in *Phaedo*, something is beautiful because it participates in Beauty (100 c 5–6). Why is this not analogous to 'knowing something means participating in it'? The answer is that the beauty in that which participates in the Form of Beauty is, as we have seen, diminished in reality or defective. Of course, it is materiality, roughly speaking, that inevitably produces the defect. If the presence of a Form to a knower were the presence of the Form defectively, then exactly what the non-representational account of knowledge intended to ensure, namely, infallibility, would be lost. One would know 'defective' beauty, not Beauty. And, as we shall see, this is exactly the case for types of cognition other than and inferior to knowledge: that is, types of cognition that are representational. But that still leaves us with the question of why only an immaterial entity can know an immaterial entity.

The answer, I believe, is to be found in the claim that knowledge is essentially self-reflexive. As we saw in the last chapter, when a subject is in a self-reflexive state, that subject is aware or cognizant of the state that the subject is in. The subject in both cases is identical. If knowledge is essentially self-reflexive, then knowers cannot be material entities. Against this, suppose that a subject knows some object of knowledge and that this subject is a material entity. Then there must be a mental state that constitutes this subject's knowledge and another mental state that constitutes his awareness of being in the state of knowing. On this scenario, though, the subjects of the two mental states cannot be identical any more than a switch can simultaneously be in the 'on' and the 'off' positions. We could devise a material entity that had both on and off switches or parallel states, one of which served to 'monitor' the other. But this material entity is not self-identical in the relevant sense.

It may be objected that 'in the relevant sense' begs the question. I think it does not so long as we insist on infallibility as a characteristic of knowledge. For if knowledge is infallible, then it is not arbitrary to hold that if a subject knows that it is in a mental state, then the subject that knows this is identical with the subject of the mental state. That is the only way that infallibility can be secured. No material process, including the monitoring of one part of an entity by another, can similarly guarantee infallibility. This is equivalent to holding that if knowledge is a self-reflexive, infallible mental state, then it must also be non-representationalist. For all representational states are fallible in their representations. Thus, there is an appropriately tight connection between the concepts of self-reflexivity, immateriality, infallibility, and non-representationalism.

Here is a further objection. In the RA the interlocutors agree that they have acquired knowledge of Forms but they do not have that knowledge presently, so they know but do not know that they know. Thus, self-reflexivity does not seem to be an essential component of knowledge. The correct response to this objection, I believe, begins by noting that the interlocutors only believe that they must have once known the Forms. They do not now know them, else they could give an account of them. This, however, does not solve the problem. If Simmias and Cebes believe truly that they have known Forms and that this knowledge can be recovered, then in some sense they know Forms now. They seem to be in the state that a knower is in but they do not know that they know.

I think we must insist that the interlocutors do not know Forms. What the RA tries to show is that they must have once known them if they are able to make the sort of judgements that they do about sensibles and that they are identical with the persons who once had this knowledge. But they do not have the knowledge now. Thus, they are identical with a disembodied ideal in a defective way, namely, as images of that. The AA tries to show that only if persons are immaterial entities could they have had that knowledge. This is a sort of transcendental argument, revealing the conditions which make certain embodied cognitive activities possible. These conditions are in a way 'personalized' since, for example, Simmias' ability to judge sensible equals defective is owing to Simmias having had knowledge of the Form of Equality. The state that each interlocutor is presently in is informed by the knowledge each had, but it is nevertheless a defective or diminished state. It is analogous to the imagistic state of any instance of a Form. It is therefore at least misleading to characterize the basic cognitive state of an embodied person as potential knowing, since potencies are not defective images of actualities. Embodied persons are images not simply of an ideal towards which they strive, but of an ideal that concurrently defines their cognitive powers. If the personalizing of the transcendental argument does not yet allow us to give anything like a robust account of personal identity, it nevertheless suggests the important consideration that the cognitive states of embodied persons are images of a disembodied ideal. Specifically, they are representational images.

There are basically three ways in which the AA as I have interpreted it can be denied. First, one can try to show that knowledge is not what Plato says it is. That is, one can try to show that a non-representationalist account of knowledge is an account of nothing actual or possible. Second, one can try to show that material entities can have knowledge as Plato understands that. Third, one can agree with Plato regarding knowledge, but claim that it is not possible for humans to have it. That is, it would take an immaterial entity to have knowledge, but since persons are not immaterial entities, they cannot have it. Perhaps gods or angels have it, but not us.

I shall not pause here to undertake a discussion of the pros and cons of each of these strategies. I am mainly concerned to have shown that the AA reveals Plato's commitment both to the immateriality of persons and to the identity of persons as ideally or paradigmatically knowers. An important part of the proof for the immortality of the soul is the discovery that one is, at least in a disembodied state, an immaterial knower and that in the embodied state one is 'deficient with respect to sameness' in relation to that immaterial knower. In discovering that one could not have judged the equals deficient in their equality without having known the Form of Equality, one further discovers that one could not have known what Equality is if one were not the sort of entity that a Form is. If one is this sort of entity, then the body does not belong ideally to one's identity: that is, a person is not a human being. Finally, one's identity turns out to consist not primarily in being able to be reidentifiable diachronically, but in being images variously occurring of a disembodied exemplar.

My analysis of the AA focuses on the immateriality of the Forms rather than their invariance or incompositeness or indissolubility. This is not the usual approach.[36] The invariance that the soul has is present, as the passage quoted above insists, only when in the company of Forms. This 'company' is, it appears, cognitive attainment. Invariance is never independently established for the soul. And incompositeness and indissolubility are said to follow from invariance (cf. 78 C 1–4, 6–7). Since the reason for holding that the soul is invariant is the possibility of knowledge, we return to the question of why this possibility should lead us to conclude that the soul is like a Form. That the soul may not be unqualifiedly invariant, incomposite, or even indissoluble means that the AA could only show that that which knows Forms is immaterial. If there are parts or modes of existence for the soul not implicated in such knowledge, this argument has nothing to say about them.

After agreement is reached on the AA by the interlocutors, a subordinate argument is introduced:

Now look at it in this way, too: when soul and body are present in the same thing, nature ordains that the one shall serve and be ruled, whereas the other shall rule and be master. Here again, which do you think is like the divine and which is like the mortal? Don't you think that the divine is naturally adapted for ruling and leading, whereas the mortal is adapted for being ruled and for serving? (79 E 8–80 A 5, trans. Gallop, slightly modified)

Cebes readily concurs that the soul resembles the divine and so, presumably, the immortal. I say this is a subordinate argument because it does not address immateriality, although this may be inferred from the contrast of the soul to the body. What the argument does in particular is introduce the relation of the soul and the body with respect to governance. The rule of the body by the soul is natural but not always the case. Indeed, the soul's very presence in the body as in a 'tomb' suggests as a condition of embodiment a state 'contrary to nature' (cf. 82 D 9 ff.). It is typically Platonic to invert the ordinary conception of what is natural. Embodiment is contrary to the true nature of the person, which is fulfilled only in separation from the body

---

[36] See e.g. Apolloni (1996), 12 ff., who argues that the key characteristic of Forms is invariance or 'constancy', and that this is the characteristic of soul that Plato is most keen to establish. Bostock (1986), 118–20, assumes that the soul must be supposed to be analogous to Forms in all the relevant respects and that if it is not the argument fails.

when 'nurtured' by what is 'true' and 'divine' and 'the non-opinable' (84 A 8–B 1). In short, the person achieves his true nature in knowing Forms.

Socrates presses the analogy of the soul to the immortal and the body to the mortal. Since even parts of the body, like bones and sinews, are practically immortal, how much more likely it is that the soul itself is immortal (80 C–D). But now he seeks to differentiate the disembodied souls of those who have pursued a life of philosophy from the souls of those who have allowed themselves to be contaminated by their bodies (80 E–81 C). The latter, owing to their previous attachments to their bodies, are doomed to wander about tombs and graves until eventually they are reincarnated into the type of animal body that suits their previous degenerated characters (81 C–82 A). Those who have followed neither philosophy nor lives of wickedness but rather lives of 'popular, that is, civic, virtue' will experience a happier fate, first being re-embodied into tamer animals and then eventually back into human beings (82 A 10–B 8).

Socrates has moved from an argument for the immortality of the soul to an argument that one's disembodied fate flows from one's embodied career. The latter is expressed in terms of the degree of attachment to bodily desires. This argument seems to fly in the face of the implication of the RA that embodiment has nothing to do with personal identity. This is not so, however, because the consequences of embodied life do not change what we are ideally, that is to say, in the disembodied state. Indeed, it is because we are ideally knowers, akin to gods, that an embodied life devoted to something other than philosophy results in re-embodiment. The failure to become what we are is what Plato represents as 'being weighed down' with bodily elements (81 C 10), 'co-operating especially in one's imprisonment' (82 E 6–7), and being 'made corporeal' (83 D 5) and 'contaminated' by the body (83 D 10).

That the soul can be corrupted by the circumstances of embodiment in general is readily understandable, and surely this is principally what being 'made corporeal' and similar metaphors convey. What it means for the soul to 'share opinions' (ὁμοδοξεῖν) and pleasures with the body (83 D 7–8) and ultimately to adopt its false opinions is somewhat less understandable. But let us recall that Plato's dualism does not require him to view the body as having opinions. Bodily pleasures that seduce are the pleasures of the same person who does or does not desire to submit to the seduction. Although

I shall reserve until the next chapter discussion of the sort of conflict this occasions, it is here most relevant to stress that the embodied person who is subject to seduction is an imperfect or incomplete creation. This imperfect person who submits or does not submit or submits occasionally to the blandishments of the body as a consequence of embodiment is an image of its perfect exemplar just as the equal logs and stones manifest an image of the Form of Equality and just as the opinions this person holds, true or false, are images of knowledge of the immaterial knowable. The conflicted state of an embodied immaterial person who finds himself to be the subject of bodily desires as well as immaterial thoughts is not unlike the images of Forms that 'are and are not at the same time', as *Republic* will put it. In one crucial respect, however, the embodied, that is, empirical, person is disanalogous to the other images. Only this image can become aware that it is an image and only it can gradually assimilate itself to its exemplar. This process of assimilation is concisely named by Plato 'the practice of philosophy'.

2.5 The Objections of Simmias and Cebes

Immediately upon the conclusion of the AA, Cebes and Simmias raise objections to the arguments that have hitherto been advanced by Socrates (84 C 1–88 B 8). Simmias objects that the soul may in fact be a ἁρμονία or attunement of the bodily instrument and Cebes objects that, although the soul might survive the body, it might eventually die on its own. The objection offered by Simmias is somewhat puzzling since it is an objection that would refute the RA, the conclusion of which he has already accepted (92 C 11–E 3; cf. 76 E). But if the soul did pre-exist embodiment, nevertheless its association with the body is obscure. The idea that the soul is an attunement would at least make that association clearer. Cebes' objection is directly aimed at the AA if that argument is read as allowing the possibility that though the soul be immaterial, it can nevertheless be dispersed or wear out in time. One might suppose that it is simply a category mistake to talk about immaterial entities wearing out, but it is no doubt fresh in the minds of the interlocutors that the (re-)embodied soul is 'weighed down' or affected by 'bodily elements'. And so Cebes might well raise the objection not against the argument that the soul is immaterial but against the argument that its immateriality guarantees its imperishability.

Simmias' argument (85 E 3–86 D 4), or rather, the argument reported by him, is in fact analogical. The soul can plausibly be compared to an attunement of a lyre. The attunement is, like the soul, invisible, immaterial, and divine. Yet, when the lyre of which it is an attunement is destroyed, so is the attunement. Analogously, when the body is destroyed, we must assume that the soul is destroyed as well. The basic thrust and relevance of this argument are perfectly clear even if it is not so clear exactly what sort of property an attunement is supposed to be.[37] The soul must be shown to be not merely immaterial but an entity that can exist independently, so that its continuing existence is not contingent on a body. Simmias' argument does not directly supply a refutation of the arguments of Socrates. The AA might seem to require only immateriality for the soul, not status as an independent entity, although I have argued that this is not so. The RA certainly concludes that the soul is an independent entity, but it infers this only from the claims about disembodied knowledge. Together, the RA and the AA want to claim that we either do or can have knowledge of immaterial Forms and that this would not be possible if we were not such as to be immaterial and to have existed prior to embodiment. A simple step to undermining both arguments is to deny that such knowledge is possible or that it has been shown to be possible. Simmias does this implicitly when at 85 C 3–4 he avers that 'clear knowledge' (σαφὲς εἰδέναι) is either impossible or extremely difficult in this life. He is talking about knowing whether the soul is immortal, but if he doubts that this can be known he might also doubt that Forms can be known. The *only* thing that Socrates has said that goes to show that knowledge is possible is that part of the RA which claims, in effect, that abstraction or conceptualization of the sensible world does not account for our ability to judge sensibles inferior to Forms. Simmias might be forgiven for being uncomfortable that the justification of his hope for an afterlife hangs by such a slim reed. In fact, Simmias opts for the truth of the RA over that of the attunement theory (92 C 11–E 3). Nevertheless, Plato thinks the objection serious enough to devote three Stephanus pages to it.

Cebes agrees with Simmias regarding the cogency of the RA. He accepts the claim that the soul is an entity with respect to pre-existence (87 A 1–2), but

---

[37] See Gallop (1975), 147–9, on the various possibilities.

he doubts that this entails its immortality. For soul might survive a succession of bodies only to wear out eventually on its own, like a weaver who outlives many cloaks he has woven, but for the last (87 D 7–88 B 8). It seems that the succession of bodies does not refer to successive reincarnations in different bodies, which is mentioned only at 88 A, but to successive reconstructions of the body of one person throughout his life. As Gallop and others have pointed out, the analogy of the weaver must be taken to specify that the weaver weaves and outlives his own cloaks. This assumption is the opposite of Simmias': it makes the body dependent on the soul rather than the other way around. This fact guarantees that the refutation of Simmias has to be entirely independent of the refutation of Cebes. Except for the eschatological myth at the end of the dialogue and the closing scene of Socrates' death, the remainder of this work is devoted to answering these two objections.

There are two intertwined arguments against Simmias' attunement hypothesis.[38] The underlying strategy of both is to show that there are crucial disanalogies between an attunement and a soul. The first argument (92 E 4–93 A 10, 94 B 4–95 A 3) seeks to show that the soul can control and oppose bodily 'states' ($\pi\acute{a}\theta\eta$), whereas an attunement can never do so. The second (93 A 11–C 10, 93 D 1–94 B 3) seeks to show that if an attunement can admit of degrees, a soul is not an attunement because a soul cannot admit of degrees. That is, no soul is more or less of a soul. But if an attunement can be said not to admit of degrees because it does not partake of non-attunement, then again it is unlike soul, for souls can be good or bad, and, on the attunement hypothesis, a good soul would be one that partakes of attunement and a bad soul would be one that partakes of non-attunement.

The first argument anticipates the argument in *Republic* 4 for the tripartitioning of the soul.[39] As we have already seen, however, prior to *Republic*, where appetites are psychic states requiring a body, they are represented here simply as bodily states. And the conflict that in *Republic* is described as a conflict between reason and appetite is here described as a conflict between soul and body. Granted that the phenomenon of conflict to which Socrates is alluding is not seriously contestable, is there any reason to be-

[38] See (Gallop 1975), 153–67, for an excellent analysis of the replies. Gallop's analysis relies heavily on that found in a paper that was actually published later; see Taylor (1983).

[39] See below, § 3.1.

lieve that such conflicts count against the claim that the soul is an attribute of a body, an attribute which is functionally related to the body? It is easy to give a precipitate negative reply to this question based on a plethora of readily available counter-examples. A complex organism with complex substates can obviously find itself in all sorts of conflicting states under a suitably defined sense of 'conflicting'. Such counter-examples seem to leave open the possibility that the relevant bodily states should be in conflict or perhaps tension with other bodily states.[40] Even so, no bodily part can be in conflict with itself, that is, in contradictory states. But that is exactly how the phenomenon of the same person desiring to drink and desiring not to drink is here described (cf. 94 B 8–9, ἐπὶ τοὐναντίον ἕλκειν). Reason's conflict with appetites at the very least supports the contention that in so far as the soul is identifiable with reason, it is not accurately described as functionally related to a body, as an attunement would be. I mean that the conflict cannot easily be represented as between a function and that of which it is a function.

The second argument is more difficult. As I read it, it in effect poses a destructive dilemma. If the soul is an attunement, then it is an attribute of a body. The sort of attribute it would be either admits of degrees, like hotter or colder, or it does not. The first alternative is excluded by the assertion that one soul is not more or less of a soul than another (93 B 4–7). This assertion follows from the establishment of the soul as a separate entity in the RA and AA. The second alternative is excluded as follows. A good soul on this hypothesis would be one that has a further attunement and a bad soul one that fails to have this (93 C 3–8). But no attunement partakes of non-attunement (94 A 2–4). So, if a soul were an attunement, it could not be bad. But this is absurd. So, whether an attunement admits of degrees or not, a soul is not an attunement. Perhaps the strange idea of an attunement of an attunement is taken from some Pythagorean source espousing the hypothesis that the soul is an attunement and trying to account for the different qualities of souls.[41] In any case, the ready acceptance by Simmias that soul is not the sort of thing that there are degrees of is equivalent to the

---

[40] See Taylor (1983), 230–1.

[41] See Kahn (2001), 68, citing the Peripatetic Dicaearchus of Messina, whose view of the soul as an attunement may well derive from Pythagorean sources.

assertion that the soul is an entity.[42] And the conclusion that souls can be good or bad but that an attunement cannot follows from an idiosyncratic account of good and bad, whether this be Plato's or some Pythagorean's. Socrates' refutation of the attunement hypothesis succeeds only in showing an inconsistency in that hypothesis, which was perhaps all that it was intended to do.

2.6 Socrates' Reply to Cebes and the Argument from Exclusion of Opposites

Socrates' reply to Cebes is prefaced by a sketchy intellectual autobiography beginning with his early interest in natural science (ἡ ἱστορία φύσεως, 96 A 8). This interest consisted in seeking to know the αἰτίαι or explanations of the generation, existence, and destruction of things in nature. Socrates relates his disillusionment with the types of scientific explanation available in his day. For example, Socrates once supposed that the explanation for an animal growing larger was consumption of food and drink and the consequent accretion of bodily mass (96 C 8–D 5); or that a large man standing next to a tall man was, say, larger because he was a head taller; or that ten was greater than eight because of having two more units. The reason for his disillusionment makes it clear enough that these are examples like the equals in the RA, namely, cases where the sorts of proffered explanation generate contradictions. A 'naturalistic' explanation of equality or largeness falls into contradiction because exactly the same explanation could be offered for the presence of the opposite property.[43]

Socrates' disillusionment and subsequent preference for a different sort of explanation for natural things, namely, his theory of Forms, is curious because nowhere does he say that the rejected explanations are irrelevant

---

[42] Aristotle in *Cat.* 3ᵇ34–4ᵃ9 takes as a criterion of substantiality that a substance does not admit of degrees but is the subject of attributes that admit of degrees. That is part of what we mean by 'substance'. Similarly, part of what Plato means by saying that the soul is an entity is that it does not admit of degrees.

[43] Cases of generation and destruction do not work quite in the same way. There is not even an apparent contradiction in saying that the cause of his getting larger was gaining 10 kilos and the cause of his getting smaller was losing the same 10 kilos. At *Rep.* 478 A 5–6 that is why Plato says 'at the same time' (ἅμα) when speaking about that feature of the sensible world that makes it less than really real.

or wrong. They just generate puzzlement. Socrates does not claim, for example, that the presence of largeness or equality alone is sufficient to make something large or equal, though it is evidently necessary. What is wanted here is an explicit distinction between an αἰτία proper and a συναιτία, or the material condition which, along with the αἰτία, is jointly necessary and sufficient for the instantiation of a Form. This is more or less implicit on the next page, when Socrates contrasts a naturalistic explanation of his sitting in prison with the true explanation (99 A–B). The appropriate distinction is explicit in *Timaeus* (cf. 46 C 7–E 6). The argument for the priority of the αἰτία to the συναιτία, and, generally, of metaphysical or supernatural explanations to natural ones, is basically the same as the argument for the priority of Forms to instances of them. That is, the reason for holding that the Form of Largeness explains why something is large is the same as the reason for holding that if something is large and other things can be large too, this is because there is such a thing as Largeness that they instantiate. The eternal possibility of instantiation guarantees the priority of that which may be instantiated.

Socrates is equally disillusioned with Anaxagoras, who reputedly offered Mind or νοῦς as an alternative to naturalistic explanations (97 B 8 ff.). As Socrates understood it, such explanations would tell us *why* things happen as they do as well as why it is best that they happen as they do. Socrates reports that in fact Anaxagoras did no such thing, rather giving somewhat banal naturalistic explanations. Socrates' dissatisfaction both with Anaxagoras and with other purveyors of naturalistic explanation leads him to fall back on his theory of Forms (100 B). He will hypothesize Forms and explain the presence of any property or attribute in anything by the presence of or participation in that Form. Nowhere does Socrates tell us, however, how such explanations cohere with the sort of explanations that he sought in Anaxagoras and failed to find, namely, explanations of why it is best for things to happen as they do. Nor does he explain the connection between the favoured sort of explanation and the naturalistic ones, those that 'confuse' him.

To the preferred explanation, Socrates adds an assumption and a sort of corollary. Just as Largeness itself is never small, so the largeness in a large thing is never small. Therefore, if the large thing is to become small—that is, small relative to that in comparison with which it was large—then either the largeness in it is removed or it perishes (102 D 5–103 A 2). Sometimes the explanation of the presence of an attribute is not the Form of that attribute but another Form which always brings with it an instance of the first Form because, presumably, these Forms are eternally necessarily connected (103 B 10–105 C 7). For example, participation in the Form of Fiveness explains the presence of oddness in a group of five things. And participation in the Form of Fire explains the presence of hotness. The simple explanation with its corollary and the assumption regarding what happens if something is to acquire a property opposite to that which it has provide the basis for the final stage of the proof of the immortality and imperishability of the soul.

The core of the proof is relatively straightforward:

(1) Soul is that whose presence in a body brings life to that body (105 C 9–11).
(2) The opposite of life is death (105 D 6–9).
(3) Soul will never admit the opposite of what it brings (105 D 10–12).
(4) What will not admit death is deathless (105 D 13–E 3).
(5) Soul does not admit death (105 E 4).
(6) Therefore, soul is deathless (105 E 6).
(7) Whatever is deathless is imperishable (106 C 9–D 9).
(8) Therefore, soul is imperishable (106 E 1–107 A 1).

Clearly, the proof turns upon the ambiguity in (1).[44] If soul brings life because soul just *is* life, then the presence of its opposite, death, occasions no contradiction. That is, life is destroyed when death is present just as evenness is destroyed when oddness is made to be present. But if soul is an entity whose presence in a body brings life with it necessarily, then death cannot be present by soul's death, for a dead soul is a contradiction in terms, like an even three or hot snow. Soul must remove itself from the body in that case. In other words, soul is deathless if life is a necessary property of soul. And why should we believe that life is such a property? Because all and only those things that have souls are alive.

The following objection, posed in the form of a dilemma, naturally occurs. The necessity of the connection between soul and life can be sustained only by identifying soul with life. But then the necessity of the connection

[44] Keyt (1963), 169, for example, takes the ambiguity as a fallacy of equivocation. See, against Keyt, O'Brien (1968), 101–3.

is trivial. If soul and life are not identified, there is no reason to accept the necessary connection, that upon which the entire proof turns. After all, if one insists that everything that is alive has a soul that brings life to it, then this proof would seem to show that the soul of every living thing is immortal and imperishable. Even the souls of plants would be held to live for ever. Although Plato apparently does believe seriously in reincarnation, this consequence would seem to be unattractive. There are really two questions here for Plato. First, why are soul and life connected necessarily in a non-trivial way, and second, why does this proof not prove too much? Why does it not prove immortality not just for those whose life is paradigmatically a cognitive one, but even for the lowest form of life?

As we have seen throughout this chapter, the key terms 'soul' and 'life' are systematically ambiguous and nowhere explicitly defined. Several points, however, may be drawn from the previous arguments. First, the arguments that the soul is an entity and not merely a property—namely, the RA and the reply to Simmias—could not be made from a third-person perspective. That is, I could not know that you have a soul in any sense other than one according to which having a soul is just equivalent to being alive unless I know that I have one. Therefore, the present argument must be 'personalized' and understood to be an argument presented to someone who has first-person evidence that he or she is a soul, not a body. This point, in effect the answer to the first question, is closely related to the answer to the second. For the broadest sense of 'life', the sense according to which it applies roughly to everything that evinces growth by nutrition, decay, and reproduction, is the sense available from a third-person perspective. By contrast, what is available to the first-person perspective is self-consciousness or self-reflexive cognition. By now, it should be clear that this is something quite different from Cartesian or post-Cartesian subjectivity. Consequently, although soul and life are necessarily connected, the connection is not in the present instance trivial. For the life is that of an entity aptly named a 'person'. The life or soul of anything else may be, for all we know, a bodily attribute like a harmony.

The comedian George Burns in old age used to joke that in the morning he would check the newspaper for his obituary and if he didn't find it there he would get out of bed. How do you check to see if you are alive? Simply the fact that one is conscious of checking seems to be enough, in an odd sort of twist on the Cartesian *cogito*. In any case, self-reflexive activity is the only sense of 'life' that is relevant to the proving of personal immortality and imperishability. Consequently, I take this argument as supporting, if anything, the conclusion that a person or soul and his self-reflexive activity are inseparable.

If *this* is what Plato is aiming at, then the simple fact that we sleep every day and are otherwise from time to time non-conscious should be sufficient to show that there is no necessary connection between the soul and life, thus understood. Plato can reply that embodied existence is merely an image of disembodied life both cognitively and affectively, and that intermittent self-consciousness is accordingly an imperfect version of its exemplar just as sensible equality is an imperfect version of *its*. In addition, he can appeal to the real distinction between body and soul, and to the fact that the intermittence of self-conscious activity is attributable to the presence of the latter in the former. That is, it is attributable to the embodied endowment of personhood. And because our ability to judge sensible equals deficient in comparison with the Form of Equality requires as a condition that we have had disembodied knowledge of this Form, we can identify ourselves with that which is non-bodily or immaterial.

Most analyses of the Exclusion of Opposites argument do not take account of its first-person orientation. I can, of course, imagine myself alive without my being aware that I am alive. In the relevant sense of 'dead', I cannot make any sense of the first-person claim 'I am dead', although perhaps I could make sense of the claim if it meant that I am not embodied any longer. Similarly, when I make the claim 'I am alive', not based indirectly on some sort of evidence, but directly, I am making a claim about the fact of self-consciousness or self-reflexivity. This, I believe, is the basis for the argument that soul and life are necessarily connected. That is, my identification of myself as an entity is necessarily connected to my recognition of self-reflexive activity. I and my self-reflexive thinking are distinct (as are any entity and its attributes), though necessarily connected.

The Exclusion of Opposites Argument is immediately followed by the drawing of a lesson by Socrates (107 C 1–D 5). If the soul is immortal, then the only refuge from ills or salvation for it is to become as good and as wise as possible. For when a soul enters Hades, it has nothing with it except its education and nurture. Here is an answer to the question 'Why be virtuous?' that makes no sense if the soul is not immortal. The reasoning is straightforwardly consequentialist (cf. 114 c 6–8). Indeed, this entire plea for 'soul care' suggests that if the soul is not immortal, then a finite embodied life of wickedness might actually be a reasonable or even desirable option. Such an option would flow as well from the conviction that embodied life was not an image of a disembodied exemplar.

In the myth at the end of the dialogue Socrates describes the punishments and rewards for souls who have been subjected to divine judgement:

But as for those who are found to have lived exceptionally holy lives, it is they who are freed and delivered from these regions within the earth, as from prisons, and who attain to the pure dwelling above, and make their dwelling above ground. And among their number, those who have been adequately purified by philosophy live bodiless for the whole of time to come, and attain to dwelling places fairer even than these, which it is not easy to reveal, nor is the time sufficient to present. But it is for the sake of just the things we have related, Simmias, that one must do everything possible to have part in goodness and wisdom during life, for fair is the prize and great the hope. (114 B 6–c 8, trans. Gallop)

This passage seems to make a distinction between the rewards for virtue and for a life purified by philosophy. The philosophers are a subset of those who have lived good lives. Their reward is everlasting bodiless existence. Superficially, the philosopher is rewarded for devoting himself to philosophy. His reward is greater than that prepared for one who devoted his life exclusively to moral virtue. Clearly, then, philosophers do not attain a greater reward because they are better than the virtuous, where 'better' means morally better. The reward of everlasting bodiless existence seems rather to be directly related to the results of philosophical purification. Given that this purification is not primarily a moral matter, it is difficult to conceive of it as other than intellectual. And here 'intellectual' does not mean 'attitudinal', because attitudinal purification would be present also in the philosophical neophyte. As Socrates says, *adequate* purification is essential. Such purification consists in becoming, in so far as this is possible for an embodied person, a knower.

The rewards for virtuous living and philosophical purification are distinguishable from the conclusion of the argument for the immortality of the soul. All persons are held to be immortal, but not all are rewarded with a permanent disembodied state. If, as I have argued, Plato believes that we are ideally knowers, how are rewards or punishments even intelligible? There must be some causal connection between the life of an embodied person and all that implies and this disembodied ideal. 'Soul care', or lack thereof, needs to be shown to be relevant to the achievement of the ideal or to the failure to achieve it. It does not seem adequate simply to insist that the embodied person is an image of a disembodied ideal. It must be shown how the transformation of the image is supposed to work. Plato needs a sharper account of the person, including an account of what features of the embodied person do not belong to the ideal and why. Such an account is to be found in *Republic*, to which I now turn.

CHAPTER 3

Divided Persons:
Republic *and* Phaedrus

Regarding the theme of persons and knowledge, *Republic* is clearly pivotal. It is in *Republic* that we find an argument—much disputed and puzzled over by scholars, but an argument nevertheless—for the tripartition of the soul. And it is also in *Republic* that we find Plato's most extensive treatment of the nature of knowledge, and cognition generally, developed against the background of his metaphysics. In this chapter I shall be particularly concerned with what tripartitioning of the soul does to the account of persons developed in the preceding chapters. In the next chapter I shall focus on the account of cognition and the corresponding graded metaphysics.

It is only with the argument for a tripartite soul that one is led to ask whether an alternative to tripartition was implicitly functioning in dialogues earlier than *Republic*. Prior to *Republic*, does Plato regard the soul as tripartite or as bipartite or as partless? Generally, I believe, there is not a non-question-begging answer to this question, since in none of the earlier dialogues does Plato use the language in which tripartition is discussed. That is, he does not speak of 'parts' or 'powers' of the soul or of 'principles' of action. Indeed, when, for example, in *Phaedo* (83 D 7) Plato says that the soul may 'share opinions' with the body, there is no evidence that a partitioning of the soul is contemplated.

There is, however, one important piece of evidence that prior to *Republic* Plato did not regard the soul as partitionable in the way it is in *Republic*, namely, the argument in *Protagoras* that ἀκρασία or incontinence is impossible. If, as I shall argue, Plato holds that the partitioning of the soul is necessary and sufficient to account for the possibility of ἀκρασία, then it would seem to follow that the denial of its possibility at least provides support for the claim that Plato did not have a partitioned soul in *Protagoras*.

As we have seen in the first chapter, the dichotomy between soul and body is crudely and somewhat disingenuously relied upon to support the Socratic paradoxes. It is crude because Socrates does not distinguish between two connotations of 'body'—that is, between the body as 'external' to the soul or the person and the body as the locus of certain states of the person. If the body is *merely* a possession, then preferring its well-being to one's own may amount to an indefensible position. But it is precisely because some bodily states are apparently states of the person that there is no obvious absurdity in preferring these over certain other states thought to be non-bodily. I have already argued that claims made about immortality and an ideal disembodied state clarify matters somewhat. But if I am a person with bodily states as well as non-bodily ones, my identity with a disembodied person having no bodily states is problematic. Part of the answer to this is the argument from recollection. The analysis of the soul into three parts is, as we shall see presently, another part of Plato's response to this problem. But that psychological analysis needs metaphysical support, too.

3.1 Tripartition and Personhood

We should not be sidetracked by the analogy of the soul and the state in book 4 of *Republic*, for that analogy is strictly subordinate to the argument for tripartition. Thus, only if the soul has three parts is it analogous to the state; it does not have three parts because it is analogous to the state (cf. 368 E–369 B). The immediate question that occasions the argument for tripartition is whether that in us by which we learn, and that by which we are angry, and that by which we desire the pleasures of food and sex are activities of different parts or of the whole soul (436 A 8–B 3). The question regards precisely agency or the ἀρχή of action, where 'action' can include both doing and refraining from doing something. In fact, I shall argue that a 'part' of the soul is just an ἀρχή of action, that is, a distinct and ultimate type of sufficient explanation for a particular action.[1] We might state the alternatives thus: when we engage in learning or are angry or desire food and sex, is that in virtue of which we do each of these a distinct principle of action or is it the soul as a whole that is the principle of action that acts 'according to each of these' (καθ᾽ ἕκαστον)? That is, are cognitive, emotive, and appetitive acts proper to distinct principles or do they 'adverbially' characterize a single principle of action so that, for example, it is the same agent who acts thoughtfully or angrily or lustfully?

Plato seems to argue for the first alternative. He does so on the basis of the intuitive principle that 'one thing cannot do or experience opposites in the same respect [κατὰ ταὐτόν] in relation to the same thing [πρὸς ταὐτόν] at the same time' (436 B 8–10).[2] Despite the vagueness of the expression of the principle, it is tolerably clear from Plato's own rather tedious explication of it that he is particularly interested in the sorts of situations in which one manifests an appetite for something and at the same time manifests a disinclination or unwillingness to satisfy the appetite.

For example, thirsty people are sometimes 'unwilling' (οὐκ ἐθέλειν) to drink (439 C 2–3). Being unwilling to drink is, of course, not equivalent to not being thirsty. On the basis of this intuitive principle, Plato concludes that there is present in the soul that which commands the person to drink and that which prevents him from drinking, overruling the former (439 C 5–7). And that which prevents arises as a result of reasoning (λογισμοῦ), while that which commands arises as a result of 'feelings and illnesses' (παθημάτων τε καὶ νοσημάτων, 439 C 9–D 2).[3] Therefore, it is reasonable to conclude that

---

[1] See esp. Woods (1987) for this view, although Woods does not go on to draw from this the conclusions about personhood that I do.

[2] For the justification of this translation see Stalley (1975), 111–13. Plato's own putative counter-example of the top that is moving at the same time that it is stationary does not, as some hold, defeat his general point, which is that multiple agency must be postulated to account for opposite actions.

[3] Robinson (1971), 44, says that Plato is unjustified in holding that 'whenever' (ὅταν) appetite is resisted it is owing to reason. One can, according to Robinson, resist drinking for many reasons, including disgust or fear or awe. This seems to me to miss the point. Disgust or fear or awe may all obviously play a role in a person's thinking that he ought not to drink, though he be thirsty. But what opposes the act of drinking is the state in which one says to oneself, 'I ought not to drink'. That disgust or fear or awe is at bottom part of the explanation for my thinking this is irrelevant, since these feelings could still have been present even if I had arrived at a different conclusion.

in the soul there is that in virtue of which we reason and that in virtue of which we have the sorts of appetites that reason can prevent, that is, prevent from being the principle of an action. The former he calls λογιστικόν, the latter ἀλόγιστον τε καὶ ἐπιθυμητικόν (439 D 4–8).[4]

The third part of the soul is inferred from the example of one Leontius, who, while walking by the wall of the city, sees the corpses of some executed criminals. He wants to stare at these bodies but he is at the same time disgusted with himself for wanting this and he averts his gaze.[5] When Leontius can bear his restraint no longer, he uncovers his eyes, berating himself for his weakness (439 E 6–440 A 2). In Leontius' case, that in virtue of which he is disgusted with his own weakness is assimilable neither to an appetite like the appetite to gaze on the corpses nor to the reasoning according to which he believes that it is shameful to do so. So, a third part of the soul is posited.[6]

Plato's central argument for tripartition has been subjected to considerable ingenious critical scrutiny. Two sorts of criticism are prevalent. First, it is argued that the various psychological phenomena Plato recognizes can be accounted for without partitioning of the soul.[7] Second, scholars have exerted much effort to show the flaw in the principle that yields three and

---

[4] Plato at 439 E 2 first calls the divisions of the soul 'forms' (εἴδη), only later referring to them as 'parts' (μέρη, 442 B 11, C 5, 444 B 3). I think there is more going on here than his relative indifference to technical terminology. The idea of a 'part' of an immaterial entity is problematic, although Plato recognizes Forms themselves as having parts in some sense. One problem with tripartition is, as Aristotle saw, that unless the parts of the soul are shown to be atomic parts, then they themselves may well be divisible. See *De anima* Γ 9, 432ᵃ22–ᵇ7.

[5] The use twice of the term 'at the same time' (ἄμα) is like the use of the same term a little later in reference to the objects of belief, i.e. sensibles, that 'are and are not at the same time' (ἄμα ὄν τε καὶ μὴ ὄν, 478 D 5). Of a chronically acratic person it will always be said that he 'wants and does not want at the same time'. It is the simultaneity that engenders the need to postulate parts of the soul.

[6] Penner (1971), 111–13, questions the argument for a *third* part of the soul. I think he is correct in arguing that the division between reason and appetite is sharper than the tripartite division and even that the former is primary, since after all, spirit is a reactive part of the soul. Nevertheless, in the sense I am going to try to explain, I think Plato has a strong case to the effect that spirit can be an independent ἀρχή of action. This comes out most clearly in books 8 and 9.

[7] See e.g. Cooper (1985), 5, who claims that 'Plato's theory that there are three parts [of the soul] is, roughly, the theory that there are three psychological determinants of

only three parts of the soul.[8] I believe that both of these criticisms have a common source, which is a misunderstanding of the psychic conflict Plato is analysing. The misunderstanding is that the conflict is primarily among desires and is not, as I think Plato intends, a conflict between an appetite and reason. There is no conflict among desires as such like the conflict between appetite and reason.[9] I would resist characterizing the conflict as between appetitive and rational desires precisely because it misses the main point of the conflict, which is to characterize and explain the phenomenon of incontinence. Of course, there *are* rational desires, as Plato repeatedly implies and explicitly states in book 9. But these do not establish the conflicting parts within the soul.[10] A conflict of desires, as we shall see presently, could not constitute a case of incontinence.

If each part of the soul is a distinct ἀρχή of action, one might wish to argue that the conflict within the soul is necessarily a conflict of desire because only desire can be an ἀρχή of action. The reply to this objection requires a somewhat more precise account of the term ἀρχή. An ἀρχή of action, as I understand that term in Plato, is a terminal or ultimate explanation for an action. It is the first moving cause. When a part of the soul provides the explanation for an action, it is said to 'rule' in the soul and the other parts are 'ruled'.[11] Desires *can* be explanations for actions, but not all explanations

choice and voluntary action.' According to Cooper, there is no need to partition the soul to account for these determinants. See also Irwin (1977), 191–5; Penner (1990).

[8] See e.g. Annas (1981), 137–8; Price (1995), 40–72.

[9] Irwin (1977), 192, flatly insists that the conflict is a conflict of desires. But see 439 c 9–D 8, where Plato is clearly contrasting reasoning and desire, not two types of desire. A more extensive expression of the same position is made in Irwin (1995), 205–9. This position was first powerfully articulated by Joseph (1935), 51 ff., who clearly recognizes that the putative conflict of desires is not a conflict of commensurable desires. But then I do not see how it is a conflict of desires at all.

[10] Price (1995), 53, defines 'part' as 'the home of a family of desires and beliefs that have a tendency to stand in relations both of strong contrariety, and of confrontation, with members of any other family, but not of their own'. Apart from the attribution of beliefs to appetites, I think the main problem with this definition is that it does not focus on the crucial contrariety, which is between appetite and reason. Kahn (1987), 80, is closer to the truth in saying that tripartition is not a division of a faculty of desire, but a division of the psyche itself.

[11] See *Rep.* 443 B 2, 444 B 3, 550 B 6, 580 D 8, where ἀρχή is used of parts of the soul and is usually translated as 'rule'. That is, it rules pro tem. If a part of the soul rules unqualifiedly in a person, then in every action it will be the ἀρχή. See *Phaedo* 98 c 5, where Socrates is

for actions are desires. If Leontius had refrained from gazing upon the corpses, his reason would have been the ἀρχή of the action that consisted in him averting his eyes. Similarly, if one acts to satisfy an appetite when the appetite's satisfaction is endorsed or mandated by reason, again, the ἀρχή of the action is reason. The agent acted because he thought that it was the best or the right thing to do. It does not matter that he would not have, say, drunk the water had he not been thirsty. Children, animals, and acratics drink because they are thirsty. In them, appetite is the ἀρχή of their actions. A man in whom reason rules drinks because he thinks that he ought to drink now, that is, given that he is thirsty.[12] This is so whether the person in whom reason rules is acting properly or not: that is, reason rules in him even if he thinks he ought to do what in fact he ought not to do. We could in such a case say also that he desires to satisfy the appetite and nothing in this analysis gainsays the existence of such a desire. Nevertheless, he desires to satisfy the appetite because he thinks that he ought to. So, the latter is the ἀρχή of action, not the former.

In general, if it is reasonable to ask for an explanation for a desire, then the desire is not the ἀρχή of the action. But if it is not reasonable, then the desire is the ἀρχή. If it is reasonable to ask *why* one desires to refrain from satisfying an appetite, then the answer, framed in language such as 'because I thought it best not to satisfy the appetite', provides the ἀρχή of the action. By contrast, if the desire itself is self-explanatory, as is the case with all appetitive desires, that desire is the ἀρχή of the action.[13] The appetite is the ἀρχή of an action if the ultimate explanation—that beyond which it is nonsense to seek—is that he did it because of the appetite. By contrast, reason could have been the ultimate explanation for the same action if appetite was not.

discussing the possible 'explanations' (αἰτίας) for his action of continuing to stay in prison. Against the sort of explanation that Anaxagoras would give, Socrates identifies the true explanation as his thinking it best that he remain (98 E 5). He then adds that it would be absurd to say that his sitting on the prison bed is an αἰτία of his action at all. An ἀρχή and an αἰτία of an action appear to be close in meaning, if not identical.

[12] Aristotle holds that the ἀρχή of action is 'deliberative desire'. See e.g. *NE* Γ 5, 1113ª11. As a result of his denial of a diversity of principles of action, he denies the possibility of the phenomenon of incontinence as Plato describes it.

[13] As we shall see below, we shall need to distinguish the ἀρχή of a particular action from the permanent or quasi-permanent disposition in the person with respect to action. An important case to take account of is the person in whom bad reason rules and because of that is susceptible to subordinating his reason permanently to appetite.

If the hapless Leontius had gazed upon the corpse because he thought that corpse-gazing was a harmless or wholesome activity, then the appetite would not have been the ἀρχή of the action of gazing.

Leontius is an acratic. If he had controlled himself rather than given in to his appetite, he would have been continent or an encratic. If he felt no compunction about doing something wicked, he would have been vicious. If he did not have the wicked appetite in the first place, he would have been, to that extent, virtuous. Part of the significance of tripartitioning of the soul as a solution to the problem of how to account for incontinence is that it gives us a way to distinguish virtue from continence and so, indirectly, a better idea of what a person is ideally.

The very idea of 'parts' of the soul or 'parts' of the person becomes odder the more literally one takes 'parts'. Plato's analogy of the hands pushing and pulling the bow and bowstring is not very helpful in this regard, for if we apply it to the soul, the 'parts' simply become instruments of a single entity (439 B 8–11). Indeed, a self or a person seems to be like a unit which, by definition, does not have parts. But interpreting the partitioning of the soul adverbially or instrumentally seems to be just what Plato wishes to reject. So, at one extreme, parts of a single entity that is soul or person makes no sense. At the other, if we insist on literal division, are we not led to a view of a nominal soul or person that is really three souls or three selves? Are we not led, as the predictable and just complaint has it, to the positing of homunculi, a little appetitive man, a little spirited man, and a little rational man, a sort of committee where each member is vying for dominance?[14] I believe that neither the trivialization of partitioning of the soul by adverbialization nor the *reductio ad absurdum* suggested by homunculization are true to Plato's intention. It is worth our effort to understand what exactly this is.

Let us look closely at the phenomenon of psychic conflict as Plato de-

---

[14] See e.g. Annas (1981), 142–6. Price (1995), 56 ff., sees the homunculus problem. He concludes (64–5) that, 'it may be wiser to attempt to interpret the ideal of appetite's being "persuaded" by "reason" (554d2) and "agreeing" that reason "must" rule (442d1) in a way that pays little attention to the literal meaning of the words. The thought may be that reason's task is to give appetite longer views by drawing to its attention long-term pains surpassing short-term pleasures, and hence sparing it the turmoil and ruefulness that fill the tyrannized soul (577e1–3); we may suppose that appetite is capable of responding to deterrent thoughts that it lacks the foresight to summon up itself.' As I argue below, such an interpretation actually reintroduces homunculi.

scribes it. Leontius 'struggles with himself' (μάχοιτο) and is finally 'overcome by the appetite' (κρατούμενος δ᾽ οὖν ὑπὸ τῆς ἐπιθυμίας) to look at the corpses. Similar militaristic metaphors are used throughout the passage to describe psychic conflict. Indeed, it is quite natural to describe someone like Leontius as being 'overcome by appetite'. And though it is equally natural to say that someone is 'overcome' by guilt or shame, it is not, I take it, natural to say that had Leontius resisted his appetite he would have been 'overcome' by reason or by rational calculation. One can hardly be said to be overcome by one's own decision or resolve, even if these be mistaken.[15] Prima facie, this is so because whereas we can rather easily distinguish between a person and his appetites or emotions, we cannot so easily distinguish between the person and his thinking, especially in matters related to action.[16]

Consider how we might appropriately analyse a claim to the contrary, say, a claim that one was overcome by an argument against satisfying a prurient appetite and was thereby led to embrace the conclusion of that argument. It seems to Plato that embracing the conclusion of an argument is something that one does whereas being overcome by an appetite is something that is done to one. And this is the reason why we cannot so easily distinguish the person from the reasoning but we can distinguish the person from the appetites. A parallel point can be made for the case of one endorsing an appetite, that is, accepting the conclusion of an argument that the appetite ought to be satisfied. If you think that you ought to satisfy your hunger, you can intuitively distinguish the hunger from the agent endorsing the proposition that it ought to be satisfied; but you cannot similarly distinguish the endorsing of the proposition from the agent, for at the moment the endorsing occurs, the agent is nothing more than the one who is doing it.

The conclusion of this line of argument is that the person is to be identified with the rational part of the soul. Although Plato does not explicitly propose such an argument, it is perhaps reasonable to read him as presupposing its cogency. Nevertheless, to leave matters thus is patently unsatisfactory for

---

[15] See *Laws* 863 D 10, and below, § 6.3.

[16] At 580 D 8 Plato assigns a type of ἐπιθυμία to each part of the soul. I shall discuss book 9 in due course. Here it should suffice to note that he is using ἐπιθυμία in another sense, according to which there can be *no* opposition between it and reason. The conflict that precedes the incontinent act is not paralleled by the entirely different sort of conflict between, say, an appetite for learning and an appetite for sex.

the very reason we encountered in the previous chapters, namely, that to identify the person with the rational part of the soul exclusively or unqualifiedly would be to treat one's own appetites as if they were virtually those of another. But this is false. The agent of ratiocination is *also* the agent of passionate appetites.

Jon Moline and many others have argued that understanding conflict within the soul requires that we assign 'a minimal level of cognitive capacity to [τὸ ἐπιθυμητικόν] and [τὸ θυμοειδές]'.[17] Moline cites a number of texts which seem to imply that the parts of the soul other than the rational part are engaged in various types of cognitive activity. For example, at 571 C 3–D 4 the appetitive part is said to devise elaborate dream plots. At 586 D 5–E 3 both τὸ ἐπιθυμητικόν and τὸ θυμοειδές are said to be capable of obeying or being persuaded by τὸ λογιστικόν. And at 603 C 10–D 7 beliefs (δόξαι) seem to be assigned to each part of the soul. These beliefs can evidently be in conflict. The possibility of conflicting beliefs within the soul seems to follow from the original deduction of the three parts of the soul, where a just soul is said to be one in which the three parts are in 'agreement' (ὁμοδοξῶσι) that reason should rule (442 D 1).[18] Finally, the class of appetites seems to comprise some that have an essential cognitive element, including the love of money or avarice.[19] Texts such as these certainly seem to make the homunculi problem all the more acute. Indeed, if the appetitive and spirited parts of the soul can have beliefs that conflict with the beliefs of the rational

[17] Moline (1981), 61. See also Fortenbaugh (1975), 38–44; Lesses (1987), 149–54; Kahn (1987), 85; Bobonich (1994), 4 n. 3, with references, 12; Irwin (1995), 217–22; Gill (1996), 243–60; Annas (1999), 133–6; Scott (2000), 30–2. Annas tends towards the view that the parts of the soul other than reason have a cognitive aspect because they can be persuaded. However, she also recognizes the 'unfortunately powerful appeal' for Plato of the idea that the parts of the soul other than reason are 'alien' to it and hence in need of domination.

[18] See also 437 B 1–C 6; 439 A 1–D 2; 554 D 1–575 A 7. Moline does not cite another relevant text, *Phaedo* 83 D 7, where the soul is said 'to agree' (ὁμοδοξεῖν) with the body regarding its desires. I take it that Moline would not wish to argue that the body has a cognitive capacity. It is clear that by 'body' here Plato is referring to pleasures and pains, and that these are felt by the same person who cognitively evaluates these. In other words, talk about the opinions of the lower parts of the soul in *Republic* is not substantially different from talk about the opinion of the body in the *Phaedo*. See Klosko (1988), 347–8, who tentatively accepts the attribution of cognitive functions to all three parts, but allows that the difficulties of working out 'a reasonable construal of this view are formidable'.

[19] See e.g. 553 C 5, 554 A 2, B 2, 580 E 5–581 A 7, 590 B 7–8.

part, and if conflicts within the soul are construed as conflicts of beliefs, the argument for tripartition self-destructs. If, for example, Leontius' appetite believes that he should gaze on the corpse and his rational part believes that he should not, then regardless of who wins this battle, no incontinence will occur. If the 'winning' belief is that he should gaze, then he is perhaps vicious, though not acratic. If the 'winning' belief is that he should not, then he will not gaze. Otherwise, there is no clear sense in which it is 'winning'. Thus, attributing cognitive powers to appetite is merely an indirect way of denying partitioning of the soul and therefore of denying the existence of the phenomenon of incontinence. Alternatively, to insist on this attribution is, it would seem, to create homunculi.

I believe there is another reason, apart from the undermining of the explanation of incontinence and the creation of homunculi, why attributing cognitive functions to the appetitive part of the soul cannot be correct, or even Plato's intention. There is no way of distinguishing the putative reasoning of appetite from the reasoning of the rational part of the soul. That I should provide myself with reasons why my appetite should be satisfied does not in any sense suggest that these reasons are coming from any other part of the soul besides the rational part. The entire ground for tripartition is a specific sort of psychic conflict. Arguing with myself pro and con about an appetite is not that sort of conflict. And once I have decided that, say, the appetite ought to be resisted in this instance, all things considered, there is no conceptual space for a partitioning of reasoning that conflicts with this. To say that I still have doubts that resisting is not the right thing to do is only to say that I am not firm in my conviction. But the considerations that contribute to this infirmity are entirely a function of reasoning.[20]

---

[20] It must not be supposed that when Plato says that A persuades B, this implies that B has cognitive capacity. Such a supposition rests on a simple philological error. For example, in *Timaeus* (48 A 2) 'Intellect' (Νοῦς) persuades 'Necessity' (Ἀνάγκη) to guide things that become towards the best. Obviously, Ἀνάγκη here is not to be taken as thinking. In fact, the primary connotation of the word πείθω in Greek is its contrast with 'violence' or βία. Reason affects a change in what exists by necessity by using intelligence, not force. You can 'persuade' a door to open by using your locksmith skills or you can make it open 'by violence'. The point is that when A persuades B, we must suppose cognitive capacity in A, not necessarily in B. So, talk about reason persuading appetite does not entail or even suggest cognitive capacity in appetite. See also *Tim.* 70 A 5–7.

How, then, are we to interpret psychic conflict? That there is a conflict within a single individual is certain from 430 E 11–431 A 1, where Plato says that phrases like 'self-control' (τὸ κρείττω αὑτοῦ) are 'absurd' (γελοῖον) because it is the 'same human being' (ὁ αὑτός, viz. ἄνθρωπος, A 4) who is doing the controlling and is being controlled. That is why his soul has to be supposed to have parts. We must, I believe, insist on keeping the unity at the same time as we try to explain the conflict. Leontius is not literally fighting with an appetite; he is, as the text explicitly says, fighting with himself. He is wondering whether he should or should not gaze upon the corpses. And when he does give in, or perhaps, when he is overpowered, there is nothing like a cognitive victory of appetite or anything that requires us to assign cognitive capacity to appetite. The entirety of the quarrelling takes place within the ambit of his rationality. The overpowering of reason by appetite occurs only after all the quarrelling has concluded—that is, after a decision has been reached.

But does this conclusion not err in the opposite direction? Does it not reduce the quarrel to the deliberative process that occurs prior to the determination of a belief and so prior to the apparent quarrel between reason and appetite? In fact, when Leontius thinks 'Should I or should I not?' he is neither quarrelling with an appetite nor figuring out what he ought to do. He already *knows* what he ought to do. The quarrel is rather between Leontius as a subject of the appetite and Leontius as a subject of rational thought. After all, the appetite is *his* appetite. It is at best an imprecision to say that the appetite is party to the quarrel. But there really is a quarrel or struggle. So, Leontius wants to gaze on the corpses and Leontius wants to refrain. The straightforward inference from this—one which is missed by those who assign a cognitive capacity to appetite—is that Leontius is not a unified agent. Indeed, only if Leontius is not a unified agent are both the principle upon which tripartition is deduced observed and a genuine quarrel possible.

This analysis takes Leontius to be a rational agent. He is the one quarrelling with himself.[21] The 'divided' Leontius, as I shall call him, is, on the

---

[21] See Gill (1996), 252–6, who represents the putative quarrels as 'dialogues within the self'. I agree with Gill's important observation. But the conclusion I draw is that the embodied person is a divided self, not that appetites or emotions actually enter into dialogue with reason.

one hand, the ruler of the entire embodied person or, on the other, the servant of his appetite.[22] This appetite to which Leontius finally submits is truly arational. When Plato says that an appetite forces a person to act contrary to 'reasoning' (τὸν λογισμόν, 440 A 8–B 1), he is not saying that false beliefs are forcing someone to act contrary to true beliefs, because λογισμός is not equivalent to true or right belief. An appetite can force someone to act contrary to his reasoning even when his reasoning is faulty and his appetite is innocent.[23] The quarrel is actually indicative of a sort of identity crisis: Leontius' struggle is over who he is, the master or the servant of appetite.[24]

According to my interpretation, all cognitive capacity belongs to τὸ λο-γιστικόν. The 'beliefs' of appetite are beliefs of the rational agent. An appetite has a belief only in the sense that reasoning can formulate a belief in the service of an appetite. All of the texts that seem to attribute beliefs or some form of practical reasoning to the appetitive part of the soul should be understood as indicating cognition in two modes: as principle of action

---

[22] I use the word 'divided' in line with the psychic partitioning at issue. But just as 'parts' of the soul do not indicate a physical division of the soul, so a divided person is not intended to indicate multiple persons. 'Psychic dividedness' could be understood as more or less synonymous with 'psychic complexity'. I tend to avoid the latter term, however, because complexity in itself does not imply the sort of opposition that Plato is concerned to emphasize. It also fails to capture the paradoxical nature of embodied personhood.

[23] Bobonich (1994), 9, analyses acratic action in terms of relative 'strength of desire'. Thus, Leontius acts acratically because his desire to gaze on the corpses is greater than his desire to refrain. In my opinion, Bobonich does not see that this turns ἀκρασία into vice. Bobonich thinks that this view which he attributes to Plato is faulty (see esp. 15–17 for further criticisms of the view) and is recognized as such by Plato himself in Laws. I believe that Bobonich and others are led to reject partitioning of the soul because they do not see this as partitioning of the person. It is the concept of a unified agent of action (as in Protagoras) that makes ἀκρασία impossible.

[24] Penner (1990), 38–9, argues that all 'executive desires', namely, desires that are effective for action, are rational. This entails not only that (1) the surrendering to appetite is a rational act, but that (2) the action based on the appetite to which reason surrenders is rational. This amounts to claiming that ἀκρασία as Plato understands and accounts for it is impossible. See 49–61 for Penner's argument against the possibility of irrational executive desires. I think Penner is wrong to infer (2) from (1). His reason for making this inference is basically that the agent of the action is identical with the agent of the executive desire. But this is in effect to deny that the embodied person can be divided. I want to argue that the embodied person is the agent of the appetite that is contradicted by reason. The embodied person becomes that agent while remaining a rational agent. That such a becoming is possible is the core notion of psychic dividedness.

and as subservient to a principle of action. If one has an appetite for drink or food or sex, one does not persuade the appetite to 'stand down', and there is, I believe, nothing in the texts that forces us to think otherwise. One tries (if one is continent) to persuade oneself not to let the appetite be the principle of action. But we must not say that in failing to persuade oneself either one has given in to a wholly alien appetite like that of another person or one has been overcome by appetite's reasons. The 'surrendering' to appetite's rule when one believes that one should not is acratic because a person is a rational agent.[25] The acratic in a way pretends to be someone he is not. He says in effect, 'I shall be an agent who acts from appetite and not reason.' But the fact that he can say that at all indicates that he is not really such an agent. He is only pretending. Why, though, is it pretence if the appetites are *his*? The answer to this question is thoroughly and distinctively Platonic. One who acts as the acratic or vicious person acts implicitly identifies himself as that which he, in fact, is not really or ideally. Persons are the only sort of being who can pretend not to be what they really are.

The basic opposition of appetite and reason is based on the contrast between the idiosyncratic or particular and the universal. Even though I can speak quite naturally about *my* reasons as well as *my* appetites, the former can be independently evaluated or appropriated in a way that the latter cannot. There is no universalizability in statements of appetite. It is not so implausible to view the spirited part as in a way between the particular and the universal, since its reactions to the quarrel of reason and appetite are neither impervious to reason in the way that appetites are nor universalizable in the way that reasoning is. When a person, on the brink of an acratic act, recognizes that he is both the subject of an appetite and the subject of the belief that the appetite ought to be resisted, he is confronted in a dramatic way with his embodied and ambivalent status. When the acratic act is committed, the ambivalence is exacerbated by the person's recognition that he is also the subject of the negative reaction. One could just deny that this ambivalence is genuine or take the homunculi approach to its resolution. By contrast, Plato's position is that the single subject of appetite and spirit and embodied reason is an image of the really real person.

---

[25] Cf. e.g. 533 c. At 550 b 5–6 the timocratic man surrenders rule to the spirited part of his soul.

The logical and psychological priority of reason in all the person's conflicted states is at least part of the basis for this view.

I suspect that one reason why many scholars have held that a tripartite soul must be a collection of homunculi is that they assume that whatever the embodied subject is, it must be permanently so. That is, if Leontius is the subject of the reasoning that leads him to believe that he should resist gazing, then he could not be another subject, much less another *kind* of subject. Since he could not be the subject of the appetite to gaze, there must be another subject that has that appetite. But it should hardly surprise us that embodied persons, situated in the world of becoming, are variable. Just as sensibles can appear to manifest opposite attributes simultaneously, so embodied persons can appear, even to themselves, as opposing subjects. They can also identify themselves as other than what they truly are, namely, subjects of reason.

There is a puzzling passage towards the end of the discussion of tripartition that actually seems to identify the person as something over and above the three parts.[26] Socrates there describes the just man as 'ruling himself' (ἄρξαντα αὐτὸν αὑτοῦ, 443 D 4) and 'binding' (συνδήσαντα) the parts of his soul together and becoming 'one from many' (ἕνα γενόμενον ἐκ πολλῶν, E 1).[27] We must not suppose that 'becoming one' means dissolving or extirpating multiplicity, for the embodied just person surely continues to have multiple parts of his soul. Similarly, the just state 'becomes one' in the sense of a harmonious whole where all the parts operate correctly (423 D 5). Presumably, the just person becomes one in the sense that he becomes a unified agent of activity, unified under the rule of reason. That is, reason is always the ἀρχή of his actions, as it is not in other persons. But the unity here, which is indicated to be a desirable achievement, cannot simply consist in the fact that in every action there is the same part of the soul in charge. For in that case there would be as much unity in someone in whom the spirited part or the appetitive part ruled as there is in the just man.

The just man has become a unity because, to put it simply, he wants what

---

[26] This is noticed by Price (1995), 56–7, who in passing refers to the general role of such characterizations as 'apposite to self-images that mould the self'. See also 550 A 4–B 7; 553 B 7–D 7.

[27] At 554 D 9–10 the person suffering from 'internal strife' is said to be 'in some way two', not one. See the same thought expressed slightly differently at *Phaedo* 83 A 7: 'to collect and gather itself together'.

reason wants.[28] He has come as close as possible to the ideal person. By contrast, every other person is a multiplicity of agents, sometimes acting against reason, sometimes acting as reason dictates, and sometimes acting purely out of spiritedness.[29] To be overcome by appetites, as is the acratic, is implicitly to identify the person with that which is overcome, namely, the rational part of the soul. Anyone in whom reason is not permanently the ἀρχή of action is 'multiple' in the sense that his identity is compromised. Even the vicious individual, who, unlike the acratic, puts his reason permanently and entirely in the service of appetite, does not achieve unity. He remains distinct from those appetites. At the extreme limit of servitude to appetites is the obliteration of the person and the transformation into another type of living thing.

This interpretation of the just person 'becoming one' helps us to understand how tripartition addresses the problem of embodied personhood. On the basis of this interpretation, we can make a distinction between personhood as an endowment and personhood as an achievement.[30] This distinction is simply an application of the fundamental distinction or bipolarity in Greek between two senses of the term φύσις or 'nature'. In one sense, 'nature' refers to what is; in another sense, it refers to what ought to be, where 'ought' includes but is not limited to a moral connotation. Thus, in the first sense of 'nature' two-headed calves are natural, but in the other they are not. The basic bipolarity allows us to speak of something that exists by nature at the same time acting to fulfil its nature. It is natural for human beings early in their development to be totally dependent on others for sustenance. It is also natural for them to achieve a level of independence. The difference between personhood as an endowment and

[28] Lear (1998), 329 n. 13, cites 433 D 4–5 as a text which indicates that in the just πόλις each person, in performing his own task, will not be a multiplicity but a unity. But this is, I think, a misunderstanding of the text. The text reads ὅτι τὸ αὑτοῦ ἕκαστος εἷς ὢν ἔπραττε καὶ οὐκ ἐπολυπραγμόνει and should be translated 'because each person, being one, performed his own task and was not a busybody'. The point has nothing to do with the unity of a tripartite soul, which is not established until ten pages later, but with Plato's claim 'one man, one job'. See 443 C 4–7.

[29] Parfit (1984), pt. III, describes persons as 'nations' and not 'Cartesian egos', a notion that deserves comparison with Plato's view of the ordinary embodied condition of at least most persons.

[30] See McCabe (1994), 264–6, who makes a similar distinction between 'that which I can take for granted' and 'that which I aspire to be'.

personhood as an achievement is the difference between what is the case for most persons and what ought to be the case. It is the difference between a life of adventitious and confused agency and a life in which the person has 'become one'.

Embodied personhood is characterized by Plato in part by the ἀρχή of action in the person. If someone subordinates his appetites to reason so that the ἀρχή of his action is reason, then though his appetites are his, they do not define the kind of person he is. Such a person acts to achieve only what reason determines ought to be done.[31] If someone subordinates his reason to his appetites, he becomes, if only temporarily, a compromised image of the person he really is. *He* identifies with his appetites—that is, he identifies himself as an agent who, when acting to satisfy an appetite, is acting on behalf of his good. As we shall see presently, Plato's division of human character is an emblematic way of talking about such endowed persons.[32] The achievement of personhood in a mature individual consists of a fixed pattern of agency. Only the just individual, later explicitly identified by Plato with the aristocratic man or philosopher, has an achievement in personhood that is truly and unqualifiedly praiseworthy (544 E 7–8).[33]

[31] Kahn (1987), 86–91, makes an important distinction between three senses of 'rule of reason': (1) reason is purely instrumental in attaining what is desired; (2) reason determines the ends of action; (3) reason constitutes the goal of human life through its own philosophical activity. Kahn notes that (1) is not, according to Plato, strictly the rule of reason, though in such cases reason may prevail. The distinction between (2) and (3) corresponds to the distinction between pre-philosophic virtue in book 4 and philosophic virtue in books 5–6. Kahn argues that 'reason just is, or essentially contains, a primitive desire for the good, an irreducible, non-derivative urge to pursue what it takes to be the good and advantageous' (89). I think this is basically correct and deeply illuminating, but I do not think it requires us to assign cognitive capacities to the other parts of the soul.

[32] See e.g. 544 E 1, 545 B 4, 548 D 4, 577 A 2 on the use of ἦθος. I take it that in the first passage ἦθος is equivalent to any one of the κατασκευαὶ τῆς ψυχῆς (544 E 5) which correspond to the five types of government: aristocratic, timocratic, oligarchic, democratic, and tyrannical.

[33] See Kraut (1991), who denies that the just man is identical with the philosopher. The only passage that might suggest that there can be virtue without philosophy is at the end of the *Republic* (619 C 7–D 1), where a soul who had previously been in heaven is said to choose the life of a dictator owing to his having never experienced evil. It is said that, having lived in a 'well-ordered state', he 'participated in virtue by habit without philosophy [ἔθει ἄνευ φιλοσοφίας ἀρετῆς μετειληφότα]'. I interpret these words to mean

Even someone who has achieved the most desirable state of person-hood is nevertheless an embodied person. To what extent that person is identical with a disembodied person is another question. Even a person who has more or less identified with his embodied rational faculty seems on the face of it radically distinct from the disembodied person understood to be a contemplator or cognizer of eternal reality. For the moment, however, I wish to point out that it is precisely at the point where we can distinguish the just man as a unified self in whom reason rules from every other kind of person that the connection between knowledge and personhood becomes clearer. For it is the presence of knowledge—or at least true belief—in the just man that produces the requisite unity. That is, by acquiring knowledge the just man acquires a new identity. It would be a mistake, I think, to suppose that what the wise man acquires is something that could be employed in the service of anything other than the ideal. Knowledge entails self-transformation. Simply stated, if one knows what is good for oneself, that is because one knows that a person is ideally or really an agent of rational activity and therefore one's primary good is found in successful rational activity. Coming to know that this is what one is represents a self-transformation. One comes to recognize that the things that one supposed were desirable really were not so. One takes an entirely different attitude towards one's own appetites. That is the real reason why the Platonically just man is unlikely to do the things that are ordinarily regarded as unjust.[34] The deeds ordinarily counted unjust arise from the appetites of those who think that their good is truly served by satisfying them. By contrast, the just man recognizes that his true good is indistinguishable from what is good simply, and that therefore his good cannot be achieved at the expense of injustice. He has appetites and he seeks to satisfy them, but in such a detached manner

that someone could, in a just state, do virtuous deeds at the behest of a just ruler. But this would not mean that they were just persons in the sense that philosophers are.

[34] See Sachs (1971). Klosko (1988) argues that there are two types of 'rule of reason'. The first is that of the philosopher, in whom reason directs the soul to the goods of reason. The second is that of ordinary people, in whom reason rules when it subordinates appetites to the good of the soul as a whole. Presumably the latter amounts to 'political' or 'demotic' virtue. I think it is correct to hold that Plato is committed to saying that one can adventitiously do that which a philosopher would necessarily do. If this is so, this supports the compromised and equivocal integrity of the endowed person.

that satisfying them at the expense of someone else is psychologically unthinkable.

With the definition of the virtues and the claim, accepted by all interlocutors, that it is intrinsically desirable to be a just person (445 A), Socrates begins to categorize types of government and types of soul (445 C 9–10). This categorization is supposed to contribute to the proof that justice is not only intrinsically desirable but is desirable for its consequences as well, though it is not immediately evident how this is so. Nevertheless, the categorization of types of government and soul is interrupted by the 'digression' that constitutes the central books of *Republic*. This digression will be the subject of the next chapter. For now, let us proceed to book 8 (544 B ff.), where, after the digression is completed, the discussion explicitly returns to the categorizations. I am particularly interested here in the five types of soul—aristocratic, timocratic, oligarchic, democratic, and tyrannical—and what the analysis of these tells us generally about personhood.

There is a striking parallel in all the descriptions of the degenerate forms of soul: (1) timocratic (550 B 5–6): 'he turns over [παρέδωκε] government in his soul to the intermediate and victory-loving part, that is, to the spirited part'; (2) oligarchic (553 C 4–8, D 1–2): 'such a man will establish [ἐγκαθίζειν] the appetitive and avaricious part of his soul on the throne and set it up as the great king . . . and under its dominion he will force the rational and spirited parts to crouch down left and right as slaves'; (3) democratic (561 B 4–5): 'turning over [παραδιδούς] the rule of himself as if to one [pleasure] chosen by lot, until each is sated'; (4) tyrannical (577 D 1–5): 'his soul is filled with much slavery and illiberality, enslaving [δουλεύειν] the best parts, and making a despot [δεσπόζειν] of the worst and most manic part'.

I suggest that we try to understand these texts by asking what sort of psychological structure must be supposed to describe phenomena as Plato does here? In each case, the person is described as in some way relinquishing rule or control to either the spirited or the appetitive part of his soul. I take it that although these types of soul are 'derived' from the aristocratic soul, we should not assume that it is in every case an aristocratic soul that relinquishes control. This certainly cannot work for the last three, but it cannot work even for the first, the timocratic man, who was never an aristocratic man (cf. 549 B 3–4). So, that which relinquishes control is not

τὸ λογιστικόν itself, which is what rules in the aristocratic soul.[35] We seem
to need a psychological component to be that which relinquishes control
to one or another part of the soul.[36] But that which relinquishes control
cannot be substantially different from that to which control is relinquished.
Otherwise, we have the problem of homunculi appearing once again. We
need a concept of a person of sufficient complexity to account for the
psychological phenomena described above.

The endowed person, I suggest, 'identifies' with one or another parts
of his soul in much the way we would say that someone identified with a
cause or an institution or another person. This identification is equivalent
to endorsing the rule of either the rational, or the spirited, or the appetitive
part of the soul. Prior to maturity, the identification is doubtless episodic and
various. At maturity, whenever this occurs, the person becomes sufficiently
like one of the types of soul described by Plato in order to be characterized
as such. At that point, rule in the soul is established. I take it that it does
not matter very much to Plato whether we characterize the acratic as an
immature individual and hence prone to episodic capitulations to appetite
or as a mature individual with a 'mixed' character.

If we try to characterize the agent involved in identification, it is difficult to do so in terms other than those that would be applied to the
characterization of the rational part of the soul. That is, if we imagine a
person 'turning over' government in his soul to the spirited part in such a
way as to fix his character, we must imagine reflective consideration on his
part. Plato does exactly this. In the development of the timocratic man, he is
viewed as struggling between the pull of his aristocratic father and the bad
influences around him. The oligarchic man is described as turning to a love
of money out of fear for his life. The democratic man is viewed as giving in

---

[35] Irwin (1995), 285–8, argues that it is the rational part that cedes control to the
other parts of the soul in the deviant individuals. This view follows from Irwin's overall
interpretation, which in my view misrepresents embodied personhood by generating a
multitude of agents or homunculi.

[36] At 589 A–590 A the relative states of the just and unjust man are finally compared.
Here it is clear that what truly benefits oneself is what serves reason and what harms
oneself is what compels or seduces reason to serve appetite. Reason is identified with
the 'man within the man' (589 A 7–8). This is what I have argued is implicit in the early
dialogues. What is different here is that the identification of the person with the rational
faculty will presently be placed within the context of an argument for the immortality of
the soul.

to his appetites owing to certain false beliefs. The same description would appear to apply to the tyrannical man who enslaves himself to his worst appetites. In all cases, the person is treated as a sort of rational adjudicator, throwing in his lot, either permanently or temporarily, with one or the other of the contestants.[37]

When the person so adjudicates between the demands of appetite and those of reason, the apparent incommensurability of appetite and reason seems to be a problem. I mean, if I want to gaze upon the corpse and I do not think that I should, on what basis do I identify with my desire or my reason? Stated otherwise, according to what criterion of judgement do I side with what I want to do or what I should do? The difficulty in answering this question is the reason why many scholars have supposed that conflicts within the soul are really conflicts among desires and that the adjudication process is a matter of recognizing the strongest desire. This cannot be correct if for no other reason than that if the greatest desire were always to win the contest, then there would be no possibility of incontinence. It is precisely because Plato came to recognize that incontinence is a fact about persons that he jettisons the model of action found in *Protagoras*, a model according to which one always acts on the greatest desire. In that model, the person is an unqualifiedly unified ἀρχή of action. For that reason, there is no conceptual space, so to speak, for describing a truly acratic action.

There is one passage in book 9 in which Plato does seem to provide support for the notion that psychic conflicts are conflicts of desires. At 580 D 7–8 he assigns proper or 'unique' (ἴδια) pleasures and 'desires' (ἐπιθυμίαι) to *each* part of the soul.[38] In this passage the specification of a desire and a pleasure attaching to each part of the soul is intended to serve the argument

---

[37] See Scott (2000), 26, who aptly characterizes the democratic man as 'quasi-appetitive' and as someone who from time to time 'has a desire of reason for knowledge and a desire of spirit for honor without basing these desires upon considerations of the good'. Although I agree that such a man can have a rational desire in a way other than the way the good man would have this desire, I disagree with Scott's view that this implies the attribution of rationality to his appetites. The democratic man *thinks* that it is good to follow whatever appetites arise in himself. He is, for all his psychic disunity, a rational animal.

[38] One might infer a desire as appropriate to the rational part from 435 E 7, where the term φιλομαθές is apparently used as an attribute of it. Cf. 581 B 9 and 586 E 4. I do not think that the desire of the rational part is a desire in the sense that it conflicts with appetitive desires. It is a desire for a particular kind of activity. It is called ἐπιθυμία because

that the philosopher is better placed than his polar opposite, the tyrannical man, or any one else for that matter, to evaluate the pleasures of each part and to declare that the pleasure of the rational part is superior. That each part should have a desire and a pleasure makes it superficially plausible that one can at least make a judgement about which of a pair of conflicting desires or pleasures is stronger. That the judgement is about the relative pleasures of different 'ways of life' (βίοι) seems evident at 581 D 10–E 4. And yet, immediately before this passage the philosopher is said to call physical pleasures 'necessary' because he would feel no need of them if they were not necessary to live. When the philosopher thus denigrates the worth of these pleasures, he is not evaluating them as pleasures, like the hedonist. To have 'no need' of a pleasure is not to make any judgement on its pleasureableness.

Commensurating desires is in general a deeply obscure project. Consider once again the case of Leontius. Was his desire to gaze upon the corpse greater or less than his putative desire to refrain? Someone supporting commensuration might say that it was the former. But what more does this mean than that he did in fact gaze? And if this is the case, then what is offered as an explanation is not an explanation at all but a restatement of the fact in need of explanation. If the explanation is instead that 'greatest desire' means that one could not have acted otherwise, then this seems to me to be equivalent to an entirely gratuitous counterfactual conditional, namely, 'If his desire to refrain had been greater, then he would not have gazed.' For this there could be no evidence: evidence is not an intelligible notion in this case. If, however, one could make sense of the idea of the commensuration of desires, and if one wanted to claim that in the case of Leontius the greatest desire won, then Leontius is not an acratic, but a vicious person (assuming, of course, the viciousness of his appetite for corpse-gazing).

The unintelligibility of the notion of commensurating the desire to do something and the desire to refrain from doing something applies to the notion of commensurating desires of different parts of the soul or commensurating their pleasures. The philosopher who judges the pleasures of philosophy as superior to those of the tyrannical man is not quantifying over

---

it is not the result of deliberation. Cf. *Phaedo* 66 E 2–3, where we find an ἐπιθυμία for wisdom.

pleasures. He employs three criteria in making his judgement: 'experience' (ἐμπειρία), 'wisdom' (φρόνησις), and 'argument' (λόγος, 582 A 5). Only the first criterion is conceivably intended to be used to compare the pleasurableness of pleasures as such. But even here, the philosopher is actually judging that he prefers the pleasures of learning and achieving knowledge to the pleasures belonging to any other part of the soul. That is not commensurating so much as making a judgement about the pleasure that pertains most to the sort of person one is. For the philosopher, of course, does not entirely forgo appetitive pleasures. In any case, that the rational faculty has a peculiar pleasure and a peculiar desire for it does not at all suggest that a desire to satisfy an appetite is countered by another desire to refrain and that these are commensurated.

The unintelligibility of the notion of commensurable desires as a way of explaining incontinence goes to the heart of the issue of tripartition and self-identity. The acratic does not desire to do what he thinks he ought not to do more than he desires not to do it. At the crucial moment, he identifies himself as one whose good is achieved by the putatively wicked appetite. And yet, contrary to Aristotle's account, he is not like the 'drunkard' whose belief that he ought to refrain is no longer occurrent or, perhaps, no longer 'operative'.[39] Embodied persons are the sort of creature who experiences disunity of agency or subjectivity. They are among the incoherent images of the really real that constitute the sensible world.

There is an interesting echo of the concept of the person which I have argued is present in the tripartitioning of the soul and the concept of a person developed by Harry Frankfurt.[40] Frankfurt thinks that what is essential for personhood is the capacity for forming what he calls 'second-order desires' (p. 83 in the 1989 reprint). Someone has a second-order desire when

he wants simply to have a certain desire or when he wants a certain desire to be his will. In situations of the latter kind, I shall call his second-order desires 'second-order volitions' or 'volitions of the second order'. Now it is having second-order volitions, and not having second-order desires generally, that I regard as essential

[39] See *NE H* 5, 1147^{b}9–12.

[40] See Frankfurt (1971), reprinted in Watson (1989), 81–95. Irwin (1995), 288–97, argues for a view of the function of reason within the tripartite soul that is very much in harmony with Frankfurt's, though Irwin accepts some sort of cognitive functioning for the parts other than reason.

to being a person. It is logically possible, however unlikely, that there should be an agent with second-order desires but with no volitions of the second order. Such a creature, in my view, would not be a person. I shall use the term 'wanton' to refer to agents who have first-order desires but who are not persons because, whether or not they have desires of the second order, they have no second-order volitions. (86)

Frankfurt illustrates the difference between a person and a wanton with the case of two narcotic addicts, one unwilling and one willing. The unwilling addict has conflicting first-order desires. He wants to take the drug and he wants to refrain from taking the drug. In addition, he has a second-order volition to have the latter first-order desire, that is, the desire to refrain from taking the drug, constitute his will. The other addict, the wanton, only desires to fulfil his first-order desire to take the drug. It never occurs to him to consider whether he does not want the desire he has to constitute his will. Even if he also has a desire not to take the drug, he does not prefer that one of these conflicting desires should prevail over the other. He is not exactly neutral with regard to these. Such neutrality would suppose that he finds these equally acceptable and that he therefore has a second-order volition. Rather, he literally has no identity apart from these first-order desires. By contrast, the unwilling addict, in addition to the conflicting desires he possesses, identifies himself, in virtue of having a second-order volition, with one rather than the other of his first-order desires. He makes one of them truly his own and in so doing he withdraws from the other:

It is in virtue of this identification and withdrawal, accomplished through the formation of a second-order volition, that the unwilling addict may meaningfully make the analytically puzzling statements that the force moving him to take the drug is a force other than his own, and that it is not of his own free will but rather against his will that this force moves him to take it. (88)

The wanton does not care which of his conflicting desires prevails. Whichever does prevail, he will be unsatisfied because he is identified with both the desire that constitutes his will *and* the desire that does not. When a person acts, the desire by which he is moved is either the will he wants or a will he wants to be without. When a wanton acts, it is neither (89).

I do not know to what extent, if any, Frankfurt's analysis of what constitutes a person and what constitutes a wanton is based on his reading of *Republic*. Nevertheless, the parallels are striking. First of all, let us note the idea of identifying with a desire. According to Frankfurt, the unwilling addict identifies with his first-order desire to refrain from taking drugs. According to Plato, the just person identifies with the rational part of his soul. In addition, *all* persons identify with the rational part of their souls when this is in conflict with their appetitive parts. According to Frankfurt, the unwilling addict can make 'the analytically puzzling statement' that the force moving him to take the drug is a force other than his own. According to Plato, the acratic believes that the appetites that are moving him are an 'alien force' against which he ought to struggle.

The Platonic doctrine 'no one does wrong willingly' implies first and second order volitions or desires.[41] The acratic *unwillingly* does his evil act. The vicious person *willingly* does his. The 'willingly' (ἑκών) in 'no one does wrong willingly' indicates what Frankfurt would call a second-order volition when wrongdoing originates in a first-order desire. In contrast to Frankfurt, however, for Plato the desire to refrain from doing wrong is not really a 'first-order' desire. It is a 'second-order' volition because it is cognitive. It is this second-order volition that submits to or rules over appetite.

Frankfurt does not provide or apparently presuppose a metaphysical basis for his claims about identification and intrapsychic conflict. His analysis operates entirely in the formal mode. Having second-order desires or volitions, identifying with first-order desires, having alien forces within oneself are on the surface strange ideas, though they are employed to describe situations, like that of the unwilling addict, that are readily understandable. By contrast, Plato's account of embodied personhood is embedded in his two-world metaphysics. For Plato, psychic conflict is a sign of the equivocal status of immaterial entities caught up in the material world.

As I argued in the second chapter, the immateriality of the person is for Plato a condition necessary for self-reflexivity. Self-reflexivity is an essential property of cognition. In Frankfurt's language, having a second-order volition is only possible for something that can, at the same time, also be the subject of the first-order desire. If it were not the same subject in both cases, then 'resisting' one's own appetite would be in principle no different from

[41] See *Ap.* 37 A 5; *Gorg.* 488 A 3; *Prot.* 345 D 8, 358 C 7; *Rep.* 589 C 6; *Tim.* 86 D 7–C 1; *Laws* 731 C–D.

resisting the appetite of another person. If one were to analyse resistance in this way, incontinence would be impossible. After all, when one's resistance to an attacker is finally overcome, that is not incontinence.

If, however, it is agreed that the subjects must be the same, why must they be the same immaterial entity? The answer is that psychic conflicts have an inseparable cognitive dimension. Even Frankfurt's wanton, on Plato's account, has self-reflexive cognition of his own desire. For Plato, the wanton is similar to the tyrannical man, living at the outermost reaches of personhood by identifying himself with his most wicked 'first-order desire'. His polar opposite, the aristocratic man, identifies himself not with a first-order desire, but with the cognitive subject, what Frankfurt calls the subject of second-order volitions. An embodied person is incapable of perfect identification at either extreme.

There are some philosophers, like the early Stoics, who reject psychic conflict of the sort Plato recognizes, precisely because they are materialists. There are others, like Frankfurt, who recognize the conflict without committing themselves to any particular metaphysical foundation for it. Plato, it seems, has a metaphysical apparatus well suited for explaining the paradoxical life of an embodied person. Discovering oneself to be the subject of a bodily appetite and at the same time the subject of the will not to have that appetite is, according to Frankfurt, the prerogative of a person. An embodied person, for Plato, like everything else in the sensible world, is an image of that which is ideal or really real. That image has a paradoxical status, literally a metaphor for what the person really is. Incontinence is a sort of emblem of embodiment, even if there be a few who have renounced it.

Embodied persons are alone among images of the intelligible world in that they can recognize themselves as images. In the very act of acknowledging a psychic conflict within oneself, one can recognize that one is living a life that is in a way false. What the anti-dualist claims is the insurmountable problem of interactionism—how the immaterial and the material can affect each other—Plato claims is the paradox of diminished reality. Perhaps if Plato was not already convinced that it is importantly true of sensibles generally that they 'are and are not at the same time' he would not also have been convinced that an immaterial entity can be the subject of material states.

From *Republic* we learn that the life of an embodied person is an ongoing identity crisis. On Plato's model of the embodied person, to make one's appetites the principle of action is to opt for a disassociated or incoherent self. For if one decides to serve one's own appetites, the decision is being made self-evidently by an entity that is different from a subject of appetites. It is a decision to seek one's good outside of one's true self. Everyone, however, naturally seeks his own true good.[42] And so the one who opts to serve his appetites has actually failed to recognize his own identity. He is deconstructing his own personhood.

Apart from the Platonic context, it would be question-begging to insist that the embodied person who variously identifies himself as the servant and the master of his own appetites nevertheless has a single identity. One could reasonably insist that whatever identity is claimed is fictional or arbitrary. But for Plato, embodied identity is controlled by a real disembodied exemplar. The endowment and the achievement of embodied personhood are measured against the ideal. That ideal is a subject of thinking or a cognitive agent. For this reason, Plato can speak about one's self-identification as a servant of appetites as the deconstruction of personhood. What I termed in the first chapter Socrates' 'absolutist prohibition of wrongdoing' can be justified on the basis of the personal deconstruction that is constituted by subordination to appetite. The argument for the tripartite soul indirectly supports the prohibition by showing that reason trumps appetite in the dynamics of self-identification. To identify oneself as other than a cognitive agent is to court incoherence. The argument for the immortality of the person is supposed to ensure that a willingness thus to court incoherence is a wholly unattractive life strategy.

3.2 Tripartition and Immortality in *Republic* Book 10

In *Republic* 10 (608 C 1 ff.) Socrates finally returns to the second part of the challenge advanced at 358 A 1 ff.: to show that the just life is better than

---

[42] See *Meno* 78 B 5; *Gorg.* 468 B 7–8; *Rep.* 438 E 3–4, 505 D 11–E 1. Irwin (1995), 293, aptly concludes, 'We want to pursue the good of the whole soul because we want to be guided by the real merits of different activities, not simply by our degree of inclination towards them. To this extent we regard ourselves as essentially rational agents who want to form and to act on true judgments about our good. Forming and acting on these judgments is not simply a useful instrumental means towards securing our good; it is also part of the rational activity that is itself part of our good.'

the unjust life with respect to its 'rewards and consequences' (τοὺς μισθοὺς καὶ τὰ γιγνόμενα). These rewards and consequences belong to the afterlife. In order to show that the just person fares better in the afterlife than his opposite, it must first be shown that the soul is immortal.

The argument Socrates offers for the immortality of the soul (608 D 13–611 A 3) is different from what we found in *Phaedo*. Here he argues that anything is destroyed only by its peculiar or natural evil. Just as the body and natural substances have their own evil by the presence of which they are destroyed, so the soul, too, has its own evil. That is injustice, licentiousness, cowardice, and ignorance (609 C), the opposites of the four virtues defined in book 4 (444 B–C). But none of these, it seems, destroys the soul. Therefore, if the soul's own evil does not destroy it, the evil of the body resulting in death is not going to destroy it either. The soul cannot be destroyed by an alien evil, that of the body.

Two questions naturally arise. First, if the soul's evil does not destroy it, how does it harm it? Second, if the soul is not destroyed by the evils it experiences, would we not then expect the entire tripartite soul to be immortal? But in that case, what would it mean for the subject of bodily states to survive the death of the body?

The subsequent passage is supposed to throw some light on the nature of the disembodied soul (611 A 10–612 A 6). The exegetical problem posed by this passage is well known.[43] Whereas it is clear in books 4, 8, and 9 that Plato views the embodied soul as tripartite, the present passage could be read as holding that the disembodied soul is without parts—is entirely rational. Such a reading at least coheres with the representation of the soul in *Phaedo* and with the account in *Republic* that views the ideal person as the subject of thinking only. The reading does not, however, seem to cohere with *Phaedrus*—usually taken to post-date *Republic*—which is generally interpreted as representing the disembodied soul as tripartite in its central myth. Even worse, *Timaeus*, again almost universally taken to post-date both *Republic* and *Phaedrus*, seems to represent the disembodied soul as consisting only of the rational part.[44] So, on the view that the disembodied soul in *Republic* 10 is partless, Plato's position would seem to have wavered

---

[43] Szlezák (1976) gives a good summary of the various scholarly positions. Additional material is referred to in Gerson (1987).

[44] See 41 C–D, 69 C 8–D 1, D 5–6, 90 A.

considerably. I shall discuss the *Phaedrus* passage in the next section and *Timaeus* in the last chapter. I wish to focus now on the disputed passage in *Republic* 10 and try to understand it in the light of the analysis of this chapter.

Socrates avers that the 'truest nature of the soul' (τῇ ἀληθεστάτῃ φύσει τοιοῦτον εἶναι ψυχήν) does not allow of 'much variety and unlikeness and difference' (πολλῆς ποικιλίας καὶ ἀνομοιότητός τε καὶ διαφορᾶς, 611 B 1–2). 'It is not easy', he says, 'for anything composed of many parts [σύνθετον ἐκ πολλῶν] to be everlasting [ἀΐδιον], if it is not composed in the best way [τῇ καλλίστῃ συνθέσει], as the soul now appeared to us' (611 A 5–7).[45] Plausibly enough, the qualification 'not composed in the best way' can be glossed by *Timaeus* 41 D–E, where the human soul is created in the 'second or third degree of purity' compared to the world-soul. Nevertheless, since the human soul is affirmed to be 'immortal' (ἀθάνατον) or everlasting (B 9), the fact that it is not composed in the best way obviously does not destroy its immortality. So, we may ask, why should the fact that it is composed of many parts compromise immortality? If it is not easy for a tripartite soul to be immortal, that does not mean it is impossible.

Socrates now insists:

'That the soul is immortal, our recent argument and others have compelled us to hold. But to view [θεάσασθαι] the soul as it really is it is necessary to view it not in its condition as maimed by association with the body and other evils, as we are now viewing it, but as it is when it has become purified. We ought to view it carefully in that way with adequate reasoning, and then one will find it to be a much finer thing and one will see more clearly its justice and injustice and all the things we have now considered. What we are saying about it now is true of it as it appears in its present state. But we have considered it now looking at it in a state like that of the sea-god Glaucus, whose original nature one would not easily glimpse. For some of his original parts have been broken off, and some have been crushed and maimed by the waves, others have been attached to him, shells and seaweed and rocks, so that he looks more like a wild animal than what he is by nature. In the same way we view our soul beset by countless evils. But it is necessary, Glaucon, to look elsewhere.'

'Where?'

---

[45] 'Now' (νῦν) seems to refer to the entire argument of the dialogue, i.e. to the conclusion that the soul is tripartite. Adam ad loc. cites 504 D 2 and 414 B 4 as parallels.

'To its love of wisdom. And we should think about the sorts of things to which it attaches itself and desires to consort with, as being akin to the divine and immortal and to that which is always, and the sort of thing it would become if it were completely attracted to this and were elevated by this impulse from the sea in which it now is, and had scraped off it the rocks and shells which, since it is now at an earthly table, grow around it in earthy, rocky, and wild profusion owing to those feasts widely regarded as happy. And then one might see its true nature, whether that is multiform or uniform [εἴτε πολυειδὴς εἴτε μονοειδής], or in what way it has [either a multiform or uniform nature] and how. But for now we have, I think, given reasonable consideration to its conditions in human life and its forms.' (611 B 10–612 A 6).[46]

Socrates does not, however, go on to describe the soul in its true nature. Yet three times in this entire passage he refers to the soul's 'true nature', which is evident only apart from the body. The task of seeing the soul apart from the body cannot mean simply considering the embodied soul in abstraction from the body, because that is what they have been doing since book 4. This insistence by Socrates must mean that the soul's true nature is revealed or recovered by it when it is disembodied. And that entails that its embodied form is somehow defective. It is defective when, as tripartite, it exists in a 'human life'.

One might suppose that if the disembodied soul can be seen to be just or

---

[46] At 580 D 11 the appetitive part of the soul is called πολυειδής owing to its motley array of appetites. This, of course, does not for Plato occasion the need to posit additional soul parts because the multitude of appetites do not contain the relevant conflict, namely, that between reason and appetite. We must suppose that πολυειδής is being used here in a generic sense. A somewhat more interesting and difficult counter-example is at 603 A 1, where Plato adduces the same principle used at 436 B 8–10 to derive tripartition, namely, that 'the same thing cannot act in opposite ways or be in opposite states at the same time and in the same part of itself in relation to the same other thing' in order to distinguish that in the soul that measures sensible objects correctly and that in the soul that 'believes falsely' regarding these. The latter presumably refers to the judgements made on the basis of sense-perception. By contrast, reasoning properly employed is not fooled. So, for example, one can believe that two objects are the same in size at the same time that one believes that they are different because one has measured. If we interpret the distinction between thinking and sense-perception as a true partitioning, then we can recur to 443 D 7, where Plato seems to leave open the possibility of parts in addition to the canonical three, or we can locate the partitioning within the rational part. Since for Plato sense-perception is a condition or 'state' (πάθος), I doubt, however, that it can be an independent ἀρχή of action.

unjust, and justice involves the proper arrangement of the parts of the soul, then the disembodied soul must be 'multiform'. But it no more follows that the true nature of the soul must be multiform for this reason than it does that the true nature of Beauty must have flesh and bones because a human bodily instance of beauty must be so. The disembodied soul is destined to experience the consequences of its embodied career. This does not require that it retain a tripartite form. Indeed, if in order to see the soul in its true nature we need to see it apart from the body, then one would suppose that tripartition, which we *can* observe indirectly in the soul in its bodily existence, does not belong to it while disembodied. Nevertheless, it cannot be gainsaid that for whatever reason Plato does not in this passage provide a decisive answer to the question of whether the disembodied soul is multiform or uniform. What is clear, however, is that one does not observe it in its true nature when it is embodied. Our previous analysis may help us to understand why this is so.

The soul's true nature is observable when it has 'become purified' (καθαρὸν γιγνόμενον, 611 C 3). This statement puts us in mind of the discussion of purification in *Phaedo* (81 B ff). But there is an ambiguity present in both passages. Does the disembodied soul, whether it be good or evil, attain its 'true nature' or is this the state only of one, such as the philosopher, who has undergone purification from all evil? Socrates' subsequent words strongly suggest the latter. He says that we must study the soul when it is not beset by evils (611 D 6–7). That is, we must study its love of wisdom. We must realize 'what it grasps and desires to have intercourse with, because it is akin [συγγενής] to the divine and immortal and what always is, and we must also realize what it would become if it followed this desire completely' (611 E 1–4). On the one hand, the soul's evil is supposed not to destroy it, in which case even the wicked leave the body essentially intact. On the other, the philosopher is here supposed to achieve what everyone else does not, namely, his true nature.

The present passage also recalls a previous description of the philosopher. At 500 C 5 the philosopher is said to 'imitate' (μιμεῖσθαι) Forms and to 'make himself a likeness' (ἀφομοιοῦσθαι) of them.[47] The type of imitation

---

[47] The word ἀφωμοιώθη is used at *Parm.*132 D 7 by Parmenides to characterize the relation of an instance of a Form to the Form itself. See also *Theaet.* 178 B, where the 'target' is god, not Forms.

Plato has in mind here is not entirely clear. It can refer either to a process whereby the philosopher makes of himself an example of the Forms of Justice, Temperance, etc., thereby becoming like these Forms. Or it can refer to the effort to be like certain properties of Forms, such as stability and uniformity. Finally, it can refer to an effort to know the Forms—that is, realizing one's nature by actually identifying with the immaterial, as in the Affinity Argument in *Phaedo*. I do not think that any of these possibilities ought to be excluded. But the third is prior to the other two. For it is in virtue of knowing Forms that one attains a state of personal equilibrium and is also able to instil the virtues in the populace over which the philosopher is to rule. This is, I suggest, what the desire to have 'intercourse' with Forms means. Whereas *Phaedo* argued that *because* we are endowed with souls that are likenesses of Forms we are similar to what is immutable, here we can become like Forms by becoming knowers. Even if the knowledge we acquired while disembodied were not directly available to us here below, by identifying ourselves as knowers we begin to ascend to an immutable-like state.[48]

We recall from the last chapter that an argument for the immortality of the soul is not necessarily an argument for the immortality of the person. Plato tries to show that the person is immortal by focusing on one psychic function, namely, the cognitive. In the light of that argument, and of the tripartitioning of the soul in *Republic*, we would expect that the only part of the soul that is immortal is the rational. Although I think this is in fact Plato's position, he also recognizes that disembodied persons may at the same time be complex. That is, they may well bear the 'scars' of embodiment and continue an orientation to a false life. One thing that can be safely asserted is that if the body is necessary for having bodily appetites, then the part of the soul that is the subject of these does not survive death. In Frankfurt's

---

[48] Miller (1985), 188–92, interprets the imitation at *Rep.* 500 c 5 as essentially ethical and spiritual. That is, by imitating the Forms (and especially the Form of the Good), the philosopher will 'come to constitute, by his own character and comportment, a kind of analogue in the context of human being to the nature of the Good'. Part of the problem with Miller's interpretation is that the Form of the Good is not introduced until several pages after the remarks about imitation are made. In addition, though it is undoubtedly true that 'consorting with Forms' will have ethical and spiritual consequences, the imitation itself is cognitive, or else it surely presumes a cognitive relation to the Forms. Kraut (1992b), 328, has a similar view.

language, there are no first-order appetites for the disembodied. A person is, however, an entity capable of identifying himself as the subject of these or as the subject of thought. The philosopher is one whose identification with the latter is, while embodied, almost complete. The non-philosopher would, when disembodied, presumably continue to have a second-order volition to have the first-order desires that he embraced when embodied. So, the answer to the difficult question of whether the disembodied soul is tripartite or a unity is that it depends on whether we are referring to the soul or to the person. Remarkably, Plato has woven together (or perhaps, on a less charitable interpretation, confused) immortality as an endowment and as an achievement.

A disembodied soul must bear the marks of its just or unjust embodied life. Although the disembodied soul will not include the capacities of the embodied soul, at least not the capacities requiring a body, the person who is the subject of these continues to be the identical subject he was when embodied. Since a person ('the human being within the human being', 589 A 7) is a rational agent or subject, self-identification as servant of appetites would produce a sort of 'duck-rabbit', looking for all the world both like a person and like something else. The disembodied soul of the just man, by contrast, looks practically like a uniform entity. That person has, in Plato's words, 'become one out of many'. There is only a residual distinction between that person and the first-order desire of its rational faculty. The qualification 'residual' is necessary, as we shall see, to distinguish reincarnatable human souls from the souls of gods.

A Platonic hell, viewed non-mythically, would be the self-reflexive state of a disembodied person who had spent his embodied existence betraying his own identity by enslaving himself to his appetites. Such a person would have nothing to do but what he least desires to do, namely, to think or reflect. A Platonic heaven would be the self-reflexive state of a disembodied person who had identified himself with his rational faculty and its desire to know. Such a person would at last be free from what here below he had rejected, in so far as that was possible.

There is a subtle but important difference between the grounds for the absolutist prohibition of injustice in the early dialogues and the position of *Republic*. It is true that in *Crito* injustice is its own punishment and justice its own reward, and though there is not a tripartite soul there, we can say much the same things we can say about the soul in *Republic* with regard to its identity or lack of identity with its rational part. Still, as we have seen, without a doctrine of everlasting disembodied existence, one might make a plausible case for the limited value of living a just life over an unjust one. So long as the play continues and real life is not faced, one can argue that it is more amusing to play the villain than the hero. That the real nature of the person, distinct from the human being, is not revealed while embodied is enough for the champion of wrongdoing to insist on the irrelevance of the contrast between images and reality. With a proof of the immortality of the soul, that argument no longer works.

The question posed in Chapter 1, namely, 'How does wrongdoing harm the soul?', can now be given a somewhat clearer answer. Wrongdoing involves the identification of the person with the subject of the desires of either of the lower two parts of the soul. In fact, it could be argued that the definition of wrongdoing just is an action in which reason serves appetite or spirit, where 'serves' connotes a false personal identification. The identification of the person with the subject of appetite or spirit necessitates a kind of deconstruction of the self or a loss of identity. Assuming that the loss is permanent, it is difficult to imagine that one could really prefer the loss of identity to its recovery. Someone who says 'I want to be a bird so that I can fly' really means 'I want to fly'. If wanting to be a bird in order to fly really meant the obliteration of personal identity, there would be no difference between wanting to be a bird which can fly and wanting a bird to fly. Desiring something for oneself seems to necessitate logically that when what one desires is achieved, one is identical with that which has been achieved. One might argue that the person who simply desires to be dead provides a counter-example to this claim. But Plato's argument in *Republic* 10 renders this view irrelevant.

3.3 *Phaedrus*

For a number of reasons, *Phaedrus* is, as Alexander Nehamas and Paul Woodruff state in the introduction to their vibrant translation, 'one of the strangest dialogues [Plato] ever wrote'.[49] One thing that is clear about the dialogue is that it argues for the immortality of soul and assumes

---

[49] See Nehamas and Woodruff (1995), xii.

tripartitioning of it in some form. In this section my central concern is to show how the discussion of immortality and tripartition serves to deepen the account of personhood in *Republic*.

In what follows I shall have little to say about the abrupt shift that occurs in the dialogue at 257 B from speeches about love to discussions about rhetoric and the nature of writing. I shall also have little to say about what is arguably the most important passage in the dialogue, where Socrates seems to undercut what has gone before by his denouncement of writing as a means of doing philosophy.⁵⁰ I do not thereby mean to suggest that a satisfying overall interpretation of the dialogue does not need to take account of all its parts. Nor do I minimize the difficulty of doing this. I do, however, write on the assumption that neither the denouncement nor the long discussion of rhetoric, finally, erases the claims made earlier. Part of the defence of this assumption will follow here; part of it I have offered elsewhere; and part of it will have been made by others.

Socrates meets Phaedrus as they are both walking outside the city walls (227 A ff.) Phaedrus has come from hearing the famous orator Lysias deliver a speech on why a boy should allow himself to be seduced by a non-lover rather than a lover. In response to Socrates' wish to have the speech read, Phaedrus proposes a spot under a plane tree by the Ilisus river. This may be the place where legend tells us that Boreas, the North Wind, carried off Oreithyia, daughter of the Athenian king Erechtheus. In response to Phaedrus' query whether Socrates believes such legends, he gives an ambiguous reply. Anyone who does not believe in them will require much time and ingenuity in order to provide an aetiological demythologizing explanation. Socrates, however, will not take the time for that since he is mindful that he has as yet failed to heed the Delphic inscription's injunction 'know thyself'. Attempts to achieve self-knowledge, he holds, should precede efforts to know such matters (230 A). Thus, the familiar Socratic passion for critical introspection is introduced. Naturally, it is not yet clear how this passion is going to be satisfied, if at all, by anything said or done in the dialogue. Indeed, Socrates explains that pastoral perambulations have little attraction for him just because they separate him from the very people who have something to teach him. The prospect of hearing a speech of Lysias recited by Phaedrus, however, serves as an enticing charm. This is certainly

---

⁵⁰ See Gerson (2000) on the latter passage.

not the Socrates we know from elsewhere, the Socrates who disdains long speeches.[51] If for no other reason, this should bolster the suspicion that the Socrates we know from the dialogues is Plato's literary creation. He is neither using the literary creation to represent the historical Socrates nor to conceal anything. He is using Socrates as an instrument of philosophical writing.[52]

The speech supposedly by Lysias recited by Phaedrus argues that a boy should prefer an older man who does not love him to one who does (230 E–234 C). By 'prefer' is meant allowing the older man to enjoy him sexually. So, both the lover and the non-lover want sex, but the boy should be persuaded that it is better to submit to the latter rather than the former. A number of reasons are offered for this view, most of which are patently specious. One remarkable thing about this speech is that it presumes that 'love' (ἔρως) is something more than sexual desire (since the non-lover has this as well), but it does not directly specify what this might be. One obvious possibility is that the difference between the lover and the non-lover is that the former cares for the beloved whereas the latter does not. But the speech directly contradicts this. The non-lover is said to do the best he can for the boy and to exercise a 'strong friendship' (ἰσχυρὰν φιλίαν) for him though he does not love him (231 A 4–6, 237 C 7).[53] It seems exceedingly unlikely that one can have a strong friendship for another without caring for that person at all. Another more promising possibility is that the lover is smitten whereas the non-lover is not. If that is the case, then the lover is someone who is 'in love' and the non-lover is not.[54] Is there any more to ἔρως than this? Not, I think, in this utterly conventional tour de force, making the worse cause appear the better, as Socrates' accusers insist that he does.

---

[51] Cf. *Prot.* 334 C–335 C; *Gorg.* 449 B–C, 461 D–462 A.

[52] Cf. 235 C–D, where Socrates says that, owing to his ignorance, the speech he is about to give could not have come from him. I see this as a clear manipulation of the literary figure, just as in the case of Diotima.

[53] This point makes it clear that preferring the non-lover to the lover does not mean preferring *any* non-lover who wants sex. At 231 E 1–2 the boy is advised to choose from among those non-lovers who are worthy of his friendship and presumably will reciprocate.

[54] At 231 C 5 ὕστερον ἐρασθῶσιν has to be understood to indicate a temporally limited episode. 'Falling in love' connotes an episode; 'loving' does not, as the translators uniformly recognize. In addition, and more importantly, falling in love is something that happens to one.

Socrates' counter-speech in defence of the non-lover over the lover simply begins where the previous speech leaves off (237 B–241 D). Phaedrus has reported that Lysias says that the non-lover is to be preferred over the lover because the lover is smitten and so is in many ways unreliable. Socrates claims, as Socrates always does, that in order to understand any subject and to avoid self-contradiction, one must first know the 'essence' (οὐσία) of the thing under discussion (237 C 3). In the present case, one must start with a definition of love and of its 'power' (δύναμις, 237 D 1).[55] As in *Symposium*, love is said to be a type of appetite or 'desire' (ἐπιθυμία, 237 D 3). But even those who are not in love can have desires for 'beautiful things' (τῶν καλῶν, 237 D 4–5). The implication of this is that all desire is for beautiful things, but love is one form of this, not distinguished by its having beautiful things as an object. As in *Symposium*, beauty and good are conflated as objects of desire.

In order to arrive at the distinguishing mark of love, Socrates explains that there are two 'principles' (ἀρχαί) of action in us, an 'inborn desire for pleasures' and an 'acquired belief' (ἐπίκτητος δόξα, 237 D 8) which pursues the best. Thus, reason and appetite variously provide the ultimate explanation of actions. This bipartitioning of the soul is familiar, too, from *Symposium* and indeed implicit in the early dialogues. I take it that it neither replaces nor corrects in any way the triparititioning of the soul in *Republic*. Indeed, we shall see the tripartite soul represented in the central myth of the dialogue shortly.[56] With this psychic division, Socrates can now say that the desire for pleasure in beauty and the related desire for beautiful bodies by the part of the soul that rules without reason and without that which drives a person to do what is right is what love is (238 B 7–C 4; cf. *Symposium* 205 A–206 A). This should immediately put us in mind of the definition of love at *Symposium* 205 D 2–3: 'every desire [ἐπιθυμία] for good things or for happiness is the supreme and treacherous love in everyone'. The limitation in *Phaedrus* and the attendant apparent contradiction between the two

---

[55] I take it that δύναμις is in this context practically synonymous with the ἔργον of love in *Symposium*.

[56] It could be argued that the third part of the soul, the spirited part, is never actually an ἀρχή of action. It is always *reactive*. I do not think this is correct for *Republic*, and I doubt it is so in *Phaedrus*, though the functioning of the third part is rather obscure in this dialogue, probably because it is rather beside the point.

definitions arise, as we shall see presently, from taking 'love' in the narrow way understood in Lysias' speech, namely, as 'being smitten'.

There is an obvious ambiguity in the use of 'desire' in the above passage. Those who are not in love can have a desire for beautiful things. Does this desire belong to the reasoning part of the soul or is it a desire of the appetitive part that is disposed in relation to reasoning other than the way the desire that is love is disposed? It is most natural to take it, as in *Republic* 580 D 8, as referring to the desire of the reasoning part. What is wrong with Socrates' definition in his first speech is that it excludes from the class of lovers those whose desire for 'good or beautiful things' arises from the rational part of their souls. In *Republic* that love is called φιλία, not ἔρως. What Socrates' recantation is going to do is extend the ambit of ἔρως without abandoning its connotation of affect and passivity.[57]

Socrates' argument for the superiority of the non-lover over the lover moves from the definition of love to its effects. The rest of the speech is true to his promise to say something beyond what is contained in Lysias' speech (cf. 235 B). But he does not say anything that exceeds in profundity that which is contained in the previous speech. All of the supposed effects that follow, says Socrates, 'by necessity' belong to love as defined. It is not difficult to show that a lover of *this* sort is to be avoided and a non-lover preferred (cf. 241 E–242 A).

Socrates' δαιμόνιον holds him back from leaving without making a recantation of his denunciation of love (242 C). The recantation or palinode in praise of love is the passage central to my concerns (242 E–257 B). In all likelihood it is the passage where we shall find that which unites all the parts of the dialogue. Socrates comes immediately to the point. The previous speech erred in taking 'madness' (μανία) as unequivocally bad. But in fact if the madness is 'divine', it is the source of the best things we have (244 A 5–7). Among types of divine madness are those that belong to prophetesses and priestesses, to those seeking expiation for ancient crimes, and to poets (244 B–245 B). So, the question becomes: is love a divine form of madness?

---

[57] This is most explicit at 255 E 1–2, where the boy who is pursued by his lover begins to 'return the love' (ἄντερως) but mistakes it for friendship. Nussbaum (1986), 205 ff., claims that the doctrine of the first speech of Socrates is strikingly similar to 'the view of the middle dialogues'. She identifies Socrates' 'recantation' with the rejection of this view. I hold that the first speech of Socrates does not represent the view of *Republic* and *Symposium*.

In order to answer this question, we must, says Socrates, first understand the truth about the nature of human and divine souls, 'what they do' (ἔργα) and 'what they suffer' (πάθη, 245 C 2–4). The forthcoming account of soul is, I want to show, an account of personhood.

The central truth about the soul is that it is immortal, and on behalf of this claim we get an argument (245 C 5–246 A 2).[58] The strategy of this argument is essentially to show that soul is a principle of self-motion and that self-movers can cause generation but cannot be generated. If souls were generated, the cause of their generation would either be a moved mover, and hence something itself in need of explanation, or it would be another self-mover. That soul cannot be destroyed is shown by arguing that if soul is the explanation of generation and soul could be destroyed, then everything that is in motion would eventually come to rest. I shall not address this strange, complex, and historically portentous argument except to point out that at 245 E 7–8 soul is said to be just what meets the definite description 'that which moves itself' (τὸ αὐτὸ ἑαυτὸ κινοῦν). We are not told what this psychic motion is or how it is the cause of motion in bodies. As in *Phaedo*, where soul is life and brings life, here soul is self-moving and brings motion to the body. Indeed, it is not at all clear that psychic self-motion is anything other than life.

Personal immortality is not plainly in focus in this argument. As many have pointed out, the words ψυχὴ πᾶσα ἀθάνατος are ambiguous between 'every soul is immortal' and 'all soul is immortal'.[59] In addition, the argument for the indestructibility of soul does not have any clear relevance to individual souls. Finally, if the argument works for every individual soul because it is a self-mover, then Plato seems committed to the immortality of every living thing. It seems easier if Plato only commits himself in this argument to the claim that soul as such is neither generated nor destroyed, but that individual souls may be both generated and destroyed. Then, the argument for personal immortality has to be of a different sort—for example, such as that in *Phaedo* or *Republic*. It is true that immediately after the proof Socrates begins to describe human

---

[58] On the structure of this argument see Bett (1986).

[59] See Bett (1986), 436–9 (in Fine 1999: vol. ii) and n. 24, where he argues plausibly for the collective sense of the phrase. See Griswold (1986), 84, who argues that 'all soul' is a mass term which is intended to apply to every individual soul.

souls, but this shift, if it be such, does not seem to me to be impossibly abrupt.

In any case, Socrates offers to describe the 'form' (ἰδέα) of soul, but instead of a straightforward account, which would be too difficult and lengthy, he suggests saying 'what the soul is like' (ᾧ ἔοικεν, 246 A 5). That is, he is prepared to offer an image of the soul in a myth. It is, he says, like a natural union of a team of winged horses and their charioteer (246 A 6–7).[60] The team of horses belonging to the gods are both of good stock. In the case of humans, one horse is good and one bad. Consequently, driving this team is always difficult work for us. Then, oddly, Socrates proceeds to describe at great length and with great power the states of divine and human souls in heaven, the causes for human souls falling to earth, the requirements for redemption, and so on. Presumably heaven refers to the disembodied state of the soul and earth to its embodied state. Let us recall that the reason for the entire speech was to discover if love is a divine madness. In order to determine this, we first have to learn the nature of the soul and then its properties. It is somewhat surprising that the speech now shifts almost entirely to the discussion of the soul in heaven, or at least from a heavenly perspective, but it will become clear presently how this serves the argument that love is a form of divine madness. Scholars, however, have struggled with the implication in this speech that the disembodied soul is taken to be tripartite, as is the embodied soul in *Republic*. But the claim that the disembodied soul is tripartite is in some tension with *Republic* 10, 608 C–612 A, and certainly conflicts with *Timaeus* 68 C 8–D 6, where only the highest part of the soul is said to be immortal and where tripartition is associated with embodiment.[61]

The complex relation between soul and personhood that is implicit in *Republic* 10 should help us to see what is going on in the *Phaedrus* myth. Suppose Plato wants to present an image of the soul with a view to answering the question about the nature of love. What is wanted is a single image that takes account of both the embodied and the disembodied forms. In addition,

---

[60] This image recalls the 'three-headed beast' of *Rep.* 588 B–590 A, where the 'human being within the human being' corresponds to the charioteer in the *Phaedrus* myth.

[61] See Gerson (1987) for an argument that Plato has one self-consistent view in all these texts. See Shiner (1972) for doubts about Plato's unambiguous commitment to the immortality only of the rational part of the soul in *Republic*.

what is wanted is an image that takes into account both the souls of those who have an embodied existence, like persons, and the souls of gods, that do not. A careful reading of our passage shows that the image of the charioteer and the horses does exactly that.

The soul has just been shown to be a self-mover. It seems that is why in the image it is said first of all to consist of a charioteer and horses naturally 'united in power' (σύμφυτῳ δυνάμει). If they were not so united, then it would be the horses that would be the self-mover and the real soul, while the charioteer would be that which was moved. But that seems to be the wrong way round. It is the charioteer who represents the person, the one who enjoys the intellectual heaven of the gods and the one who is re-embodied according to his heavenly existence.[62] The image offered is in fact of the soul in abstraction from its disembodied or embodied state. It is a mistake to see the motion of the soul in heaven provided by the horses as other than an image of psychic motion, just as it is a mistake to see the motion of the embodied soul as being provided by appetite and emotion.[63] Perhaps viewing embodied motion in this way would be intelligible if it were not the *only* means of motion available for the soul in the image. For nowhere does Plato ever suggest that psychic motion is exclusively non-cognitive. Once we realize that it is a mistake to view the motion of the soul as accurately represented by the motion of the horses, we shall perhaps be a little less willing to suppose that the disembodied soul is unequivocally tripartite.

If we understand that the embodied person is an image of its own disembodied self, we can appreciate that the image of the charioteer and horses includes both and does not entail a disembodied tripartite soul.[64] As I have tried to show, in *Republic* the embodied person is the subject of both appetites and emotions. In the image in *Phaedrus* the good and bad horses of the disembodied soul have appetites and emotions over against those of

---

[62] See e.g. 248 D 2, where the charioteer is the implicit subject of the phrase 'who has seen the most'.

[63] See below, § 6.1, for a discussion of psychic motion in *Timaeus*.

[64] At 253 D ff. the tripartite image is applied to the embodied soul. See Robin (1985), cxxiii, who argues that the embodied tripartite soul is an 'image dégradée' of its disembodied exemplar, which is tripartite only in the sense that it is 'composed', as in *Timaeus*, of the ingredients Sameness, Difference, and Existence.

the charioteer.[65] Their satisfaction has nothing to do with the satisfaction of the desire of the charioteer. By contrast, when the image is applied to the embodied soul, the desires of the horses are identical with those of the charioteer, as we should expect.[66] Here it seems that the image is differently applied to the soul in its embodied and disembodied states.

One clue regarding the relation between the disembodied and embodied soul or person is that, as part of his description of successively inferior forms of reincarnation, Socrates says that (1) a human soul can be reincarnated as a 'wild animal' and (2) the soul of a wild animal can be reincarnated as a human, provided that it had once been human (249 B 3–5). Only (3) a soul that has never experienced the knowledge of eternal truth can never be reincarnated as a human. Presumably in both (1) and (2) some sort of personal identity is retained, else we can hardly call it reincarnation. We should have no more or less difficulty in conceiving of a person being reincarnated as a wild animal than of a person being identified as a purely rational agent. Just as the tripartite embodied soul can be imaged in a purely appetitive, i.e. animal, nature, so it itself can image a purely rational one. Just as one's embodied life can justly lead to one's embodiment as an inferior, so one's embodied life can lead to one's eternal vindication. What this means in general is, I take it, that rationality and hence personhood are affected by embodied life. This in itself is not very surprising. One who has almost completely delivered himself over to his appetites has become a fitting candidate for animal reincarnation. In a disembodied state such a person would be a thinker barely functioning, perhaps like someone utterly deranged.[67]

The image of the charioteer and horses, like the image of the three-headed

---

[65] See 247 C 7–8, where the charioteer is identified as 'intelligence' (νοῦς). Bett (1986), 443 (in Fine 1999), says that the horses 'play an indispensable role in [the] eternal traversing, and in transporting the charioteer'. From this Bett concludes that the disembodied soul is represented as being tripartite. But Bett does not say how the indispensable role in the image is supposed to translate into an indispensable role in reality for the rational soul.

[66] See 253 E 5–6, where it is the 'whole soul' that is smitten by the beloved. So, too, 251 B 7–8, where the 'whole soul heaves and throbs'.

[67] Griswold (1986), 144–7, argues that there is no literal immortality in *Phaedrus* in part because this would, according to the myth, involve disembodied tripartition. I disagree that the myth entails that the disembodied soul is tripartite and I disagree with Griswold's inference from the claim that the myth is not to be taken literally to the claim that literal immortality is not being mythically represented.

beast in *Republic*, should be construed in the context of the distinction between immortality as an endowment and immortality as an achievement.
Whatever requires a body—that is, all bodily states—disappears at death.
But the person is left with his achievement. This achievement is measured by the extent to which he has identified himself as a thinker or as
the subject of appetite. Various forms of reincarnation await those whose
self-identification with thinking is imperfect. Plato imagines the results of
embodied wrongdoing as reflected in the subject of thinking.

When an embodied soul recollects what it saw while disembodied,
namely, the Forms, it longs to return to heaven. Here, recollection is loosely
described as a cognitive process wherein one categorizes sense-perceptions
according to 'what is called form' (κατ᾽ εἶδος λεγόμενον, 249 B 7). As in
Phaedo, the ordinary judgements that result from the categorization of
sense-perceptions are not equivalent to knowledge of Forms. Cognizing
that a Form has been instantiated in such-and-such a manner is not equivalent to the knowledge of the Form itself. The implication of the myth is that
knowledge is present only to disembodied souls. The philosopher stands
out above all other embodied cognizers because 'in so far as is possible'
(κατὰ δύναμιν, 249 C 5) he 'uses' (χρώμενος, 249 C 7) the knowledge he
previously had.

The longing engendered in a philosopher by recollecting and 'using'
his previous knowledge of Forms is the divine madness Socrates seeks to
explain (249 D 4 ff.). Specifically, when someone sees sensible beauty and
thereby recollects the Form, his 'eagerness' (προθυμούμενος) to return is
what is called a form of madness (249 D 6–7). Since only someone who has
at least glimpsed these Forms can be (re)incarnated as a human, everyone is
susceptible to being in love. The divine madness thus connects the passivity
of the state of being in love and the appetitive desire for sex with the
rational desire paradigmatically belonging to a disembodied soul.[68] The
divinely mad lover seeks to recover knowledge lost. We could say with
equal justness that he seeks to recover himself, that is, his true identity.[69]

[68] The passivity of being in love is to be distinguished from the passivity of the boy in
sex, who, conventionally, is not in love and does not enjoy being the passive sexual partner.
See Price (1989), 86–8, for a treatment of Plato's 'embarrassment' when he explains why
the boy will eventually reciprocate love.

[69] See esp. Griswold (1986), 87 ff., for an analysis of the myth which ably makes the
connection between self-knowledge and personhood.

This astonishingly clever linkage gives us in effect two forms of being in love, depending on whether the one smitten is aware that the object of his affection is an image of the Form of Beauty or not. In fact, it would seem to be sufficient that the object of affection appear to be an image. The divine madness does not—and this is surely crucial—exclude the πάθος of love (cf. 250 A 7). Thus, the one who is divinely mad is essentially no different from the lover condemned in the previous speech. The difference is, of course, that he who is divinely mad is ruled by reason, not appetite.[70] This is evident in the description of the charioteer who disciplines and restrains his bad horse with the support of his good one (253 D ff.). So, in the ordinary lover and in the divinely mad lover there is the same πάθος but a different ἀρχή of action. The image of the charioteer and horses presents a picture of embodied personhood even more compelling than that contained in the argument and martial metaphors of *Republic* 4. But it should not lead us into thinking that disembodied life for Plato includes appetites and emotions as opposed to the scars these may leave on a purely rational agent.

The mad lover in Lysias' speech and implicit in Socrates' first speech is someone who endorses his own desire to have sex with his beloved. His being smitten is in a way a type of addiction or madness. By contrast, the divinely mad lover does not want his desire for sex to rule. He willingly restrains himself, though he cherishes the desire he restrains. After all, on the image of charioteer and horses, to abandon love is to weaken at least one of your horses. It is to abandon desire, an essential element in philosophy. The divinely mad lover, by force of will, controls his madness but does not seek to eliminate it. The idea of 'controlling madness' is not so strange if we realize that divine madness implies not frenzy but, as Socrates says, 'release from normally accepted behaviour' (ἐξαλλαγῆς εἰωθότων νομίμων, 265 A 9–11).[71]

The difference between an ordinary lover and a divinely mad lover is, finally, the realism of the latter. He does not mistake his beloved for anything more than an 'image' (εἴδωλον, εἰκών, ἄγαλμα) of the Form of Beauty. As

[70] That the divinely mad lover experiences the same πάθος as 'ordinary' lovers is clear from 250 E–252 C 2.

[71] Cf. 256 E 5, where the 'human self-control' of the non-lover is pejoratively compared to divine madness. See Price (1989), 56, who rightly notes that the possibility of a conflict of reason and desire implied here is not evident in *Symposium*.

Socrates carefully notes, a terribly powerful love would be awakened if there were an image of Wisdom as readily available to us as an image of Beauty. The ordinary lover sees the same image but mistakes it for what it is an image of. And since he longs to possess beauty, as we all do, he seeks to possess the image in the only way known to him (cf. 250 E). Since, as we have seen, apparent beauty is sufficient to awaken love, everyone is potentially a beloved image of the Form, at least for psychological purposes. That is, the lover, however ineptly, has to make the connection between the putative image and its model.[72]

I think it is reasonably clear that the relation between the image and the model is not the relation between means and end, and accordingly I reject Gregory Vlastos's charge that the Platonic lover does not love the beloved 'for himself' but rather as a means to achieving his own end, enjoyment of immortality.[73] The issue turns entirely upon metaphysics. The beloved is not just the bearer of an image of the Form of Beauty, he is an image of an ideal person or self. The lover strives to make the beloved into that ideal in so far as this is possible for embodied persons.[74] From this perspective, loving a person 'for himself' or 'for his own sake' evanesces into triviality or pathology. All that is contained in the phrase 'for his own sake' is accounted for by the lover's persistent state of passion. He is smitten by that unique person. But it is precisely the non-lover and the ordinary lover who have no inkling how to disassociate the image of beauty from the person's other qualities and who therefore think that being in love is being in love with the 'whole' person, including those qualities. To mistake the relation between the beloved and the eternal objects of knowledge for a means–end relation is to disassociate Plato's account of love entirely from his metaphysics. That such an approach is insupportable should be evident from the insertion of the proof of the immortality of the soul in the middle of the dialogue.

Vlastos thinks that the beloved is treated as a means to an end because he supposes that the ideal person is embodied. Were we to suppose this, it would be reasonable to conclude that the lover loves something other

---

[72] As Price (1989), 84 ff., notes, the lover is initially confused. He does not know whether the boy is a god or a statue of a god. It is clear, though, from 252 D ff., that the divinely mad lover does in time make the distinction between beloved and god, turning to the project of making the beloved an even better icon than he already is.

[73] Vlastos 1973*a*), 3–34. See in reply Kosman (1976); Griswold (1986), 128–9; Price (1989), 89–102.   [74] See 253 A 6–B 1; B 8–C 2, where this is most explicit.

than the person. But if we take seriously the view that the ideal person is a disembodied thinker whose goal is to be cognitively at one with Forms, then love for the embodied person is love for an image of the 'real thing'. When the idiosyncratic is excluded, love for the real thing coalesces with love for the person.

The last section of the palinode describes in mythical terms encounters of a lover with a beloved (253 C 7–257 A 2). It gives us a vivid portrayal of the sort of psychic conflict upon which the partitioning of the soul in *Republic* depends. The conflict between reason and appetite, which, I have argued, is really a conflict within a divided person, is represented as a conflict between the charioteer and the dark horse. An acratic 'charioteer' would be one who gives in to his dark horse against his better judgement and sexually gratifies himself with his object of desire. An encratic 'charioteer' restrains the horse despite its violent opposition (253 E–254 E). A virtuous charioteer is one who is no longer tempted to give in at all (cf. 254 E 5–255 A 1).

The difference between the virtue of the embodied philosopher and the self-restraint of the encratic is not that the former has renounced sexual appetite and the latter has not (256 A). It is that the philosopher is permanently in control, whereas the encratic is apt to relinquish control on occasion (256 C–D). Why should the philosopher not from time to time follow his appetite as well? I believe the best way to understand the difference is in terms of the personal self-identification I have described. In a true philosopher appetite would never be the ἀρχή of action. But the enslavement of the appetites is not equivalent to their obliteration. This cannot be an ideal situation. In such a person an appetite for sex and an appetite for illicit sex are perhaps not so easy to distinguish, especially when this appetite is in both cases interpreted as a desire to possess beauty.

By contrast, we may well ask why encratics ever restrain themselves. What is their motive for *not* giving in to their appetites? Plato says that they do not habitually give in because 'they have not endorsed [δεδογμένα] what they are doing with their whole mind [πάσῃ τῇ διανοίᾳ]' (256 C 5–6). I think it is most natural to take this reticence as indicating imperfect self-identification. Otherwise, restraint would be based purely on expedience.

The way of the encratic is in fact the way of 'popular and civic virtue' as described in both *Phaedo* and *Republic*.[75]

With the defence of divine madness completed, the conversation moves to a discussion of excellence in speech-writing and delivery (259 E–274 B) Just as the divine madness of the philosopher is distinguished from the human madness of the ordinary lover, so an ordinary form of rhetoric that aims simply at persuasion is distinguished from a philosophical rhetoric that aims at implanting truth in the audience by persuasion. The two forms of rhetoric obviously mirror the comparative states of the souls of the two lovers. A divinely mad lover is one who has implanted in him the truth that *any* human represents only an image of what is really real. An ordinary lover is a victim of those who have implanted in him the untruth that one possesses beauty in the person of the beloved. The philosopher is not only the true lover; he is the true speech-maker and the true practitioner of 'soul guidance' (ψυχαγωγία, 261 A 8, 271 C 10 ff.).

The potential self-referential meaning of these claims leaves much scope for speculation. Both Lysias and Socrates have been practising rhetoric. Is Socrates' speech in praise of the non-lover to be counted as inferior rhetoric while his second speech is true rhetoric? Certainly there is much in his description of the analytic requirements of true rhetoric that is reflected in his own second speech. Still, Socrates disavows possession of the science of speech-making (262 D 5–6). But his disavowal is compatible with the gods speaking through him. Further, he cautions that in his speech, when he used an image to convey the erotic state, he 'probably hit upon some truth, though it may also have led us astray' (265 B 6–7). This is one of the main passages used by those who think that Plato is here undermining all that has previously been said. But this passage can be simply and naturally taken to refer to the image of the charioteer and horses, and the caution to the fact that it is an image of an image and that tripartition does not refer unqualifiedly to disembodied souls. Indeed, the exigencies of *any* myth call for a disclaimer of this sort. I am not persuaded that this passage gives us cause to jettison the conclusions of Socrates' second speech.

---

[75] See *Phaedo* 69 B 6–7, 82 A 10–B 3; *Rep.* 365 C 3–4, 500 D 8, 518 D 3–519 A 6. The latter passage describes those without philosophical virtue as not yet having had their 'souls turned around'.

Another passage often used to draw even more far-reaching conclusions occurs near the end of the dialogue, when Socrates recounts the myth of the gods Theuth and Thamus and the latter's condemnation of writing as a danger to remembering (274 E ff.). This passage has been frequently used to argue for the undermining not only of Socrates' speech but of all the claims made by Socrates or anyone else in all the dialogues. This is excessive. The criticism offered in this passage is of writing in relation to discourse. The former is an image of the latter (276 A 8–9). From the fact that speech is superior to writing in conveying truth, in so far as truth can be conveyed, it does not follow that what is written is false or even necessarily misleading. He who is convinced of the superiority of speech to writing will not be, as Socrates says, serious about writing (276 C 7–9). But this only means that he will not expect writing to be the vehicle for communicating knowledge. This is something we know from *Republic*, and indeed it is something that is absolutely foundational for Socratic dialectic. For if discourse does not convey knowledge, then certainly an image of it will not. As the image of the charioteer and horses is an image of the embodied tripartite soul which is an image of the disembodied exemplar, so the written word is an image of the spoken word which is itself an image of the truth. None of this should lead us to believe that Plato is placing a mental negation sign before every single assertoric statement of Socrates in *Phaedrus*. Rather, we should recognize that the effort to employ images to convey the truth about images themselves and what they represent is the embodied philosopher's burden.

The characterization of the philosopher as the supreme lover, speech-maker, and soul guide brings us back to the beginning of the dialogue and Socrates' preference for acquiring self-knowledge over knowledge of the natural explanations behind myths. Though it cannot be lost on the reader that Socrates' longest speech is precisely a myth, there is really no discord between his aversion to seeking out naturalistic explanations behind myths and his offering a defence of the lover that is partly myth. Central to that defence is the account of the soul, its nature, and its properties. It hardly needs pointing out that an account of the soul would at least contribute to self-knowledge. Virtually all commentators on this dialogue have said as much. I have, however, been arguing that self-knowledge in the dialogues is something more than the knowledge of the kind of thing a soul is. It is the first-person knowledge of my personhood. What *this* amounts to is the knowledge that among the states of the embodied me some of these are not states of the real me. Self-knowledge is the recognition that I am an image of an ideal. First-order desires that I experience while embodied do not belong to me ideally. Self-knowledge consists in the recognition of my true identity as a subject of thought. From this recognition follows the enslavement of appetite so that I come to treat them *almost* as if they were those of another. The enslavement of appetite is, however, not its elimination. But precisely because appetite cannot be eliminated, its enslavement is motivated entirely by the recognition that I am not, really or ideally, the subject of those appetites. I have the appetite but I lose interest in it.

A philosopher who has achieved such a level of self-knowledge is appropriately enough a superior soul guide. His beloved sees him as the image he is and thereby achieves his own self-knowledge. That is, he comes to love the lover as an image of the ideal, union with which is what he truly desires.[76] The beloved sees someone who has come to identify with the rational part of his soul and the beauty of this sight inspires him to do the same.

Finally, soul guidance, provided by the superior embodied images of ideal disembodied persons, is conveyed by philosophical talk, itself an image of truth. The best and perhaps the only way that one can achieve the sort of self-knowledge that Plato undoubtedly believed was possessed by Socrates is to have a Socrates for a lover. The recognition of one's true identity is not acquired by an examination of one's occurrent desires. Performing such an examination, one is as likely to find urgent bodily desires as prominent as anything else. To pass from 'these are the things I desire' to 'these are the things I really desire' requires active participation in philosophical dialectic.[77] After all, if one really or ideally is a thinker, it is plausible that it

---

[76] See the difficult lines 255 D 3–E 2: 'Then the boy is in love, but has no idea what he loves. He does not understand, and cannot explain, what has happened to him. It is as if he had caught an eye disease from someone else, but could not identify the cause; he does not realize that he is seeing himself in the lover as in a mirror. So when the lover is near, the boy's pain is relieved just as the lover's is, and when they are apart he yearns as much as he is yearned for, because he has a mirror image [εἴδωλον] of love in him—backlove [ἀντέρωτα]—though he neither speaks nor thinks of it as love, but as friendship.'

[77] See Griswold (1986), 232, for a similar point: 'The unique knowledge of the soul

should be by self-reflexive thinking that one achieves one's true identity. As a tool for achieving self-knowledge understood as recognition of one's true identity, it is easy to see the superiority of speech over writing, speech that can persuade and respond to the hearer's stage of learning.

that neither reduces it to a special type of abstract object nor confines it to the images of edifying poetry is exhibited in dialectical discourse.'

CHAPTER 4

Knowledge and Belief
in Republic

I have been trying to make the case that for Plato a person is ideally a knower. I have explored some of the ethical and psychological facets of this identification in the previous chapters, and would now like to turn to the epistemological side. It is in *Republic* that Plato provides his most complete account of knowledge. By understanding what knowledge is for Plato we shall, I believe, be in a better position to see what the self or person is for him as well. Specifically, we shall be able to appreciate both what the state of the ideal person is supposed to be and also how the inferior states of embodiment are images of that.

4.1 Knowledge vs. Belief

As Aristotle tells us (*Metaphysics M* 4, 1078^{b}30 ff.), one of the ways that the Platonists differ from Socrates is that they separated the Forms. Much has been written regarding the meaning of 'separation' in Plato and Aristotle's interpretation of that.[1] Minimally, it seems that Aristotle thought that for Plato it meant 'independent existence', that is, ontological priority.[2] Thus,

---

[1] For clearly opposing views see esp. Fine (1984), (1986), and Devereux (1994), with full references to the scholarly literature.

[2] See Arist. *Metaph. M* 9, 1086^{b}4–11, for the meaning of 'unqualified separation', which I take to be extensionally equivalent to the ontological priority of Forms to sensibles. On ontological priority or priority in substance as equivalent to unqualified separation see

Forms would exist even if everything in the sensible world did not. But even if, as Aristotle claims, Plato separated the Forms, this in itself need not occasion a revision of the view about how Forms are known, unless separation excludes access to them in or through sensibles. The question of whether Forms are 'in' sensibles and whether our contact with the latter somehow enables us to know the former is a large one, to which I shall return.

For now, let us begin with two obvious epistemological questions that arise from the separation of Forms. First is the question of whether *we* need to be separate from our bodies in order to know them. This is a question that *Phaedo* (66 E–67 B) seems to answer by claiming that knowledge of Forms is not possible in this life. This claim is made between the passage in which separate Forms are posited and the passage in which the sensible world is said to be 'defective'. By contrast, an assumption that seems to be accepted throughout the early aporetic dialogues is that the interlocutors might actually succeed in acquiring the knowledge of Forms.

The second question is whether knowledge is *only* of Forms or whether there is knowledge of other things. *Meno* claims that true belief is said to become knowledge when it is 'tied down with an account' (98 A 1–8), whereas *Republic* (478 B 1–2) claims that the objects of knowledge and the objects of belief cannot be the same. Since *Meno* also argues that learning or coming to know is recollection and presumably this knowledge is of separate Forms, it might seem that *Republic* contradicts *Meno*, and it has frequently been taken to do so.[3] That is, whereas *Meno* seems to hold that there can be knowledge *both* of Forms and of that of which there can be true belief, *Republic* claims that the objects of knowledge and belief are mutually exclusive.

The putative contradiction between the two dialogues is not obvious to me. For *Meno* does not literally say that when true belief becomes knowledge that knowledge is of the same things of which there was true belief. If the 'account' transforms true belief, perhaps it also transforms the object of cognition. This would not be so implausible if the objects of true belief and knowledge are in fact related as image and model or paradigm. Stated more

---

Δ 11, 1019ᵃ2–4, where Aristotle explicitly attributes this view of Forms to Plato. Cf. *Θ* 8, 1050ᵇ7; *M* 2, 1077ᵇ1–9.

[3] Stokes (1992), 132, for example, simply assumes that the accounts in *Meno* and *Republic* contrast strongly, for in *Meno* 'knowledge supervenes on belief *in the same proposition or other object of cognition*' (my italics).

positively, if the objects of true belief are images or copies or representations of Forms, it might well be Plato's view that the account produces knowledge of the original and not knowledge of the copy.[4] I mean that if the separation of Forms in *Meno* entails the diminished reality of the sensible world, as it does in *Phaedo*, it is not clear that the transformation of true belief into knowledge in the former dialogue is a transformation that is unlike that even in *Republic*. If, however, it is the case that *Meno* is to be read as assuming that it is possible to have knowledge of that of which one can have belief, then in so far as the objects of belief are propositions, so, too, would be the objects of knowledge. *Phaedo* seems to distinguish two sorts of knowledge (74 B 2–3 and 76 B 8–9), the first of which is perhaps equivalent to knowledge in *Meno*, and the second of which is primarily or exclusively disembodied and hence of different objects. *Republic* identifies the objects of the only sort of knowledge there is as radically distinct from those of belief. This knowledge, as we shall see, is not propositional.

As we turn to *Republic*, we can hardly be surprised to see things to be said about knowledge which follow from the separation of Forms. Whether *Meno* is a 'transition' dialogue or not, it does not provide evidence that should lead us to conclude that separation is assumed while the epistemology remains the same. The argument at the end of *Republic* 5 and its adumbration in books 6 and 7 is and deserves to be among the most controversial texts in Plato. In the argument distinguishing philosophers from lovers of sights and sounds Plato makes an extremely bold claim based upon an obscure argument the conclusion of which is that knowledge and belief are radically discontinuous. That is, each has different objects; there can be no knowledge of that of which there is belief and vice versa. The argument is highly contentious for many reasons, among which is that it seemingly flies in the face of reasonable accounts according to which knowledge is a kind of belief or entails belief. In addition, if knowledge is only of Forms, then not only is one committed to the existence of Forms if one is committed to the existence of knowledge, but one is faced with the possibility that,

---

[4] Fine (1990), 85–6, is, I think, mistaken in holding that the account of the distinction between knowledge and belief in *Republic,* on the traditional interpretation, 'radically rejects the *Meno*'s account of knowledge' because for the *Meno* 'knowledge implies true belief'. This is false in the case of the disembodied knowledge which is the condition for the putative knowledge in this world. It is even false on the assumption that in *Meno* knowledge and true belief are of the same things, if knowledge replaces true belief.

as in *Phaedo*, knowledge cannot be had in an embodied state. Alternatively, if knowledge is what Plato says it is, then if one denies the existence of Forms, one is perhaps forced to deny the possibility of knowledge. Finally, at least on Platonic principles, if knowledge is not possible, the result is not the relatively benign one that we can nevertheless aspire to some form of cognition close to or for all practical purposes as good as knowledge. No. If knowledge is what Plato says it is and it is not possible to have it, then true belief, or at least *justified* true belief, becomes problematic.

The traditional interpretation of the argument at the end of book 5 of *Republic* has been challenged in recent times, implausibly and unsuccessfully, as I shall hold. Answering this challenge will enable us to see the critical role that the account of knowledge there has for Plato. The account of knowledge will provide us with indispensable insights into what Plato takes persons to be. By understanding what knowledge is we shall be able to see generally the gradations of cognition and the corresponding gradations of personhood.

Let us turn to the argument itself. The entire argument goes from 476 A 9 to the end of book 5. This ending is indicated at the very beginning of book 6, where Socrates states that they have completed their distinction between the lovers of sights and sounds, lovers of crafts, and practical people on the one hand, and philosophers on the other. The argument purports to distinguish these two groups 'apart from each other' (χωρίς . . . χωρίς). It can be conveniently divided into three stages. In the first stage (A), 476 A 9–D 6, lovers of sights and sounds and philosophers are distinguished by the objects of their love: the former love beautiful sights and sounds whereas the latter are interested in beauty itself. Lovers of sights and sounds are unable to follow anyone who could lead them to Forms. They believe in (νομίζων) beautiful things but not in beauty itself (C 2–3). Since they do not believe in beauty itself, they think that its likenesses are in fact what beauty is. They are like someone in a dream state compared with someone awake. By contrast, someone who does believe in beauty itself can differentiate it from its 'participants' (τὰ μετέχοντα). He is truly awake. His 'thought' (διάνοιαν) is rightly called 'understanding' (γνώμην), whereas that of his opposite is rightly called 'belief' (δόξαν).

The second stage of the argument (B), 476 D 7–478 E 5, seeks to establish the distinction between the modes of thinking or cognition belonging to the lovers of sights and sounds and those belonging to philosophers, based upon a distinction between the objects of cognition. The argument proceeds as follows:

(1) 'One who knows' (ὁ γιγνώσκων) knows 'something' (τι) (476 E 7).

(2) The something that is known 'is (or has being)' (ὄν) (476 E 10–477 A 1).

(3) What is (or has being) 'completely' (παντελῶς) is completely knowable, whereas what is not (or has no being) is completely unknowable (477 A 2–4).

(4) Whatever is (or has being) and is not (or has no being) is 'intermediate' (μεταξύ) between what is (or has being) completely and what is not (or has no being) completely (477 A 6–7).

(5) Then, as knowledge is 'directed to' (ἐπί) what is (or has being) and 'ignorance' (ἀγνωσία) is directed to what is not (or has no being), there should be (a mode of thinking) directed to the intermediate, that is, what is (or has being) and is not (or has no being), assuming there be such a thing (477 A 9–B 1).

(6) 'Belief' (δόξαν) is something (that is, it exists) (477 B 3).

(7) Belief is a 'power' (δύναμιν) different from 'knowledge' (ἐπιστήμη) (477 B 5).

(8) 'Therefore' (ἄρα), belief 'has been ordered to' (τέτακται ἐπί) one thing and knowledge to another, according to their respective powers (477 B 7–8).

(9) Knowledge is by nature directed to what is (or has being) to know what is 'as it is' (ὡς ἔστι τὸ ὄν) (477 B 9–10).

(10) Powers are a class of things by which we are able to do what we are able to do (477 C 1–2).

(11) A power is named according to what it is directed to and what it 'accomplishes' (ἀπεργάζεται) (477 C 9–D 2).

(12) A power that is directed to the same thing and does the same thing is the same power; what is directed to another thing and does another thing is another power (477 D 2–5).

(13) Knowledge is a power (477 D 7–8).

(14) Belief is a power (477 E 1).

(15) Knowledge and belief are not 'the same' (ταὐτόν) [i.e. power] (from

7) because the former is infallible (ἀναμάρτητον) whereas the latter is not (477 E 6–7).[5]

(16) Belief does not believe the same thing that knowledge knows (478 A 10–11).

(17) So, the 'object of knowledge' (γνωστόν) and the 'object of belief' (δοξαστόν) cannot be the same (478 B 1–2).

(18) Belief is directed to something (478 B 7).

(19) Belief is directed to some one thing (478 B 10).

(20) That which is not (or has no being) is not one thing but no thing (478 B 12–C 1).

(21) But knowledge is directed to what is and ignorance to what is not (478 C 3–4).

(22) Therefore, belief is directed neither to what is nor to what is not (478 C 6) (from 8).

(23) Therefore, belief is neither ignorance nor knowledge (478 C 8).

(24) Belief is therefore intermediate between knowledge and ignorance (478 D 3).

(25) So if something could be shown to be and not to be at the same time (ἅμα), it would be intermediate between what purely is and what altogether is not, and what is directed to it would be something intermediate between knowledge and ignorance (478 D 5–9).

(26) It is belief that appears to be intermediate between knowledge and ignorance (478 D 11).

(27) So, we need to identify what participates in what is (or has being) and what is not (or has no being) and is not purely one or the other and, if there is such a thing, it can be said to be an object of belief (478 E 1–5).

The third stage of the argument (C), 478 E 7–480 A 13, seeks to identify (from 27) that which participates in what is (or has being) and what is not (or has no being). That argument goes as follows:

(1) All the beautiful things appear somehow ugly. Similarly, just things

---

[5] It is true that this claim is actually stated rhetorically: 'How could someone who has any sense put down that which is infallible as the same as that which is not infallible?' I express this assertorically as (15).

appear unjust and pious things appear impious. So too for the double, the big, and the heavy (479 A 5–B 7).

(2) All of these participate in opposites, that is, they are no more than they are not what they are said to be (479 B 8–10).

(3) They are 'ambiguous' (ἐπαμφοτερίζειν). One cannot understand these as securely being or not being or both being and not being or neither being nor not being (479 C 2–5).

(4) They are then appropriately classified between being and not being, since they are not more than what is nor not more than what is not (479 C 6–D 1).

(5) We have therefore discovered that the many conventions of the multitude about beauty and the rest roll about between what is not and what purely is (479 D 3–5).

(6) We have already agreed that such a thing should be called an object of belief and not of knowledge, a wandering intermediate grasped by an intermediate power (479 D 7–9).

(7) Therefore, those who study the many beautiful and just things and so on and do not see the beautiful itself and the just itself and do not follow those who do, these people are said to have beliefs and not to have knowledge of the things of which they have belief (479 E 1–5).

(8) Those who study the things themselves which are always the same, are said to have knowledge but not to have belief (479 E 7–8).

(9) So, just as these latter love the things which are the objects of knowledge, so those others love the things that are the objects of belief (479 E 10–480 A 1).

(10) They will be called 'philodoxers' ('belief-lovers'), whereas the former are philosophers (480 A 6–12).

There are numerous complex issues arising from these arguments, although their main thrust is clear enough. This is that knowledge and belief are distinct powers corresponding to distinct objects, that which is, and that which both is and is not. Among the most contentious interpretative issues are these: are the powers distinguished according to their objects or vice versa? what does Plato mean by the objects of belief being intermediate between what is and what is not? and what does he mean by 'object of knowledge' and 'object of belief' and, most puzzlingly, 'object of ignorance'?

Among the most difficult philosophical issues raised by the arguments are: why should a distinction between the two powers of cognition lead one to hold that they have mutually exclusive objects? why should knowledge be thought to be infallible? and why is that which is completely, completely knowable? Needless to say, all of these issues are closely related in the sense that answers to all the questions, interpretative and philosophical, ought to be mutually supporting. In fact, I think there is only one completely coherent account that can be given of the entire passage, and this is more or less the traditional one.

Let us begin with the distinction between knowledge and belief. At B5–7 it appears that knowledge and belief are distinguished according to their objects. At B11 we have the additional complication that powers are distinguished by their 'objects' (ἐφ' ᾧ) *and* their effects or 'what they accomplish'. It has been frequently objected that thus laying down two criteria for the differentiation of powers is logically inept.[6] The problem is that if two powers differ in their effects or products, they might yet have the same object, and Plato has not given any reason for thinking otherwise. For example, my speaking to the same person in two different manners may have two different effects. Of course, everything depends upon how we are to understand these objects and what it means to distinguish modes of cognition 'according to' them. Although the objects are apparently to be identified as Forms and sensibles, and although we may be entitled to assume that these are separate in some way, it does not seem to follow from the distinction between knowledge and belief and the separation of Forms and sensibles that there cannot be knowledge of sensibles and beliefs about Forms as well.[7]

The only reason given for the distinction of knowledge and belief in

---

[6] See Stokes (1992), 119–32. Denyer (1991), 56–9, tries to rescue Plato from what he takes to be the absurdity of a general acceptance of the two criteria, but his attempted rescue entails a denial of the distinctness of knowledge and belief in the way that I argue Plato maintains. Ebert (1974), 117–30, argues that in this argument the differentiation of powers is made from the perspective of one who has only belief about what knowledge is. Therefore, the entire argument is not to be taken as Plato's own. Rather, it is intended by Plato to be understood as fallacious.

[7] Smith (1996) argues that the objects of cognitive states can be different from the objects of the powers that produce these states. So, though the objects of the powers of belief and knowledge are clearly different, namely, the knowable and the opinable, the objects of different cognitive states can and in fact are identical. I take a cognitive state to be the actualization of its power and so not to have different objects. But the more

themselves is in B15, namely, that the former is infallible whereas the latter is not. Even if this is so, it does not, however, seem to follow that there cannot be knowledge and belief applied to the same object, the one perhaps infallibly and the other fallibly. For example, perhaps God could infallibly count up the number of hairs on my head, whereas I would do so fallibly. If the reason for isolating knowledge and belief is not in B15, then B16 and B17 are completely question-begging. But if it should turn out that infallibility and fallibility are functionally related to objects, such that one could infallibly cognize only something that is really different from that which one could only fallibly cognize, then it would be true both that infallibility and fallibility would provide a genuine reason for distinguishing the objects of knowledge and belief and that, the objects being what they are, the only mode of cognition relative to each is different.[8] And as I shall argue, it is owing to the distinction between an infallible and a fallible mode of cognition that Plato is justified in holding that their corresponding powers differ both in their objects and in their effects.

'Infallible' cannot be simply equivalent to 'unmistaken' or 'not false' if one kind of belief is true belief. If that were what it meant, true belief is no less unmistaken than is knowledge, and the claim of B15 would be hopelessly confused. Assuming that Plato can see this simple point, we might begin by asking what in his opinion distinguishes a true belief that is, by definition, unmistaken from knowledge? What is the difference between 'unmistaken' and 'unmistakable'? It is simply that one might have a true belief without knowing or even believing that it is a true belief.[9] The truth of the belief

fundamental point is that different powers are inferred from different states and their difference is incommensurable.

[8] I mention now only in passing the text that will concern us later, namely, *Theaet.* 152 C 5–6, where two criteria of knowledge are laid down, that knowledge be of 'what is always' and that it be 'without falsity' (ἀψευδής). The meaning of 'without falsity' is equivocal. But when it is understood as infallibility, as opposed simply to 'not false', it will become clear that these two criteria are not adventitiously conjoined. That is, infallible states are possible only in relation to 'what is always', and the only mode of cognition possible for 'what is always' is an infallible one.

[9] In *Meno* 97 A–98 A Socrates gives as a reason why knowledge is preferable to true belief that it does not 'run away', i.e. it is not unstable. As Socrates explains, true beliefs run away because they are not tethered by a 'calculating of the explanation' (αἰτίας λογισμῷ). When they are so tethered, they are stable. This cannot mean, then, that what makes a true belief unstable is that its objects come and go or are contingent, because adding the

is, one might say, 'externally grounded'. Thus, its truth (however this be construed) is not logically dependent upon the psychological state of the believer.

By contrast, if knowledge is infallible, it is impossible that it should be mistaken. It is 'internally grounded': that is, the cognitive state itself guarantees the truth of what is known. The cognitive state is not adventitiously connected to the truth. What is known is therefore self-evidently true. If this were not so, and if what is known is not true adventitiously, then what is known would be known on the basis of or as entailed by something else. And this, of course, would have to be known either self-evidently or on the basis of something else, and so on. So, even if there is inferential self-evident knowledge for Plato, the necessity of the inferences would have to be self-evident as well.

Perhaps reflecting on the issues raised in *Meno* led Plato into arguing that the objects of belief and knowledge must be different. Consider the following. Assume that the objects of true belief and knowledge can be the same and what differentiates them is, as *Meno* holds, 'binding them with the calculation of an explanation'. It is fairly obvious that the metaphor of binding conceals an embarrassing problem. Does one know or merely truly believe the explanation that does the binding? Clearly, it cannot be the latter, for it would be absurd to hold that true belief in p is transformed into knowledge of p by true belief in q. So, assume that one *knows* the explanation. There are two things wrong with this. First, knowing q is not equivalent to knowing p, and it is therefore quite opaque how knowing q turns believing p into knowing p. Second, and even more obviously, on this account one can apparently know q without binding *it* down with an explanation. If so, why not p as well? But if belief in q has to be turned into knowledge by binding *it* down with an explanation before it can bind down belief in p, one has commenced on a vicious infinite regress. In fact, it does not seem possible that truly believing p can be turned into knowing p either by truly believing or knowing q. When one has the account that binds the true belief, it certainly does not then follow that the knowledge is of the same thing as the true belief. Indeed, this is precisely the sort of

reason or explanation would not change that. So, it seems that what the one who has mere true belief is missing is an understanding of why it is a true belief. Perhaps this is not different from not knowing that it is a true belief.

consideration that would lead someone to distinguish belief and knowledge as different powers with different objects.

An obvious objection to tying knowledge to what is self-evident is that there simply is no entailment from 'It is self-evident to me that p' to 'p'. Even if it is *inconceivable* to me that p should be false, this does not guarantee the truth of p. After all, perhaps I have a very limited ability to conceive of things. Inconceivability does not entail truth because no psychological state of mine seems to be a condition for the truth of p, especially if p is not a proprietary truth, that is, a truth about me. Thus, if p can be known by someone else, nothing about me alone or anyone else alone would seem to be able to guarantee the truth of p. But surely the truths about which Plato is interested are universal truths potentially available to all. In that case, how can it be that that which is self-evident to me must be true? This is, I suppose, the reason why infallibility is sometimes not taken seriously as the criterion that distinguishes knowledge from belief even though the text seems to offer it as such. So, the reasoning goes, since there is no such thing as infallibility, there is no such thing as infallible knowledge. And if Plato thought there was, then he did not understand what knowledge is.[10]

Whether Plato is wrong about knowledge is a question different from that of the correct understanding of his argument and his claims. Perhaps it is worth stressing here that we must resist building into our interpretation of Plato's use of ἐπιστήμη contemporary views about the term 'knowledge'. But this caution can be overstated. I believe not only that the interpretation of ἐπιστήμη that I am developing is correct but that if the concept of knowledge has a clear and distinct meaning, then it is going to be not far removed from what Plato takes ἐπιστήμη to be.

In any case, I think we can discern even in the *Republic* passage the reasons for Plato's taking infallibility as the criterion of knowledge. The reason why there is no infallible cognition of sensibles and the reason why there is no fallible cognition of Forms are, as one would expect, virtually the same. The distinction between appearance and reality that applies to sensibles does not apply to Forms. By 'appearance' I do not mean what is necessarily false but rather what is possibly false because it is not identical

---

[10] See Penner (1987), 33–40, 57–140, who uses the term 'incorrigible' instead of 'infallible' and argues similarly that the 'genuine a priori' 'presupposes incorrigible conceptual states'.

with reality. In this sense, an appearance is like a representation. For the moment 'representation' may be taken to apply to beliefs, propositions, words, or concepts indifferently. No representation or appearance exhausts sensible reality, at least for the realist tradition to which Plato unquestionably belongs. If I believe truly that 'Theaetetus is sitting now' when he is sitting, then my belief in some way represents sensibles as they are. Theaetetus appears to me as he is. But there is more to Theaetetus than his sitting here and now. If I repeat the claim that 'Theaetetus is sitting' with the indexical 'now', I can produce an endless series of 'takes' on Theaetetus and his sitting. All belief is fallible because no belief, with its psychological component, entails anything about reality. No state I am in entails anything about the world except that the world includes me in my state.

It might seem that all that I have said about sensibles should apply to Forms as well. Representing them seems the easiest thing to do. All that is necessary is to choose a symbol or sign for a Form. Do not all of Socrates' interlocutors in the early and middle dialogues represent Forms in this way? And do they not accordingly have beliefs about them? Fallible beliefs to be sure, even false beliefs, but beliefs none the less? I think that once Plato separated the Forms, he came to hold that the answer to these questions was unequivocally no.

Note that in stage A of the argument the lovers of sights and sounds do not believe in Forms. Therefore, they falsely believe that the likenesses of Forms are what they are in fact likenesses of. This cannot be like someone who, knowing both Socrates and Plato, confuses one for the other as he enters the agora.[11] A lover of sights and sounds who confused a Form and a sensible manifestation of it in this way would have to believe in the Form in the first place, that is, minimally, believe in its existence. So, the philodoxer who held, say, that 'beauty is in the eye of the beholder' would not be like someone who mistook the Form of Beauty for something else. He is rather like someone who thinks that the word 'beauty' represents or stands for something other than what, for Plato, it in fact does. And in so far as the sensible

---

[11] Stokes (1992), 111, slips into claiming that the sight-lovers 'confuse' the beautiful itself with the many beautiful appearances. But that is exactly what Plato takes pains to explain that they are not doing when they believe that likenesses are reality. Cf. the difference between ordinary and divinely mad lovers in *Phaedrus* as discussed in § 3.3. The latter, unlike the former, knows that his beloved is merely an image of the ideal.

manifestation of the Form is a representation or appearance of it analogous to the representations and appearances mentioned above, they believe that these appearances are in fact reality. Believing that the appearance is the reality in this case is different from someone who believes that 'Theaetetus is sitting' represents the fact that consists of Theaetetus sitting and 'Theaetetus is standing' does not because he can see that Theaetetus is sitting. The lovers of sights and sounds do not believe what they believe about beauty because they have some *other* cognition of the Form.[12]

The above contrast between knowledge and belief suggests that knowledge is non-representational whereas belief involves a representation of some sort. Propositions are one example of representation. They represent facts or states of affairs or whatever one's ontology mandates. Accordingly, if knowledge is non-representational, then knowledge is non-propositional.[13] If it were propositional, then it would seem that one could alternately know or believe the same proposition. The resistance to this traditional reading of the above arguments in *Republic* arises, I think, from a subtle shift in thinking about knowledge. This shift arises when one stops thinking about belief and knowledge as psychological states like dreaming and imagining and starts thinking about belief and knowledge from a criteriological perspective, that is, from the perspective of what would turn a true belief into knowledge. We have seen that Plato does ask that very question in *Meno*, but it is not obvious that the question is understood in the same way. For the assumption behind the modern question is that *all* cognition

---

[12] One might conjecture that a lover of sights and sounds has knowledge of Forms acquired prior to embodiment. Even if this is so, unlike the interlocutors in *Phaedo*, they do not acknowledge the existence of Forms.

[13] Sorabji (1982), esp. 299–301, argues that in *Republic* (and perhaps *Theaetetus* as well) knowledge of Forms is for Plato propositional. He rejects what has been called 'knowledge by acquaintance'. The only evidence for this interpretation that Sorabji actually cites, *Rep.* 534 B 3–C 5 (see below), is a passage in which Plato asserts that the dialectician acquires 'an account of the essence of each thing' and that no one who does not have such an account can be said to have 'understanding' (νοῦν) about these things. That the account itself is propositional is evident. What is false, however, is the assumption that either the account or the ability to give the account is what knowledge is for Plato. It is in virtue of having knowledge that one has that ability. A related point is made at *Crat.* 439 A–B, where Socrates claims that it is better to learn the truth and therefore recognize that a name is a good image of it than it is to learn a name and thereby learn what the image is an image of. The latter alternative is only given as a hypothetical possibility.

is representational and so belief and knowledge are to be understood as different propositional attitudes. For Plato, once the distinction between separate Forms and their sensible instances is made, one must not suppose that the question is to be asked with the same assumption. Perhaps I can put this another way. Let us suppose that Plato did wonder how belief about sensibles could be turned into knowledge about the same things. Surely, he had to ask himself the question whether this putative knowledge was the same sort of thing as knowledge of Forms. I take it that the answer to this question would have to be clearly no if, as in *Republic*, infallibility is the criterion of knowledge.[14]

If knowledge of a Form is an infallible mental state, representations or appearances, including especially propositional representations, have to be rigorously excluded from the account of what knowledge is.[15] It is quite common for the question 'What is knowledge?' to be answered by saying that knowledge is of propositions. This is, of course, irrelevant as a direct answer to the question 'What is knowledge?' Telling us what one knows when one knows is not telling us what knowledge is any more than telling us that one eats food is telling us what eating is. With reference to Plato in the middle dialogues, it is equally obvious that knowledge is not *of* propositions, but rather of 'what is' or Forms. If a proposition were meant by Plato to be included among 'what is', then it is extremely difficult to see what the object of belief, 'what is *and* what is not', is supposed to be. Gail Fine tries to deal with this problem by arguing that 'what is' includes true propositions and 'what is and what is not' includes true and false propositions.[16] In reply

[14] Gonzalez (1998), 252–3, avers that 'the characterization of non-propositional knowledge as infallibly true is a category mistake. One can say of such knowledge only whether it is present and in what degree.' Gonzalez seems to me to equivocate on 'true'. I agree with him that when referring to propositions it makes no sense to say of them that they are true unless it makes sense to say of them that they are false. But in referring to the cognitive state that is knowledge, 'true' does not mean the same thing.

[15] Gulley (1962) rightly holds that δόξα is propositional, but confusedly he identifies ἐπιστήμη with a priori knowledge and δόξα with empirical knowledge, and hence thinks that ἐπιστήμη is propositional as well.

[16] Fine (1990), 91. Gosling (1968) appears to hold this view: see esp. 129. Although Gosling recognizes that infallibility vs. fallibility is the crucial mark distinguishing knowledge and belief (119), he does not explain why the same object cannot be fallibly and infallibly cognized. Stokes (1992), 103, agrees with Fine's interpretation of *Republic* 5. Like Fine, he holds that that text does not commit Plato to a 'two-world' theory. But Stokes's

to the objection that 478 A 12–B 2 (B16, 17) says that what is known and what is believed cannot be the same thing, Fine says that this 'might mean only that the set of propositions one can believe is not co-extensive with the set of propositions one can know—for one can believe but not know false propositions. More weakly still, Plato might mean only that the properties of being known and of being believed are different properties.'[17]

The fact that lovers of sights and sounds do not believe in Forms (476 C 2–3) might suggest that if they *did*, then there could indeed be belief about Forms. For example, suppose a quondam lover of sights and sounds came to believe in Forms, that is, he came to believe that Forms exist and proclaimed, 'It is false that Forms do not exist.' Could he not be said then to have a belief about Forms? According to this line of thinking, we would either have to say that his false belief had not been about Forms though his true belief now is, or else we would have to say that both his false belief and his true belief were about Forms. In either case, there would be *some* belief about Forms.

This interpretation is implausible and is not supported by the text. First, there is nothing in the text to suggest that the object of knowledge is propositions as opposed to the Forms themselves. Second, though it be true that one can believe but not know false propositions, it is also true that one can believe true propositions. On Fine's interpretation, then, one can believe and know the same thing, namely, the true proposition. It does not seem that this conclusion can be reasonably held not to be in direct contradiction with B16, 17. Only if 'object of belief' (δοξαστόν) is a class

reason is different from Fine's. He holds that the entire argument is dialectical. Briefly, what this means is that Plato is showing how the sight-lovers who deny the existence of Forms are thereby led into saying contradictory things about knowledge and belief. Plato himself is not committing himself to their separation.

[17] See White (1977), who takes the objects of belief to be kinds or types of sensibles, not concrete particulars. Reeve (1988), 58–71, claims that 'the argument with the sightseers and craft-lovers is an ingenious and philosophically penetrating attempt to show that only reliable belief-forming powers, with access to unique, intelligible, immutable properties, which satisfy the law of non-contradiction, can produce knowledge . . . The argument is not, as many have claimed, a failed attempt to prove that particulars have contradictory properties and are too unstable to be known, or that forms are the only things that can be known.' I agree with Reeve that the instability of sensibles does not prohibit them from being cognized, but I would deny that there is anything in the argument upon which to base the claim that things other than Forms can be the objects of ἐπιστήμη.

encompassing the class of 'object of knowledge' (γνωστόν) would it follow that in some cases they could be the same. Apart from the fact that this would be a trivial point, hardly in keeping with its crucial role in the central books of *Republic*, there is no textual warrant for this gloss at all, nor, indeed, anything in the structure of the argument that supports it. Third, B22, which says that belief is directed neither to what is nor to what is not, would seem to contradict the claim that belief differs from knowledge because it is directed to the same thing as knowledge *and* to something else, namely, false propositions. Finally, B25 identifies the object of belief as 'what is and what is not at the same time'. I fail to see how this can be taken to refer to propositions.[18] Though it may be true that 'Theaetetus is sitting' is true and 'Theaetetus is standing' is false at the same time, on Fine's interpretation one can know that 'Theaetetus is standing' is false, but one can believe that it is true. But why should this fact alone make the modes of cognition different, since what makes the 'knowledge' true and what makes the belief false are the same thing, in both cases external to the cognition?[19]

Perhaps another unspoken reason for insisting that Plato *must* have meant that there can be beliefs about Forms is this. Even if there is non-propositional knowledge of Forms, there must also be propositional knowledge of them, namely, the propositional knowledge expressed in a λόγος. Thus, if a λόγος of a Form is a true one, a person could have knowledge that the λόγος is true, especially if that same person had the knowledge of the Form and therefore the reason *why* it is true. But if there can be such propositional knowledge, then it immediately follows that there can also be belief about the Form. This might be the state of one who did not have the knowledge of the Form. What is wrong with this line of reasoning, in my view, is that it does not take seriously the infallibility of knowledge. As we shall see in our discussion of *Theaetetus*, one does not have knowledge of a

---

[18] We need to distinguish what is believed from the object of belief, as in '*s* believes *p* about *x*'. Here, *x* is the object of belief. Thus, δόξα requires three terms: the believer, what is believed, and the object of belief (what the belief is 'about'). Hence the reason for saying that belief is propositional, that is, *s* believes *p* about *x*. But there is no basis in the text for transferring this threefold analysis to knowledge.

[19] See Gonzalez (1996) for a thorough refutation of Fine's position, with which I largely agree. See also White (1984), 344–53, for additional considerations on behalf of the view that Plato did not intend to allow knowledge of the sensible world.

proposition even if that proposition is true and even if one believes it. This is not because there is something missing in a true belief that could turn it into knowledge. Rather, it is because there is no infallibility in belief. There is no infallibility in belief because of the nature of the objects of belief.

There are only two texts Fine appeals to in support of her claim that Plato allows the possibility that there could be knowledge of sensibles and beliefs about Forms.[20] At 506 c Socrates claims to have no knowledge about the Form of the Good but only belief, and at 520 c he says that the philosopher who returns to the cave knows sensibles.

Regarding the first passage, Socrates is someone who wants to posit the existence of Forms as explanatory entities (507 B 5–7) but who also strongly implies that he does not have knowledge of them (506 c 2–3). So he is neither in the position of a successful philosopher nor in that of the lovers of sights and sounds in A above. What Socrates proceeds to do is speak about the analogy of the sun, the 'offspring' of the Form of the Good which he says is 'most like it' (ὁμοιότατος ἐκείνῳ, 506 E 3–4), and its relation to cognition in the sensible world. When Socrates moves on to develop the analogy of the divided line, he says that the object of belief is to the object of knowledge as the 'likeness is to that which it is like' (τὸ ὁμοιωθὲν πρὸς τὸ ᾧ ὡμοιώθη, 510 A 8–10). His talk about the sun is thus talk only about a likeness and so not about a Form. But Socrates is not like the lovers of sights and sounds in this regard and the text tells us plainly why. The lovers of sights and sounds do not believe in the existence of Forms and so they take likenesses for reality (534 c 5–6).

Socrates is, by contrast, someone who does not believe that the likenesses of Forms are reality. He truly *does* believe in the existence of Forms. But this does not imply that he knows the Forms themselves. Nor does it imply that his beliefs about the likenesses are beliefs about the Forms. They are in fact beliefs about likenesses *as* likenesses, not as originals. That is, he believes them to be likenesses of intelligible entities. Roughly, what this means is that the beliefs are not about the sensible properties of sensibles but about their intelligible structure.[21] This is the difference between someone who

---

[20] Fine (1990), 97.

[21] One might compare in this regard Socrates' remark at *Phaedo* 98 c–99 A that some would confuse the conditions for his sitting in prison at that moment and the true reason for his being there.

believes that Helen is beautiful because of her flesh and bones (which is in one sense true) and someone who believes that Helen is beautiful because of the instrumentality of the Form of Beauty. But I submit that someone who holds that Helen is beautiful owing to the Form of Beauty is not thereby committed to claiming that he has knowledge of the Form of Beauty. So, we need not take Socrates to be expressing beliefs about Forms but rather beliefs, in this case, about likenesses of Forms. The account of the sun in relation to the objects of sight depends upon a postulated likeness between this relation and the relation between the Form of the Good and the other Forms.

Perhaps this argument will be thought to depend on a quibble. After all, when Socrates says, 'The many things are the objects of sight but not of thought, while the Forms are the objects of thought but not of sight' (507 B 9–10) and similar things, is he not expressing belief about Forms? I think the answer must be no if the above arguments for the distinction between lovers of sights and sounds and philosophers is here in force. For according to B22, δόξα is applied neither to what is nor to what is not. If there is δόξα of Forms, then what is said in B22 is simply false. In that case, when Socrates says that 'Forms are the objects of thought and not of sight', is he expressing a δόξα about something other than Forms? If it is not about Forms, what is it about? I shall attempt to answer this question later in this chapter. For now, let me simply note that it does not require much ingenuity to construe Socrates' claim in a way that does not require direct reference to Forms, just as it does not for a philodoxer's claim that there is no such thing as a Form.

The text in which Fine claims that the philosopher returning to the cave displays knowledge of the sensible world (520 C 3–6) actually says that the philosopher, having seen the truth about things noble, just, and good, will then be able to 'recognize' (γνώσεσθε) each of the 'images' (εἴδωλα) for what they are and of what they are images.[22] Unlike Socrates above, these philosophers appear to have seen the Forms. They are exactly like those in

---

[22] We see here that the word γνώσεσθε is the same as that used in B17. But here it seems that it can be used in the loose colloquial sense, not the technical sense according to which it is distinguished from δόξα. We would need very strong evidence indeed to conclude that Plato is using the word in exactly the same way here and so repudiating what he has argued for a few pages earlier.

stage A of the main argument—that is, they can differentiate originals and likenesses on the basis of their own experience. The simplest explanation of why even though they know Forms they cannot know sensible likenesses is that knowledge requires infallibility and there can be no infallibility with regard to the recognition of sensible likenesses. Because they know Forms, they can recognize and are likely to have true beliefs about their likenesses. This is in contrast to the beliefs of most people about things noble, just, and good.[23] Though ordinary people may have true beliefs, they cannot know that they are true or indeed have the true reason why they are true. Further, their true beliefs, when they (inadvertently) have them, are likely to alter. Nevertheless, true beliefs are the best that anyone can have about these likenesses.

If it is thought that Plato intends that there should be two species of knowledge, one having infallibility as a property and one not, then it is still the case that philosophers are not said to have knowledge of sensibles in the manner in which they have knowledge of Forms and in the manner in which our main argument distinguishes it from belief.[24] In effect, the putative knowledge of sensibles would be close to and perhaps indistinguishable from justified belief.[25] Reflecting upon what for Plato would be presupposed in the claim that there are two species of knowledge, namely, that they are both knowledge because they have an identical nature in common,

[23] 520 C 3–6 is obviously intended to be compared with 479 D 3–5: τὰ τῶν πολλῶν πολλὰ νόμιμα καλοῦ τε πέρι καὶ τῶν ἄλλων. The beliefs of the many are, of course, not always false, and so they will sometimes be identical with those of philosophers. At 484 C 6–D 3 again those without knowledge are contrasted with those with knowledge in regard to their ability to establish νόμιμα καλῶν τε πέρι καὶ δικαίων καὶ ἀγαθῶν.

[24] This is the approach of Szaif (1998), 183–222, 300–24. Szaif argues (300) that 'Das Erkennen eines Gegenstandes wäre ein Modus von Gegenstandskognition, das eines Sachverhaltes ein Modus propositionaler Kognition. Erkenntnis eines Gegenstandes kann wiederum grundsätzlich in zwei Weisen konzipiert werden, nämlich entweder als eine vorpropositionale Form von Erkenntnis, etwa im Sinne einer geistigen Schau, oder als eine propositionale Erkenntnis, durch die ein bestimmter Gegenstand kognitiv gleichsam "erschlossen" wird, nämlich insbesondere indem er seinem Wesen nach erkannt wird. Im letzteren Sinne würde Gegenstandserkenntnis auf propositionaler Erkenntnis aufbauen, insofern sie sich in Urteilen über den fraglichen Gegenstand vollzieht oder artikuliert, sie würde aber nicht einfach mit dem Begriff propositionaler Kognition zusammenfallen.'

[25] This is the approach taken by Gregory Vlastos in Vlastos (1985), repr. in Vlastos (1994), 39–66. He claims that Socrates does not have 'certain knowledge' but rather 'elenctic knowledge', which is nothing but justified true belief (46 in the reprint).

proponents of the above view might agree that there is no light at the end of this tunnel. I admit, though, that one's disinclination to accept such a view depends upon one's conviction that, for better or worse, Plato means what he says when he unequivocally separates knowledge and belief in separating philosophers and lovers of sights and sounds and in the divided line.[26]

Here we might recall the previous discussion about the Recollection Argument in *Phaedo*. According to that argument, all people have had knowledge of Forms prior to having entered their bodies. Clearly, what philosophers have is something more, though it need not be so much as occurrent knowledge of Forms. Someone who accepted the Recollection Argument would be apt to recognize images as images of Forms, that is, as deficient in reality, though he would not thereby be claiming to have occurrent or actual knowledge of these Forms. The latter is not necessary for the former. Though Plato speaks as if there were two kinds of knowledge (75 A 5–B 2), in the light of the more technical argument of *Republic* I doubt that he would continue to countenance such loose talk.

As I argued in Chapter 2, the knowledge that is acquired while disembodied cannot be the knowledge that is acquired from sense-perception. I argued that in order to make the judgement that sensibles were inferior in the relevant way, one would have to make that judgement on the basis of a claim that one previously knew the paradigm, although one does not have occurrent knowledge of it. This seems certainly to be the case with Cebes and Simmias. Indeed, anyone who comes to acknowledge that sensible equals are deficient in their equality, though they be exactly equal, and who also acknowledges that the sensible equals are equal owing to the instrumental causality of the Form of Equality, must acknowledge that the sensibles are deficient with respect to the Form of Equality itself. Such a person is neither in the position of one who has occurrent knowledge of the Form of Equality nor in the position of one who does not believe in Forms. As we shall see in the next section, Plato accommodates the status of such a person in the divided line.

An issue that I have not yet dealt with and which in itself might be thought to cast doubt upon the seriousness with which Plato makes the separation

---

[26] Cf. 529 B 7–C 1, where the denial of ἐπιστήμη of the sensible world is emphatically reaffirmed.

of knowledge and belief is the curious description of ignorance as related to what is not (B5). Surely, it can be argued, if one cannot have beliefs about Forms, one can at least be ignorant of Forms. And if one can be ignorant about the same thing of which one can have knowledge, then there is one case in which the stratification and isolation of modes of cognition (or absence of cognition) do not pertain. So, if it does not work in one case why should we suppose that it will not fail in other cases, whether that means knowledge of sensibles or belief about Forms? First, though it is admittedly odd to say that ignorance is directed to or in relation to anything, Plato does not say that ignorance is a power or a mode of cognition. One can, of course, be ignorant of the existence and nature of Forms. That ignorance, however, is distinct from the state of someone who, owing to ignorance of Forms, believes that likenesses are reality. The 'object' of ignorance is 'what is not' which is said to be distinct from the object that combines 'what is and what is not'. Note that belief here is not just false belief; true belief has 'what is and what is not' as its object as well. But both true and false belief are about something, whereas ignorance refers to nothing. Ignorance is also not an alternative mode of cognizing Forms, because then it would be indistinguishable from false belief about Forms, if there were such a thing. For example, one might claim that one could be ignorant of how the Form of Oddness and the Form of Threeness were related. But either this would be entailed by the fact that one was ignorant of the Forms altogether or else it would be equivalent to a false belief about Forms. If, however, as Plato says, and I have argued he means, there is no belief about Forms, there is then no false belief about them.

Nevertheless, ignorance seems to be perfectly possible in regard to 'what is'. So, though 'what is not' may be an 'object' of ignorance, it does not seem to be exclusively the object of ignorance.[27] One way of addressing this sort of criticism is to begin by pointing out that it supposes that ignorance is a sort of relation between cognizer and 'what is'. But that is not at all the way Plato thinks of it. Ignorance is not a cognitive state like knowledge and belief. The word ἀγνωσία indicates an absence of something. The question is whether this absence is to be understood as an absent relation or an absence in the state of the cognizer. In the first case, ignorance would be the absence of that the presence of which would be knowledge. That is,

---

[27] So Stokes (1992), 114.

the lack of relation between subject and object would be the contradictory of the presence of the relation between the same subject and object. But according to Plato, ignorance does not have the same object as knowledge. To take ignorance as ignorance about that of which one can have knowledge is to identify what is with what is not. Such a view confuses the object of cognition with a relation between subject and object.[28]

My interpretation is not intended to dismiss what was said in the first sentence of the preceding paragraph. Indeed, being in the state of ignorance entails that the one who is in this state is ignorant about what is in some sense. This becomes clear when we realize that ignorance for Plato is not a relation primarily but a property of a cognizer. The difference between ignorance and knowledge in this regard is the difference between the mind 'being empty' and the mind 'being full'. If I am ignorant about a Form, this means, roughly, that the Form is not present to the mind. That is all it means. This ignorance does not preclude the presence of belief about sensibles at the same time. The absence of the Form in the one who is ignorant is the 'what is not' or non-being. It does not seem to me to matter for the purposes of this argument that I could not say that I am ignorant about a Form, where this is taken to imply that I am referring to that Form. That this claim can only be a third-person claim seems to me to mirror the fact that knowledge is primarily first-person. In short, I do not see any basis for holding that the possibility of ignorance of Forms requires us to accept that there can be knowledge and belief about the same objects.

I return now to the question of what 'what is' and 'what is and what is not' are supposed to mean. For without some answer to this question, the point of separating knowledge and belief in the way that Plato does is going to remain vague and unpersuasive. Much has been made of the distinction between veridical and existential and predicative senses of 'is' in Plato in relation to this passage.[29] Fortunately, we do not, I think, have to try to make the text fit such categories. Rather, we can simply ask what Plato believes he establishes and why within the context of the argument. I take it that in C1 the 'appearances' of things are not meant to contrast with the way they 'really' are. First, what appears double and half is not really something else

[28] See Glidden (1985) for a view similar to mine.

[29] See Smith (2000), with references, for a good discussion of the alternatives in the literature.

or really one rather than the other. Second, if 'x appears f' is meant to be contrasted with 'x really is g', then as far as the text goes, the philodoxer would be in no worse a position than the philosopher in discovering what this is. The first puzzling step is made in C2, where it is said that what participates in opposites, that is, something that is both f and not-f, is no more f than not-f. What does 'no more f than not-f' add to 'both f and not-f'? Presumably, all it need mean is that being f does not preclude being not-f. But if that is all it means, then we have certainly not advanced very far. And we have no reason for denying that what appears to be f really is f, despite the fact that this does not prevent it from being not-f.

The crucial step is made in C3, where it is next claimed that what participates in opposites cannot be securely understood to be (a) being or not being; (b) both being and not being; (c) neither being nor not being. As is evident from C4, what is referred to in C3 is in contrast to the classification of the objects of knowledge and ignorance as being and not being, respectively. The objects of belief are thus identifiable neither with (a) the objects of knowledge or ignorance; (b) both the objects of knowledge and ignorance together; (c) what is neither the object of knowledge nor the object of ignorance. The last alternative must naturally not be understood as meaning that belief does not have an object that is different from the objects of both knowledge and ignorance. That is exactly what the argument will conclude. It seems that it must mean that just as it is wrong to claim that the object of belief partakes of both being and not being, so it is wrong to claim that it partakes of neither just because of what was claimed in C2, namely, that being f does not preclude something from being not-f. But this cannot be right because being f and being not-f does not mean 'neither being nor not being f'. Rather, I believe the point is that what is f and not-f is therefore something like a 'mixture' of being and not being. It shows two 'aspects' depending on perspective or situation, which is exactly what the word ἐπαμφοτερίζειν conveys.[30] The 'mixture' is specifically of the perfectly intelligible with the perfectly unintelligible, yielding the equivocally intelligible, what is 'between being and not being'. If this is right, then being and not being do not represent primarily existence, for the 'mixture' of what exists with nothing is no different from what exists. On the other hand,

---

[30] Cf. *Phdr.* 257 B 5. Aristotle frequently uses the term in his biological works to refer to animals that manifest contrary properties belonging to different species.

if being means primarily what is intelligible or transparent to an intellect, then there is good sense to be made of a claim that the objects of belief are a sort of mixture in this way.[31]

It might be claimed at this point that we are no better off if we take this approach. For what is f and not-f is nevertheless perfectly intelligible. Or rather, the fact that something is not-f does not reduce the intelligibility of its being f one bit. But consider that if δόξα is derived from 'sense-perception' (αἴσθησις), then a belief that something is f is going to be a belief the evidence for which is rooted in the deliverances of the senses.[32] That is, one believes that x is f because of its shape and colour and so on. But according to Plato, whatever is f is also not-f at the same time, which means that the evidence for claiming that x is f is the same evidence for claiming that x is not-f. If the basis for understanding the claim that x is f is the same as the basis for understanding the claim that x is not-f, it seems entirely legitimate to argue that the intelligibility of x in so far as it is f is qualified or compromised or, indeed, something like a mixture of intelligibility and unintelligibility. Thus can Plato hold that the objects of belief are neither the object of knowledge nor the object of ignorance nor both of these. The objects of belief are exclusively sensibles, sensibles that are in principle diminished in reality.

That the objects of belief—sensibles—are a mixture of being and not-being helps explain why the objects of knowledge are 'completely' knowable and the objects of ignorance are completely unknowable (B3).[33] Forms are

---

[31] This is basically the 'predicative' reading of 'is and is not', but not all those who agree with this reading would take 'is and is not' to imply something like a mixture of being and non-being. See Vlastos (1973b), who rightly rejects the 'existential' reading of 'being and not being' and argues for the meaning of 'being' in this context as 'cognitively reliable F' and 'reliably valuable' (49–50). The former is close to what I mean by 'intelligible'.

[32] See Sprute (1962), 40–4, and Lafrance (1981), 225–49, on the connection between δόξα and αἴσθησις in Plato generally.

[33] The repeated use of the term 'purely' (εἰλικρινῶς) for the intelligible at 477 A 7, 478 D 6, 479 D 5 suggests the aptness of the metaphor of a mixture for sensibles. In *Timaeus* (35 A–B, 41 D–E) both the world soul and human souls are composed out of a mixture of two kinds, that which belongs to the intelligible and that which belongs to the sensible or material. Each kind has three subtypes, being, sameness, and difference. The mixture that is the soul is analogous to the mixture that is the object of embodied cognition, as it should be if sensibles are to be cognizable. The metaphor of 'clarity' (σαφήνεια), 478 C 10–11, 518 C 5–10, 532 C 6–8, has roughly the same force as the metaphor of purity.

transparent to the intellect. That is why cognition of them is infallible. Sensibles are a sort of mixture of what is transparent to the intellect and what is utterly opaque, like darkness. For when one tries to understand sensibles on the basis of the deliverances of the senses, one is *necessarily* going to have a type of cognition that is diminished in relation to the cognition that has as its objects what sensibles are images or likenesses of.[34] The fallible belief that Helen is beautiful, even for someone who knows the Form of Beauty, is a belief that is inseparable from the belief that this beauty is constituted by, say, her shape and colour.[35] Her beauty is an image of the Form diminished in intelligibility. Certainly, one dramatic way of expressing this is to say that it is midway between being and not-being, where 'being' is understood as what is transparent to an intellect. Another way of making the same point would be to say that the λóγος of Helen's beauty is diminished in intelligibility with respect to the λóγος of the Form of Beauty. The reason for this is, again, that the λóγος of Helen's beauty (*not* its instrumental cause, which is the Form) is bound to include elements that belong equally in a λóγος of her ugliness.[36]

A more general objection to the position for which I have argued may be put as follows. Plato's use of the terms γνωστόν and δοξαστόν are improperly interpreted as indicating *objects* of knowledge and belief. In fact, the putative objects of belief are really just appearances or images of the objects of knowledge. Plato does not have a 'two-world' ontology but rather

---

[34] See e.g. 598 B 1–5, 602 D 1–4, where φαντάσματα are said to be corrupted φαινόμενα.

[35] At *Soph.* 264 B 1–2 Plato says that the meaning of φαίνεται is a 'mixture' (σύμμειξις) of δόξα and αἴσθησις: that is, when one says 'it appears to me thus and so' or '*x* is *f*', one is claiming to have acquired a belief about a sense-perception. The problem is not that the senses are deceptive, but that the information they deliver to judgement is tainted or compromised. When one sees Helen's shape or colour and makes a judgement based on *that*, one is bound to be speaking about what is and is not at the same time.

[36] Gallop (1965) argues, correctly in my view, that λóγοι of Forms are for Plato verbal images. He cites *Phaedo* 99 D–100 A, *Crat.* 439 A–B, and *Statesman* 277 C in this regard. The imagery follows inevitably from the use of the sensible world as a starting point for producing accounts of the Forms that explain things. Thus, it is one thing to say that the Form of Justice is what makes things just and quite another to try to give an account of what all just things have in common, an account which is necessarily rooted in sensible attributes. Gallop contrasts the verbal image with dialectic, which is supposed to deal exclusively with Forms. However, it is difficult to see how dialectic, which operates with language, can be exempt from verbal imagery.

a unitary ontology with various modes of apprehension of that world. To have beliefs regarding sensibles is to have beliefs regarding the appearances of Forms; belief is different from knowledge but the 'objects' of belief are not really things different from Forms.[37]

Such an argument, I think, rests upon two mistakes. First, the sense of 'object' according to which knowledge and belief cannot have the same objects does not entail that sensibles are ontologically independent of Forms. Indeed, Plato holds that without Forms there would be nothing sufficiently intelligible to have beliefs *about*. The sense of 'object' relevant to the argument is the sense according to which whatever it is that one has beliefs about cannot be identical with a Form and that which one has knowledge of cannot be identical with that about which one has beliefs. Second, the argument presumes the anodyne sense of 'appearance' according to which a thing's appearance is identical with the thing but is conceived in relation to a cognizer. So, to have a belief about an appearance of x would be to have a belief about x. However, it is Plato's view that the sensible world consists of appearances not in this anodyne sense, but in the sense that is *contrasted* with reality. It is this sense that inspires much of Greek ontological speculation, going back at least to Parmenides. So, beliefs about sensibles may in a way be said to be beliefs about appearances of Forms, but this is not the way according to which a belief about the appearance of x could be compared with knowledge not about the appearance of x, but about x itself, where 'x' is used unequivocally.

4.2 The Form of the Good

The account I have offered of Plato's distinction between knowledge and belief will, I suppose, have minimal force in isolation from an interpretation of the rest of the central books. My immediate concern is how this account squares with the famous sun, line, and cave analogies. The hypothesis with which I shall approach these texts is that knowledge and belief remain fundamentally distinguished in the way explained above. Indeed, we shall see that at one point Plato even makes the distinction sharper.

At the beginning of book 6 Socrates begins to describe for his interlocutors Glaucon and Adeimantus the character of the true philosopher and to argue

[37] This line of argument is well expressed, for example, by Perl (1997).

that some such person must rule the ideal state. He then begins to describe the course of study to be undertaken by those suited by nature to become rulers. The study of the virtues belonging to the three parts of the soul, that is, the pursuit of the knowledge of the Forms of the Virtues, is one major goal of the course of study. But the 'greatest study' (μέγιστον μάθημα) is of the Idea of the Good (505 A 2). The first point to note here is that the knowledge to be sought and acquired by the student-philosophers is obviously different from whatever we choose to call the mode of cognition appropriate for the definitions of the virtues arrived at at the end of book 4.[38] We shall return to this point.

Regarding the Form of the Good, there are many complex issues which have elicited a great deal of speculation.[39] Several claims made are directly relevant to my purposes. First, Socrates suggests that our 'knowledge of this Form is inadequate' (οὐχ ἱκανῶς ἴσμεν, 505 A 5–6). Whatever such inadequacy consists in, this is a new claim in relation to what was said in book 5, where it did not appear that any gradations of knowing were possible.

Socrates proceeds to elaborate the analogy between the Form of the Good and the sun. The terms are straightforward enough: just as we see the objects of sight with our eyes by the light of the sun, so we know the Forms with our minds by the truth of the Form of the Good. In addition, just as the sun not only provides for the objects of sight the capacity for their being seen but also provides for the nourishment, growth, and generation of the objects of sight, so the Form of the Good not only provides the knowability of the objects of knowledge but also provides for their 'existence and being' (τὸ εἶναί τε καὶ τὴν οὐσίαν, 509 B 6–7).[40]

[38] At 442 C 5–6, σοφία is said to be the ἐπιστήμη of what is good for each and every part of the soul. But just as the definitions of the virtues arrived at are not knowledge properly speaking, so it would seem that the knowledge that wisdom is here said to be is also not knowledge properly speaking. The loose use of the term ἐπιστήμη in book 4 is consistent with the provisional nature of the conclusions therein.

[39] See esp. Ferber (1989) for an excellent and detailed study and an extensive bibliography; also Baltes (1997) and Santas (1999).

[40] I am assuming that the words τὸ εἶναί τε καὶ τὴν οὐσίαν are a hendiadys on the basis of the following line ἐπέκεινα τῆς οὐσίας. Mistaking this for two distinct 'facts' about Forms is what must have led some to think that the Good is completely beyond being. Adam (1963), i. 172, for instance, thinks that the Form of the Good is the cause of the existence of the other Forms as well as the cause of their essence.

One more extremely important point made is that since the Form of the Good is the cause of knowledge and truth, it is considered to be itself 'an object of knowledge' (ὡς γιγνωσκομένης μὲν διανοοῦ, 508 E 4). This claim is not strictly speaking made to be a part of the analogy. It is not clear how the analogy is supposed to work here. For it is not clear what it means to say that if x is the cause of the φ-ing of y by z, x is φ-ed by z as well. Consider the following example. A is the cause of B getting angry at C. Does it follow that B is angry at A as well? Obviously not. The problem is evidently what it means to say that the Form of the Good is the cause of knowledge. We are also told that this Form gives to him who knows the 'power' (δύναμιν) to know (508 E 2). Perhaps we can interpret 'cause of knowledge' and 'gives the power to know' in the same way, as meaning 'makes it possible for knowing to occur'. The basis for taking the Form of the Good thus as the condition for knowledge would then be found in some relation between the Good and the primary objects of knowledge, that is, all the subordinate Forms. Still, one might reasonably ask what sort of relation between a cause and an effect makes the cause related to something else just as the effect is. Why is the cause of what is knowable thereby itself an object of cognition?

One may offer an interpretation. The Form of the Good is virtually all of the other Forms, roughly in the way that 'white' light is virtually all the colours of the rainbow or in the way that the algebraic formula of a circle is virtually a circle or in the way a function is virtually all of its arguments or in the way an artist is virtually all of his creations. The point of the last analogy is clear when we say of the artist, for example, that 'He still has great work left in him.' I shall in due course address some of the issues raised by this interpretation both systematically and historically. For one thing, we shall have to ask why the Form that is at the pinnacle of Plato's intelligible world is called 'Good'. But for the moment I shall focus on a narrower issue, namely, why there should need to be any Form serving as the cause of other Forms—a cause, I stress, of their being as well as their knowability. After all, the Forms are supposed to be immutable and eternal entities. These are among the attributes that make Forms the objects of knowledge. The introduction of a cause of what 'always is what it is' seems otiose.

One reason for postulating a cause of Forms has its ultimate origin in the reductionism implicit in Presocratic cosmological speculation. Attempts to understand and explain the complexity of phenomena by positing a minimum number of principles are legion. It is not a great speculative leap to ask about the complexity of the principles themselves and whether they can be reduced further. That the ultimate principles of reality should be an infinity of Forms must have seemed to the mathematically minded Plato intellectually intolerable. I suppose that one reason for positing a single superordinate Form is just such a reductivist presumption.

Another reason may be found in the earliest expressions of the theory of Forms. A simple-minded theorist of Forms takes Forms to be eternal and immutable 'ones-over-many', existing in splendid isolation from the sensible world and from each other. There is no problem with viewing immaterial entities as 'separate' from the sensible world so long as we understand separation basically as independence. But there is a very grave problem in viewing Forms as separate from each other. For if, say, the Form of Five and the Form of Odd are separate, there is no explanation within the theory of Forms of why instances of the former are always accompanied by instances of the latter. The point is easily generalizable. Every proposition expressing an eternal or necessary truth, other than those contained in identity statements, must, for the Platonist, represent eternal complexity.[41] But such complexity is impossible if Forms are perfectly simple in their intelligibility. And yet one wants to say, reasonably enough, that the nature of fiveness and the nature of oddness are just what they are. Each is simple.[42]

Such a line of thinking is perhaps what led Plato to suppose that there must be some *tertium quid*, something which serves a unifying function among simples such that the result is complex.[43] Thus, the necessary con-

---

[41] Cf. *Phaedo* 104 A 1–3: The words μηδέποτε ἀπολείπεσθαι indicate the necessary connectedness of the Forms of Threeness and Oddness.

[42] See e.g. McCabe (1994), 4 and *passim*, who argues that Forms are 'austere' individuals: that is, they are 'entirely simple entities, having no properties and standing in no relations that might impair their simplicity'. Since, however, Forms cannot be simple in this way *and* explain necessary connectedness in nature, the Form of the Good is introduced.

[43] If there is development in Plato's thinking about Forms, I would locate one major phase of that development in *Phaedo* precisely in Socrates' distinction between his 'simple' and 'cleverer' hypotheses. The simple hypothesis is that something is called *f* owing to the instrumentality of Fness. So, something is correctly called 'hot' owing to the Form of Hotness. By contrast, the cleverer hypothesis tells us that something is correctly called 'hot' not owing to the Form of Hotness but owing to the Form of Fire, because Fire and Hotness are necessarily connected. One point is more or less clear from the distinction

nectedness between fiveness and oddness is owing to the fact that they are aspects or parts of what one thing is. If one likes, this is an ontological mirror image of analyticity. But if one were to say that, accordingly, the Form of the Good is just the totality of Forms, as a class is the totality of its members or even as an organism is the totality of its parts, then the reductivist motive for positing the Form of the Good in the first place would be lost. Complexity would be insinuated into the first principle of all. That is why the Form of the Good should be seen as *virtually* all the Forms. The first principle of all is *per se* unique and simple. It is complex only as known.

The idea of virtuality is fairly precise. To add to the above examples, the premisses of a valid deductive argument contain together virtually their conclusion. A properly functioning calculator contains virtually all the answers to the mathematical questions that its rules allow it to be asked. An omniscient simple deity may be said to know virtually all that is knowable. Virtuality is distinct from eminence. The Forms are eminently their images, but the Form of the Good is not eminently the other Forms. This is a logical constraint. If the Form F is eminently that which its name names, this means that no other Form, even the Form of the Good, could be eminently that which the Form F's name names. The obvious vicious regress occasioned by making the Form of the Good eminently what the other Forms are is intolerable and unnecessary and unsupported by any text.[44]

It is impossible to overestimate the consequences of such a view for Plato and, indeed, for the entire Platonic tradition. If knowing a Form means really knowing the Form of the Good and therefore knowing one thing, then one cannot, it seems, know any Form without knowing the Forms comprehensively. And what this means is either that knowledge—the infallible cognition of all that is knowable—is such an exalted and impossibly

between the two hypotheses. It is owing to the eternal necessary connectedness of at least some Forms that participation in one entails participation in another. Presumably, the fact that Forms are necessarily connected is not in contradiction with the previous claim made in the so-called Affinity Argument that a Form is ἀσύνθετον and μονοειδὲς ὂν αὐτὸ καθ' αὑτό. Nevertheless, the claim that Forms are necessarily connected is of monumental significance and brings with it serious difficulties.

[44] It should be clear from this account of the superordination of the Form of the Good that, though I recognize the intra-Academic discussions that Aristotle represents as ἄγραφα δόγματα, I dissent from Krämer (1969), who traces the positing of a Form of the Good as Plato's appropriation of an Eleatic opposition of one–many.

demanding goal that it is practically unattainable or else that knowledge is something less than the ultimate cognitive attainment. The former view finds its expression in scepticism. The latter finds its expression in forms of mysticism within the Platonic tradition. And to the extent that the Form of the Good becomes somehow identified with a god possessing even attenuated personal attributes, the mysticism takes on a religious character.

For Plato and for our immediate purposes, the consequence is that gradations of cognition are required. Knowledge remains the highest of these, although its attainability by embodied individuals is still problematic. Knowledge does indeed require comprehensiveness, but this suggests a reductionism among Forms prior to their ultimate reduction to the Form of the Good. That is, certain Forms are seen as somehow more basic than others, and these basic Forms are what the Form of the Good is virtually. These basic Forms are possibly mathematical. For the mathematical reduction of Forms we have tolerably good evidence, both in the dialogues and externally. If knowledge is indeed something exalted, infallible, and direct, Plato needs to account for other lesser types of cognition. I mean the concepts and words that are used to represent what is, ultimately and virtually, the Form of the Good. So, for example, when one says that 'gold is heavier than water' or that 'justice is a virtue' or that 'pleasure is not the ultimate good' or even that 'a triangle is a three-sided plane figure', one is not expressing knowledge, because gold and water and justice and so on are not objects of knowledge; rather, one is, accurately or not, representing what is knowable.

I think that for anyone who believes that there is anything in the dialogues that expresses Plato's real views, then 'pleasure is not the sole human good' would be one such view. But if this claim is held by Plato to be true, it is not so because there is a Form of Pleasure and a Form of Good and these are related in a specific logical manner—that is, good is predicated of pleasure but not exclusively. So, if knowledge is for Plato of Forms, then the statement 'pleasure is not the sole good' is not an example of what knowledge is of. But it is not so much a question of a name for the relevant mode of cognition; rather, if 'pleasure is not the sole good' is true, what is it true *of*? I do not think the Platonic answer is that it is true of concepts or that it is an empirical truth about sensibles. The words 'true of' have to be understood in a peculiarly Platonic way.

The words are true of Forms roughly in the way that an image can be true of its model. One represents what is in a different medium. Ultimately, it is Forms that make 'pleasure is not the sole good' true, but the words do not correspond to Forms as in a correspondence theory of truth. The words do not represent in this way. Or, if one claims that '5−3 = 2', this is true ultimately because of the way Forms are, but it is not a representation that corresponds to a Form of Five, a Form of Three, a Form of Two, a Form of Minus, and a Form of Equality. I am not sure that what I take Plato to be implying here is all that different from *Phaedo*, where it is owing to our pre-embodied knowledge of Forms that we can, through sense-perception, recognize or recollect truths about instances of Forms here. As we saw, the knowledge of Forms had when disembodied is not the same thing as this recognition. We do not reacquire knowledge of Forms when we recollect equality. This recollection or recognition is not knowledge of Forms because it is essentially representational. Although I think *Republic* is going further than this, it is going along the same path. Therefore, the question of whether there can be partial knowledge of Forms is probably to be answered in the negative if, as I believe, reductionism is true and there are far fewer Forms than one might have supposed, and if the representations like 'gold is heavier than water' do not constitute knowledge.[45]

As a principle and cause, the Form of the Good must stand apart from that of which it is a principle.[46] For example, in Greek mathematics the unit is the principle of number and is not therefore itself a number. That the Form of the Good is a first principle of Forms tells us why it is itself not οὐσία. It is not nothing. It is just not a limited something or other.[47] The fact that it is a principle of the knowable in this way means that knowledge of it is not a bit of knowledge in addition to the knowledge of Forms themselves. The 'power' of the Form of the Good consists in its unifying function. That is, it accounts for the fact that there is an ontologically complex unity in virtue of which necessary truths are true. If, say, a theorem in Euclid represents an eternal necessary truth, then there must be some complex unity that

---

[45] If the words 'we do not know adequately [the Form of the Good]' just mean that, though we believe that it exists, we do not have knowledge of it, then partial knowledge of Forms is completely unsupported in the text.

[46] Cf. 533 c 8–d 1. See Krämer (1969), 4, for references to this Greek commonplace.

[47] See Baltes (1997), 1–11, for a thorough refutation of the view that the Form of the Good is non-existent because it is 'beyond οὐσία'.

makes this so.[48] Understanding the Form of the Good in the above manner helps us to see the justification for its name. If persons are ideally knowers, then the good for persons is attained in knowing. The Form of the Good represents the culmination of personal achievement. Without the unifying function of the Form of the Good, Forms would not be knowable.

4.3 The Divided Line and the Allegory of the Cave

The refinements in the account of knowledge initiated by the analogy of the Form of the Good and the sun are deepened in the two following analogies, that of the divided line and that of the cave, to which I now briefly turn.

The analogy of the divided line is supposed to develop the previous analogy of the sun (509 D).[49] It aims to analyse the two realms of the intelligible and the visible or sensible, over which the Good and the sun preside, respectively. The analysis is both ontological and epistemological. A line divided into two unequal parts represents the two realms, now named epistemologically, the 'object of belief' (τὸ δοξαστόν) and the 'object of knowledge' (τὸ γνωστόν), rather than ontologically (510 A 9).[50] Each part of the line is itself apparently to be divided according to the same ratio as the whole line, though we are not told what this ratio is.[51] The 'lower' part of the line includes animals, plants, artefacts, in short, sensible entities, and their images. Corresponding to these are two modes of cognition, actually 'states of the soul' (παθήματα ἐν τῇ ψυχῇ) called 'trust' (πίστις) and 'imagining'

[48] The idea of immaterial complexity seems to be inseparable from Platonism or from any ontological theory of necessary truth. If it is an eternal and necessary truth that iron rusts, we might say that this is owing to the nature of iron. But then the nature of iron must be complex in itself and different from, say, the nature of water.

[49] See Smith (1996) with references for a good analysis. See Annas (1981), 242–71, on some of the issues around the connection of the three analogies.

[50] The line is of unequal parts, but we are not told which part is larger, the part representing the sensible world or the part representing the intelligible world.

[51] The phrase ἀνὰ τὸν αὐτὸν λόγον (509 D 7–8) does not necessarily mean 'according to the same ratio'. It could simply mean that the two subsections of the line are also to be divided unequally. I agree, however, that the words probably refer to the same ratio. But they do not therefore imply, as some hold, that, on the entire line A–E, B–C and C–D must be equal. This is only one possibility, which is not required by the text and so cannot be essential to the argument. In addition, if B–C and C–D are equal, so must A–B and D–E, but no one, I think, wants to argue that the objects of νοῦς and εἰκασία must be identical. See Pritchard (1995), 91–2.

(εἰκασία). With regard to truth and untruth, as the objects of belief are to the objects of knowledge, so are the objects of εἰκασία to those of πίστις.

In the 'upper' part of the line the soul uses as images what before were models (510 B 4–5). These are the sensibles that were the models for their images. In this section of the line one is forced to investigate from hypotheses, proceeding not to a first principle but to a conclusion. The examples of the sort of cognition operating in this section are mathematical. A geometrician, for example, uses drawings of lines and figures as images of the mathematical objects he wishes to investigate. These drawings belong, I take it, to the 'visible figures' referred to at 510 D 5–E 1 and their shadows and reflections in water.

In the highest section one proceeds to the unhypothetical first principle, starting with a hypothesis without the images of the previous section, using only Forms (511 B 3 ff.). Here we are dealing with what reason grasps by the power of dialectic. Its hypotheses are the starting points for reaching the first principle of all. Having attained this, the soul goes 'downward' by means of Forms to conclusions that are Forms. The four sections of the line are then graded with respect to clarity.

The general analogy is: as sensibles are to intelligibles, so images in the sensible realm are to sensibles, and objects of mathematical science are to Forms. And as the sun reigns over the sensible realm, so the Form of the Good reigns over the intelligible realm. The central interpretative difficulty in this passage has generally been taken to be concerned with the objects of mathematical science. Are these Forms? And if so, are they Forms of a different sort from those which are the objects of 'understanding' (νοῦς)? If they are not Forms, what is the justification for recruiting into the intelligible realm some new kind of entity? A related question is this. It seems obvious that the unhypothetical first principle to which the highest section of the line is directed is the Form of the Good.[52] What does the Form of the Good have to do with mathematical science?

One important clue is at 533 C 7–E 2, where Plato explains that earlier διάνοια was loosely though improperly identified as ἐπιστήμη, the mode of cognition applied generally to the top part of the line. In fact, διάνοια is a mode of cognition 'clearer than δόξα but more obscure than ἐπιστήμη'. Plato adds that ἐπιστήμη should only be used of the higher section of the top

[52] 510 B 7; cf. 511 A 5, B 6–7, C 8.

part of the line. If we put this passage together with 511 D 4–5, where διάνοια is said to be 'midway' (μεταξύ) between δόξα and νοῦς, it is evident that Plato wishes to identify ἐπιστήμη and νοῦς. Only with dialectic, proceeding to the unhypothetical first principle, is certainty attained. Not only are the objects of νοῦς 'clearer' (σαφέστερον, 511 C 4) than those of διάνοια, their objects have more truth (511 E 2–4). The objects of διάνοια are not cognized other than by διάνοια (511 A 1).

But immediately before the lines seeming to distinguish the objects of διάνοια and νοῦς, something different appears to be going on. At 511 C 8–D 2 it is implied in some sense that νοῦς and διάνοια have the same objects, namely, the 'hypotheses' or Forms, only that the former approach these from a first principle whereas the latter do not. What it would mean for this passage to be claiming that the objects of νοῦς and διάνοια are the same is that these objects are Forms, for these are unquestionably the objects of νοῦς. But this interpretation makes nonsense of the explicit claims about the different objects in the last paragraph. It is also unnecessary. That the objects of διάνοια are 'intelligible' (νοητῶν ὄντων) to someone who has νοῦς does not mean that it is νοῦς that cognizes them. The νοῦς applied to the objects of διάνοια is νοῦς of what they are essentially—what, say, a plurality of mathematical triangles have in common, namely, the Form of Triangularity. The mathematicians presume this (cf. 510 C 2–D 3) but have no νοῦς of it because they do not view it in the light of the Form of the Good, which means that they do not understand the nature of triangularity even though they recognize that this exists.

A mathematician, according to Plato, is an excellent example of someone whose work presumes the existence of Forms, but who at the same time has no knowledge of them because he does not 'go back to a first principle', namely, the Form of the Good. Here Plato is again making the point that the Form of the Good is the cause of the knowability of the subordinate Forms. Do the hypotheses 'let there be a triangle' or 'let there be a right angle' made by the mathematician constitute a type of cognition of the Form of Triangularity other than knowledge? In short, do such hypotheses compromise what was argued at the end of book 5? It might appear so, for at 510 C 6–D 1 the mathematicians are said to 'make these [mathematical hypotheses] their hypotheses and don't think that it is necessary to give any account of them, either to themselves or to others, as if they were clear to everyone'. So, one might reason, the accounts of these hypotheses, presumably provided by dialecticians, not mathematicians, would be accounts of the very same things. One reason for denying that the hypotheses of mathematicians are Forms themselves, and so for denying that in making these, mathematicians are cognizing Forms, is that at 533 c 8 dialecticians 'eliminate' (ἀναιροῦσα) the hypotheses made by mathematicians (cf.c 1). Surely, they do not eliminate these hypotheses understood as positing the existence of Forms. Another reason is that at 511 b 2–c 2 the dialecticians begin with hypotheses and, after reaching the Form of the Good, end up with Forms. The hypotheses with which they begin seem to be in contrast to the Forms with which they end. These hypotheses are the one mentioned at 510 c 3–5. A dialectician, it seems, starts out with the hypothesis that a triangle or a line or the odd or the even exists, and is eventually able to give an account of the Form of each of these.

According to this interpretation, the objects of νοῦς are virtually the objects of διάνοια just as the Form of the Good is virtually the object of νοῦς. Thus, for example, the Form of Triangularity is virtually what mathematicians study. The main point I wish to insist upon is that we are here introduced to a mode of cognition, διάνοια, that, unlike δόξα, presumes the existence of the objects of ἐπιστήμη, but is different from ἐπιστήμη. And this ἐπιστήμη is here characterized as operating deductively within the realm of Forms.

The question of whether the objects of διάνοια must be the same as the objects of πίστις turns largely on the interpretation of 510 b 4–5: 'the soul, using as images those things which were then imitated'.[53] I tend to the view that neither the analogy of the line itself nor the analogy of the cave (as we shall see shortly) requires us to posit mathematical intermediaries as the sole objects of διάνοια even if Plato did in fact hold that mathematical intermediaries exist.[54] But the analogy does very strongly require us to dis-

[53] See Adam (1963), vol. ii, appendix 1 to book 6; Brentlinger (1963); Annas (1975); and most recently, Pritchard (1995), 91–118, with references to the most recent literature on the intermediaries. All of these scholars argue for the traditional view that the objects of διάνοια are not identical with sensibles. There is also a good summary of the opposing positions on 'mathematical intermediaries' in Chen (1992), 215–27.

[54] I take seriously Aristotle's testimony that Plato did believe in mathematical objects. See *Metaph. A* 6, 987^{b}14–17. But Aristotle's reason, that mathematical objects are multiple, whereas Forms are not, is not employed in this passage. I suspect that mathematical

tinguish two modes of cognition, namely, διάνοια and πίστις, and it suggests how. The first uses as images what are models, namely, sensibles. That is, it recognizes that sensibles are images. The implication is that the second, πίστις, is the mode of cognition which takes sensibles as models and not images (cf. 511 A 7–8). That a mode of cognition between πίστις or δόξα and ἐπιστήμη is required is evident generally from the stringent requirements of ἐπιστήμη. Plato needs a mode of cognition that is discursive in principle and essential to the non-philosophical sciences. Although his examples in the line analogy are mathematical, such employment of hypotheses in order to draw conclusions is easily and plausibly generalizable. We do not need to go further than the sun analogy to see Socrates hypothesizing the Form of the Good and the other Forms and drawing conclusions about its offspring, the sun. The philosophers, distinguished from the lovers of sights and sounds, seem to be in the same position. They, unlike the lovers of sights and sounds, 'believe in' (νομίζων) Forms, which seems to be a sort of hypothesis. Their mode of cognition is even termed διάνοια (476 D 6).[55] This hypothesizing is apparently not mathematical in the stated case of beauty, nor is it δόξα, as we have seen. It is exactly what Socrates does in *Phaedo* as well when he hypothesizes Forms to solve puzzles about the sensible world and to prove the immortality of the soul.

The hypotheses of one who is in a state of διάνοια *may* involve Forms, but they may not. In general, these hypotheses seem to be of the form 'x is something (τι)', which in Greek has an existential implication.[56] The difference between a philosopher and a mathematician who does not believe that Forms exist is that the former will not attempt to give an account of x without understanding it in the light of the Form of the Good, whereas the latter thinks that he can give a suitable account of x by itself. The hypothesis 'triangularity is something' or 'let there be a triangle' is distinct from the hypothesis that the Form of Triangularity exists if Forms are only knowable in relation to the Form of the Good. We must not suppose that

intermediaries belong to a later phase of Plato's thinking, a general phase of mathematical reductionism. I do not wish to argue the point here and it is not directly relevant to *Republic*.

[55] Cf. 527 B 10: φιλοσόφου διανοίας the product of practice in geometry.

[56] For example, at 476 E 7–477 A 1 Plato moves from the claim that the object of knowledge is 'something' to the conclusion that the object of knowledge has being. See also e.g. *Phaedo* 100 B–C, which moves from 'x is τι' to 'x is ὄν'.

the mathematician is to the Form of Triangularity as someone looking at a droplet of water with his naked eye is to the scientist looking at the same droplet with a microscope. There is nothing in the text to warrant such a comparison. The interposition of the passage on the Form of the Good between the passage distinguishing knowledge and belief and the passage on the divided line ought to remove the temptation to see Forms as variously accessible, that is, as variously the objects of διάνοια and νοῦς.[57]

My point can be made in a different way. Recurring to *Phaedo*, we are obliged to distinguish, say, the largeness in someone from the Form of Largeness.[58] This entails a distinction between a Form of Largeness and largeness or the nature of largeness. The nature of largeness is paradigmatically in the Form and derivatively in all large things owing to participation. Given this basic distinction, Plato can consistently recognize a plethora of cognitive relations to various derivative versions of a Form's nature without conflating these with knowledge of a Form or without suggesting that these are relations *to* a Form. For example, when a mathematician reasons about triangularity with the help of 'images' or drawn figures, he is really thinking about 'triangularity itself' (510 D 7–8).[59] It is no part of Plato's theory to maintain that in doing so he is cognizing the Form of Triangularity. And the above distinction explains why. Of course, the dialectician, like the mathematician, will maintain that if triangularity is something, then triangularity exists; indeed, he will claim that there must be a Form of Triangularity. But this is an argument that non-dialecticians do not endorse.[60] These non-

---

[57] See Brentlinger (1963), 156–9, who sets forth what he describes as 'the really appalling amount of evidence against the theory that in the *Republic* Plato held that the proper object of the dianoetic sciences were ideas'.

[58] See 102 D 6–7. Cf. *Parm.* 132 A. Aristotle, *Top. E* 7, 137[b]3–13, makes the relevant distinction, though he denies that it is available to Plato for use in defeating objections to his theory.

[59] Cf. 511 A 1, αὐτὰ ἐκεῖνα. The use of the '*x* itself' language recalls especially *Phaedo* 74 C 1–5, αὐτὰ τὰ ἴσα. Recall as well the two 'knowledges' in the Recollection Argument. The knowledge obtained from sensibles, namely, that they are deficient examples of Equality, is not identical with the knowledge of the Form of Equality. It is this first type of knowledge that has now been identified as διάνοια.

[60] See 533 A 4–6, where Socrates gets Glaucon to agree that though he (Glaucon) is in no position to follow a discussion of Forms themselves, he must admit that they exist. Plato must have been keenly aware that many of his associates, including no doubt Aristotle, acknowledged that, say, triangularity exists though they denied that a Form

dialecticians, whether they be mathematicians or others, in effect think they can be realists about universals without being Platonists.

The existence of a mode of cognition like διάνοια is obviously indispensable to Plato given the great gulf between ἐπιστήμη and δόξα. It is a mode of cognition not in principle limited to mathematical objects. But it is wedded to images.[61] For the philosopher who recognizes the images for what they are, διάνοια is what the interlocutors in *Phaedo* had when they recognized that sensible equals were deficiently equal. They recognize that the Form exists, and are led to conclude that they had knowledge of it prior to being embodied, but they do not now have that knowledge. So, διάνοια is not an alternative mode of cognition of Forms, a sort of low-grade ἐπιστήμη. Its scope is as broad as the class of universal propositions. By contrast, ἐπιστήμη is very narrow in scope, especially if we accept the above interpretation of the role of the Form of the Good in making it possible.

All types of cognition other than knowledge are representational for Plato. That is why they all involve images. Among these images are the λόγοι used to represent Forms. Even if knowledge is necessary for 'being able to give a λόγος of each thing', the knowledge is not that λόγος (534 B 2–3). Knowledge stands apart from the other modes of cognition owing to its infallibility. I take it that infallibility entails and is entailed by the non-representational nature of knowledge. If knowledge is non-representational, it is non-propositional, because all propositions are representations. Philosophers are distinguishable from those who are unaware that, cognitively, they swim in a sea of images. But philosophers, at least in so far as they trade in λόγος, are also tied to images. They differ from everyone else in being aware of this. Because they are aware of this, they are best placed to practise the artful and beneficent manipulation of images.

The allegory of the cave (514 A–517 B), which immediately follows the divided-line analogy, seems to support the view that διάνοια has a distinct type of object. Plato explicitly tells us (517 B) that the allegory is to be

of Triangularity exists. Euclid, for example, regularly uses the locution 'the *x* itself' in referring to geometrical elements. I would disagree, therefore, with Karasmanis (1988), 156, who argues that there are no mathematical objects in the divided line because mathematicians have Forms as objects.

[61] See Cooper (1966), who identifies the objects of διάνοια generally with images of Forms.

compared to what has been said already, that is, at least to the divided line.[62] Life in the cave is taken up with the observation of images of the artefacts being paraded behind the fettered cave-dwellers. The cave is like the world of δόξα. The images on the cave wall are like the objects of εἰκασία, whereas the artefacts themselves are like the objects of πίστις. Outside the cave is like the intelligible world. There natural entities are likened to Forms and their images are likened to images of Forms. The sun once again stands for the Form of the Good. Later, in the discussion of education, Plato will again refer to these images of natural entities (532 C 1–2), this time calling them 'divine' (θεῖα). He leaves no doubt that these images are analogous to the objects of διάνοια (533 A 1–12), as he recalls the mathematical sciences and their use of hypotheses (533 B–C) and how these differ from dialectic. That mathematicals can be grasped *only* by διάνοια is stressed at 526 A 6–7. These mathematicals here include 'units' that are specifically identical but numerically multitudinous (529 C 7–D 6).

Against the interpretation that the images of the objects seen outside the cave correspond to distinct objects of διάνοια is the fact that in the line analogy the objects of πίστις include both natural entities and artefacts (510 A 5–6). What the cave allegory has actually done is to divide this class into two, placing the images of the first outside the cave and the second inside.[63] Strictly speaking, if the cave follows the line, we should resist dividing the class of objects of πίστις into the two different groups of objects required by the positing of separate objects for διάνοια. The shadows and reflections of the natural entities and the artefacts are two different sorts of sensible images of Forms.[64] That the artefacts in the cave are in fact images of images, that is, the natural entities, does not seem adequate grounds for

---

[62] The words ταύτην . . . τὴν εἰκόνα . . . προσαπτέον ἅπασαν τοῖς ἔμπροσθεν λεγομένοις are imprecise. But a comparison of 532 B–C with 534 A–B makes it evident that at least the cave and the line are being rather strictly compared.

[63] See Strang (1986) and Pritchard (1995), 101–3.

[64] If we anticipate 596 B–C, we find the distinction between the Form of Bed, the bed made by the carpenter, and the picture of the carpenter's bed made by the artist. The first is 'made by god' and the latter two are images of it, at one remove and at two removes. The status of natural entities is unmentioned here, but it is not too difficult to fit them into the picture. The artefacts in the cave are explicitly said to be images of natural entities, which are themselves, of course, images of Forms, as the line indicates. Wilson (1976) argues that the images are in fact visible images of moral qualities which are themselves images of moral Forms. Thus, the prisoners are habituated in judging morality by the inferior

equating the latter with mathematical entities. He who possesses διάνοια has the capacity to distinguish among sensibles different types of images.[65] If the natural entities of the cave allegory are analogous to Forms, then their images are properly contrasted with the artefacts in the cave in that the former are understood (by those who have escaped) to be images and the latter are not (by those chained in the cave). The shadows of the natural entities are divine because the gods are the makers of the former.[66]

Having explicitly connected the cave with the line and the sun analogy (517 B), Socrates turns to a discussion of how to produce human beings who will leave and then return to the cave to govern once they have experienced true reality. He is talking about nothing less than a 'psychic conversion experience' (περιαγωγή, 521 C 5–8).[67] The instruments of this conversion are the mathematical sciences, beginning with arithmetic (522 C 5 ff.).[68] Why are these especially apt for 'leading the soul upwards', as Plato says (525 D 5)? Because they compel one to focus on intelligible reality rather than the realm of becoming or sensible images. There is more to it than this, I think. One wants to know why the mathematical sciences have this power to produce a reorientation of one's soul, not just a temporary diversion of the focus of attention. Surely, it is because the soul is by nature akin to intelligible reality. The underlying argument, drawing on *Lysis*, *Symposium*, and *Phaedo*, is something like this: all things desire their own good; what is something's own good is what is akin to it; what is akin to the soul is intelligible reality; so, the soul, when led to experience intelligible reality, is naturally drawn to it. The mathematical 'ascent' of the soul is the process of self-recognition or identification.

images of behaviour. This is a plausible and fruitful interpretation, and is supported by the distinction between inferior or 'popular' virtue and philosophical virtue.

[65] Strang (1986), 29, argues that one can thus have beliefs about Forms via their images. I think this violates the requirement that belief requires reference. On the contrary, cognition of images of Forms does not require reference to Forms because it can occur without awareness that the images *are* images. And even if one is so aware, one is not thereby referring to Forms.

[66] See *Soph.* 266 C for the explicit identification of images as 'divine' for this reason.

[67] Cf. 518 D 4, E 4, 533 D 3. A similar idea is expressed with the word μεταστρεπτικῶν at 525 A 1.

[68] The 'mathematical sciences' here are clearly distinguished from the use of mathematics for practical or applied purposes (525 B–C). See Miller (1999) for a careful study of this passage.

Those who have undergone or are in the process of undergoing mathematical training are likened to those who have escaped from the cave and can now gaze upon images of natural entities (532 C). Only those who have been practised in dialectic are able to see the natural entities themselves. Whereas the students of mathematics merely lay down hypotheses, dialecticians aim to give an account of what is hypothesized (533 C 1–3). This account evidently goes beyond both an existential hypothesis and the sort of nominal definition that must go with a hypothesis if it is to be a part of any mathematical demonstration. In addition, dialecticians eliminate (ἀναιροῦσα) these hypotheses and ascend to the first principle (533 C 8).[69] It is in virtue of reaching this first principle that the dialectician has genuine knowledge. Thus, only the highest part of the divided line, that which has Forms as objects, deserves to be called ἐπιστήμη (533 D 4–7). As for the line in general, as being is to becoming, so is νόησις, now used of both sections of the upper part of the line, to δόξα (534 A 2–5).[70]

Whatever the exact nature of dialectic is, the relationship between dialectic as described at 531 D–535 A and knowledge is not as unproblematic as it is generally made out to be in the literature.[71] For one thing, the practice of dialectic in itself does not guarantee any sort of success (cf. 537 E). In particular, engaging in it does not guarantee knowledge. For another, re-

---

[69] The idea here is obscure. See esp. Robinson (1953), 160–2, who thinks that 'eliminating the hypotheses' means moving from an attitude of tentativeness to certainty with regard to them. This does not seem very plausible to me, particularly since the text does not say 'eliminate the hypotheses as mere hypotheses in order to make them something else for us'. I would suggest that, in the light of the discussion of the Form of the Good, the unhypothetical first principle, 'eliminating the hypotheses' means that the hypothesis of an individual, isolated Form as a starting point in explanation, as is posited in *Phaedo*, for example, is what is being eliminated.

[70] Here νόησις is used of the two sections of the top half of the line, whereas in 511 D–E it was used only of the first section. So, whereas the notion of ἐπιστήμη has been refined to refer only to the top section, the notion of νόησις has been broadened to refer to both. I take it that the reason for this shift is in part that the basic distinction is between that which is sensible and that which is intelligible. See for a similar explanation Jäger (1967), 89.

[71] Annas (1981), 282–3, seems to identify dialectic and knowledge and to equate both with the ability to give an account. For this reason, she seems to view knowledge as propositional. Robinson (1953), 157, claims that 'Plato is not nearly so ready to assert . . . that dialectic or right manipulation of hypotheses *is* knowledge. Although that is here the obvious and inevitable tendency of his thought.' Robinson, too, views this knowledge as propositional.

gardless of how we characterize dialectic, it is, unlike knowledge, a method, not a state.[72] This method is practised by the future philosopher-guardians for at least five years prior to their practical apprenticeship in the state, which lasts all of fifteen years (539 D–540 A). Only at the age of 50 do these dialecticians attain a vision of the Form of the Good. But a vision of this Form seems to be required in order to turn the 'hypotheses' into objects of genuine knowledge.[73] Thus, not only is the scope of knowledge strictly limited as compared with διάνοια, but the actual period of time in one's life in which it could be present is alarmingly small. It is simply false to insist that anyone who practises dialectic—even the most rigorous and pure type of it—is thereby either engaged in knowing Forms or guaranteed to attain knowledge of them at some time in the future.[74]

We can discern three distinct steps in the refinement of the notion of ἐπιστήμη prior to as well as in *Republic*: (1) knowledge is true belief tied down with an account (*Meno*); (2) knowledge and belief are mutually exclusive; (3) knowledge is distinct from a lower type of cognition of intelligibles, namely, διάνοια. The explicit refinement in the notion of ἐπιστήμη is inspired by the interposition of the passage on the Form of the Good between (2) and (3).[75] If the Form of the Good is virtually all of the Forms, then all of the Forms are virtually one. Knowledge of any one of them would imply knowledge of all.[76] If this is so, then such comprehensive knowledge would seem to be rather hard to come by. One might improve one's chances in this regard if one had available a sort of ontological heuristic, that is, a device for

---

[72] At 539 D 8–10 the one engaged in dialectic is said to be engaged in a kind of intellectual, as opposed to physical, 'exercise' (γυμναζομένῳ). It is quite implausible that Plato should identify the highest state attainable by a person—namely, knowledge—with exercise. The latter is always instrumental. In this regard, one might compare *Parm.* 135 C 8–D 1, where Parmenides tells the young Socrates that he has mistakenly tried to define Forms prior to just such an intellectual exercise.   [73] See Robinson (1953), 153.

[74] The assumption that knowledge is to be identified with an account or the ability to give an account is perhaps what leads some scholars to hold that knowledge is constitutive of the dialectical process.

[75] Miller (1999), 83–4, provocatively argues that the five propaedeutic mathematical sciences lead up to the study of Forms as expressed in and as ratios. I do not see why, if this is so, ἐπιστήμη would need to be distinguished from διάνοια, the mode of cognition used by the mathematical sciences.

[76] At 537 C 7 the person dialectical by nature is said to have the 'power to see things as a unity' (συνοπτικός).

reducing the scope of the task: for example, if all the Forms were reducible to Forms of Numbers and these were reducible to their principles, such as a One and an Indefinite Dyad. I do not wish to argue here that this is what Plato actually did, although we must recognize that the Platonic tradition beginning with Aristotle unquestionably testifies to Academic discussions along these lines.

The claim that δόξα is to νόησις as γένεσις is to οὐσία is usually taken as an inconsequential reiteration of the divided-line analogy. One wants to understand, however, what exactly is the point of the comparison here. We should start with what Plato says elsewhere in *Republic* about the relation of the sensible world to the world of Forms. As we saw at the beginning of the chapter, the sensible world is neither being nor nothing but midway between the two. It is also the world of images of Forms (cf. 520 C 4–5; 534 C 5). If becoming is an image of being, and δόξα stands to νόησις analogously, then the cognitive state or states on the lower half of the line stand to the higher analogously to the way images stand to their originals.[77] The state of belief is itself a sort of image of the state of one who has νόησις. The ascent from the cave or from the sensible world to the intelligible world begins with the recognition that what were models are really images, including one's own cognitive states. As with the lovers of sights and sounds, one's life is a dream state because one thinks that a likeness is not a likeness but the reality which it in fact resembles (476 C 4–7).

Mathematical sciences are crucial to the awakening or conversion. They lead the soul to the study of reality and truth (525 A–B). Specifically, they seem to be crucial for the philosopher 'who is to rise up out of becoming by seizing hold of being, or else he will never become rational [μηδέποτε λογιστικῷ γενέσθαι, 525 B 6]'. These odd words are often translated as if they meant that the philosopher is to become good at calculation, as we might say that someone has become 'numerate'. But that is not the goal of mathematical studies in Plato's curriculum. One is supposed to achieve a sort of personal development. These words recall the exhortation to 'become one out of many' (443 E 1). It is by 'seizing hold of being' that one identifies oneself with τὸ λογιστικόν, the rational part of the soul. By associating with the invisible, one identifies with that (cf. 529 B). This association encourages

---

[77] At 479 D 3–6, for example, the νόμιμα of the many are said to stand between being and not-being.

one to a rehabilitation from the idiosyncratic and imagistic. Beliefs that are images though their holders are unaware that they are so tie one to the sensible world and to the parts of the soul that do not belong to the ideal person. To be content with the images of the really real or worse, to mistake them for what they are images of, is to live the life of a false self.

Even the philosopher has beliefs about the sensible world, though for the successful philosopher returning to the cave these are certainly going to be preponderantly true beliefs.[78] The philosopher's legitimacy as a ruler depends on the fact that, having had a vision of the Form of the Good, that is, knowledge of the Forms, he can be expected to mould the state according to these true beliefs. He can put his knowledge into practice. The question of whether we are to take literally the implication that embodied knowledge is thus possible depends entirely on how we answer the question about the possibility of the ideal state. Naturally, this is a large and portentous question. But there is at least some reason to believe that Plato does not feel he is in a position to claim that his ideal state is actually possible.[79] If it is not, then the promise of dialectic is at least open-ended if not vain, for there is no guarantee that its practitioners will attain the knowledge that would legitimize them as philosopher-rulers. Even if we grant that such knowledge is possible, there is no basis here for finding access to the Forms

[78] Many scholars have puzzled over why the philosopher, having had a vision of the Form of the Good, would have to be compelled to return to the cave to rule over the members of his community. See the entire passage 519 C 8–521 B 10 that develops the remarks at 499 B 5 and 500 D 4. See Gill (1996), 287–307, for a full discussion of the problem as viewed by contemporary scholars. Gill concludes by acknowledging what he terms a 'tension' and a 'motivational gap' evident in Plato between his claim that knowledge of the Good is the highest value and his claim that the philosopher must be compelled to carry out the duty incumbent on philosophers to enter into practical politics. The tension is presumably that if the philosopher does indeed know the Good, then he should *want* to assume the burden of rule since he is alone capable of bearing it successfully. According to my interpretation, even if we stipulate that the philosopher has succeeded in acquiring the highest knowledge, his embodied status guarantees that he will not be a perfectly objective reasoner or perfectly identical with a subject of contemplation. That is, he will retain a residual attachment to his own personal well-being. That well-being he now identifies with contemplation. And that is why he must be compelled to return to the cave. But the compulsion is not physical; he is compelled by the force of reason to do what is just. We could equally say that he compels himself.

[79] See esp. 472 D–E, where Socrates concedes that he cannot prove that the picture of the ideal state he is painting can possibly be realized.

independently of cognition of the superordinate Form of the Good, that is, independently of a comprehensive and synoptic vision of Forms.

This lengthy chapter on knowledge in *Republic* is intended primarily to provide support for a relatively straightforward claim, namely, that for Plato the ideal for a person is to be in a state of knowledge. At a general level, Aristotle's claim that knowledge of eternal truth is what the immortal gods enjoy and what we enjoy intermittently is not essentially different.[80] But Plato believes that we are souls and that we are immortal. Even if he does believe that we can enjoy this knowledge while embodied—and I have argued that there is scant evidence for this—we have a much bigger stake in knowledge because we are immortal. Our intimate connection with Forms characterizes our lives prior to embodiment as well as our post-mortem destiny. That intimate connection is the self-reflexive awareness of our own cognitive state. That cognitive state comprises an identification of the knower with what is known. Since, for Plato, what is knowable is immaterial and eternal, that identification does not preclude a multitude of knowers. Knowledge is an infallible state because the awareness of the presence of that state itself guarantees that presence—that is, the identity of the knower with the known. And so knowledge is not, ideally, merely the central focus of persons' lives or characteristic of the best life. It is quite literally constitutive of what we are.

Just as types of cognition other than knowledge are images of it, so embodied cognizers are themselves images of their ideal. All embodied cognition, as well as its linguistic expression, is representational. Just as Forms ultimately account for the intelligibility of their images in the sensible world, so knowledge of Forms accounts for its cognitive images. The self-reflexive awareness of one's own belief states reflects the paradigm of self-reflexivity in knowing. Thus, the fact that one is aware of what one occurrently believes does not guarantee the truth of that belief. But if embodied persons were not the sorts of creatures who could be knowers, they could not be themselves genuine images of knowers. In that case, they could not have beliefs. Nor could they identify themselves as subjects of appetites. The endowment of embodied personhood is a conflicted one. That endowment, however, also includes the possibility of the achievement of an ideal state.

[80] See *Metaph.* Λ 7, 1072^{b}14–15.

CHAPTER 5

Theaetetus:
What is Knowledge?

5.1 Interpreting *Theaetetus*

If for Plato persons are ideally disembodied knowers, then his account of knowledge is obviously of the utmost importance for this study. Discovering the nature of knowledge is the key to discovering the deficiencies of other types of cognition. In addition, it should open a further window onto some of the deficiencies of embodied persons, who, even if bereft of knowledge, are primarily cognizers.

The central thesis of this chapter is that *Theaetetus* reinforces the account of knowledge in *Republic*. *Theaetetus* does this despite the nominal ἀπορία at the end of the dialogue. This view seems increasingly to be out of favour, for it has recently been argued, most forcefully by Myles Burnyeat, that *Theaetetus* rejects the discontinuity of ἐπιστήμη and δόξα, strongly implying, on the contrary, that ἐπιστήμη of the sensible world is possible. If this is so, then presumably there can be ἐπιστήμη and δόξα of the same objects. And if this is so, then there would seem to be nothing in principle against there being δόξα of the Forms or knowledge of sensibles. Accordingly, the criteria for knowledge, which, as I argued, entail that there is knowledge only of immaterial entities, would have to be revised. Indeed, it has also been held that Plato's willingness in *Theaetetus* to countenance the possibility of knowledge of sensibles is a result of his disenchantment with the Forms as knowable or even as the really real existents they are claimed to be in

Republic. If Burnyeat and others are correct, *Theaetetus*, generally considered to post-date *Republic*, stands as a major impediment to treating the doctrine of *Republic* as a guide to the thinking of the later dialogues.[1] In addition, if Plato himself came to see the error of his ways in *Theaetetus*, who would dare gainsay this revelation? That is, there would seem to be little prospect for a view that Plato himself came to jettison.

If, as I have argued, Plato's concept of personhood is inextricably bound up with his concept of knowledge, it is obviously essential for us to consider carefully the question whether the extreme things that are said in *Republic* are contradicted or even qualified in any way in *Theaetetus*. If Burnyeat and others are right, then the connection between ideal personhood and knowledge is not nearly so tight as it earlier seemed to be. In that case, knowledge would seem to be something that we may strive for or attain but not something that is constitutive of what we are. Indeed, I do not think it is excessive to insist that on the view that I shall oppose in this chapter, more than just Plato's epistemology is implicitly revised. Since his epistemology is organically related to his metaphysics and psychology, a Plato who now claims that there can be knowledge of the sensible world should probably be differently designated, say, as 'Plato' or 'Plato$_2$'. Many will, of course, be happy to maintain that this is all to the good. Be that as it may, we should look carefully at the revisionist's evidence.

Theaetetus raises the question 'What is ἐπιστήμη?' (cf. 146 E 9–10).[2] After an abortive attempt to define knowledge by listing instances or cases of it (145 C–148 E), three definitions are offered: it is 'sense-perception' (αἴσθησις, 151 D–186 E), 'true belief' (ἀληθὴς δόξα, 187 A–201 C), and true belief with an 'account' (λόγος, 201 C–210 A). All of these are found to be faulty, leading the dialogue into a concluding ἀπορία. It is notoriously difficult to draw

---

[1] See Bostock (1988), 1–31, 146–55, for an argument that *Theaetetus* revises the epistemological account of *Republic* and that therefore, among other things, *Timaeus*, which basically endorses that account, must be dated earlier than *Theaetetus*. Bostock, like Burnyeat, believes that *Theaetetus* assumes that knowledge of the sensible world is possible.

[2] That the theme of the dialogue is posed by means of the traditional 'What is *x*?' type of question does not in itself, of course, indicate that Plato understands that question as he did, for example, in *Euthyphro*. In addition, even if Plato continues to suppose that the objects of knowledge are what he supposed them to be in *Republic* and elsewhere, it does not follow that he supposed knowledge to be what he did there.

positive conclusions from one of Plato's aporetic dialogues, particularly one which actually follows those dialogues of the middle period that are filled with assertoric statements. For example, it is much more tempting to suppose the doctrines of *Republic* in reading *Theaetetus* than it is in reading the *Euthyphro*. On the other hand, just as Plato was perfectly capable of rejecting what was said in one dialogue (say, *Protagoras*) in another dialogue (say, *Republic*), so it is certainly possible that he should abandon or seriously qualify what he says in *Republic* when he comes to write *Theaetetus*.

Those who would urge that the aporetic character of *Theaetetus* portends a new start by Plato, one in which nothing about Forms should be assumed, reasonably enough point to *Parmenides*, which was almost certainly written close enough in time to *Theaetetus* to be taken as relevant to that dialogue. *Parmenides* submits the theory of separate Forms to an explicit critical analysis, something that Plato never does to what are frequently taken to be Socratic doctrines. The view of Burnyeat and others regarding *Theaetetus* garners at least some of its plausibility from the possibility that that critical analysis actually introduces a new phase of Plato's thinking. In this putative new phase Plato either rejects separate Forms or rejects them as the exclusive focus of his account of knowledge.

Regarding *Parmenides*, it will be justly said in reply that when Parmenides ends his criticism of the theory of Forms he adds that unless it is admitted that these Forms exist, there will be nothing on which 'thought' (διάνοια) can fix and all dialectic will be impossible (135 B–C).[3] It seems that if *Parmenides* is to be used as relevant background to *Theaetetus*, then such a passage cannot be excluded. But including it as background requires some care, for *Parmenides* does not say that knowledge is of Forms. He merely claims that if Forms are not postulated as the 'ones' over and above any genuine 'many',

---

[3] The phrase τὴν τοῦ διαλέγεσθαι δύναμιν (135 C 2) is certainly used elsewhere by Plato to refer to the technical method of dialectic; see *Rep.* 511 B 4. Charles Kahn has suggested to me in conversation that the *Parmenides* passage should be read in this narrow sense. But διαλέγεσθαι is also used for 'conversation' in general. Even διαλεκτική is used in this way as well; see *Rep.* 454 A–B. The latter passage seems more relevant to *Parmenides* than the former because in the latter it is argued that without properly dividing Forms, those who discuss such matters as the best way of life for different people will be arguing and not 'conversing'. In the *Parmenides* passage it is *of course* true that if Forms do not exist, dialectic in the technical sense will be impossible. It seems more to the point to claim that if Forms do not exist, then all serious conversation will cease because there will be no objective basis for the samenesses and differences upon which all language depends.

then thought and dialectic will be destroyed. I take it that what this means minimally is that we must assume that when we intelligibly call many things by the same 'name'—say, 'just' or 'beautiful' or 'tall'—we could not do so without postulating Forms. But even if this is true, it does not follow that there cannot be knowledge of things *other* than Forms, or, indeed, that there can be knowledge of the Forms themselves. So, Parmenides' resounding endorsement of Forms even despite his criticisms is not evidence that Plato is committed to an epistemology that rests upon Forms in the *Theaetetus*. Accordingly, I am not going to argue that the discussion in *Theaetetus* assumes that Forms are the objects of knowledge.[4]

A more puzzling and important preliminary issue is this. In the course of the definition of knowledge as sense-perception, Socrates gets Theaetetus to admit that if sense-perception is knowledge, αἴσθησις ἄρα τοῦ ὄντος ἀεί ἐστιν καὶ ἀψευδὲς ὡς ἐπιστήμη οὖσα (152 C 5–6). The way this line is usually understood is 'Sense-perception is then always of what is and, being knowledge, it is unerring.' This makes the most sense in the context of the discussion, although we could conceivably take ἀεί with τοῦ ὄντος, in which case Socrates would be making a claim that would or should end the dialogue right there. For neither sense-perception nor belief, in so far as belief includes sensibles as objects, could be knowledge, since in neither case are their objects those things that 'are always'.[5] So, it appears that Socrates is claiming that sense-perception is always of what is, not of what is always.

But 'what is' is ambiguous. The most natural way to take the phrase is as 'what is real', as opposed to what is not. For Plato, however, 'real' is not an unproblematic term. On the one hand, we might conjecture that 'real' is to be distinguished from 'that which is really real' (τὸ ὄντως ὄν), where the latter refers narrowly to Forms or the intelligible world and the former

[4] All the same, it is hard to read the references at 174 B and 175 C in the 'digression' on philosophy as pertaining to anything but Forms. If, as this passage seems to suggest, philosophers aim for knowledge of Forms, at least the option that knowledge is *not* of Forms is excluded. See Cornford (1934), 81–3, for the argument that Forms are 'hinted at' in this passage as the objects of knowledge. Cornford is one of the principal and most influential exponents of Burnyeat's Reading A. Reading B, tentatively preferred by Burnyeat, hypothesizes that in *Theaetetus* Plato is exploring the nature of knowledge on the assumption that knowledge of the sensible world is in some way a possibility.

[5] At *Tim.* 27 D 6, for instance, we find τί τὸ ὂν ἀεί referring to Forms.

refers more broadly to everything else this side of nothing.[6] This conjecture is in line with the view that Plato is extending the meaning of 'knowable' to include the sensible world. On the other hand, as we saw in the chapter on knowledge and belief in *Republic*, the object of knowledge is identified as 'that which is' (τῷ ὄντι, 477 B 9–10, 478 C 3–4) and the object of belief as 'that which is and is not at the same time' (ἅμα ὄν τε καὶ μὴ ὄν, 478 D 5–6), and this would suggest that 'what is' or 'what is real' in *Theaetetus* is limited to the intelligible world.[7] Consequently, we shall have to examine with care what the ensuing arguments tell us about what the objects of knowledge must be like.

Another ambiguity in this passage is whether one or two conditions for knowledge are being asserted: is it just that knowledge is unerring, as was claimed in *Republic* 477 E 6–7, or is it also the case that knowledge is always of what is?[8] Is the first part of 152 C 5–6 referring only to sense-perception or is the entire line about knowledge? Grammatically, the former is perhaps easier, but the sense of the passage suggests the latter. Socrates has just got Theaetetus to agree that Protagoras' view is that things are as they are perceived to be. And the identification of knowledge as sense-perception will ultimately be defeated by showing that in fact sense-perception is not of what is (186 A–E).[9] We recall that *Republic* says that knowledge is of 'what is' (477 A 9–B 1, 9–10, 478 C 3–4). So, it seems fair to say that having 'what is' as an object is taken to be as much a necessary condition for knowledge as that it be unerring. Let us call these the reality criterion and the inerrancy criterion.[10]

---

[6] Cf. *Tim.* 52 C 5–6; *Soph.* 240 A 3.

[7] It is true that Plato also says in the *Republic* passage that 'what is completely [παντελῶς] is completely knowable' (477 A 2–4), which might suggest that something that is, though not completely so, might be (incompletely?) knowable. In the present chapter I am arguing that Plato firmly rejects this possibility.

[8] The *Republic* passage, it will be recalled, has ἀναμάρτητον, not ἀψευδές. I discuss below the reasons for the shift.

[9] In this passage the word οὐσία is used instead of τὸ ὄν. But at 160 C 5–6 sense-perception is said to be 'true for me' because it is of 'my οὐσία', clearly harking back to 152 C 5–6.

[10] Burnyeat (1990), 238, says, 'We could well read the *Theaetetus* as a long meditation on that brief passage of the *Republic* (477 D–E). The *Theaetetus* is the work in which Plato explores the difficulties of accommodating together, on the one hand, the idea that knowledge is unerring, on the other, the idea that a capacity which is not unerring and

If these conditions are sufficient as well as necessary, then it would hardly seem to require any further effort to discover the definition of knowledge. But it seems that they are not sufficient. To say that knowledge is of what is and that it is unerring does not seem to tell us what knowledge itself is. Whether the reality criterion refers exclusively to Forms or whether, as in the interpretation of Burnyeat and others, it includes sensibles, a definition of what knowledge is certainly seems to require more. Even if we supply, once again from *Republic*, the statement that 'knowledge is a power' (477 D 7–8), we would then have 'an unerring power (relating to) what is' or perhaps 'a power (relating to) what is that when used is unerring'. I shall argue that, contrary to appearances, the two necessary conditions laid down in *Theaetetus* at 152 c 5–6 are jointly sufficient and that only if one stands unerringly in relation to what is does one know.[11]

Further, one cannot cognize 'what is', suitably defined, without cognizing it unerringly.[12] That is, there is no type of cognition of what is other than

allows mistakes must nevertheless contain a partial grasp of the truth.' I would demur at this excellent statement only in that 'partial grasp of the truth' is a misleading way to characterize what δόξα does. Rather, δόξα attains an image of the truth.

[11] McDowell (1973), 120–1, reads the line differently. He takes 'what is' to be incomplete. The words need to be completed by something like 'the way one perceives it as being' so that what is being claimed is that 'what one perceives always is the one way one perceives it as being'. That is, if one perceives something as being *f*, then it is *f*. He also claims that the word ἀψευδής adds nothing to the claim that perception is veridical. McDowell seems to me to mistake the ὡς clause as pertaining only to the latter claim. If it pertains to both, then it is implausible that the claim that perception is of what is should be read as McDowell does because, as the passages from *Republic* cited above show, the criterion that claimants to knowledge must meet is that the cognition must be of what is. Further, as a criterion of knowledge ἀψευδής cannot simply mean 'veridical', as the argument that true belief cannot be knowledge will show. However, I think McDowell is, as it were, accidentally correct, since the criteria here are offered loosely, according to dialectical exigency.

[12] At *Soph*. 249 D 3–4 the outcome of the dialectical examination of the gods and giants is that 'being and the all' (τὸ ὄν τε καὶ τὸ πᾶν) include both 'such things that are immutable and such things that are in motion' (ὅσα ἀκίνητα καὶ κεκινημένα). If τὸ ὄν includes both things that move and things that are immutable, then presumably either τὸ ὄν has a broader scope than it does in *Republic*, or it is implied that knowledge has a broader scope. Either alternative would seem to add support to Burnyeat's interpretation of *Theaetetus*. On the other hand, 249 B 12–c 4 seems to imply that knowledge is only of what is immutable. I think the most reasonable way to reconcile all the problematic elements of this passage is to insist that (1) the meaning of τὸ ὄν is here being expanded,

knowledge. Belief does not have 'what is' as its object because there is no infallible belief. As it will turn out, the term ἀψευδής is radically equivocal. In the course of the argument it means variously 'true', 'incorrigible', and 'infallible'. Knowledge must be infallible, whereas sense-perception is incorrigible and true belief is, of course, just true. Only *infallible* cognition is cognition of 'what is'. Thus, the two criteria—reality and inerrancy in the sense of infallibility—are logically inseparable. And that is just what we should expect for defining criteria of the non-arbitrary. Finally, the dialogue is intended to support these claims with a series of *reductio* proofs, the only non-question-begging way of proving a definition. In short, *Theaetetus* is an extensive defence of the bold claim made in *Republic* that ἐπιστήμη and δόξα are radically discontinuous.

5.2 Knowledge is Not Sense-Perception

The first and longest part of the dialogue examines Theaetetus' claim that ἐπιστήμη is nothing but αἴσθησις. The section ends with the conclusion that this claim is false. Little else in the section has been found to be beyond dispute. The central interpretative issue is this. Is the rejection of the definition of knowledge as nothing but sense-perception meant to suggest that knowledge is not at all of sensibles or just that knowledge is not to be equated with sense-perception, even though there might be knowledge of that which is available to us only by means of sense-perception? Clearly, the latter interpretation is in a way more circumspect than the former, and assuming that the text is not decisive either way, ought to be preferred for that reason. In fact, I think the dialectical path of the dialogue demands this interpretation. For the second definition—that true belief is knowledge—rests upon the ruins of the first. That is, it assumes that if knowledge is not sense-perception, then perhaps it can be derived from sense-perception. If this dialectical path is correct for the definition of knowledge as true belief, then it is probably also correct for the definition of knowledge as true belief plus an account. So, the coherence of the examination of the three

but that this does not require the expansion of the scope of ἐπιστήμη; (2) *Theaetetus* is dialectically exploring the requirements of such a new meaning on the assumption that the two criteria are inseparable; (3) in order to retain their inseparability, one must come to recognize that knowledge is only of τὸ ὄν in a limited sense—that is, knowledge is only of what is immutable.

definitions of knowledge depends on holding that the second builds on the first and the third builds on the second. By 'builds on' I mean 'remedies the defects of' while retaining the presumed element of truth.

The main source of contention is the uncertainty regarding whether the refutation of the definition of knowledge as sense-perception implies that it is impossible to have knowledge of sensibles or not. And the answer to this question depends upon determining how seriously Plato means to take the argument that leads to this conclusion. The answer to *this* question is complicated by the fact that whereas Plato conflates Theaetetus' definition first with Protagorean relativism (151 E–152 C) and then with Heraclitean flux theory (152 C–152 D), the actual argument that shows that knowledge is not sense-perception (184 B–186 E) does not seem to depend on this conflation.

It seems to me that a fairly plausible answer to this last question can be obtained directly from the text alone. The conflation is of Theaetetus' definition of sense-perception as knowledge with Protagorean relativism. The account of Protagorean relativism is not offered independently of the claim that sense-perception is knowledge. In other words, one who holds that knowledge is sense-perception is, according to Plato, taking a Protagorean approach because Protagoras believed that knowledge is sense-perception. To say this is to make no claim whatsoever about the true nature of sense-perception, although Plato might in fact have endorsed a Protagorean account. A similar point may be made about the conflation of Protagorean relativism with Heraclitean flux theory. Heraclitus' theory is represented as Protagoras' 'secret doctrine' (152 C 8–10). This transparent fiction refers evidently to the 'account regarding knowledge' that Socrates says was Protagoras' (151 E 8–152 A 2). So, we are still within the scope of an identification of sense-perception with knowledge, not an independent account of sense-perception. Accordingly, the refutation of the identification of sense-perception with knowledge commits Plato not at all to any particular account of the former. But it does tell us quite a bit about the nature of knowledge.[13]

---

[13] McCabe (1994), 270–87, argues perceptively that the refutation of Protagoras' relativism also tells us quite a bit about Plato's concept of a person. She writes that 'the *Theaetetus* allows [Plato] to confront four different questions that arise about the unity of persons. The first is about the *persistence* of persons over time . . . the second, Cartesian

If we look closely at the ways that the definition of knowledge as sense-perception fails, we can deduce quite a bit about the relation between the criteria that the true definition would have to meet. We have already seen that knowledge must be of what is and that it must be unerring. It is implausible that such defining criteria should be unrelated, when what is being sought is a real, not a stipulative, definition. Compare the defining criteria for Athenian citizenship. At different times these included, among other criteria, being born in Athens and having one or both parents who were Athenian citizens. There is no logical connection among these, and the precise criteria changed over time. I think that we are entitled to assume that Plato did not regard the search for the defining criteria of knowledge in this way. Nor is he particularly interested in 'the concept' of knowledge. Whose concept, after all, would this be? Rather, he is interested in what the 'thing' knowledge is. And if knowledge is of that which is or is real and is unerring or, as I shall argue, infallible, that is because of the necessary connection between the criteria. My claim is that the dialectical refutation of the three definitions of knowledge aims to show this connection. For there to be knowledge, both criteria must be jointly met.

This, of course, leaves open the possibility that one or the other criterion should be met in a mode of cognition other than knowledge. So, it would seem that we ought to be able to cognize that which is in a manner that is not unerring and we ought to be able to have unerring cognition in regard to what is not or at least in regard to something other than what is. If this is so, then perhaps there is nothing to be said against having, say, beliefs, including false beliefs, of that which is and having unerring cognition or even infallibility in regard to objects that are not. But if this is not so—if it is impossible to cognize that which is other than infallibly and if infallibility is only of that which is—then the failure to meet one criterion will entail the failure to meet the other. A mode of cognition that is not infallible cannot be knowledge and we can conclude that whatever its object, it is not that which is in the requisite sense. Similarly, if the putative object of cognition is not that which is, then there can be no infallibility in regard to it.

question is about the subject and its *first personal perspective* . . . the third concerns the *unity of consciousness* . . . the fourth is about the *autonomy* of the subject in its dealings with the external world' (274).

The central interpretative difficulty in the first section of the dialogue seems to turn upon this point. Everyone agrees that in the conclusion to the first section of the dialogue sense-perception fails to meet the reality criterion in some sense. But if it also necessarily fails to meet the inerrancy criterion, we should not expect to find either criterion met independently by any other putative claimant to knowledge. Those who think that Plato is aiming towards a definition of knowledge that at least includes sensibles as objects will want to hold that cognition of sensibles can meet the reality criterion. Assuming this is correct, how is the inerrancy criterion supposed to be met? It is certainly clear that the way to meet it is not by stipulation, as the refutation of true belief as knowledge shows. When Theaetetus says that true belief is knowledge because it is true, that is, 'without error' (ἀναμάρτητον, 200 E 4), Socrates argues that if this were so, there would be no difference between believing the truth adventitiously or second-hand and knowing.[14] But there is such a difference. So, meeting the criterion must, on the present assumption, involve some sort of 'account'. Since none of the sorts of account proffered in the last section of the dialogue is adequate, it is supposed that some additional sort must be found. Either Plato knows but is not saying or he is genuinely puzzled as to what this might be. In either case, there must be such an account that turns true belief into knowledge, whether the object is a sensible or not. And since Theaetetus manifestly confuses truth with infallibility when he identifies true belief with knowledge, the account must presumably guarantee the latter.

Before returning to the refutation of the definition of knowledge as sense-perception, I should like to say a bit more about this point. It is very difficult to think of how any account of the object of a true belief or of the belief itself will turn that belief into something that is not merely true, but infallible. The simple reason is that if an account is needed to turn true belief into knowledge, then either there is no knowledge of that of which there is no account or else there are at least two kinds of knowledge: the one with an account and the one without. But the latter is wholly implausible, not just because Socrates rejects it in the third part of the dialogue in the refutation

---

[14] Bostock (1988), 147, thinks that the point of the refutation is that an eyewitness to a crime may know who committed it. Cf. Vlastos (1994), 50–1, who correctly notes in this passage the distinction between 'inerrable' and 'inerrant'.

of the 'dream theory', but because accepting it would just throw us right back to the beginning of the dialogue. What I mean is this.

Let there be knowledge of that of which there is no account. On the face of it, this is just what true belief is. But we want infallibility, not just truth. This seems to take us back to sense-perception. But as the first section of the dialogue (151 D–186 E) will show, we cannot both have truth or attain to what is and have infallibility at the same time. In fact, as I want to argue, we cannot have either in regard to the sensible world. It does not seem, then, that there is knowledge without an account from the perspective of this dialogue. But if in order to distinguish knowledge from true belief we need an account, and it turns out that there is no account, there is no knowledge. That is, there is no knowledge that is equivalent to true belief plus an account. This does not mean that there is no knowledge or that knowledge does or does not require an account. It just means that no form of belief is going to be turned into knowledge because no form of belief is going to meet both the reality and the infallibility criteria.

Does sense-perception as explained in section one of the dialogue meet the inerrancy criterion? At 160 D 1–2 Socrates gives a sort of summary of the claim that sense perception is knowledge: 'How if I am unerring [ἀψευδής], and never stumble in my thinking [διανοίᾳ] in regard to the things that are or to the things that become, can I not be a knower in regard to the things of which I am a perceiver?' The alternatives 'the things that are' and 'the things that become' are evidently a reference to 160 B 5–C 2, where Socrates, in explaining the conflation of the theories of Protagoras and Heraclitus, says that we can use 'is' or 'becomes' to characterize the relation of a perceiver to that which is perceived. That is, sense-perception is the result of an interaction between perceiver and perceived at a particular time. What results from this interaction can be said to be or to become for each other. The perceived at the time of perception is or becomes what is perceived by the perceiver, who is or becomes a perceiver in the act of sense-perception. Thus, we should not take 160 D 1–2 as indicating two forms of sense-perception, but rather alternative ways of characterizing the single activity of sense-perception.

Another interesting point about this passage is the casual conflation of sense-perception with thinking. The term διάνοια has not been used before in reference to the theory of sense-perception. Here it seems to be synonymous with the way that the perceiver is characterized in the lines immediately preceding: 'then my sense-perception is true for me—for it is always sense-perception of the being that is mine, and I am judge [κριτής], according to Protagoras, of the things that are that they are for me and of the things that are not that they are not'. One wonders what sort of a sense-perception is the judgement that something that is not is not.[15] If the wind is chilly for me and warm for you, then, on this theory, it is not warm for me. It is easy enough to understand that I can judge it to be not warm for me, but is this equivalent to perceiving something? Surely, I do not perceive it to be chilly and to be not warm in the same sense of 'perceive'. In addition, if I judge that I am not warm because I feel chilly, do I also judge that I am chilly because I feel chilly? And is that judgement, if it occurs, part of the activity of sense-perception or something over and above it?

That a judgement can be of 'the things that are not that they are not for me' suggests that a judgement can be distinguished from the act of sense-perception. Yet we want the judgement(s) to stay within the scope of that which is ἀψευδής, as the text insists. How is that possible? I suggest that the text trades on an ambiguity in the meaning of this term, an ambiguity between 'true' or 'veridical', 'infallible', and 'incorrigible'. A cognitive act is incorrigible if there is no possible way of its being shown to be false. This does not, however, entail that it is true. But that is precisely what infallibility does entail. The conflation of the identification of sense-perception with Protagorean relativism and Heraclitean flux theory ensures that no one else could be in a position to correct my judgements about the 'being that is mine'. Indeed, I myself am not in a position to make such a correction, for on the theory proposed, the one making the correction is different from the one who made the original judgement (cf. 159 E 1–160 A 3). So, the fact that my judgements about my sense-perception are incorrigible does not mean they are infallible provided it can be shown that 'truth' or 'being' do not equal 'true for me' or 'being that is mine'. That is precisely what the ultimate refutation of Theaetetus' definition is intended to do.[16]

[15] At 152 A 3–4 Protagoras himself is quoted as claiming that 'man is the measure of all things, of the things that are that they are and of the things that are not that they are not'. But it is Plato who conflates this claim with a definition of knowledge as sense-perception. So we cannot assume that 'the things that are not' means for Protagoras what Plato is taking it to mean.

[16] Bostock (1988), 110–45, gives an admirably lucid exposition of what he calls the

The refutation consists in showing that while we perceive sensible qualities, we do not perceive 'common terms' (τὰ κοινά) that 'apply to everything'.[17] Among these common terms are 'being' (οὐσία) and 'not-being' (τὸ μὴ εἶναι), 'likeness' and 'unlikeness', 'sameness' and 'difference', 'one' and 'numbers', 'odd' and 'even', and so on (185 C 9–D 4).[18] These are not perceived by us; rather, the soul operating through itself investigates and reaches out to them (185 E 1–2, 186 A 4). For example, the being and number and contrariety of two qualities are 'judged' (κρίνειν) by the soul; they are not perceived (186 B 6–9).[19] To Theaetetus' list of common terms Socrates adds 'beautiful' and 'ugly', 'good' and 'bad'. He then argues: it is not possible to 'attain' (τυχεῖν) truth if one does not attain being; it is not possible to attain knowledge if one does not attain truth (186 C 7–10).[20] Therefore, if one does not attain being, one does not attain knowledge. But attaining being is not equivalent to having a sense-perception. Therefore, sense-perception is not knowledge.

The 'common terms' are cognized by the 'mind through itself' (185 E

'orthodox view' of this refutation and of alternatives to that, including the interpretations of Cooper (1970) and McDowell (1973). Bostock rightly rejects the interpretations of both, opting finally for the orthodox view. Space does not allow me to comment on all of the details of his argument. Suffice it to say that my interpretation is a variant on the orthodox view. Where I differ from Bostock and others will be evident.

[17] This strong claim seems to be in conflict with passages such as *Phaedo* 75 B–C and *Rep.* 523 C, where sense-perception does seem to attain to at least some of these 'common terms'. These passages, however, do not connect the reality criterion and the inerrancy criterion, as does *Theaetetus*. This fact suggests to me that *Theaetetus* does mark a certain advance in Plato's analysis of knowledge.

[18] Cornford (1934), 105–6, is very confident that τὰ κοινά are Forms. I do not think that this is at all clear from the text, and in this I agree with both McDowell (1973), 189–90, and Bostock (1988), 118 ff.

[19] The words at 186 B 6 τὴν δέ γε οὐσίαν καὶ ὅτι ἐστόν are translated by McDowell (1973), 191, as 'but their being and what they both are', thus suggesting that what is wrong with sense-perception is that it does not cognize the essence of the things perceived. This is what judgement will add. But, as Bostock (1988), 139–40, argues, this translation is eccentric and apart from it there is no evidence that what judgement putatively attains to is essence, or essence exclusively. Burnyeat (1990), 59–60, understands οὐσία as corresponding to the 'ordinary, everyday use of "is" '. Thus, what sense-perception is unable to do is grasp propositional truth as in '*p* is the case'. This seems to me anachronistic and an illicit translation from the material into the formal mode.

[20] 'Attaining truth' is a nice compression of the two criteria of knowledge.

1–2), whereas the objects of sense-perception are cognized by the mind through the senses (184 D 2–5). The obvious question is why acts of sense-perception do not attain being even though each act is ἀψευδής. When we have answered this question, we should know why such acts do not attain truth—why, for example, the judgement that this feels hard or hot cannot be true, if indeed that is what attaining truth means. Presumably the refutation of the identification of knowledge as sense-perception is to be taken as retaining the account of sense-perception that has preceded. This is sometimes implicitly denied by scholars who complain that sense-perception does indeed attain to truth about the experiences of the one who senses. In support of this complaint, one might ask what else ἀψευδής can mean. But the theory of sense-perception being scrutinized holds that truth equals 'true for me' and being equals 'being for me'. So, the refutation must show that these are not equivalent. But the only *reason* given for claiming that sense-perception does not attain being is that being is cognized by the 'mind through itself'.

My contention is that the theory under scrutiny tries to fulfil the criteria by substituting 'being for me' for 'being' and by using one possible meaning of ἀψευδής, namely 'incorrigibility', as opposed to 'infallibility'. Moreover, these substitutions amount to the same thing. At 156 E 7–157 C 3, as Socrates explains the theory of sense-perception he is advancing, he asserts that this theory is committed to maintaining that perceptual qualities like hard and hot do 'not have being in itself' (αὐτὸ μὲν καθ᾽ αὑτὸ μηδὲν εἶναι).[21] Rather, they arise only in the perceptual act *relative to each perceiver*. So, at 186 B 2–9, when Socrates is contrasting what the mind attains by itself and what it attains through the senses, he seems committed to the implication that what the mind attains through the senses is not 'being in itself', where this means 'objective' or 'non-relative'. Thus, I interpret τὰ κοινά in contrast to 'private' or 'unique' terms (τὰ ἴδια).[22] That the mind attains universals or common

[21] Cf. 158 A 7, 160 B 8–C 2, 162 D 1, 166 D 4–E 4, 167 C 5.

[22] See Liddell and Scott, s.v. κοινός, for the meaning 'public' or 'objective'. I disagree with Cornford (1934), 106, who asserts that τὰ κοινά are here simply to be identified with Forms. This identification is unnecessary and pre-empts the dialectical force of the argument. Plato does not need to adduce Forms to defeat the view that sense-perception is knowledge. He need only argue that being or objective reality is not attained through the senses. Broadie (1977), 32–3, indirectly supports this interpretation when she argues that Protagoras' relativism is 'a relativism not of truth but of fact'. By this she means

predicates is just an irrelevant point. It is objectivity, not universality, that is germane.[23] If being is attained by the mind itself, then what is attained by sense-perception is not identical with being and one who holds that 'is' and 'is for me' are identical is mistaken.[24]

That the mind attains being by itself is a claim that is neither rhetorical nor hypothetical. It is based on the account of sense-perception which holds that in having a sense-perception I can only claim that I am having the experience I am having. If, for example, someone says, 'it tastes salty to me', the question is, I think, whether or not from 'it tastes salty to me' one may infer that 'it is salty'. The point is simply whether or not the question is an intelligible one, that is, whether or not there is a genuine or ampliative inference to be made. If it is, then one does not attain being by using the senses. If it is not, then that is because 'it is salty' means nothing but 'it tastes salty to me'. In general, one who admits to a distinction between perceptual appearance and reality and who holds to the theory

that there is for Protagoras no ontological distinction between an appearance and that of which it is an appearance. The refutation contradicts this.

[23] This interpretation is given by Kanayama (1987), esp. 51–81, and bears at least some resemblance to that of Crombie (1963), 13–14, 26–7. Bostock (1988), 134–6, raises two objections against Crombie: (1) that on Crombie's view, it is not clear that sense-perception does not attain being or truth; and (2) that τὰ κοινά cannot bear the connotation of objectivity. Rather, they must be 'concepts of a special and rather abstract kind'. In reply to (1), I argue that any interpretation of the passage must show that sense-perception does not attain being and truth; otherwise, the argument is hopeless. Against (2), I claim that the contrast is not, as Bostock holds, between τὰ κοινά and παθήματα but between τὰ κοινά and τὰ ἴδια, as in 166 c 4, where Protagoras refers to the ἴδιαι αἰσθήσεις of his theory. The terms 'being', 'non-being', 'likeness', 'unlikeness', 'sameness', 'difference', 'one', 'numbers', 'odd', 'even', 'beautiful', 'ugly', 'good', 'bad' are all, it is agreed by virtually all interpreters, supposed to be unavailable to the senses. But this is not because they are 'abstract'. They are no more 'abstract' than are 'hardness' and 'hotness', which are available to the mind through the senses. It is owing to the relativity of sense-perception that τὰ κοινά are not available to it. See also Sayre (1969), 62–3, 95–100, for a similar argument.

[24] Frede (1987), 5–8, interprets 'attains being' as being sharply contrasted with the passivity of sense-perception. Thus, the mind attains being because it actively scrutinizes the deliverances of sense-perception in order to arrive at a belief. I agree with Frede that in this argument Plato is showing that the mind attains something that sense-perception alone cannot. But when we put the inerrancy criterion together with the reality criterion, we see that belief, including true belief, does not attain being in the relevant sense because belief is not infallible.

of sense-perception developed earlier in the dialogue cannot maintain that sense-perception attains to being. Then, why should the proponent of that theory not just insist that perceptual appearance and reality are identical or that 'it is salty to me' is equivalent to 'it is salty'? I suppose that one answer to this question is the *reductio* argument against Heracliteanism earlier. But Plato also *could* have argued, rightly I think, that any attempt to sustain the extreme solipsism that the conflation of appearance and reality requires is incoherent.[25]

If this is so, what does it mean to say that sense-perception is ἀψευδής? I suggest that the word ἀψευδής here is being used to mean 'incorrigible' or 'unfalsifiable'. This expresses what sense-perception is when it is understood not to attain being. It is clear from the argument that that which does not attain being does not attain truth (186 c 7–8). But this does not change the account of sense-perception according to which each perceptual event is ἀψευδής or incorrigible. Sense-perception is incorrigible because at every moment there is a different perception constituted by a different perceptual object and a different perceiver (159 e 7–160 a 3). What one person perceives is unique to that person and so in principle inaccessible to another or even himself at another time (160 c 4–5). But a perception is not infallible because it does not attain being. And because it does not attain being, it does not attain truth. 'True for me' does not mean 'true' as 'being for me' does not mean 'being', after all, counter to the claim of one who wants to hold that knowledge is sense-perception. That the ambiguity in the meaning of ἀψευδής should be revealed by Plato dialectically, so to speak, seems to me typical. That sense-perception should be held to be ἀψευδής only in a sense, despite the fact that it does not attain being, makes more compelling the implicit claim of the inseparability of the criterion of reality and the criterion of inerrancy understood as infallibility.[26]

---

[25] See Burnyeat (1990), 39–42, for a perceptive discussion of the refutation of Protagoras' relativism, emphasizing that the relativism is opposed by a claim to objectivity.

[26] Bostock (1988), 135–7, thinks that sense-perception obviously attains truth. I think he has simply missed the ambiguity in ἀψευδής. Further, in holding that sense-perception attains truth, he must ignore the inference at 186 c 7, that without attaining being one does not attain truth—that is, if he agrees that sense-perception does not attain being. But if Bostock believes that sense-perception attains being, counter to the explicit argument in the text, then why is sense-perception not knowledge? That is, in what sense does it not meet both criteria?

Returning to the being that is crucial to the above argument, it is part of the interpretation of scholars like Burnyeat, Bostock, and others that we are to take the reference to indicate that sensibles are included in the reality of which there can be knowledge. Indeed, long before they argued in this way, G. E. L. Owen held that this passage indicates Plato's new recognition that sensibles are to be included in the realm of οὐσία, the realm which is contrasted with that of γένεσις.[27] The view of all three scholars on this point seems to me simply to ignore the dialectical nature of the discussion. That knowledge is not attained without attaining being does not entail that there is knowledge of the sensible world, *even if* the sensible world has being in the appropriate sense. The fact that sense-perception does not attain being or truth also does not entail that sensibles have being or truth. Finally, the fact that the mind judges the being of sensibles, which sense-perception does not, entails neither that such judgements constitute knowledge, nor that they can be infallible, nor even that the judgements could meet the reality criterion.

To see the last point we need to ask what exactly οὐσία stands for in the argument. Translators understandably vacillate between 'being' and 'essence' and 'existence' in translating this word. It seems that the word is being used in a broader sense than it is in 185 c 9, where it is just one among many 'common terms'. Here the vaguer term 'reality' is probably least misleading and best makes the connection between the criterion laid down at 152 c 5–6 and the argument at 186 c 7–10: if one does not attain οὐσία one does not attain truth, and if one does not attain truth, one does not attain knowledge. The use of the term is systematically ambiguous as is the term ἀψευδής. The translation 'reality' is most appropriate because it is the term that has the closest connection with the connotation of objectivity, which preserves the contrast between what sense-perception attains and what knowledge must attain.[28] The fact that in some passages 'existence' seems to fit best and in others 'essence' is secondary, because these are each features of reality.

It is misleading to focus on the special features of these terms. This is what has led Owen and others to believe that οὐσία is being attributed by Plato

---

[27] Cf. Owen (1986), 71–3.

[28] See Kanayama (1987), 65–74, for a detailed argument that οὐσία is to be understood in this way.

to the sensible world and that some form of δόξα will qualify as knowledge. It is exactly right that one should be led dialectically to believe the latter, given what is said at 186 B. But it will turn out that δόξα no more attains being than does αἴσθησις. In addition, the truth of true beliefs will be true though not ἀψευδής in the sense of 'infallible', just as sense-perception is not infallible though it is ἀψευδής in the sense of 'incorrigible'.

What Bostock calls the 'orthodox interpretation' of the refutation of the theory that sense-perception is knowledge holds that there is no judgement in sense-perception. For there to be judgement, there must be a grasp of τὰ κοινά. John Cooper challenged this view, arguing that what Plato is contrasting are two different sorts of judgement, the one perceptual (that is, what one perceives to be the case) and the other propositional (that is, what is the case).[29] I think this dispute is somewhat beside the point. If by 'judgement' is meant what Plato means by the terms he uses in the argument, namely, κρίνειν, συλλογισμός, τὰ ἀναλογίσματα, then it is precisely his point that αἴσθησις includes none of these. If, however, 'judgement' is intended to include cognition that one is having the sense-perception that one is having, and indeed, having it incorrigibly, then in this sense Plato is recognizing a sort of perceptual judgement. But this fact is not to be taken as the same sort of thing that 'attaining being' is supposed to indicate. I mean that, contrary to Cooper, attaining being is not to be understood primarily as an existential judgement as opposed to another predicative judgement. Finally, returning to the point about the dialectical nature of the argument, that Theaetetus is led to define knowledge as true belief immediately upon the recognition that sense-perception is not knowledge because it does not attain being should alert us to the fact that, when this definition is proven to be inadequate, the grounds for making the new definition need to be carefully scrutinized. Naturally, one could say that defining knowledge as true belief is better than defining it as sense-perception and closer to the true definition, which is true belief plus an account of some sort. But since the dialogue ends in ἀπορία, it is hard to see on what basis one definition is an improvement over the other, where the goal or trajectory of the putative ἐπαγωγή is invisible. The only way of telling that one definition is closer to the truth than an other would be, so far as I can see, according to the criteria of knowledge already laid down.

[29] See Cooper (1970), 138–44; also Kahn (1981).

212 · CHAPTER 5

But if these criteria are logically connected, nothing is going to meet just one of them.

If sense-perception does not attain reality and therefore does not attain truth, then it is unclear why our 'reflections' on our sense-perceptions or on the states we are in when we perceive should remedy this defect (cf. 186 D 2–5). Presumably these reflections are related to τὰ κοινά. But it is not clear how exactly τὰ κοινά are related to the sense-perceptions. Furnishing clarity in this matter is part of the dialectic. I mean that we are to expect a dialectical clarification of how these reflections do and do not meet the criteria of knowledge, just as we had a similar clarification for sense-perception.[30]

One final point. Like the fruitless debate over whether sense-perception involves judgement, the debate over whether Plato actually endorses the theory of sense-perception developed here is bound to go nowhere. For what we in fact have is a theory of sense-perception based on the assumption that sense-perception is knowledge. That is, we have a theory of what sense-perception must be if it is to meet the inerrancy and reality criteria. Since it does not meet these criteria, it is really beside the point to ask whether Plato endorses this theory. I think in all probability he does not.[31] But we cannot know this for certain because he is only developing a theory of knowledge based on the proposed criteria. Telling us what knowledge is does not reveal what the criteria for sense-perception are.

Before turning to the argument against the identification of knowledge and true belief, I would like to say something about the 'digression' at 172 B–177 C regarding the difference between philosophy and rhetoric.[32]

---

[30] Bostock (1988), 146 ff., argues that the refutation of the identification of knowledge with sense-perception commits Plato to the view that there is knowledge about perceptual objects, that is, that the 'reflections' on perceptual states will include cases of knowledge. This seems to me quite false because (1) the dialogue ends without an agreement that knowledge is δόξα at all; (2) there is nowhere in the dialogue a claim that in attaining being one is attaining anything about sense-perception; and (3) the sense in which true belief is ἀψευδής is not the sense required to meet the inerrancy criterion, where this is understood as inseparable from the reality criterion.

[31] To this extent, I agree with the interpretation of Burnyeat (1990), 9, 52–61. But Burnyeat implicitly denies the linking of the reality and inerrancy criteria, and so believes that despite the fact that sense-perception is not knowledge, knowledge of sensibles is possible.

[32] Plato himself designates it as such at 177 B 8: πάρεργα τυγχάνει λεγόμενα. Never-

This passage contrasts the lives of philosophers and 'speakers in courts' or rhetoricians, though the latter group is described more broadly than that. The implied occasion for making the contrast is that these rhetoricians apply Protagorean relativism to the moral sphere.[33] Such a position is, for example, attributable to Thrasymachus in book 1 of *Republic*. The passage famously goes on at some length about how foolish philosophers look when they have to confront rhetoricians on their own ground and vice versa. Socrates has no trouble in persuading Theodorus of the superiority of the life of the philosopher. Theodorus in turn avers that if more people were persuaded of this, the world would be a better place (176 A). Replying to him, Socrates insists that evil is in fact inseparable from 'our mortal nature' and its region, the sensible world.

Socrates then makes a pronouncement in a passage that was to become enormously influential in the later history of Platonism.

Therefore, it is necessary to try to flee from here to there as quickly as possible. And flight [φυγή] is assimilation to god [ὁμοίωσις θεῷ] as much as possible. And assimilation is becoming just and pious with wisdom. But, my good man, it is not at all an easy thing to persuade people that it is not for the reasons some say that it is necessary to flee wickedness and pursue virtue. It is not in order not to appear evil to others but to appear good that wickedness should be fled and virtue pursued. This is just an old wives' tale, or so it appears to me.

Let us state the truth in this way. God is in no way unjust; rather, he is as just as is possible, and there is nothing more like him than one who would become as just as possible. It is in this matter that someone shows his true toughness or his insignificance and weakness. For the grasp of this is true wisdom and true virtue, whereas the ignorance of this is clear folly and evil. (176 B 1–C 5).[34]

What has especially puzzled scholars about this passage is the seeming identification of the 'flight' from this world with the practice of virtue.[35] The supposed tension is, however, considerably mitigated, though perhaps not totally resolved, if we recall the previous contrasts made by Plato

theless, it can hardly be doubted that what is said in this rather long passage is relevant to what has gone before or even what is to follow.

[33] See Cornford (1934), 81–3.
[34] See below, § 6.1, for a discussion of the parallel text in *Timaeus*.
[35] See Annas (1999), 70–1.

between philosophical virtue and 'ordinary virtue'.[36] This philosophical virtue is closely connected with a process of 'purification' in *Phaedo* and 'imitation' of the divine in *Republic*.[37] As I have interpreted these properties of philosophy, they imply the identification of oneself as an ideal knower. I see no reason to interpret the 'assimilation to god' in any other way.[38] The virtue that this is supposed to involve is philosophical virtue, not its counterfeit. The 'flight', therefore, is not to be glossed principally as 'other-worldliness' or withdrawal from human affairs. It does not consist simply in the practice of intellectual, as opposed to moral, virtue.[39] It consists mainly in the transformation of the person, first through the practice of moral virtue and then through the practice of intellectual virtue, as Plato's educational system for the philosopher-kings indicates. The one who has thus transformed himself (as much as is possible for an embodied person) will, of course, practise moral virtue in the ordinary sense, though he will do so from a radically different perspective.

If the above interpretation of the account of assimilation to god is correct, then the location of the 'digression' in a dialogue devoted to discovering what knowledge is makes very good sense. This is especially so if knowledge is confirmed as being the sort of thing that *Phaedo* and *Republic* have shown it to be. If there is no knowledge of the sensible world, then 'becoming like god' means becoming like a disembodied knower. The 'flight' from this world is the identfication of oneself and hence of one's good as coincident with the deliverances of reason. Knowledge of the sensible world is no more an option than embodiment is an ideal achievement.

5.3 Knowledge is Not True Belief

The basic structure of this section of the dialogue is straightforward. It was shown in the last section that knowledge is not sense-perception because knowledge is supposedly somehow contained not in acts of perception but

[36] See *Phaedo* 82 A 10–B 3. Cf. 69 B 6–7, where this sort of virtue is called an illusory façade (σκιαγραφία), fit for slaves; and *Rep.* 365 C 3–4 and esp. 500 D 8 with 518 D 3–519 A 6, where the 'popular' virtues are identified as the 'so-called virtues of the soul'.

[37] See above, chs. 2–3; also below, ch. 6, on *Tim.* 90 B 1–D 7.

[38] See Sedley (1997), 332, who argues that the assimilation to the divine consists in 'identifying your true self with the immortal part of your soul'.

[39] In this respect I would dissent from Sedley (1997), 334.

in judgements the mind makes by itself. But knowledge cannot be simply 'making judgements' (δοξάζειν) because there is such a thing as 'false belief' (ψευδὴς δόξα). So, it would seem plausible to identify knowledge with true belief. But this appears to lead to the problem of how there can be any belief that is not true. Socrates and Theaetetus fail to arrive at a satisfactory explanation of false belief. But like the refutation of the definition of knowledge as sense-perception, which was, as we have seen, independent of the long discussion that precedes it, so the refutation of the definition of knowledge as true belief proceeds independently of the failure to explain false belief. That refutation, as already mentioned, consists in the distinction between the jury and the eyewitness. Knowledge is evidently more like the belief that the eyewitness has than the belief that the jury has. So, the final section of the dialogue tries to identify this difference as some form of 'account' (λόγος).

There is some ambiguity in the above summary that is naturally indicated by distinguishing 'judgement' and 'belief', even though the Greek words have the same root. I agree with Bostock that the ambiguity does not make any difference to the argument.[40] It is worth adding, however, that whereas beliefs are generally both dispositional and occurrent, judgements are typically assumed to be only the latter. But Plato will shortly (197 B–D) distinguish between dispositional and occurrent knowledge and argue that the latter is logically prior to the former. If true belief is knowledge, it is occurrent true belief that is the focus, not dispositional. And between occurrent belief and occurrent judgements there is very little difference if both are propositional, as Plato seems to hold (cf. 189 E 6–190 A 6, C 5). So, Plato is not, I think, being unintentionally imprecise or sloppy. Rather, he is trying to treat the definition of knowledge as true belief as if true belief really does meet the relevant criteria. That is why we can speak indifferently of belief and making a judgement.

The consideration of true belief as knowledge also explains the difficulty of giving an account of false belief. This part of the dialogue has attracted

---

[40] As Bostock (1988), 156, notes, 'belief' is the most appropriate translation for δόξα, although occasionally, as at 190 A 3–4, 'judgement' seems more appropriate. The main distinction between belief and judgement is that the former is usually understood to be dispositional whereas the latter is episodic or occurrent. It is, however, not unusual in ancient Greek generally and in Plato in particular to elide in one word a process and its result, as in αἴσθησις and γένεσις. The distinction does not affect the present argument.

a great many charges of sophistry against Plato. Plato is not in my opinion displaying puzzlement or confusion regarding the nature of false belief at all. Rather, he is trying to show that *if* knowledge is true belief, then false belief cannot be explained because there is no such thing as false knowledge (cf. 188 c 5–7).[41] This is in line with the dialectical nature of the entire dialogue. It is easy enough to see that ignorance is not false knowledge. It is somewhat more difficult to see that the impossibility of false belief if true belief is knowledge depends upon the failure of true belief to meet both the reality and the inerrancy criteria. This failure is not going to be remedied by adding an 'account' to true belief.

Three attempts are made to describe how false belief is possible if true belief is knowledge: (1) 187 E 1–188 C 7; (2) 188 C 8–189 B 9; (3) 189 B 10–190 E 4. According to (1), false belief is a case where what one knows are things one does not know or where things one does not know are things one knows. According to (2), false belief is believing things that are not. According to (3), false belief is 'mistaking one thing for another' (ἀλλοδοξεῖν). Each of these failed accounts actually tells us about knowledge and not false belief. Simply put, it is not possible for one not to know what one knows. Of course, it is also not possible to believe falsely what one believes truly. But it is in fact possible to have false belief about *something*, as Plato will demonstrate in the *Sophist* (259 D–264 D).[42] The reason why true belief is not knowledge is *not* that false belief is impossible. Rather, the reason is that both true and false belief require a sort of psychological complexity, wherein one first cognizes something and then formulates a belief about that thing.[43] If true belief were knowledge, then knowledge would require a similar complexity. The first stage of this complex psychological operation consists in referring to or otherwise picking out the subject of the subsequent belief. Referring, then, cannot be unpacked as a belief or else a vicious infinite regress would ensue. But it also cannot be unpacked as knowledge of the subject to which

---

[41] So Fine (1979a) and Benson (1992), though these scholars differ on precisely why true belief is not knowledge.

[42] The account of how false belief is possible does not precede Plato's recognition that in fact it is possible. For example, it is owing to knowledge of Forms that false beliefs about sensibles can be securely replaced by true beliefs.

[43] Bostock (1988), 194–5, agrees that beliefs must be complex, though he holds that knowledge must be complex as well—that is, its objects must be complex. And he holds this because he holds that knowledge is a form of belief. So, apparently, does White (1976).

reference is made, since then true belief would be derived from knowledge; it would not be identical with it.

If this is the reason for the failure of true belief to count as knowledge, then obviously *no* definition which includes belief is going to count as knowledge. For if the subject of the belief must first be picked out or referred to, and then a judgement made about it, the lack of complexity within knowing would seem to prevent it from being a form of belief or including a belief. Otherwise, it is difficult to see why there could not be false knowledge if there can be false belief (as Plato surely thought there could). The obvious objection to this line of reasoning is that adding something to true belief, say, an account, actually transforms true belief into knowledge. I think that the refutation of the final definition in fact forecloses this possibility in principle, but it will perhaps still be urged that some unexplored sense of 'account' can fill the bill. This means that knowledge would, finally, turn out to be a form of true belief. An account no doubt adds something to mere true belief. But would it transform a true belief such that either the true belief was divested of the relevant complexity or else there was no longer any need to assume that knowledge is without complexity? I do not see how the former could be the case so long as it is held that knowledge can be had of the same things of which there can be true belief. As we have seen, that is one of the main motives for the revisionist interpretation of Burnyeat and others. As for the latter, if we hypothesize that knowledge can be complex in the way that true belief can, then the above three cases where false belief is shown to be impossible would be irrelevant. False belief is shown to be impossible if true belief is knowledge. But if knowledge is just true belief plus an account, how does adding an account make false belief possible? In other words, why should thinking that true belief is knowledge make false belief impossible, if knowledge is just true belief plus an account?

The complexity / simplicity distinction as applied to belief and knowledge is parallel to the distinction between propositional and non-propositional cognition. We should not be tempted to identify it as a distinction between different types of knowledge, say, propositional and simple apprehension.[44] There is, as I argued in the last chapter, no such thing as propositional knowledge according to Plato, for the complexity involved in identifying

---

[44] As, for example, Bostock does (1988: 272–3).

the subject of a proposition and asserting something of it removes infallibility. It is always possible that error may occur. Far from being infallible, propositional beliefs are typically not even incorrigible. This point is addressed in the next passage of the section, where cases of false belief are actually discovered.

Those cases involve the image of the wax tablet in which memories of things we have perceived are stored (190 E–195 B). False belief can occur when a perception is 'misfitted' to the residue of a previous perception in the wax tablet. Three cases are envisaged: (1) x is known, y is known and perceived; (2) x is known, y is unknown but perceived; (3) x is known and perceived, as is y (192 C 9–D 1).[45] For example, I mistake the person I see in the distance for Theodorus. In all three cases, the perceptual residue or memory is said to be something that one 'knows' (οἶδεν). Although the term used here is different from the main term, ἐπιστήμη, it is natural to wonder whether these are supposed to be synonymous and if so, whether Plato thinks that one truly knows what one remembers, having once perceived it. The answer is pretty clearly no. If false belief is possible, then true belief is not knowledge. If true belief is knowledge and false belief requires knowledge, as in the case of 'knowing' Theaetetus and mistaking Theodorus for him, then this 'knowledge' is true belief as well. But then if being acquainted with Theaetetus is having true belief about him, once again it does not seem that false belief is possible. For the putative false belief would require one to be acquainted with him already. Or else, false belief would just be a matter of being unacquainted with him. And as we have already seen, this is *not* what false belief is. So, it appears that 'knowing' (οἶδεν) is not being taken as a case of 'knowing' (ἐπιστήμη).

The demonstration of how some cases of false belief work is sufficient to show that true belief is not knowledge just in those cases where a false belief is possible. That is, if false belief is possible regarding that about which true belief is possible, then in those cases true belief is not knowledge. Perhaps one might argue that there is a kind of true belief where false belief is not possible, and that kind of true belief is knowledge. To say that false belief is not possible regarding that of which there is true belief is not the same

---

[45] The summary at 194 A 8–B 6 seems to exclude case (2), although this is perhaps just a looseness in the language used. There is no reason for excluding this case and nothing else suggests its exclusion.

thing as saying that the true belief is infallible. If it is impossible for me to be mistaken about something, it does not follow that someone else could not be mistaken. It is clear enough, however, that none of the cases of false belief endorsed here is a case where the corresponding true belief would be infallible. For my belief that Theodorus is standing before me now, even if true, certainly does not entail that Theodorus is standing before me now. No attempt to discover an infallible form of true belief where there is no corresponding case of false belief is made in the dialogue. But if in some case there could not be false belief and true belief about the same thing, this would be because the true belief was in fact really knowledge, which is just to say that there cannot be knowledge and belief about the same thing. In all the recognized cases of false belief the complexity referred to above is manifest. The difference between a false belief and a true one here is not the difference between what is psychologically complex and psychologically simple.[46] Only when true belief is recognized not to be infallible is false belief possible.

The account of false belief generally as 'misfitting' perception to imprint is found to be wrong in the immediate sequel. For though one could not falsely believe that '11' is '12', one could certainly have the false belief that $7+5=11$ and not 12 (196 A–B). This is obviously not a case of misfitting perception to imprint. On my interpretation, a general account of false belief, although independently desirable, is not going to yield a definition of knowledge. No such account is forthcoming anyway. But the attempt to explain false belief in the present case might lead one to suppose that true belief is much closer to knowledge than I have made it out to be. The Platonist, as I understand him, has a ready reply. It is that just as the sensible world is an image of the intelligible world, so cognition in the sensible world is an image of immaterial intellection. Understanding false belief as a kind of image of true belief is, as this entire section of the dialogue shows, invaluable for understanding belief generally as an image of knowledge.[47] It is not only heuristically apt. If knowledge is what I take Plato to understand it to be,

---

[46] At 194 B 2–6 it is evident that both true and false belief are psychologically on a par, even though the aetiology of each may be different, as Socrates goes on to explain at 194 cff.

[47] After showing that false belief can exist (263 D–264 B), *Soph.* 264 D identifies false beliefs with μιμήματα τῶν ὄντων. These ὄντα are true beliefs.

we embodied individuals are obliged to access the paradigm exclusively through its images.

The metaphor adduced to account for false belief in a case like $7+5=11$ is that of the aviary (196 D–199 C). The distinction upon which the use of the metaphor turns is between 'possessing' ($\kappa\epsilon\kappa\tau\hat{\eta}\sigma\theta\alpha\iota$) and 'having' ($\check{\epsilon}\chi\epsilon\iota\nu$) knowledge (197 B 8–10). The former refers to its initial acquisition and the latter to its 'recovery', that is, to an occurrent state. The distinction is easily illustrated by the case of someone who learns something, forgets it or simply does not attend to it, and then recalls it. The aviary and the birds in it stand for the soul and its 'pieces' of acquired knowledge. According to this metaphor, believing that $7+5=11$ when one knows that $7+5=12$ and also knows that 11 is not 12 is explained by reacquiring or having the wrong piece of knowledge—that is, 'getting hold' of 11 instead of 12.

This explanation is obviously inadequate, as the text proceeds to show. In fact, it is no explanation at all (199 C–D). On the assumption that one knows that $7+5=12$, how could one come to 'get hold' of the wrong answer? If one looks carefully at the putative explanation, it turns out that in fact one cannot get hold of the wrong answer just when one has the right answer. But then the only conclusion to draw from this is that 'possessing' the knowledge that $7+5=12$ is *not* knowing it.[48] If it were knowledge, then the false belief that $7+5=11$ would not be possible, analogously to the case of the wax block. And yet the existence of such false beliefs is uncontroversial. So, we can conclude that knowledge is not dispositional true belief.[49]

The distinction between a dispositional and an occurrent sense of 'know'

[48] Cornford (1934), 136–8, thinks that Plato is not taking $7+5=12$ as a piece of knowledge but rather that the one who is mistaken is somehow supposed to take 11 for 12. But at 196 A 6–7 Plato describes one man as believing truly that $7+5=12$ and another as believing falsely that $7+5=11$. I fail to see why the first man is not presumed to have knowledge, since we are still within the scope of the hypothesis that true belief is knowledge. In addition, at 199 B 7–C 2 the man who has captured a piece of knowledge in his aviary is said to have true belief. Indeed, he is said to meet the two criteria of knowledge, that it be $\dot{\alpha}\psi\epsilon\upsilon\delta\acute{\eta}s$ and of $\tau\grave{\alpha}$ $\check{o}\nu\tau\alpha$. On Cornford's interpretation, this man must have the true belief that 12 is 12, but this is completely implausible.

[49] Cornford (1934), 137, thinks that the aviary can serve to explain the false belief that $7+5=11$ on the model of the wax block—that is, a misfitting of two pieces of knowledge, 11 and $7+5$. This is a confusion on Cornford's part. There is no such thing as the knowledge $7+5$. And presumably no one would or could misfit their knowledge of 11, whatever that is, with their knowledge that $7+5=12$. Bostock (1988), 181–3, thinks that

is crucial.[50] Even if, as this section demonstrates, occurrent true belief is not knowledge, a comparison of dispositional and occurrent states of true (or false) belief yields more insight into the nature of knowledge as Plato conceives it than commentators have noticed. One who has the dispositional belief that $7 + 5 = 12$ without thinking about it now may be thought to know it without activating that knowledge or even without being aware that he knows it. In many cases it is quite natural to say that people know things without being aware that they know them. After all, that is what Socratic questioning and the doctrine of recollection depend on.

Presumably, if knowledge is occurrent, a disposition to have that occurrent state is still different from ignorance. The occurrent state adds a sort of 'awareness' to the dispositional 'content'. But awareness of what? Not of the content, for then moving from a dispositional to an occurrent state of knowing would not differ from moving from ignorance to knowing. It must be rather awareness of having the content. And if this is to differ from awareness of the content, it must be awareness that *I* have the content. I am aware that I have the content. At this point we need to press the metaphor of 'having', for we must distinguish the situation from one in which, say, one has learnt something and then forgotten it but is confident that one can remember it. In short, one is aware that one has the content. What is missing in this case? What is the difference between my being aware that I 'have' the answer to a question 'in me' though I cannot remember it now and my being aware of 'having' the answer now? It seems that 'have' does not mean the same thing in each case. In the first case, 'having' is just the presence of the content, a presence that would be explained according to one's theory of cognition generally. In the second case, 'having' is a relation between me and me-and-the-content. In short, if knowing is essentially occurrent, it is essentially reflexive: that is, it involves me in relation to myself.

If knowledge is occurrent and the occurrent is reflexive or self-reflexive, these facts help explain the logical connectedness of the two criteria of knowing. Cognition of what truly is must be infallible if that cognition is of one's own occurrent state. The distinction between incorrigibility and infallibility is in play here. As we have seen, the reason why an incorrigible

Plato is simply puzzled about how to account for false belief in a non-perceptual case such as mathematics.

[50] Here I disagree with McDowell (1973), 221.

perceptual state is not infallible is that it does not guarantee the truth. That is because what is presumed to be is other than my cognition of my own perceptual state. But the occurrent cognition of my own state of 'having' a content ought to guarantee truth. What I am aware of when I am aware of having the content is that I am in a certain state, that of being identical with the object of knowledge. It is impossible that the knower should be aware that he is in the state without being in the state. But the state he is in is a state which consists of identification with the object known. To be fallibly aware of that state would mean that I could be aware that I am in the state I am in without being in that state. But this is impossible.

But even if we assume that '7 + 5 = 12' is true and I am self-reflexively aware that I am in a state in which I am aware of this, it certainly does not follow that my self-reflexive awareness entails the truth of '7 + 5 = 12'. Even if I find it inconceivable that '7 + 5 = 12' is false, it does not follow that it is true. Hence, we should not suppose that Plato's mathematical example is a case of something that can be known rather than a case of true belief that is only hypothesized as knowable for the sake of the argument. In fact, it is difficult or perhaps impossible to find occurrent embodied cognitive states that guarantee anything about the world other than the presence of that state. That is, these states might be incorrigible; they cannot be infallible. For example, that I am aware that I am in pain and that I could not be mistaken about this implies only incorrigibility, not infallibility. My self-reflexive awareness of a pain state does not imply that I am in pain where 'pain' is construed according to objective criteria. Again, the reality criterion and the inerrancy criterion are seen to be inseparable.

The final argument of the section that ends with the dismissal of the identification of knowledge with true belief is superficially detached from what has gone before. True belief is not knowledge, because if it were there would be no difference between a jury's true belief about the perpetrator of a crime and what an eyewitness has. But surely there is such a difference. Therefore, true belief is not knowledge. As I have already argued, one conclusion that *should not* be drawn from this refutation is that the eyewitness account is an example of knowledge. The contrast is purely dialectical or analogical.[51] I mean that the eyewitness is to the juryman

---

[51] See *Meno* 97 A 9–B 3, where there is a distinction between one who knows the road to Larissa first-hand and one who merely has true belief about it because he did not obtain

as a knower is to a true believer.[52] True belief about events or states of affairs acquired second-hand is not equivalent to what is acquired at first hand. The latter could only be supposed to be knowledge if knowledge is true belief plus whatever it is that the first-hand cognizer has. Indeed, that possibility is what the last section of the dialogue examines and finally rejects.

As we shall see in a moment, none of the proposed additions to true belief describes what it is that the first-hand cognizer has. But that does not mean that some hitherto unadduced addition to true belief could turn true belief into knowledge as instanced by the eyewitness. For the reason why true belief could not be knowledge was that if it were, false belief would not be possible. The following dilemma presents itself. Either the putative addition to true belief as represented by the eyewitness is, as it were, extrinsic, in which case it is still true belief and the reason for rejecting the identification of true belief as knowledge still applies. Or else the addition is intrinsic and with that addition true belief is transformed into something else. That is, the putative knowledge is no longer true belief. But it is very difficult to see what sense to make of the latter horn of the dilemma. The jury believes that so-and-so committed the crime based on the testimony, and the eyewitness believes that so-and-so committed the crime based on his own sense-experience. If what makes the eyewitness different from the jury is sense-experience, then either knowledge is once again sense-experience alone and we are back at square one or else it is sense-experience plus true belief. In that case, the eyewitness's claim to have knowledge can be doubly deconstructed according to whether we stress the true belief he has or his sense-experience. In short, the refutation of knowledge as true belief

his belief first-hand. That the first man does not unqualifiedly know is suggested by 98 A 3–4, where it is said that knowledge is based on explanation. It is far better to read the present passage as an analogy: first-hand experience (including that of the eyewitness) is to second-hand experience (including that of the jury) as knowledge is to (true) belief. See Scott (1995), 46, for the same suggestion. Lewis (1981) argues, too, that Plato is not claiming that eyewitnessing is a form of knowledge. Rather, he is relying on ordinary canons of epistemic appraisal to make Theaetetus uneasy about equating true belief with knowledge.

[52] The analogy is, of course, limited. It does not include the implication that knowledge is to belief in the way that the eyewitness is to the juryman, namely, that they cognize exactly the same thing.

includes the rejection of the eyewitness as a knower in so far as he has true belief.

Nevertheless, it will be said that, after all, a true belief is true. It may be reasonably inferred from this that one attains being by having a true belief, reversing the implication at 186 C 7. So, true belief seems to meet at least one of the criteria of knowledge. And indeed, in a sense a true belief is ἀψευδής, so it can be said to meet the other criterion as well. So much is more or less explicitly stated in the aviary example at 199 B 7–C 1. I am quite certain that the overwhelming reason for some scholars holding that knowledge *must* be true belief plus an account is that knowledge is, *at least*, true belief.[53] I have already stated why I regard this view as mistaken. I would like to add several further considerations.

First, the sense in which true belief is ἀψευδής, namely, 'not false', is irrelevant to knowledge. The easiest way to express this is to say that one can have a true belief without knowing that it is true. It will not do to reply that it is the account that turns the true belief into knowledge, because even if one 'has' the true account one may still not know that it is true. Thus, there is no necessary connection between believing something and its being true. No proposition is true because I believe it. By contrast, if knowledge does not entail that what I know is true, then there could be false knowledge, which is impossible. Of course, there is a necessary connection between my truly believing something and its being true. But since I can truly believe something without knowing it, true belief does not become knowledge just because it is true.

Second, the sense in which true belief attains being is not the appropriate fulfilment of the reality criterion. The basic metaphor underlying the words used to express the 'attainment' of being, τυγχάνειν, ἅψασθαι, indicate touching or connecting. The attainment of being must involve an immediate connection between cognizer and being such that the only alternative is an absence of that connection. That is why there is no such thing as false

---

[53] See e.g. McDowell (1973), 227–8. Burnyeat (1990), 125–7, clearly sympathizes with the view that the jury *could* possess knowledge if it were in possession of the facts of the case. Although White (1976), 176, thinks that this passage 'suggests what Plato has oftentimes earlier denied, that there can be knowledge about matters in the sensible world', he goes on to say, rightly, that the passage is an attempt to say what knowledge is 'quite apart from the question what sort of objects it may be concerned with'.

knowledge. One either knows or one does not.[54] And that is why, on the singular assumption that true belief is knowledge, there is no such thing as false belief. Only if true belief is separated from knowledge, that is, only if it recognized as *not* fulfilling the criteria of knowledge, is false belief possible. Having a true belief does not include the attainment of being because we can obviously say of someone that he believes truly without knowing—for example, when he guesses correctly and believes his guess, or as in the example of the jury vs. the eyewitness. The jury has no 'contact' with reality, as does the eyewitness. But we should not then conclude that the eyewitness really knows, for the reasons given above. What we should conclude is that knowledge does not consist in being in a representational state. Since all beliefs consist in representational states, no belief can be knowledge.

Finally, in supposing that a true believer attains truth, and therefore attains being, not only does one ignore the previous inference, but one must do this by ignoring completely the two-world metaphysics of *Republic*, wherein the sensible world is not really real and true belief is accordingly discounted. Naturally, it begs the question against Burnyeat and others to suppose that Plato could not have changed his mind here and repudiated that two-world metaphysics. I am rather arguing that there is no good reason for denying what was argued for in *Republic* and, more importantly, much reason for insisting that everything Plato held in *Republic* about knowledge and belief and the sensible and intelligible worlds still holds in *Theaetetus*. True belief attains the truth only in a diminished sense of 'truth'. True belief meets neither the reality criterion nor the inerrancy criterion, when ἀψευδής is properly construed neither as 'true' nor 'incorrigible', but as 'infallible'. More profoundly, it could not meet either criterion without meeting them both.

Theaetetus concedes only that knowledge is not true belief. And indeed he will try to remedy the faulty definition by suggesting that true belief plus an account is knowledge. The suggestion is doomed to failure, as is the suggestion that knowledge is true belief made in response to the

---

[54] At 191 A 8–B 1 Socrates allows that if false belief is to be accounted for, then we shall have to give up the condition that a man cannot think the things he knows are things he does not know. I take it that this implies that false belief is possible only if true belief is no longer being considered as knowledge.

failed definition of knowledge as sense-perception. It is doomed because the problem with true belief is that it is belief. It is quite astonishing that some scholars have given so little weight to *Republic*'s claim that knowledge and belief are mutually exclusive that they do not even countenance the possibility that this is the case in *Theaetetus*. They assume that *some* form of account added to true belief must be knowledge. Even without knowing the various types of account on offer, we can anticipate from what has already been said that one needs to know the account and that this knowledge will have to amount to more than true belief. Either the knowledge of the account will consist in true belief plus an account of the account, which manifestly leads to a vicious infinite regress, or else the knowledge of the account will not be true belief, in which case one would like to know why knowledge of the account is something different from the knowledge that is true belief plus an account.

5.4 Knowledge is Not True Belief with an Account

Theaetetus reports the following view about knowledge: it is true belief with an 'account' (λόγος); the things of which there is an account are 'knowable' (ἐπιστητά) and the things of which there is no account are not knowable (201 C 9–D 3). It is ambiguous whether or not the 'things' in each case can be the same. Indeed, what these 'things' are is wholly indeterminate. We cannot, for instance, be confident that adding an account to true belief would produce knowledge of the object of true belief. That an account should turn the true belief about something into the knowledge of something else is admittedly a very odd idea—in a non-Platonic context. But for Plato the oddness disappears with the consideration that the sensible world, the object generally of belief, and the world of Forms are related as copy to model. Instances of Forms in the sensible world are and are not the same as their paradigms in the manner that is worked out in the middle dialogues and that is the despair of Plato's critics. The above view about knowledge does not claim that the things that are not knowable are objects of true belief or of belief at all. So, it is well to keep two issues separate: first, whether knowledge is supposed by Plato to be true belief with an account in some sense of 'account'; and second, if it is, whether or not knowledge can be had of the same things of which there can be true belief. I claim that Plato holds that there is no sense of 'account' such that knowledge is true belief with an account. The reason why knowledge is not true belief with an account is that having an account or giving an account of what you know is extraneous to what knowing is.[55] If, however, one wishes to argue that an account or an ability to give an account is a property of knowledge, it is still another matter entirely to determine what there is knowledge of and whether there can be knowledge of that of which there can be belief.

It is also unclear exactly what an account is supposed to be. One might suppose that it is what the eyewitness has but the juryman does not. But this is difficult to maintain. The jury has the right answer, we might say, but the eyewitness *knows* that it is the right answer. His putative account might then consist in his statement of this fact.[56] Surely, it does not consist in his being able to give other reasons—that is, other evidence—why someone is guilty, since the jury could have these as well. Yet, as we shall see, the sort of account both in Theaetetus' and in Socrates' definitions consists not of statements but of explanations or analyses.

Socrates interprets the view expressed by Theaetetus in his 'dream', representing yet another view (201 D 8–202 C 6). According to this view, elements are simple components of all things. These elements can only be perceived and named; we can say nothing further about them in any way. We cannot legitimately say that the element 'is' or 'is not', nor can we in relation to an element use the words 'itself', 'that', 'each', 'alone', or 'this', because using these words would add to the name it has. Thus, there is no account of them. By contrast, things composed of elements can have an account. The account of these is just the 'nexus' (συμπλοκήν) of names. So, elements are not knowable and have no account, although they are

---

[55] See Nehamas (1984), esp. 20–4, who argues somewhat similarly against what he calls 'the additive model' of knowledge, that is, the view that Plato claims that knowledge is true belief plus some sense of λόγος. Nehamas, however, also argues that there are some beliefs, namely, those regarding essences, that can be transformed into knowledge of the same essences (25–6). His alternative to the 'additive model' is that 'those beliefs can qualify as ἐπιστήμη concerning something that are expressed in or through that thing's λόγος' (30).

[56] Bostock (1988), 202–11, argues that λόγος throughout this part of the dialogue must mean 'account' in the sense of definition or analysis and not 'statement'. He does not consider that at least the initial use of λόγος in the argument should be applicable to the eyewitness example.

perceivable. Things composed of elements are knowable because there is an account of them.

If the elements are perceivable and the complex is knowable, where is true belief? Socrates, puzzlingly, says that true belief differs from knowledge where knowledge is understood as the ability to give an account in the above sense (202 B 8–C 5). What would true belief be in the case where knowledge is a statement of the elements? Even if the account is a description or analysis, there seems to be no difference here between knowledge and the true belief that *that* is the correct description or analysis. And since the elements are perceivable alone, there would be no true belief about them either. This odd disconnect between the theory offered and the agreement that knowledge should be taken to be true belief plus an account has not been much noticed. It is, as I shall argue, inevitably a feature of *any* attempt to define knowledge as true belief plus an account.[57]

The generality of the proposal in the dream has encouraged a great deal of speculation.[58] But, even apart from the occlusion of true belief, the difficulty with the proposal is fairly obvious, as Socrates' following analysis shows (202 D 10–206 B 11). Either the complex is the sum of its parts or not. If it is the sum of its parts, then knowing the sum is just a matter of knowing each part. But the parts are unknowable. Therefore, the sum cannot be knowable. If, however, the complex is not a sum of parts, but something simple, then, again, it is no more knowable than the putatively unknowable parts. The two horns of the dilemma are not making exactly the same point. In the first, it is concluded that the sum is not knowable. Socrates does not say that it does not have an account. In the second, he says that the complex considered as simple is both unknowable and has no account (205 E 3). The apparent remedy is to deny that simples are unknowable,

---

[57] At 206 C 1–5, at the end of the refutation of his dream theory, Socrates seems to separate that theory from the effort to show that adding an account to a true belief produces knowledge. This might suggest that we should not have taken the dream as a response to the refutation of the definition of knowledge as true belief. Nevertheless, the exclusion of true belief from the 'knowledge' that is an account of the elements raises what I take to be an insurmountable problem for any attempt to define knowledge as true belief plus an account.

[58] Burnyeat (1990), 134–87, has a thorough and penetrating discussion of the passage. The indeterminacy of the dream, clearly displayed by Burnyeat (163–4), in my view supports the above interpretation. See also McDowell (1973), 231–40.

which would either allow the complex as a simple to be knowable or else would allow the complex as a sum to be knowable because its parts are knowable. But if simples are knowable, then knowledge cannot include an account in so far as that account precludes simplicity.[59] Even if it is thought that both complexes and simples or elements are knowable, the definition of knowledge cannot include an account if that account implies that only complexes are knowable.[60]

It is sometimes said that only certain meanings of 'account' are to be excluded from the definition of knowledge and that the appropriate meaning is to be sought. Either Plato knew this or he should have known it.[61] Indeed,

[59] Burnyeat (1990), 182, holds that the conclusion of the dream refutation (206 B) clearly intends to show that elements or simples are knowable. 'This', says Burnyeat, 'does not entail that the dream was also wrong to say that elements are perceivable.' But if there are elements that are perceivable and knowable, then it would seem that we are back to defining knowledge as perception or as true belief about what it is that is perceived.

[60] Bostock (1988), 212–19, has argued that the refutation of the dream theory is 'a wholly unsatisfactory argument'. He argues that Socrates fails to distinguish a 'structured whole' from a mere sum. So does McDowell (1973), 233–4. The syllable SO is neither the mere sum of S and O nor is it a mere simple. Thus, Socrates has posed a false dilemma and his demolition of either horn therefore does not result in his conclusion that the dream theory cannot account for knowledge as an account of a complex. But the perfectly legitimate distinction Bostock draws is not relevant to the argument. The absurdity of the first horn of the dilemma is that one should know a complex and not know the elements (cf. 203 D). If knowing the complex also includes knowing the structure, this changes nothing. If the complex is really a simple, then it is unknowable even if we take this simple as ordered. Further, Bostock argues that the putative absurdity of the first horn of the dilemma rests upon a straightforward fallacy of division: it assumes that if the whole is knowable, then the parts must be knowable as well. But why, after all, is it not absurd to say that what is knowable consists ultimately of what is not? See Burnyeat (1990), 195–6, for some obvious examples, although Burnyeat agrees with Bostock that the dilemma is a false one. I think the confusion is Bostock's and not Plato's. Plato is taking the dream theory to hold that one knows the first syllable of Socrates' name if, when asked, one replies 'SO'. But could one then go on to say that one did not know the first letter of his name? I think not. The point is the inconsistency of holding that the complex is knowable, *as knowledge is here being understood*, and the elements are not (cf. 203 D).

[61] See e.g. Sayre (1969), 120–37, who argues that Plato recognized that a refinement of the third sense of λόγος would lead to an adequate definition of ἐπιστήμη; also Cooper (1995), 82–3, who argues that 'the critique of the old conception of λόγος is . . . the intended moral of the third part of the *Theaetetus*'. That old conception is of an account in words, written or spoken, that are 'dead' and so insufficiently 'dynamic'. Cooper's point

it is only a slight exaggeration to say that all modern analytic epistemology begins with the assumption that *some* meaning of 'account' added to true belief will yield the definition of knowledge. Actually, I do not think there is a shred of evidence to indicate that this is what Plato thought. On the contrary, the refutation of the dream theory, whoever it may be that holds it, opens the way to seeing why no sense of 'account' is going to turn true belief into knowledge.[62] Further, it is odd, to say the least, to assume that focusing on the appropriate sense of 'account' will be of any use until a definition of knowledge is had. That is, assume that one does have true belief plus an account in any sense of 'account' one likes. Why take that to be knowledge unless the inerrancy and reality criteria are suitably met?

Whether one who knows has an account dispositionally or occurrently, either the account is identical with the knowing or not. If it is, then there is no difference between someone who apes an account without the slightest understanding of what it is and someone who is not like this. So, let us suppose that the account is not identical with the knowing but follows as a result of the knowing. If you know, then you are in a position to give an account. This sounds reasonable enough, but it is evident that the account then has nothing to do with what knowing is. So, one might suppose that the knowing is just the state of one who has true belief plus the account. Once again, however, this does not exclude the one who apes the account.

Further, the reason why false belief was shown to be impossible on the hypothesis that true belief is knowledge was that there is no such thing as false knowledge. And that is because knowing does not admit of the complexity that false belief requires, the 'misfitting' of an attribute to a subject. Knowing cannot require an account if an account presumes the sort of complexity in the knowable that is excluded in the last section of the dialogue.

The failure to explain the account that turns true belief into knowledge as an analysis of parts of a complex is followed by three successive attempts to give an account of an account: (1) an account is the expression of a thought

---

is, I take it, that the conceptions of λόγος in *Theaetetus* are inadequate to the demands of knowledge acquisition through dialogue.

[62] It thus seems to me to be a mistake to hold that if Plato supposed that there was *no* sense of 'account' that would turn true belief into knowledge, he would have then indicated that the three senses discussed here are exhaustive.

in speech (206 C–E); (2) an account is the enumeration of elementary parts (206 E–208 B); (3) an account is a statement of a distinguishing mark (208 C–210 B).

The first sense of 'account' does not distinguish true belief from knowledge because anyone who expresses his true belief would then know. The second sense ignores the qualification of Socrates' 'dream' that the elements are unknowable though the complex is knowable. In effect, it concedes the possibility that Bostock took as being illicitly excluded by the false dilemma of the dream theory, namely, that the complex can indeed be knowable when the elements are not. Nevertheless, a mere list of the parts or elements of the complex does not yield knowledge. The reason for this appears to be that knowing the elements of a complex requires that one know how the same elements might comprise any other complex of which they are part. This is a surprisingly strong condition, but it seems just irrelevant to suppose that for that reason it is one which Plato did not want to impose.[63]

It certainly does seem odd that if one can give an exact enumeration of the elements of A, that is supposed to entail the ability to give an exact enumeration of the elements of B that are the same as those of A. After all, if one knows A because one knows all the elements of A, what does it matter if one does not know B because one does not know all the elements of B even if some of those elements are the same as those of A? The counter-example Socrates gives is itself odd. One cannot be said to know the first syllable of the names 'Theaetetus' and 'Theodorus' if one thinks that in the first case it is 'The' but in the second case 'Te'. An error about epistemic opacity seems to have been made. Just because the first syllable of Theaetetus' name is in fact the first syllable of another name, ignorance in regard to the second should not invalidate the claim to knowledge of the first. The oddness is, however, only apparent if we realize that we are here dealing with the claim that the enumeration of the elements is putatively knowledge. Of course, one can enumerate the elements of A without being able to enumerate the elements of B. The point is that such enumeration is not knowledge. Against the interpretation of Burnyeat and others, if the moral of this story is that knowledge of the sensible world is taken by Plato

---

[63] Burnyeat (1990), 209–18, struggles with the prospect of attributing to Plato this extreme view, and though he clearly does not want to conclude that that is in fact what Plato intended, he has to admit that it is a legitimate interpretation.

to be possible, then it is hard to see why the rejection of (2) would not need to be rescinded.

Someone who can correctly name the first syllable of 'Theaetetus' but cannot do so for 'Theodorus', though these sound the same, has something less than a perfect grasp of that syllable. I suspect that Plato's readers understood the syllable 'The' as that which corresponds to or represents the sound made when one says names like 'Theaetetus' and 'Theodorus'. If someone responded that 'The' is the syllable for the first but 'Te' is the syllable for the second, then it would seem that he does not know the syllable 'The'. What is missing, I suspect, is the transparency of infallible recognition. Getting the right answer in the first case and failing to get it in the second strongly suggests that the right answer is adventitiously cognized. If one had obtained the right answer in the first case because one *knew* that it was the right answer, one could not get the wrong answer in the second case, any more than someone who knew '11' could mistake it for '12'. In the case of the syllable, the very possibility that one should be able to give the right answer in one case without being able to give it in another indicates that the account adds nothing at all to true belief.

It is easy enough to accommodate the idea of partial knowledge within an empirical framework. One can know (in the ordinary sense of 'know') that water is H_2O without, say, having the faintest idea what hydrochloric acid is. Indeed, partial knowledge seems entirely unsurprising even in non-empirical contexts when viewed from the perspective of empirical knowledge. What I mean is, for example, that there is no puzzle in someone knowing the answer to a simple mathematical problem without knowing the answer to a harder one. But this is, I suspect, because mathematical knowledge is being viewed as something very like empirical knowledge. By contrast, as we have seen in *Republic*, Plato came to recognize that the interconnectedness of Forms was essential to explaining necessary truth. In addition, Plato explicitly distinguishes knowledge of the nexus of Forms from the reasoning that mathematicians engage in. The refutation of the enumeration of elements as knowledge seems to echo precisely Plato's refusal to call what the mathematician does knowledge. Someone who can give the factors of one number correctly might or might not be able to give the factors of another. But this is not knowledge. So much is clear in *Republic*. The only issue is whether Plato is here reinforcing this view or abandoning it. I think there is no evidence in the text to support the latter alternative.[64]

Apart from such considerations, I think there are actually good philosophical grounds for believing that Plato is not backing away from what he says in *Republic*. That is, what makes mathematical truths true must be such that the comprehensive all-or-nothing description of knowledge is really the only possibility for it. If $5 + 3 = 8$ is true it is not because there is a Form of Five, a Form of Three, a Form of Plus, and so on, each eternally existing in splendid isolation, although that is an easy error into which one may fall. Whatever it is that makes this equation true—what really is, according to Plato—is a complex unity whose 'parts' are *not* duplicable. Therefore, knowing one 'part' or element really means knowing the 'whole' comprehensively because that is the only knowing there is.

We can express this point yet another way. Knowing cannot be explained as knowing that the elements of something are so-and-so. For one thing, it is obviously of no use to define knowledge by claiming that knowing *A* is knowing the parts of *A*. For another thing, 'knowing' *that* these are the parts of *A* is not equivalent to knowing the parts of *A*. Consider someone who can give a list of the parts of a tree but has no idea what a phloem is. Finally, if knowledge is true belief plus an account in the sense of the enumeration of parts, the enumeration adds nothing to the true belief that *these* are the parts. The enumeration of the parts of *A* might be knowledge of something different from knowledge of what it is, but there is no suggestion here that such is the case. None of these considerations would have much weight if Plato were suggesting that knowledge of the sensible world is possible.

The final effort to define 'account' has from time to time been taken as an improvement over its predecessors, indeed as something rather close to the truth.[65] The claim is that an account gives a 'sign' ($\sigma\eta\mu\epsilon\hat{\iota}ov$) of how

---

[64] McDowell (1973), 252, complains that the argument against the second sense of 'account' shows 'how far Plato is from showing insight into the notion of knowledge, in general, that something is the case. His concern in this passage is still, evidently, with what he thinks of, interchangeably, as knowledge of a thing or knowledge of what the thing is.' I believe that McDowell is mistaken in thinking that Plato is concerned with what McDowell understands knowledge to be. Plato is concerned with $\dot{\epsilon}\pi\iota\sigma\tau\dot{\eta}\mu\eta$, which is not what McDowell understands by 'knowledge that something is the case'. For Plato, there is no $\dot{\epsilon}\pi\iota\sigma\tau\dot{\eta}\mu\eta$ that something is the case.

[65] See Burnyeat (1990), 219 ff., who, however, glosses the meaning of 'account' here as

234 · CHAPTER 5

something differs from everything else. So, if knowledge is true belief plus an account in this sense, one has true belief about something plus the account of how that object of belief differs from everything else.

There are two rather obvious difficulties with this view, as Socrates shows. First, to have true belief about something already implies the ability to pick that thing out as a subject of belief (209 D). But that is what the account was supposed to do. Second, having an account can mean nothing but knowing the differences. That is, knowledge becomes true belief plus the knowledge of the differences (209 E–210 A).

The principal complaint made about Socrates' first objection is that he falsely assumes that in order to have a belief about something one must already have the sign or distinguishing mark, in which case what is supposed to turn true belief into knowledge is superfluous.[66] But as we have already seen, belief requires reference to a subject. One cannot have a belief about a subject without referring to it. I do not think that this is quite the same as holding, as Bostock claims Socrates does, that one cannot have a 'notion' of something without a distinguishing mark. Obviously, I can have a 'notion' of someone or something that is so vague that it fails to refer to one thing uniquely. A distinguishing mark does add something to *that*. But the problem Plato is uncovering is rather that belief, or especially true belief, requires unique reference if it is going to be the basis for knowledge. I mean that if the sign or distinguishing mark is going to turn true belief about *x* into knowledge about *x*, then the reference to *x* in both true belief and knowledge must be the same. That is, of course, what those who take Plato to be arguing that it is possible to have knowledge and belief about the same thing think is the case.[67] On their view, Socrates is offering a weak argument

'identification plus the ability to give proof of the basis for the identification'. The latter is Burnyeat's own addition to the text, but I think there is a fairly obvious Socratic objection to it.

[66] See Bostock (1988), 226–33. Bostock, like Cornford, translates the various forms of δοξάζειν in this argument by the vague expression 'having a notion' rather than 'believing' or 'opining' or 'making a judgement'. I think this is subtly mistaken, as I explain below.

[67] Bostock (1988), 267, goes so far as to say that one conclusion of the dialogue is that 'some knowledge is simply true belief and nothing more'. Burnyeat (1990), 133–4, identifies as 'the central conundrum' of this part of the dialogue whether there are some objects of which there is an account and others of which there is no account. If this is so, then there may be two different kinds of knowledge, of the former and of the latter sorts

for a conclusion that they accept. If, by contrast, true belief about x were to be transformed by a distinguishing mark into knowledge about y, then the patent fallacy of equivocation would undercut the proffered definition of knowledge. Plato's point, I take it, is that if the addition of a distinguishing mark produces knowledge, then true belief will already be knowledge. And that has already been rejected in the dialogue. If true belief cannot be knowledge, then true belief cannot be transformed into knowledge of the same thing by the addition of a distinguishing mark. One further point in this regard is that even if it should turn out that one who knows can give a distinguishing mark, that ability is not constitutive of what knowledge is, nor is it entailed by the possession of knowledge. So, the absence of such an ability does not show the absence of knowledge.

There is some unclarity regarding the circularity that is apparently present in the requirement that one must have knowledge of the account that turns true belief into knowledge.[68] The circularity cannot be equivalent to the vicious infinite regress that is contained in the contemporary analysis of knowledge as justified true belief. For as that account typically goes, the proposition q that justifies belief in p is that which entails p in virtue of its evidentiary nature. So, in order to know p, one must know q, but if q is known, then there must be some r, the evidence for q, that must be known, and so on. But in Socrates' argument the account that must be known is the distinguishing mark or sign and the putative knowledge of this is not the knowledge of evidence for the knowledge of that of which one has true belief. Knowing the distinguishing mark must just be knowing the thing, unless there are, counter to the assumption of the argument, other distinguishing marks. So, it appears that knowledge of the distinguishing mark does not add anything to the true belief that requires a distinguishing mark.

of objects. I think this is quite fanciful. If there are different kinds of knowledge, I would assume that the Platonic question 'What is knowledge?' would be a question about that which all kinds have in common. Further, if I am right about the reality and inerrancy criteria, there is not likely to be conceptual space for a mode of cognition that does not meet the criteria but still deserves to be called 'knowledge'. See also 231–3, where Burnyeat appears to suggest that Plato recognizes 'mundane recognitional knowledge' that is compatible with mistakes. Thus, on this view, Socrates could have knowledge of Theaetetus and still on occasion mistake him for someone else.

[68] See Bostock (1988), 236–8.

The dialogue ends in ἀπορία immediately after this final refutation. It has been my contention that the ἀπορία precisely turns on the attempt to define knowledge on the assumption that knowledge is either not infallible or not of what is—that is, what *really* is. It is a kind of *reductio ad absurdum*. This interpretation admittedly begs the question in its own favour in so far as it assumes that what is said in *Republic* and *Phaedo* still represents Plato's view. On the other hand, without evidence to the contrary—evidence I have argued is not present—it is reasonable that in *Theaetetus* Plato should, from a different point of view as it were, seek to show the force of the position to which at least for a time he was committed.[69]

From a historical perspective, it should be clear that Plato's successors were not being naïve in seeing *Theaetetus* as belonging to the documents of the doctrine of Plato as evidenced in *Republic*. Philosophically speaking, the indirect reaffirmation of the doctrine of knowledge in *Republic* reinforces what we have learnt about personhood from the earlier dialogues. Knowledge is an occurrent, self-reflexive, infallible cognitive state. Many philosophers, including many sceptics, have, I suppose, maintained roughly this position. Few, if any, have combined it with the account of personhood I have tried to expose in the dialogues. If a person is ideally a disembodied agent of reason—a disembodied thinker, if one likes—one can see at once that the state of knowing so defined identifies that person. Viewed thus, there is little if any room for personality or the idiosyncrasies of personhood generally thought to be bound up with the very idea of being a person. In Platonic heaven, what one philosopher knows is exactly what any other knows and there is nothing more to them than being in that state of knowing. Although the universality of knowing excludes the particularity of personality, it does not exclude, at least for Plato, the desirability of attaining a disembodied state.[70] It does not exclude the individuation of those in such

---

[69] White (1976), 182–3, argues that, while Plato still believes at the end of the dialogue that the ability to give a λόγος is a necessary condition for knowledge, 'he did not see *how* he could uphold this view'. I think White, like many others, confuses knowledge with what is in effect a πάθος of knowledge, namely, the ability to give a λόγος that is indefeasible. See e.g. Cooper (1995), 77–8, who insists that the ability to give a λόγος is a 'necessary condition' of knowledge and then slides into identifying knowledge with that ability (see 87).

[70] See Nussbaum (1986), 187–99, for a very interesting analysis of the speech of Alcibiades at the end of *Symposium*. There she claims that we are meant to see in that speech 'the

states. That is, the state that I am in (ideally) is distinct from the state you are in. That you and I know exactly the same thing certainly does not entail that my knowing is the same event or state or act as yours.[71]

The logical inseparability of the reality and inerrancy criteria indicates that Plato is thinking of knowledge as an ideal state, one which is unavailable to embodied persons. Thus, one can know only when one infallibly knows and one infallibly knows only when the awareness of the presence of the cognitive state entails the presence of the knowable. And this is only possible if the knowable consists of immaterial objects or what for Plato is 'really real'. A person has knowledge only when that person is self-reflexively aware of his own cognitive state and where that awareness guarantees that what is known is not other than as it is known. The guarantee consists in the fact that the content of the cognitive state is the knowable.

Much of this book so far has attempted to show the implications of the above for embodied life. Plato typically thinks in ideal terms not merely as a theoretical exercise but in order to address decidedly mundane problems. There are countless examples in the dialogues of Plato arguing that a particular practical question cannot be answered until a particular theoretical question is answered such as the 'What is x?' question. Questions like 'How ought we to live?' or 'What is the best life for human beings?' patently require an answer to the question 'What is a human being?' The evidence of the dialogues hitherto discussed suggests that Plato approached this question somewhat obliquely by asking first, 'Am I identical with a human being?' His answer is 'No, I am identical with a soul.' More specifically, I am identical with a subject of thinking. Then, the question 'What is the

deep importance unique passion has for ordinary human beings; we see its irreplaceable contribution to understanding'. Since I think Plato distinguishes persons and 'ordinary human beings', I do not exactly disagree with Nussbaum. But I would claim, apparently against Nussbaum, that Plato believes that the destiny of persons is not the destiny of ordinary human beings, and for the former the idiosyncrasies of human attachments are not a snare and a delusion only if they are channelled 'upward' into the impersonal.

[71] See Hall (1963), 143, who avers that 'if in its real nature the immortal soul is a simple unity equivalent to the rational aspect λογιστικόν, then its immortal condition will be devoid of any psychical characteristics that would serve to separate it from other souls'. Hall seems to me to equate psychical characteristics that 'separate' one soul from another with 'idiosyncratic personality traits'. Given the self-reflexive nature of knowledge, this seems to me to be a mistake.

best life for me?' amounts to the question 'What is the ideal state for such a subject?' The answer to that question is 'A state of knowing.'

Since we manifestly do not experience ourselves as being in such an ideal state or indeed experience ourselves as being exclusively subjects of thinking, Plato needs to account for the discord between our self-perceptions and the ideal and to develop a strategy for attaining that ideal. The account is situated, broadly speaking, within a hierarchical metaphysics. The most concise name for the strategy is 'philosophy'. To practise philosophy is both to approach the ideal state and to 'identify' with it in the sense of that term I explained earlier. If, as I have argued, Plato held that knowledge, ideally conceived, is not available to us while embodied, he surely also held that there was a huge gap between those who came as close to the ideal as an embodied person might on the one hand and almost everyone else on the other, a gap between, say, a Socrates and an ordinary Athenian.[72] If Socrates was not a living refutation of the claim that embodied knowledge was impossible, he was yet a stellar example of someone who was transformed by love of that ideal state.

If knowledge must meet the reality and inerrancy criteria, then it is perhaps inevitable that it is unavailable to embodied persons. What transforms *Theaetetus* into a powerful piece of Platonic argument is adding to it the assumption that knowledge is, despite being unavailable to embodied persons, possible for us. Many other philosophers either accept the criteria in one form or another or else they accept this assumption. Rarely do other philosophers accept both. Since few will question Plato's adherence to the assumption, it is important to have a clear picture of what *Theaetetus* aims to achieve. If that aim is what I have argued it to be, then Plato is in this dialogue actually reinforcing his previous account of ideal personhood. The possibility of knowledge would not exist for us unless persons are, ideally, nothing but knowers.

---

[72] See *Symp.* 205 D 5 for the characterization by Diotima of love 'as between wisdom and ignorance' and the manifest representation of Socrates as the ideal lover.

CHAPTER 6

Personhood in the Later Dialogues

In this chapter I want to focus on some texts in what are generally regarded by scholars as late dialogues of Plato. The relative lateness of *Timaeus*, *Philebus*, and *Laws* has been thought to provide the basis for showing that Plato came to moderate some of his more extreme views about personhood. For example, it is held that in *Timaeus* Plato began to move away from dualism towards a more hylomorphic account of the person. It is claimed that he abandoned the tripartitioning of the soul in *Laws* and took a less other-worldly view of human happiness in *Philebus*. I am here as much concerned to show that in all essentials Plato's views did not change as I am to show the trajectory of his late speculations.

6.1 *Timaeus*

In *Timaeus* Plato adds a cosmological dimension to his treatment of human psychology. That is one of the few uncontroversial things one can say about this dialogue. In this section I want to gather together the evidence from *Timaeus* that supports the interpretation I have hitherto developed.

That tripartition of the soul is maintained in *Timaeus* seems certain, although Plato adds that each kind or part has its own 'motions' (κινήσεις).[1] What is equally clear is that the two lower parts are said to be 'mortal'

---

[1] See 89 E 4–5: τρία εἴδη ψυχῆς ἐν ἡμῖν, as in *Rep.* 435 C 5 etc. At *Laws* 896 E 8–897 A 3 Plato describes these motions of the parts of the soul as their various cognitive, affective,

and only their highest part, the rational, 'immortal'.[2] The mortal parts correspond to the spirited and appetitive parts of the soul in *Republic*. Several important points, however, are added. First, the parts of the soul are 'housed' (κατῴκισαν, 69 D 7, 70 A 3, E 2; οἰκεῖν, 90 A 4) in different parts of the body: the rational part in the head, the spirited part in the heart–lung region, and the appetitive part in the belly. Nothing can be directly inferred about the nature of the parts of the soul from the spatial metaphor of housing. The immortal part is undoubtedly incorporeal, though it is in the head; the mortal parts are presumably also incorporeal, though this is not quite as clear.[3] At best, one can infer their incorporeality from 69 C 5–6, where the Demiurge's created assistant gods fashion mortal soul to be housed in mortal body. It is difficult to see from this how the mortal soul could be corporeal, for in that case it would be part of the mortal body. That the parts of the soul are housed or 'in' the body does not therefore mean that they are corporeal. Furthermore, the fact that all three parts are housed in a body—though one part, the rational, does exist apart from the body and the other two do not—means that we should not suppose that there is to be found here anything like a straightforward account of mind–body interaction. I mean that 'in' does not simply indicate a dependence relation.[4]

and emotional activities. For example, 'investigating', 'being pained', and 'being afraid' are all 'motions'.

[2] See 41 C–D, 69 C 5–6, 69 E 1, and 90 A for the distinction between immortal and mortal. That the mortal comprises two parts follows from 70 A 2 with 70 D 7. At *Rep.* 611 B 9–12 A 6 we find the immortal part of the soul identified with that which is separable from body. This is presumably the rational faculty. Robinson (1990), 103, challenges the traditional view, arguing that 'the tripartite soul is everlasting (albeit not immortal) and there is no escaping the cycle of rebirth'. Robinson's central point is that the immortality of the highest part of the soul does not actually preclude the everlastingness of the other two parts, citing 41 B as evidence suggesting that the gods made the lower parts of the soul to be everlasting. The crucial issue seems to me to be embodiment. If we are necessarily embodied, then we are necessarily tripartite. But there is a great deal of evidence against embodiment as an ideal state for persons. See below on *Laws* 954 A 4–B 7, for example. See also Mason (1994) for a criticism of Robinson and a defence of the traditional interpretation.

[3] Sedley (1997), 330, for example, does not doubt the incorporeality of the mortal parts, but he cites no clear textual support for this.

[4] Cf. *Phaedo* 83 D, where the soul is 'riveted' to the body by pleasure. Distinguishing soul and person as we have done, we must suppose that there is a dependence relation between the mortal parts of the soul and the body, but not the person and the body.

It is more likely that the location of all three parts of the soul in a body follows from the initial explanation of the motive for creation. The Demiurge, ungrudging, wished to make something as good as possible out of the pre-existing chaos (29 D 7–30 C 1). He foresaw that in the visible (i.e. corporeal) world a product possessing intelligence was better than one without, and for that a soul was required. Therefore, in making the universe, the Demiurge put reason in soul and soul in the world's body. A similar motive is given for the production of individual types of mortal living things (41 A 7–8). Among these, it was 'fitting' (προσήκει) that there should be one kind possessing an immortal element. But if this kind were to possess *only* this immortal element, then it would be equal to gods. That is, it would be redundant to make human beings who were just immortal living things, because they would then be gods.[5] So, the assistant gods are bidden to weave mortal elements with the immortal. These mortal elements are the body and the two lower parts of the soul. In short, organic individuals, including especially rational ones, are a necessary part of the economy of creation. Thus, what is fitting, what is possible, and what is necessary, given the goodness of the Demiurge, are merged. That there *must* be human beings—that is, body–soul composites—if there can possibly be such, is as close as Plato comes to explaining why the incorporeal is located in a body. More important, however, is that here the primary dualism is between immortal and mortal parts of the soul, not between incorporeal and corporeal. The mortal parts are a necessary concomitant to a type of creature called 'human'.[6]

The immortal part is differently related to each of the two mortal parts. The spirited part of the soul is placed 'within hearing distance of reason so that together with reason it can restrain with force the appetitive kind [γένος] whenever it is not willing to be persuaded by the command, that is, reason, from the citadel' (70 A 4–7). The appetitive part is placed in the region of the liver:

---

[5] This suggests that even those who manage to 'achieve' immortality and become like gods do not actually become gods. Persons belong to a stratum of creation separate from gods.

[6] Cf. 70 E 4–5: 'There [in the liver] they tethered it [the appetitive part] like a beast untamed but necessary to be maintained along with the rest if a mortal race were ever to exist.'

And, knowing that it would have no grasp of reason, and that even if it did in some way partake of a perception of some aspect of reason, it would not be in its nature to pay any attention to these, but that it would be mesmerized [ψυχαγωγήσοιτο] night and day by images and shadows, god took advantage of this fact and constructed for it the liver and he placed it in the dwelling of the creature. This was done so that the mind's power [ἡ δύναμις ἐκ τοῦ νοῦ] of transmitting thoughts [διανοημάτων] would be [reflected] in it [the liver] in the way a mirror is receptive and reflects impressions [τύπους] and images [εἴδωλα] to look at. (71 A 3–B 5)

The reflections in the liver are primarily the substance of haruspical divination, but also divination by dreams (71 D 3–4). The liver also seems to serve to 'translate' the deliverances of reason into a form that the appetitive part of the soul can assimilate. The impressions and images seem to be what one would discover if one could observe one's own liver or perhaps what one would feel as a result of some physical disorder. What one observes are the effects on one's own constitution of reason's operation on the liver.[7] Perceiving these effects is, of course, a rational activity.

Notice that in this passage the possibility of appetite being persuaded by reason is envisaged even though appetite has no share in reason. The persuasion is accomplished by the translation of thoughts into impressions and images. And though these may be *intelligible*, when available for interpretation in divination, it is not in virtue of their intelligibility that they affect the body and hence the appetitive part. Reason does, however, directly affect the spirited part through its commands. But obedience to reason no more requires the presence of an independent cognitive capacity than does being persuaded by reason.[8] The direct result of reason's determination that a misdeed has been committed, whether from 'outside' or 'inside' (70 B 5), is anger. Reason in this instance is translated into anger. As puzzling as this may be, assigning to the spirited part a cognitive capacity would only shift

---

[7] This is, I believe, the sense of the very difficult passage 71 B 5–E 2. See Taylor (1928), 514–15. Cornford (1937), 286–9, says that the passage is limited to forms of divination, but I take one effect of reason's operation on the liver to be the 'pain and nausea' of c 2, a 'warning' of sorts, no doubt.

[8] The persuasion by reason of necessity at 48 A 2 does not, of course, presume cognitive capacity in necessity. See Archer-Hind (1888), 263, who, however, believes that, unlike the appetitive part, the spirited part of the soul can actually obey reason, where 'obey' implies some sort of cognition.

the problem into one of how the cognitive awareness by the spirited part of the deliverances of reason is translated into the affective response.

In Chapter 3 I argued that the putative quarrelling between reason and appetite did not imply cognitive capacity in the latter but that it did imply a divided rational subject. The spirited part might seem to be somewhat different. As in *Republic*, it is the inevitable ally of reason precisely because it can obey reason. Does this imply that the spirited part has its own cognitive power? I think not. First, as we have seen, obedience to *A* by *B* does not in itself imply cognitive powers in *B*. Obedience is just the obverse of persuasion and need only imply a type of submission having no cogntive connotation. More importantly, there is an argument that suggests that the answer to this question of whether spirit has a cognitive capacity is no. Reason is reason and when reasoning is going on in the human being, there are no grounds for assigning this to something other than the immortal part besides a wish to produce homunculi. True enough, the spirited part *always* obeys or aligns itself with reason when reason and appetite quarrel. But the grounds, if any, for assigning cognitive power to the spirited part cannot be just this. The obedient response of spirit to reason's quarrel with appetite is anger. To assign to spirit cognitive power as well as the power for anger and other emotions makes entirely opaque Plato's insistence that spirit is one part, not two. But then what does it mean for spirit to obey reason? A person becomes angry when he thinks that anger is justified or that it is the appropriate response. The obedience to reason by spirit is not assent to an argument; it is simply the angry response. The assent to the argument is just part of the process of reasoning. And yet it *is* the same person who reasons and is angry.

What does all this tell us about the person and the human being? First, it seems that the immortal part of the soul must be distinguished from the composite that consists of this immortal part plus the other psychic mortal parts plus the body. The entire composite is identical with what Plato later calls 'human nature' (90 c 3). The person or self is the immortal part alone. This is made explicit in a passage in *Laws* that I shall examine later in this chapter. If the disembodied person is just the immortal part of the soul, then the embodied person is something else, though it is not identical with the human being. The embodied person is the identical subject of appetites and emotions as well as the subject of thought. That person can perceive or be aware of himself as the subject of bodily states. This fact implies, as I have argued, the immateriality of the person. Remarkably, in *Timaeus* Plato is eager to acknowledge that a condition for embodied psychic complexity or dividedness is physical separation of the bodily parts which are the instruments of embodied personal life. The physical division does not preclude the psychic or personal complex unity.

I have also argued that the embodied person is an image of its disembodied exemplar. Embodied subjectivity of organic animals is an image of the pure disembodied thinking attributable to the Demiurge and to us in an ideal state. On the psychological side, we can express the imagistic nature of the embodied person by saying that the life of an embodied person never frees itself entirely from dividedness or complexity in its desires. On the epistemological side, we can express the imagistic nature by saying that embodied cognition consists essentially of images of eternal reality. Propositional belief represents in the images that are concepts images of Forms. The life of embodied persons is not a life of what is really real interacting with images, but a life of images interacting with images. The path of philosophy is the path leading to the recognition not just that the sensible world is an image of ultimate reality, but that *we* are images of ideal, disembodied persons. Only an immaterial person is capable of the unequivocal self-reflexivity necessary for recognizing this.

Remarkably, images reach straight down to the liver. Just as embodied cognition consists of images of the cognition of the disembodied exemplar, so the appetitive part of the soul contains images or impressions of thinking. When the appetitive part of the soul is controlled by reason, the moderation or limitation of appetite will literally reflect the reasoning that produced the moderation. This is less strange than it seems when we realize that discursive reasoning itself is only a reflection of eternal being. The moderate appetite for, say, drink reflects one's belief that drinking in moderation is good just as that belief reflects, say, an eternal relation among the virtues and the Form of the Good. Embodied subjectivity images thought; it does not stand in polar opposition to it.[9]

The appropriate linkage between the disembodied and the embodied is

---

[9] The production of images in the appetitive part by the rational part of the soul, especially at 71 C 3–4, parallels the effect produced by artists in *Republic* 10 on the appetitive part; see 605 A–B. In addition, the susceptibility of the appetitive part of the soul to εἴδωλα

provided again by the Demiurge, whose words imply that he who lives well here below and controls with reason his arational part will return to his first and best state.[10] We should similarly understand the creation of human souls in 'the second or third degree of purity' (41 D 7) and the statement that purification by education of a suitable nature consists in becoming more rational.[11] That is, purification of the soul is release from the body, but not in the sense in which everyone can achieve this simply by dying. Purification of the soul is explicable as a path to rationality, but not the rationality that is an endowment. That is, it does not consist in getting better at, say, mathematical calculation. Growth in rationality is, physically, described in terms of the 'circles' of the 'same' and 'different' in the soul. Psychically, it is a constriction of the person into the rational faculty or an identification of the person with it. The person becomes less divided, which does not contradict the sense in which the embodied person is permanently divided. A residual division is unavoidably bound up with embodiment. Epistemologically, the person on the path to purification gradually divests himself of false beliefs and, most importantly, strives to recognize cognitional images for what they are.[12]

Towards the end of the dialogue Plato takes up the matter of physical and psychic disease and cure and care. There are two passages in particular which throw light on the above argument. First, there is the passage where Plato makes the claim that practically all that is called incontinence with regard to pleasure is not justly blamed because no one does wrong willingly (86 D 7–E 1).[13] The reason given for this claim is, on the surface, fairly clear. People are overcome by pleasures. But pleasures originate in the body's constitution and people have no control over this (86 B–D). So, we should not blame people for being overcome by pleasures any more than,

---

and φαντάσματα at 71 A 5–6 should be understood according to the distinction between two kinds of image-making at *Soph.* 235 A–236 C.

[10] 42 D 1–2. Taylor (1928), 263, ad loc., takes the words ἄλογον ὄντα . . . λόγῳ κρατήσας to mean 'without ratio' and 'by rule', referring to the literal construction of the soul. But I think the point about return to the ideal state is the same in either case.

[11] See *Phaedo* 67 C 2–3, 69 A 6 ff., and 69 B 8–C 3; and Robinson (1995), 105.

[12] See esp. 44 B 6–7, where becoming a rational person is promoted by the acquisition of true belief.

[13] That no one does wrong willingly is consistently held by Plato. See *Ap.* 37 A 5; *Prot.* 358 C 7; *Gorg.* 488 A 3; *Rep.* 589 C 6; *Laws* 731 C–D.

say, their being undone by a bad heart or lungs. The interesting difference between the two cases is that, as we have seen in *Phaedo* and *Republic*, the subject of bodily infirmity is the body, whereas the subject of pleasure is the person, not the body, which is the person's possession. And so, if one is unwillingly overcome by pleasure, one is overcome neither by something completely alien nor by oneself.[14] The phenomenon of ἀκρασία is not here being denied; it is just that ἀκρασία does not contradict the fact that no one does wrong willingly. The 'no one' means no person. All persons are permanently oriented to their own good, as Plato has always maintained. If embodied persons are sometimes overcome by pleasure contrary to what they regard as their own good, it is because their embodied fate is dividedness. Sometimes they see their own good in pleasure, sometimes they see their own good in resistance to pleasure, and sometimes they see their own good in pleasure and resistance to pleasure at the same time. A person who is divided in this way, who at the same time does and does not want to 'give in' to pleasure, who does and does not want what is really good for himself, is, I think, not implausibly described as an image of a united person or self. But even if he should overcome his incontinence and never again desire other than that which reason dictates ought to be desired, he would still be an image of an ideal person. For his practical desiring is only an image of the desire for knowing, a desire that can only be fulfilled while disembodied.

The second and related passage describes soul care, identifying it with 'assimilation to god' (ὁμοίωσις θεῷ).[15]

Now if someone is engrossed in appetites or ambitions and spends all his efforts on these, all his beliefs [τὰ δόγματα] will necessarily be mortal and, in so far as this is possible, he cannot fall short of becoming mortal altogether, since he has nourished this part of himself. But if someone is a lover of learning and zealous for true wisdom and has especially exercised this part of himself, his thoughts will necessarily be immortal and divine, so long as he grasps the truth, and in so far as it is possible for human nature to participate in immortality, he will not

---

[14] Recall *Rep.* 430 E 11–431 A 1: 'Isn't the expression "self-control" absurd? The stronger self that does the controlling is identical to the weaker self that is controlled, so that it is the same [person, ὁ αὐτός] referred to in both cases.'

[15] See Sedley (1997) on the entire passage. See also *Symp.* 207 D 1 and *Rep.* 498 E, 500 C, as well as the discussion of *Theaet.* 176 B–C above, § 5.2.

lack any part of this. And because he has ministered to the divine part in himself and has kept in good order the guardian spirit that dwells in him, he must be happier than anyone. (90 B 1–C 6, trans. Cornford)

There are a number of remarkable features in this passage. First, it appears that the tripartite soul provides the framework for the claims being made here. 'Appetites' (ἐπιθυμίαι), 'ambitions' (φιλονικίαι), and 'love of learning' (φιλομαθία) are the distinguishing features of the three parts of the soul in *Republic* (581 B–E). Within this framework, it is also clear that the individuals here described are supposed to be able to choose to devote themselves to different sorts of lives. As we have seen in Chapter 1, without a claim for personal immortality, the basis for such a choice is obscure, especially if it is suggested that one should alter one's natural disposition. Here, the preferred choice is explicitly linked to immortality as something quite evidently assumed to be desirable.

If the embodied person is the sort of self-reflexive subject I have claimed Plato takes him to be, then his 'training' (παιδαγωγία) will be a life-or-death exercise in identity recognition. As someone capable of identifying himself as the subject of his appetites and emotions, he should be able to understand that that very identification belies his true nature. Thinking 'immortal thoughts' or, more precisely, the *images* of genuine immortal thoughts is the antidote to false identification. If images are the bane of our embodied existence, they are also the instruments of our salvation, provided that they are the correct type of images. The person who identifies himself as a 'lover of learning' unmasks his own false self-images. He does not cease to have appetites; he only ceases to suppose that his true identity is found as a subject of these.

The most curious feature of this passage is that, in virtue of the sort of commitments one makes, one is supposed to be able to become or participate in mortality or immortality 'in so far as this is possible'. We have already learnt, however, that the human soul is one part immortal and two parts mortal and that the human being is the combination of this type of soul with a mortal body. Obviously, immortality and mortality as achievements are different from immortality and mortality as endowments. The passage makes good sense, however, if we keep the above distinctions in mind. A person, who is essentially immortal, can, when embodied, decide to identify himself as the subject of the mortal parts of his soul, the parts which require mortal bodily parts. Such a person renounces his destiny by renouncing his identity. One who opts for the philosophical life participates in immortality 'in so far as this is possible for human nature'.[16] That persons—rational subjects—are immortal is not in question here. But human nature, composed of immortal and mortal parts, participates in immortality in so far as one identifies oneself with philosophical activity. Thus, Plato is referring to participation in immortality in *this* life, not after separation from the body, when immortality is assured.[17]

That the identification with a life of philosophy is assimilation to god is stated in the remainder of the passage. The way to accomplish the assimilation is remarkably concrete:

Now for everyone there is one form of care for all the parts: to give to each part its own proper nourishments and motions. Regarding the divine part in us, the motions that are akin to it are the thoughts and revolutions of the universe. Everyone ought to follow along with these, straightening out the corrupted revolutions in our head concerned with becoming [τὴν γένεσιν] by means of learning the harmonies and revolutions of the universe, making that which thinks similar to [ἐξομοιῶσαι] that which is thought according to its archaic nature [τὴν ἀρχαίαν φύσιν];[18] and by producing this similarity achieving the end that is the best life offered to humans by god for the present and future time. (90 C 6–D 7, trans. Cornford)

As Sedley remarks, the process of assimilation to the divine described here is principally, if not exclusively, intellectual.[19] In one sense, just as persons are already immortal and do not need to achieve immortality, so are they

[16] Sedley (1997), 333, understands the qualification as a limitation on our ability to have astronomical knowledge. This seems unnecessarily limited.

[17] See Sedley (1997), 332, for a similar interpretation. He aptly compares the ideal described in this text with Aristotle's ideal of contemplation as participating in immortality.

[18] Cf. *Symp.* 193 C 5.

[19] Sedley (1997), 334. That it is not exclusively so is indicated by *Lysis* 221 D–E. There the lover loves the beloved because he is missing what 'belongs to' (οἰκεῖον) himself. The connection and distinction between the sense of τὸ οἰκεῖον in *Lysis* and in *Timaeus* can be expressed succinctly by saying that we all desire what belongs to us or that to which we belong, but we do not all know who we really are so we are unclear about our proper belongings. For that reason, our desire is sometimes other than an intellectual desire. See also *Symp.* 193 D 2. At 205 E–206 A Diotima explains that one does not really desire one's 'other half' unless that is good, and only that which is good is οἰκεῖον to oneself.

already likenesses of god just in so far as they are possessed of a divine part.[20] The sense in which we are exhorted to become like god is surely not the sense in which we are already like him. On the basis of the bipolarity of the term φύσις connoting both endowment and achievement that we have already noticed, Plato can say without straining the language at all that we are being exhorted to become what we are.

The association of 'likenesses' (τὰ ὁμοιώματα) with 'images' (εἰκόνες) is a central feature of Plato's metaphysics.[21] It is true generally that two things can be like without one of them being an image of the other. In *Timaeus*, however, the Demiurge makes the world and all the living things in it to be both likenesses and images of the Form of Living Animal which contains within it the Forms of all living things.[22] In addition, he wanted the world to be as 'near to' (παραπλήσια) himself as possible (29 E 1–3). The meaning of 'near to' is not clear, for it is not immediately obvious how making a complete copy of the Form of Living Animal, that is, making a world with all the possible things in it, makes that world 'near to' its maker. Perhaps we can at least say that because the Demiurge is good, he strove to make things as good as possible, thereby making them 'near to' him. But the central point is that the production of likenesses by the Demiurge is an act of image-making. And that means that mortal creatures, including human beings, are made to be images of a part of the Form of Living Animal. So, human beings are like the Demiurge because they have an immortal part and like the Form because that Form contains the Form of Humanity as a part. The assimilation to god can be rather precisely, if simplistically, situated within the two sorts of likeness. Embodied persons, inhabiting human bodies, must strive to transcend their human endowment. Embodied persons can never assimilate themselves to the Form of Humanity. But they can assimilate to

---

[20] Cf. 41 C 6–7: 'in so far as it is appropriate that there is something in them [viz. mortals] that shares in the name [ὁμώνυμον] of the immortals'.

[21] See esp. *Parm.* 132 D 3. Patterson (1985) has a careful and perceptive study of the issues surrounding this association.

[22] 30 C 2–D 1 and 92 C 7. The phrase νοητὸν ζῷον is easy to misconstrue. It need not refer exclusively to a Form of Animal if when the Demiurge introduces figures and numbers into the pre-cosmic chaos, he is using this very Form. In fact, in ordinary Attic Greek τὸ ζῷον is regularly used for something in 'real life' when that is what an artist draws. That is why an artist is called ὁ ζωγράφος. Just as an artist here below may draw an image from real life, so the divine artist employs an intelligible model for the entire cosmic image.

a divine life, a life of contemplation. A person is an image of the divine in so far as he has an immortal part; he is an image of a Form in so far as he takes on mortality, too. Owing to its immortal part—his reason—he can assimilate 'human nature' to the divine. He can make the image a better version of its original.

That the Demiurge wants to make the world as 'near to' himself as possible *and* that he made it according to an eternal paradigm has suggested to most Plato scholars up to the twentieth century that the Forms are somehow to be identified with the Demiurge.[23] This view has also been widely criticized, for a reason that seems to me to be patently circular. It is held that the view is Neoplatonic and since Neoplatonism is not a reliable guide to Platonism, the view cannot be correct. I have elsewhere argued for the traditional interpretation.[24] Here, I add a slightly different consideration.

I have been arguing throughout this book that knowledge is a state in which there is cognitional identity between knower and known. It is frankly unbelievable that Plato supposed that the Demiurge has mere concepts or images of Forms in his mind. So, the question naturally arises how the Demiurge is related to the Forms. I suggest that the self-transformation we seek is present paradigmatically in the Demiurge, who is identifiable as a pure subject of knowing. The Demiurge does permanently what we aim to do ideally, namely, contemplate Forms. This contemplation is just cognitive identity between knower and known in which the knower is self-reflexively aware of the identity. Thus, a further way of characterizing the assimilation to god is divinizing of the contents of the mind by acquiring knowledge. As we have seen, knowledge is supposed by Plato to produce a self-transformation. Our endowment is as immortal rational subjects; our goal should be to take on the divine life of contemplation. The fact that so long as we are embodied we do maintain mortal parts of our self, that is, mortal desires and emotions, suggests to me that transformation into a divine state is not available for us here below. That is, we should not expect to be able to acquire knowledge while embodied. So long as we are embodied, we are images striving to emulate our maker 'as far as possible'.

[23] See Perl (1998) and his notes for references to the major ancient and modern proponents of this view.

[24] See Gerson (1990), 69–70.

6.2 Philebus

This complex and conceptually untidy dialogue cries out for a comprehensive interpretation, one which situates convincingly the ethical claims made within the cosmological and methodological framework. Fortunately, I do not think I need to be so ambitious. I want to focus on what this dialogue tells us about embodied personhood through its discussion of pleasure, especially its rejection of false pleasure as an element in the good life.

One way of approaching this matter is by asking the following question: what does this dialogue on the good life tell us that is not already contained in Republic? The straightforward summary of Philebus is that the contenders for the prize of the good life are pleasurable experiences, on the one hand, and intellectual activity, on the other.[25] It is quickly determined that neither a life containing exclusively one or the other could be the best life for a human being (22 B 3–4). Rather, some combination of the two components is best (22 C 7). What is contentious, however, is which of the two components is primarily 'responsible' (αἴτιον) for the goodness of the best life. Socrates contends that it is intellectual activity and his interlocutor, Protarchus, contends that it is pleasure (22 D 2). In order to resolve this issue, it turns out to be necessary to understand, among other things, what goodness is. Goodness is analysed into three aspects: beauty, measure, and truth (65 A 1–5). Intellectual activity or 'intellect' (νοῦς) itself is seen to be more akin (συγγενές) than pleasure to each of these aspects of goodness.[26] Hence, intellectual activity is closer than pleasure to that which is responsible for the goodness in a good life.

This conclusion to what is indisputably the central theme of the dialogue hardly seems like anything new. Specifically, Republic, as we have seen, identifies a type of pleasure that belongs to each part of the soul, including the rational part (581 C 6). Thus, the best life, the life of the philosopher in whom reason rules, is a life that includes pleasure. Indeed, the life of the philosopher is by far the most pleasurable life (583 A 1–3). So, it hardly seems a revelation that the so-called mixed life is best or that the dominant component of that life is intellectual activity. That Philebus provides a more

---

[25] 11 B 4–C 3. I use 'intellectual activity' for what is obviously meant to be a representative list: τὸ φρονεῖν, τὸ νοεῖν, μεμνῆσθαι καὶ τὰ τούτων αὖ συγγενῆ, δόξαν τε ὀρθὴν καὶ ἀληθεῖς λογισμούς.

[26] Truth: 65 C 4–D 3; measure: 65 D 7–10; beauty: 65 E 4–68 A 3.

rigorous account of the nature of pleasure than is to be found in *Republic* or *Gorgias* or anywhere else for that matter is undoubtedly one part of the answer to the question 'What is added that is new?'[27] Is there more?

It will be recalled that in the first chapter I argued that Plato faced a problem in his account of embodied personhood. Persons are subjects of pleasures and pains as well as subjects of cognition. It is not at all obvious why a person, aiming for his own good, should not prefer, say, doing injustice to suffering injustice if the former produces more pleasure than the latter. I argued further that at least part of the solution to this problem is that the embodied person is not the ideal and that embodied life came to be viewed by Plato as a self-constructed image of that ideal. Accordingly, the reason for preferring suffering injustice to doing injustice is that ideally a person lives without a body and hence without bodily pleasures. So, in aiming for our own good we must come to realize that that good does not include bodily pleasures, though as *Republic* insists, it includes the pleasure specific to rational activity.

That which *Republic* adds in what is really an offhand manner actually reintroduces the problem. For even if it is true that the philosopher prefers a philosopher's pleasures and even if it is true, as Plato says, that his life is 729 times more pleasurable than that of a tyrant, still the fact that the presence of pleasure should be a criterion of the good life leaves a puzzle about the relation of the embodied person to the ideal. I mean first of all that if what makes a life good is in part pleasure, then one might actually choose the pleasures of the tyrant despite the superiority of those of a philosopher— superior, that is, from his perspective. Second, what sense does it make to strive to attain the ideal if that involves the elimination of pleasure? I shall argue that *Philebus* is very much concerned with these issues.

I begin by laying out what I take to be Plato's strategy and then proceed to the relevant details. The strategy is not unlike that employed in *Sophist* or even that of an important argument in *Republic* 1. In *Sophist* Plato aims to show that the sophist is someone whose *métier* is not just different from that of the statesman and the philosopher, but inferior. In order to do this he shows first that the stock-in-trade of the sophist is false belief, and then that false belief does indeed exist and that it is something not just different from

[27] See Frede (1992), 437, who argues that *Philebus* offers 'a new ontology of pleasure and pain'.

true belief but inferior as well. The metaphysics of false belief serves the practical goal of showing the reprehensible nature of sophistry. In *Republic* 1 Socrates forces Thrasymachus to admit that if justice is a 'craft' (τέχνη), then it must follow objectively determinable rules. But Thrasymachus' claim that justice is the interest of the stronger is undercut by this admission, for he views his position as one that allows unlimited domination unconstrained by anything other than self-interest.

Similarly, in *Philebus* almost half of the dialogue is devoted to the examination of the nature of pleasure, specifically the establishment of the existence of false pleasures and their difference from true pleasures. The basic strategy is to get the interlocutors, including, always, the readers, to agree to the very reasonable assumption that the good life will be a mixed life, a life of pleasure and intellectual activity. That having been agreed, Plato can argue that it is reasonable that they proceed to an analysis of pleasure in order to determine its causal role in the good life. That is, the rather commonsensical position that one ought to seek pleasure unqualifiedly and at all costs is, on a moment's reflection, unsustainable. Therefore, one can reasonably wonder what the constraints on pleasure's role in the good life actually are. And in order to answer *that* question, an analysis of pleasure is appropriate. What this analysis eventually shows is that there is a distinction between true and false pleasures and that the latter ought not be allowed into the good life. Exactly that which shows why false pleasures are not part of the good life shows that even true pleasure has a qualified or restricted role in that life. That is, one who argues that false pleasures are inferior to true pleasures will have already prepared himself for admitting that even true pleasures are not that for which we ultimately aim. This conclusion does not generate an exhortation to asceticism for the embodied person. Still, it orients the person to an identity other than as a subject of bodily pleasure.[28]

It is important to observe here that Plato never directly urges one to invert one's value system. His basic protreptic strategy is to draw one into

---

[28] The 'most divine state' is the one in which there is neither pleasure nor pain (33 B 6–7). But as it turns out, a life deprived of pleasure is neither self-sufficient nor complete (67 A 5–8). I think the conclusion we should draw from this is the one that Plato has drawn already many times, namely, that embodied life is only an image of a divine disembodied state. We should, however, strive to come as close as possible to that state so long as we are embodied. The best life for a human being is not identical to the best life overall or, more to the point, the best life for us.

an argument on behalf of a position to which he is evidently opposed. It is to the recognition of the inconsistency of that position that one is led. Plato does not say in effect that pleasure is to be shunned. Rather, he says that if you agree that what you want is true pleasure and not false pleasure, then you will see that what you *really* want is something quite different after all, that the reason for wanting true pleasures is inconsistent with principled hedonism in any form. This does not eliminate intellectual pleasure as desirable, but only as that at which one primarily aims. This basic strategy serves the doctrine that I have attributed to Plato throughout this book, namely, that self-knowledge is not a means to happiness but constitutive of it. The way to dislodge the hedonist is not by denigrating pleasure but by enticing the interlocutor into an ἀπορία about what he really wants which can only be resolved by coming to realize who he really is.

The basis for the proof of the existence of false pleasures is, naturally enough, the definition of pleasure (and pain). Socrates offers the following λόγος:

When the natural state of a living organism, constituted, as I said previously, of the Unlimited and the Limit, is destroyed, that destruction is pain; conversely, when such organisms return to their own nature [τὴν αὐτῶν οὐσίαν], this restoration [τὴν ἀναχώρησιν] is in all cases pleasure. (32 B 2–4)

This λόγος is supposed to work for all pleasure and pain. It cannot escape our notice first of all that a condition for the possibility of pleasure here is in some way an 'unnatural' state. This seems to stack the deck against hedonists because if returning to a natural state is desirable, that seems to be because being in a natural state is even more desirable. Indeed, Socrates goes on to argue that a state in which neither pleasure nor pain is present, a state that he identifies as belonging to one exclusively devoted to intellectual activity, is the most divine life (33 B 6–7). On this basis, it is child's play to argue, in the abstract, as it were, that the closer to the divine life one can live the better. But this will hardly impress the hedonist for the plain reason that he need not and almost certainly will not concede that the divine life is best for *him*. Socrates does not in fact take the facile approach. Rather, with the distinction between true and false pleasures, he aims to win over the hedonist on the hedonist's own terms.

In order to show how this is done, I shall begin with the discussion of true pleasures, not false ones. A true pleasure, says Socrates, is one in which the 'deficiencies' (ἐνδείας), that is, the deviations from the natural state, are 'unperceived' (ἀναισθήτους) and so painless, but the 'fillings' (πληρώσεις) are 'perceptible' (αἰσθητάς) and pleasurable (51 B 5–7). Thus, a true pleasure is a pleasure because it consists in a filling or, as the original definition says, a restoration of the natural state. It is a *true* pleasure because there is no perception of the deficiency and so no concurrent pain.

A close reading of this definition of a true pleasure reveals the crucial assumption that there are neither unperceived pleasures nor unperceived pains. What is unperceived in the case of a true pleasure is the deviation from the natural state. This assumption appears to contradict the original definition of pleasure and pain, where the destruction and restoration themselves are identified as pains and pleasures. But this definition is agreed to by Protarchus only as a sort of 'sketch' (τύπος, 32 B 5) and it precedes the argument by Socrates that perception occurs independently of the deficiencies that occur in body and soul.[29] In other words, a deficiency may occur either in body or soul and be unperceived. This stipulation about perception undercuts the claim that there can be unperceived pains or pleasures. If, as it appears, pleasure and pain and their perception go necessarily together, this does not mean that they are identical. Indeed, it is absolutely crucial to the argument that there are false pleasures that they be distinct. They must be distinct because perception provides the possibility of falsehood with regard to the pleasure. That is, what allows Plato to say that there are genuine pleasures that are nevertheless false is that the falsehood depends upon a cognitive defect in what is inseparable from the pleasure. If there are no unperceived pleasures, then judgement is inseparable from pleasure in human beings.

Socrates discusses four types of falsity in pleasures: (1) arising from miscalculations of anticipation; (2) arising from misperceptions of relative mag-

---

[29] 32 D 2–34 A 5. Gosling (1975), 122, claims that Plato 'acknowledges the existence of pleasures that are not replenishments or lacks'—specifically, the pleasure of anticipation and the pleasure in malice. I believe that the latter claim is refuted at 47 C–D, where the general claim about replenishments of 'mixed' pleasures includes malice. As for pleasures of anticipation, I see no acknowledgement in the text that this pleasure, whether false or true, does not involve replenishment. On the contrary, given what is said about desire at 35 C–D as the reaction to a lack, it would seem that the presence of a desire, implicit in anticipatory pleasure, is *eo ipso* evidence of the presence of a lack.

nitude of pleasure and pain; (3) arising from confusion of pleasure and pain; (4) arising from intrinsic connection of pleasure with pain.[30] It is a frequent complaint of commentators that 'falsity' is used equivocally by Plato.[31] Even those sympathetic to the argument presented accept the equivocation, trying to make it a virtue.[32] I think that if we accept the equivocation as obvious or irremovable, we shall miss what Plato is trying to do. If we put together the definition of pleasure and what is subsequently said about true pleasure at 51 B 5–7, then, generally, a false pleasure should be one in which the deviation from the natural state is perceived: that is, when a pain accompanies the pleasure. But in fact the falsity of a false pleasure is only explicitly connected with pain in (2), (3), and (4) above. It is the difficulty of fitting (1) into the general account of pleasure that leads some scholars to question that account. So, what do all false pleasures really have in common?

The argument for the existence of false pleasure is based on a similarity with 'belief' (δόξα). Just as there can be true and false beliefs, so there can be true and false pleasures. A false pleasure is no less a pleasure than a false belief is a belief (37 A 11–B 3; cf. 40 C 8–10). The cogency of the analogy is immediately suspect. Plato seems to base the similarity on the claim that pleasure, like belief, has an intentional object (37 A 7–9). But it is generally supposed that states like pleasure and pain do not have intentional objects. Pleasure is not an object of feeling as a proposition is an object of belief. The failure to see the difference in intentionality in the two cases misleads Plato. For the truth or falsity of a belief is irrelevant to whether one actually has a belief just because truth or falsity are external to the intentional relation. So Plato, the objection continues, incorrectly assuming that pleasures are intentional objects, thinks that one can have a pleasure, like a belief, whose truth or falsity is external to it or an added feature.[33]

This analysis is mistaken for several reasons. First, and most importantly,

---

[30] (1) 36 C–41 B; (2) 41 B–42 C; (3) 42 C–44 D; (4) 44 D–50 E.

[31] See e.g. Gosling (1975), 212–13; Gosling and Taylor (1982), 134–7.

[32] See Frede (1992), 442–3.

[33] At 37 B 10 truth and falsity are said to 'supervene' (ἐπιγίγνεσθον) on the belief. Penner (1970) and Williams (1974) both think that Plato fails to distinguish between believing and the product of believing, a belief. It is only the latter that may be true or false, whereas pleasure is in fact analogous to the former.

if pleasure is inseparable though distinct from the perception of pleasure, the correct intentional object of a feeling of pleasure is oneself in a pleasurable state. It is a feature of persons, as they are described in *Republic*, that they can cognize affective states in which they themselves are the subjects. This feature is owing to the immateriality of persons. If one is in a pleasurable state, therefore, one is able to cognize this state. The cognition includes the ability to articulate to oneself what the pleasure consists in even if one is not presently focused on that.[34] That is why there are no pleasures or pains that are unperceived. Because the pleasure is *both* felt and cognized, falsity can attach to it. That is, falsity is a permanent possibility for the representational content of the intentional object.

Second, if there is a necessary belief component in pleasures, then the similarity between pleasure and belief does not consist in the fact that being pleased is a sort of belief. Rather, pleasure, in so far as it has this component, is like a belief that has nothing to do with any states of pleasure and pain—for example, the belief that Australia is a continent. The similarity is between 'pleasure-involving' beliefs and 'pleasure-neutral' beliefs, not between a feeling of pleasure and a belief. The similarity consists in the fact that the former are susceptible to alteration just as the latter are.

Thus, third, the externality of truth and falsity to belief is a subtler matter than the above objection recognizes. No one holds a belief supposing it to be false.[35] It is for this reason that if one comes to believe that a proposition is false, one immediately stops believing it. Continuing to believe it is not, it seems, a psychological option. That beliefs can be true or false does not change the fact that beliefs are held without exception as true. That is what it means, after all, to hold a belief. What for Plato makes pleasure relevantly similar to belief is the supposition that if the belief that attached to a pleasure came to be recognized as false, and were therefore jettisoned, the pleasure would cease.[36] But is this in fact true?

---

[34] The point is well made by Frede (1985), 179–80.

[35] See e.g. *Rep.* 382 A–B, 412 E–413 A.

[36] At *Rep.* 583–5 Plato argues that there are false pleasures as well as false pains. Their falsity rests upon a perceptual error in those who experience them. There is an intermediate state, a certain calmness or tranquillity (ἡσυχία), between pleasure and pain (583 C 7–8). The recovery from a pain or the removal of a pleasure is often mistaken for a true pleasure or pain. The appearance of a pain or pleasure that is really the return to the 'neutral' state is clearly cognitive. People in such a condition are 'deceived'

Socrates' entire argument for the existence of false pleasures rests upon the similarity of pleasure and belief. I have interpreted this similarity as between 'pleasure-involving' beliefs and 'pleasure-neutral' beliefs. In both cases the recognition of the falsity of one's belief produces a rejection of the belief. In the former case the pleasure is thought to disappear as well. For example, someone who got pleasure from imagining the possibility of winning the lottery would, at least as I interpret the argument, immediately cease to have that pleasure if he came to believe that his ticket had been removed from the batch and that it was in fact impossible for him to win.[37] Persons such as acratics and encratics may desire something and also simultaneously desire the opposite. But persons cannot believe and not believe the same thing.

It could be said in response to this that the cognitive element originating in perception and inseparable from the pleasure itself is true or false just because it amounts to a belief. And if this is the case, then the truth or falsity does not, as claimed, belong to the pleasure, but only to the belief. This is in fact precisely the objection Protarchus makes (37 E 12–38 A 2). If this objection is correct, then the belief can vary independently of the pleasure. That is, there is some belief associated with the pleasure that is held and held as true and the subject can come to reject the belief, now thinking it false, without the pleasure being eliminated. But if changing one's belief does necessarily affect the pleasure, then pleasure can have falsity, albeit a

---

(ἀπατῶνται, 585 A 5). But Plato is not so clear regarding whether these false pleasures are truly pleasures. He calls them 'so-called' pleasures and 'shadow-painting' (583 B 5), and later (586 B 8) 'images' of true pleasures. If false pleasures are not pleasures at all, then Plato's argument seems confused. See Frede (1992), 436–7. Presumably, false pleasures have roughly the compromised or equivocal status of sensibles generally. They 'are and are not'. The account in the *Philebus* passages does seem more refined especially in its definition of pleasure, although there Socrates also calls false pleasures 'apparent' (51 A 5–6). The crucial point about the cognitivity of pleasure, however, remains the same in both dialogues.

[37] I suppose that anticipatory pleasures provide especially good cases of belief having an effect on one's occurrent states. See 40 D 7–10. Tuozzo (1996), 504–8, argues that in the case of false anticipatory pleasures the pleasure is caused by images in the subject of the conditions of psychic restoration and their consequences. They are false because they are generated by false beliefs about conditions contrary to future facts. As I understand him, this is consistent with my argument.

falsity that might be termed 'borrowed' (cf. 42 A 7–9).[38] In fact, all the false
pleasures discussed by Socrates are supposedly of this sort. It is assumed
that if the associated belief were to be changed owing to the fact that it was
recognized to be false, the pleasure would be gone. This supposed causal
relationship dramatically indicates the unity of the embodied person despite
its dividedness or tripartitioning.

Pleasures are said to be able to 'miss the mark' (ἁμαρτάνουσαν) regarding
their 'object' (τὸ ἐφ' ᾧ, 37 E 5–7). Presumably 'object' refers, roughly, to
that which is the cause of the filling of a deficiency. Such an object fulfils its
causal role independently of the associated false beliefs. But surely it is odd
to say that a pleasure is 'aiming' at anything. Indeed, a pleasure no more
aims at something than it throws up arguments against reason. It is in fact
the subject of the pleasure who is doing the aiming. And this is made all
the more plausible if we accept that this subject has an attendant belief that
is constitutive of the pleasure. The subject, if he is a consistent hedonist,
believes that what he is aiming at and achieving with this pleasure is his own
good. If the pleasure is false, what he supposedly fails to achieve is just that.

It is no coincidence that Plato uses the word ἁμαρτάνειν here, the word
that appears in the portentous claim 'No one goes wrong willingly [οὐδείς
ἕκων ἁμαρτάνει]'. In fact, when we unwillingly go wrong, it is often with
regard to our pleasures. And the remedy is the same in either case, namely,
the recognition that one has missed the mark at which one is truly aiming.
If Socrates can persuade his interlocutor that a hedonist typically misses
the mark in this way, though he indeed experiences pleasure heaped upon
pleasure, he has practically won the day. For missing the mark implies that
there is a mark at which one aims. That mark is not the pleasure itself;
that has been achieved. What is it then? The simple answer is that what
one desires or aims at is the good and in hitting upon false pleasures one
has not achieved it.[39] But surely the hedonist contends that pleasure just is

---

[38] The verb is ἀνεπίμπλασαν, literally 'fill up'. Gosling translates it as 'infect' and Frede
as 'affect'. In any case, the problem is how the cognitive state of belief is related to bodily
states of pleasure. It is, I think, appropriate to connect the explanation of how belief can
'fill up' pleasure with the explanation of how reason and appetite can quarrel. See above,
ch. 3.

[39] That the good is the aim of all is the common assumption of the interlocutors at
the beginning of the dialogue (11 B); cf. 20 D, 35 D, 61 A . Hampton (1987), 257–9, has a
slightly different analysis of the falsity in false pleasures, but her conclusion is substantially

identical with the good and that when one has the former one necessarily has the latter.[40] So, it cannot simply be taken for granted that attaining false pleasures is not attaining the good just because these pleasures are false.

A somewhat more satisfactory answer is that he who identifies the good with pleasure cannot reasonably deny that a *false* pleasure is not the good. Such pleasures, Protarchus agrees, are 'imitations' (μεμιμημέναι) of true ones (40 c 5).[41] But as it turns out, the reason for preferring true pleasures to false pleasures is the reason for rejecting hedonism as the best way of life. Let us see why this is so.

Recall that the issue is what is the best way of life for a human being, a life of pleasure or a life of the mind. There is no disagreement that a life bereft of either pleasure or intellectual activity would be less than the best. It is a way of life that is in question, and a way of life is more than an individual pleasure or activity. Hedonism is the view that a certain way of life is the good, not the view that pleasures are pleasurable or, as such, good. Someone who pursues false pleasures as a way of life is wedded to a precarious position. First, it is difficult to see how someone could pursue a false pleasure believing it is false any more than one could embrace a belief believing it to be false. No doubt, a false pleasure is enjoyed when it is experienced. After all, it is a pleasure. But let us not forget that we are here talking about a way of life in the abstract and something like one's plans for the future. No one, it could reasonably be argued, would actively pursue false pleasures as a way of life, recognizing them to be false. So, if the putative hedonist agrees that the best life is one that includes as part of its plan only true pleasures, he is going to conceive the good life in a radically different way from any hedonist who ever lived. For true pleasures, as we have seen, do not involve a perceived deficiency in body or soul. The hedonist must now be pursuing pleasures that do not arise from any deficiency or pain that he can generate on his own. That is,

the same as mine. According to her, pleasures are false when they reflect an incorrect evaluation of reality.

[40] So Protarchus' position is summarized at 11 B.

[41] Cf. 65 c 5, where Protarchus asserts that pleasure is the 'biggest imposter of all' (ἁπάντων ἀλαζονίστατον). One interpretation of this claim is that precisely because false pleasures are pleasures, they can deceive and mislead us through their cognitive component. Literally, the deception is self-deception because the subject of the pleasure along with the cognitive component is also the subject deceived.

he cannot be a calculating hedonist striving to produce the conditions for pleasurable experience since that would involve the production of states that are perceived to be painful. He can at best be an opportunistic or adventitious hedonist, grasping pleasures when they fortuitously arise. But that is not in any sense sufficient to constitute a way of life. To recognize that false pleasures are to be rejected amounts to giving up pleasure as the good or as the principal constituent of a happy life.[42] If, as Socrates and Protarchus agree, desire for the good is the starting-point for the activity of every living thing (cf. 20 D 7–10, 54 C 9–11), and a way of life is best if in living that life one achieves what one desires, then, though pleasure may be a part of that life, it cannot be the good.

In true pleasures one pursues the activity, not the pleasure, because one does not perceive the deficiency. By contrast, with a false pleasure one is pursuing the pleasure because of the perception of a lack where the pleasure is coincident with its desired removal. This point is reinforced by Socrates when he argues that true pleasures are 'becomings' and are completed in a state other than themselves, namely, being (54 A–55 B). It is interesting that the criticism of pleasure as a means to an end other than itself belongs to the discussion of true pleasure rather than false pleasure. The proponent of what are in fact false pleasures might wish to hold that he pursues pleasure for its own sake. Indeed, Socrates heaps scorn on one who holds this (54 E). But the proponent of false pleasures as constitutive of the good life has already been defeated. The point that true pleasures are a means to an end is directed to a supposedly more 'refined' hedonist. If it is the case that true pleasures do not follow upon perceived pains, then no one pursues true pleasures as such but must be otherwise motivated to engage in the activities that in fact produce such pleasure. The proponent of hedonism is thus made to accept that he does not desire pleasure at all! In reshaping his concept of what he desires, he reshapes his concept of himself.

One who is experiencing a false pleasure could no doubt insist on the sheer pleasurableness of his pleasure, claiming that he is completely uninterested in whether it is true or false. But the hedonist is making a larger claim, namely, that the best life is the life of pleasure. If he agrees that this claim should be limited to true pleasures, then he gives up his position, which is what Protarchus does. If he claims that it does not matter if the pleasures are

---

[42] Essentially the same argument is made at *Rep.* 586 A–B.

true or false, then he is committed to pursuing at least some false pleasures. But he cannot be aware that they are false beforehand. If he were, he could not embrace the false belief that is constitutive of the false pleasure. So, he has to hope that he never finds out that such a pleasure is in fact based on a false belief.[43] If the hedonist intends to incorporate false pleasures into his overall life plan, he has to resist the reformation that spontaneously occurs in any person who comes to the realization that he has a false belief. But the reason why we drop our false beliefs the moment we recognize they are false is the same as the reason why we do not seek out false beliefs. If the hedonist is going to pursue pleasures on the assumption that they are true, how will that differ from a commitment to seek out *only* true pleasures?

What makes a true pleasure true and a false pleasure false is the belief or beliefs associated with each. The overarching false belief of all those who pursue false pleasures is that one's good is achieved by pursuing pleasure. False pleasures, as opposed to true ones, are those that involve the removal of pain (51 A–B). Since the removal of pain is not identical with true pleasure, the indiscriminate hedonist is, it seems, bound for failure in achieving his own good time and again.[44] A hedonist who resolved only to pursue true pleasures would, from a Platonic perspective, have a view of his own good more in line with the philosopher than with the tyrant or libertine. Though such a person would not actually be a philosopher, surely he would be apt for conversion.

It has often been noted that the definition of a true pleasure as involving a deficiency seems to preclude the pleasure of learning—that is, the plea-

---

[43] Perhaps it is the unreformable hedonist, dismissed at the beginning of the dialogue and at the very end, who would choose such a life. He is one who is beyond argument. See Irwin (1995), 329–30, for a similar account of the hedonist's indefensible strategy. This account has been challenged by Carone (2000), esp. 271–80. She argues that the rejection of false pleasures is not a rejection of hedonism, but an indirect endorsement of true pleasures. The best life is in fact a 'mixture' of pleasures and intellectual activity, and the hedonist can reasonably claim to employ intelligence in maximizing pleasures. Such a hedonist is perhaps best represented by the highly refined aesthete. Since it does not adduce considerations relating to immortality, *Philebus* may not be in a strong position to show that this sort of life is inferior to the philosophical life.

[44] At 44 A 9–10 Socrates claims that pleasure and removal of pain are distinct. But he seems to mean 'true' pleasure based on his later identification of true pleasure with a state in which there is no pain to remove (51 B 1–2).

sure of the rational part of the soul mentioned in *Republic* (583 A).[45] The very terms of the argument in *Philebus*—pleasure vs. intellectual activity— seem to make inevitable the denial that learning is a pleasure. It is not so clear, however, that learning does not involve something like an unperceived deficiency being filled up, though admittedly when such a deficiency is corrected there is no more pleasure of that sort. This fact makes all the more remarkable Plato's claim that a hedonist can be brought round to agreeing that, finally, he does not want to pursue pleasure as his primary aim.

All of this discussion of the relative merits of the life of pleasure and the life of the mind takes place entirely outside the context of any recognition of the immortality of the soul. We saw in Chapter 1 that similar claims made by Socrates in the early dialogues ran up against those made by the recalcitrantly wicked person. The doctrine of the immortality of the soul and the consequent possibility of rewards and punishments in the afterlife surely count as one way of supporting Socrates against his opponents. As I have argued, however, the most important result of the introduction of immortality is the reform in the concept of the person. If persons in their embodiments use bodies and have bodily states that are images of an ideal disembodied state, then the good for a person is intrinsically psychic. The demolition of the hedonist's position in *Philebus* is at once a recognition that embodied life imperfectly represents the ideal and a kind of tour de force of argument for the basis of the Socratic paradoxes, immortality notwithstanding. Especially remarkable is the fact that here, in contrast to *Gorgias*, the hedonist himself concedes. Callicles in that dialogue is, of course, beaten in a sense, but he does not himself believe it. Protarchus, however, really does concede. There is no discernible irony in his enthusiastic agreement with Socrates. I imagine that Protarchus represents for Plato a model of how he conceived conversion might go.[46]

The last part of the dialogue takes up the claim of intellectual activity to be the principal component in the good life (55 C–59 C). It attempts to grade various forms in a way parallel to the grading of pleasures. In particular, it aims to grade types of knowledge with respect to accuracy and purity (56 C, 57 B 1). The use of 'knowledge' here in the plural does not contradict

---

[45] See e.g. Frede (1992), 453.

[46] And Socrates as a model of the facilitator of conversion. See Frede (1996), esp. 246–7.

its use in *Republic* and *Theaetetus* for a unique cognitive state.[47] The word in the plural is commonly used by Plato for 'fields of study or expertise' wherein knowledge in the sense of a special cognitive state may or may not be available.[48] The array of fields of study or 'knowledges' and at least the criterion of accuracy closely mirror *Republic*. In both, dialectic is the supreme cognitive enterprise.[49] Its supremacy rests on its clarity, accuracy, and truth. Pointedly, it does not rest on utility.[50] The denial of practical value to the highest form of cognition is remarkable in comparison with *Republic*, where it is precisely because of the practical value of dialectic that philosophers ought to be made kings. Indeed, in *Philebus* 'knowledges' with practical value are admitted into the good life because they provide something dialectic does not (62 A–D).

Once false pleasures are eliminated from the contest, gradations of cognitive states or fields of study are irrelevant. Protarchus does not need to be convinced that he ought to throw in his lot with philosophers in order to be convinced that pleasure is not the good. No doubt, once one is convinced of this, one is likely to be much more receptive to conversion to the philosophical life. And presumably there is available to Plato an argument about the relative truth of the various fields of study parallel to the argument about the relative desirability of true to false pleasures. Such an argument, however, is irrelevant to the present context.

Philebus confronts hedonism on a level playing field. It does not use the trump card of immortality. In this it is similar to *Theaetetus*, which confronts opposing accounts of knowledge without assuming that Forms are its only possible objects. *Philebus* implicitly rejects an account of embodiment that is hylomorphic in any way. Someone who thought that persons really are the subject of bodily states as much as or in the same way that they are the subjects of mental states could be the sort of intransigent hedonist

---

[47] See 66 B 9, where ἐπιστῆμαι, τέχναι, and δόξαι ὀρθαί are distinguished.

[48] See e.g. *Charm.* 165 E 4; *Laches* 199 C 1; *Symp.* 235 A 3. The word is also used in *Theaetetus* in the plural to refer to putative 'pieces' of knowledge. The plural use for fields of study also appears even in *Republic*: see e.g. 522 C 2, 530 D 8, 533 D 4.

[49] 58 E 2–3; *Rep.* 534 E 3.

[50] 58 C 2–4. Socrates in this passage actually sets aside the criteria of excellence and utility. It is perhaps more correct to insist that he detaches these criteria from those of clarity, accuracy, and truth, leaving it an open question whether dialectic meets the former.

that Protarchus is not and Callicles presumably is. Of course, one can be a hylomorphist and an anti-hedonist. Plato's most famous pupil comes to mind in this regard. The point is that Plato thought that one could not consistently be so. If, as he argues, all desire is in the soul, and desire is for that which is good for oneself, then one will be forced on pain of inconsistency to prefer a life oriented to intellectual goods rather than to pleasure.

6.3 Laws

If, as the most common reading of the doxographical tradition has it, Plato died while his work Laws was still in 'draft' form, we are entitled to assume that it contains something like the last written expression of his thoughts on personhood. It is particularly worth asking whether the elaborate theoretical claims made in Republic are here rejected or qualified in any way. It is universally recognized that Laws acknowledges the phenomenon of ἀκρασία. As we have seen, and as is more or less universally recognized, the partitioning of the soul provides the theoretical underpinning for the explanation of ἀκρασία in Republic. But Laws does not seem to use partitioning of the soul in order to explain how ἀκρασία is possible. So, the obvious question is: did Plato think it was a mistake to partition the soul in the first place? And if so, does he offer an alternative explanation of ἀκρασία in Laws? It is on these questions that I shall focus in the present section.

Christopher Bobonich has argued that the partitioning of the soul by Plato in Republic was an error and that this error is rectified in Laws, where Plato offers a superior theory to account for the phenomenon of ἀκρασία.[51] I shall take Bobonich's argument as a lucid and forceful expression of the sort of approach to psychic partitioning and incontinence that I find mistaken. Bobonich raises basically three problems for the partitioning of the soul: (1) it is difficult to state clearly what the principle of opposites is that generates just those parts of the soul posited by Plato; (2) the explanatory

[51] Bobonich (1994). Bobonich has kindly let me see chapter 3 of his forthcoming book on Laws, which is an elaboration of the argument in his 1994 paper (I shall refer to the latter). The book contains a wealth of argument, including an extensive discussion of how, according to Bobonich, the account of incontinence in Laws differs from the account in Republic. Bobonich thinks that the account in Laws is superior because it abandons 'agent-like' parts of the soul. These are the homunculi I argue were never part of that account.

power of a psychological theory that divides agents into agent-like parts is dubious (the 'homunculi problem'); (3) partitioning presents a problem for the unity of the self.[52] I have already addressed these problems in Chapter 3. Recognizing that the embodied person *is* divided or, stated otherwise, is an unstable and complex unity turns (3) on its head. It also undermines the homunculi problem, for the embodied person is always the agent of action, operating and identifying himself either as the master or as the servant of appetite. Appetite is never an agent of action because embodied human action requires rational agency.

Let us examine the evidence that leads Bobonich to the conclusion that the above three problems were recognized by Plato as requiring an abandonment of partitioning. Against Bobonich, I want to argue that, properly understood, the account of *Republic* is retained in *Laws*. There is no fundamentally new account in Plato's last work.

The first text, cited at length by Bobonich, is in book 1:

Let us suppose that each living thing among us is a divine puppet [θαῦμα θεῖον][53] whether made as a toy for the gods or for some serious purpose—which one it is we do not know. But we do know this, that these states [πάθη] in us, like certain sinews or cords, drag us and, being opposites, pull against each other towards opposite actions. Here is where the division [διωρισμένη] between virtue and vice lies. For, as our account declares, there is one of these pulling forces which each person ought [δεῖν] to follow along with and in no way leave hold of, pulling against the other cords. This is the golden and holy leader, reason [τοῦ λογισμοῦ], having the sobriquet 'public law of the state'. The other cords are hard and iron, likenesses of all sorts of shapes, while this one is flexible, being made of gold. It is necessary for us always to co-operate with that most noble leader, the law, for reason, being noble, is gentle and not violent, and needs assistants so that the golden cord in us can be victorious over the other kinds. (644 D 7–645 B 1, trans. Saunders)

The image of the puppet could be taken as making a Stoic point about fate or determinism. It does not count against such an interpretation that we are urged to co-operate with reason and generally to participate in our own

---

[52] Bobonich (1994), 15–16.

[53] The emendation τῶν θεῶν is quite unnecessary, as England notes (1921: i. 255, ad loc.). The puppet is divine owing to its possession of reason. Cf. *Tim.* 41 C 7, where the rational part of the soul is called 'divine'.

moral improvement. That was certainly the Stoic position. What *does* count against the interpretation is that the image of the puppet and its controlling cords is intended, as the Athenian Stranger goes on to say, to explain the phrases 'being better than oneself' and 'being worse than oneself' (645 B 1– 2).[54] These phrases were introduced earlier (626 E, 633 E) to describe a man being overcome by pleasure, which is, as we recall, the way Plato describes ἀκρασία in *Republic* (430 E 6–9). But the early Stoics, at any rate, reject the possibility of ἀκρασία precisely because they take the soul to be a unified ἀρχή of action. That is, they reject partitioning of the soul. Bobonich, it seems, wants to make Plato something of a Stoic while still allowing him to explain ἀκρασία rather than explain it away.

How is this done? Bobonich argues that the πάθη or states which drag us against the pull of reason are not, as they are in *Republic*, 'agent-like' parts. 'None, for example, is described as having beliefs or desires.'[55] As I have argued, however, agent-like parts with their own beliefs and desires are not what is involved in partitioning. The one who desires pleasure is not the appetitive part of the soul but the person. And the quarrel that the person has with his appetites is not a quarrel with a separate agent who has beliefs about the satisfaction of pleasure. Therefore, we should not suppose that agent-like parts ever belonged to Plato's explanation of ἀκρασία. Nevertheless, against Bobonich, the Stoics were right to hold that without some sort of division in the soul no explanation is possible. Does the present passage offer an alternative explanation?

Bobonich thinks that it does. He argues that Plato acknowledges in agents

---

[54] Fortenbaugh (1975), 24, says that the image of the cords 'makes clear that what has seemed to be a threefold division is to be construed as a dichotomy'. Surely, however, it does not follow from the fact that some cords are set over against one, namely, reason, that the soul is being bipartitioned rather than tripartitioned, just as, for example, this does not follow in *Phaedrus*, where horses are set over against the charioteer, or in *Timaeus*, where the mortal parts of the soul are set over against the immortal. Fortenbaugh thinks that the latter division in *Timaeus* might be viewed as an anticipation of Aristotle's bipartite psychology (40); so Rees (1957), 117–18. He also thinks that 'the dichotomy implicit in the *Laws* is fundamentally a distinction between calculations and reflections on the one hand and pleasant and painful emotions such as fear and confidence on the other' (25).

[55] Bobonich (1994), 20. But see 863 B–C, for example, where pleasure is said to achieve, 'with deceit' (μετὰ ἀπάτης), what its 'will desires' (βούλησις ἐθελήσῃ). This seems to me to be exactly on a par with the way the appetites are spoken of in *Phaedo* and *Republic*; cf. *Phileb*. 65 C 5.

the possibility of a desire to do something that is stronger than the desire
to refrain, where the latter desire is based upon what the agent thinks, all
things considered ('ATC calculations'), is best to do.[56] Bobonich's analysis
drives a wedge between ATC calculations and desire. This in itself is what
Plato himself does in *Republic* (439 C 9–D 8). But Bobonich wishes to do this
and insist that the agent is unified, which is exactly what Plato sees cannot
be the case in *Republic*. According to Bobonich, the agent can believe that
ATC, X is better to do than Y, but the agent desires Y more. The word 'more',
however, conceals the problem. If the agent ATC thinks that X is better than
Y but desires Y more, then the agent desires *less* what he thinks is better
and apparently we have a violation of the principle that no one does wrong
willingly, a principle that is equivalent to the claim that all desire their own
good. But the principle is affirmed later on in *Laws*.[57] So, Bobonich has to
say that 'no one does wrong willingly' does not mean for the agent that he
desires less what he thinks is better ATC. His calculation that ATC X is better
than Y must be completely severed from his desire. But if this is so, it is very
difficult to see what 'all desire their own good' is then supposed to mean.
Either the agent does desire what he thinks is ATC better, in which case one
wants to know how his pursuing what he desires less is being explained, or
else his calculation of what is ATC best is actually irrelevant to his action.
Figuring out what ATC the best thing to do is has nothing to do with what
he desires to do. Alternatively, one would have to say that the agent does
indeed act according to his greatest desire, in which case he is not acratic at
all, though he may be vicious or stupid.

The problem with Bobonich's analysis is not with his description of how
an acratic agent operates. The problem is with his claim that this description
works for a unified agent. True, the agent is one person (cf. 644 C 4). That
is exactly what Plato claims in *Republic* when he says that the expression
'self-control' or 'being better than oneself' (τὸ κρείττω αὑτοῦ) is laughable
because the one who controls and the one who is controlled is the same
person (ὁ αὐτός, 430 E 11–431 A 1). Nevertheless, he immediately adds that
such an expression does indicate that there is in the person a better and

[56] Bobonich (1994), 20.

[57] See 731 C 2–3: ὁ ἄδικος οὐχ ἑκὼν ἄδικος; cf. *Tim.* 86 D 7–E 1. I take it that 'all desire
their own good' can be construed as an ATC desire. See Roberts (1987), esp. 31–2, for an
interpretation of 'no one does wrong willingly' in *Laws* similar to mine.

a worse part, and that being 'self-controlled' (ἐγκρατής) amounts to the ruling of the better part over the worse part. In short, Bobonich thinks that in *Laws* Plato has abandoned what in *Republic* he thought was necessary to account for ἀκρασία, namely, partitioning of the soul.[58]

Without partitioning of the soul, either explanations of ἀκρασία amount to *explaining away* the phenomenon or, as with Bobonich, these explanations are incoherent. Bobonich's agent, like Leontius in *Republic*, is overcome with desire. It is his desire. The way Bobonich tries to render this unproblematic is by making the calculation that refraining from acting or doing something different ATC has no implication whatsoever for what the agent desires. So, in Leontius' case, for example, his belief that he ought to refrain from gazing on the corpses does not entail or is not otherwise connected to a desire not to refrain. Apart from the general obscurity of this, the passage from *Laws* with which we started certainly seems to suggest that the 'states' in us, which include reasoning, draw or incline us to actions. A desiderative element seems inescapably present. Bobonich seems to recognize this when he says parenthetically 'the desire for Y that is associated with . . . calculation'.[59] But if Leontius' desire to refrain from gazing on the corpses associated with his calculation that this is the right thing to do is commensurably less than his desire to gaze, in what sense is he an acratic? For in that case he would be acting on his greatest desire. If, on the other hand, his desire to refrain is incommensurable with his desire to gaze, and he is overcome with his own desire, some sort of partitioning of the person seems inevitable.

Let us recall that the sort of analysis Bobonich favours results in *Protagoras* in the denial of the phenomenon of ἀκρασία. Socrates says that it is 'absurd' to hold that, 'though a man knows what is good, he is not willing to do it because he is overcome by immediate pleasures' (355 B 1–3). The absurdity here, which is I suspect very close to the absurdity of the commonsensical

---

[58] Bobonich (1994), 32, concludes his paper: 'In the *Laws* . . . there are no agent-like lower parts of the soul to be persuaded, and the only ultimate protection against acratic action is the individual's power of self-control.' Bobonich in effect concludes just where Plato in *Republic* begins to construct a partitioned soul, namely, with an explanation of how self-control is possible.

[59] Cf.. 'it seems to be quite common for the recognition that one course of action is ATC best to lead to the diminishment of the strength of desires for incompatible options and to an increase in the strength of my desire for what I now realize to be ATC best' (22).

term 'self-control' used in *Republic*, is removed by partitioning. So far as I can tell, Bobonich's agent does something that *Protagoras* holds is impossible and that *Republic* recognizes is possible but only if the soul is partitioned. So long as we can give an interpretation of partitioning that avoids the problems noted by Bobonich, we should not hesitate to insist that Plato is still committed to it. In fairness to Bobonich, he does not think that his analysis leaves Plato's account of ἀκρασία without problems. But he does think that it leaves him without a partitioned soul.

The evidence for parts of the soul in *Laws* is inconclusive but not so nugatory as Bobonich and others believe. In book 3 the Athenian Stranger is characterizing what he calls 'the greatest ignorance' (ἡ μεγίστη ἀμαθία):

> [It is] that type of ignorance which we see in the man who hates, instead of loves, that which he believes to be noble and good, while loving and cherishing that which he believes to be ignoble and bad. That discordance [διαφωνίαν] between pain and pleasure in relation to rational belief is, I say, extreme ignorance, in fact the greatest of all, because it belongs to the mass of the soul [τοῦ πλήθους τῆς ψυχῆς]. For that in the soul which feels pain and pleasure [τὸ γὰρ λυπούμενον καὶ ἡδόμενον αὐτῆς] is like the populace or mass of the state. So, whenever it opposes [ἐναντιῶται] those things that by nature rule, forms of knowledge, beliefs, or reason, this I call 'folly' [ἄνοιαν], whether it be in the state, whenever the masses disobey the rulers and the laws, or in the individual, whenever the noble principles in the soul are ineffectual, but what is entirely contrary to them occurs.[60] (689 A 5–B 7)

Here, I do not think that the words 'that in the soul which feels pain and pleasure' should be understood as referring to a part, if 'part' indicates agency. The one who feels pain and pleasure is here and is always for Plato the same person who is capable of resisting these. Nevertheless, it seems very difficult to deny that partitioning of some sort is a consequence of distinguishing 'the mass of the soul' from that to which it is opposed. In addition, opposition within the soul is here recognized exactly in the man-

---

[60] The words ὁπόταν καλοὶ ἐν ψυχῇ λόγοι ἐνόντες μηδὲν ποιῶσιν πλέον, ἀλλὰ δὴ τούτοις πᾶν τοὐναντίον are somewhat ambiguous. I doubt that καλοὶ λόγοι is to be understood as the subject of the last clause, since it is hard to see how they can produce something wholly opposite to a good effect. It seems rather that we are to understand loosely as subject the group mentioned at the beginning of the passage, namely, feelings of pain and pleasure.

ner that occasions the soul's partition in *Republic*. Indeed, the comparison between the parts of the state and the parts of the soul in *Republic* is irresistibly brought to mind here. Finally, the opposition between the rational and that which produces pleasure and pain is recognized in action, in the last difficult sentence. Everything depends on whether reason or opposing principles dominate.

Another passage, much later in *Laws*, provides a similar description of the soul, emphasizing in particular the difference between the rule of reason, which is identified with justice, and the rule of passion, fear, pleasure, pain, appetite, and so on, which is identified with injustice (863 E 5–864 B 4):

> My general description of injustice is this: the mastery of the soul by anger, fear, pleasure, pain, envy, and desires, whether they lead to any actual damage or not. But no matter how states or individuals think they can achieve the good, it is the belief about the best [τὴν δὲ τοῦ ἀρίστου δόξαν] that should govern every man and hold sway in his soul, even if he is in some respect mistaken [κἂν σφάλληταί τι]. If it does, every action done in accordance with it, and any part of a man's nature that becomes subject to such control, we have to call 'just', and best for the entire life of mankind—and this in spite of the popular belief that damage done in such circumstances is an 'involuntary' injustice. (863 E 5–864 A 8, trans. Saunders, slightly modified)

The passage seems on all fours with those in *Republic* in which tripartition is clearly asserted. More to the point, as Plato explains, the rule of reason is not equivalent to true opinion or knowledge about any practical matter. Those who are just may well do things that are ordinarily termed 'involuntary' injustices.[61] Even if they have a belief about what is best, which I take it is an ATC belief, they can err. If the person is unified in the way that Bobonich

---

[61] Roberts (1987), 26–9, argues, rightly in my view, that this passage indicates that ignorance is compatible with being a just person. Those who have denied this have been reluctant thus to sever the link between knowledge and virtue. See Roberts (1987), 35 n. 5, for criticism of M. J. O'Brien (1967), Saunders (1968), and Mackenzie (1981) in this regard. But if the justice here implied to be compatible with ignorance ('even if he is a little mistaken') is a part of the popular virtue of *Phaedo* and *Republic*, there is no need to suppose that philosophical virtue and knowledge are being separated here. See Görgemanns (1960), 142. Of course, if we suppose that philosophical knowledge is unavailable to embodied persons, the scope of popular virtue will be universal. Saunders (1991), 149–50, replying to Roberts, admits that a person who is ignorant may be just, though his justice would be 'a relatively fragile thing'.

takes Plato to be claiming in *Laws*, his desire to follow pleasure and so to be under its rule is either the desire of a separate agent, which, as Bobonich insists, is absurd, or it is really his desire, but he is a divided self.

If a person can be just and still err, is justice now being reduced to a 'good conscience'?[62] I think not. The person who acts according to a belief about the best is acting, minimally, according to a belief about what is best for himself. Reason is the ἀρχή of his action. But that belief may be false, and even culpably so, in a legal sense. Whether the belief be true or false, a person in whom reason is the ἀρχή of action is not acting because of appetite or spirit. He does not identify himself as a subject whose good is achieved in that way. There is a remarkable statement by the Athenian Stranger earlier in the dialogue that connects identity and virtue in the way that we have found Plato doing throughout this book:

The greatest of evils found naturally [ἔμφυτον] in the souls of most human beings is one that everyone forgives himself for having and so makes no effort to escape. This is what people are talking about when they say that every human being is by nature a friend to himself and that it is proper for him to be so. In truth, however, the explanation [αἴτιον] each and every time for all the mistakes [ἁμαρτημάτων] that human beings make is excessive self-love [τὴν σφόδρα ἑαυτοῦ φιλίαν]. This is a love that blinds the lover in regard to the beloved, so that he judges badly matters of justice and goodness and beauty, always thinking that he should honour that which belongs to himself [τὸ αὐτοῦ] before the truth. But anyone who would be a great man should not adore himself or what belongs to him. Rather, he should adore just deeds whether they are his or—even more so in this case—if they happen to be done by another. It is stemming from this same mistake, too, that there is in everyone the lack of learning that appears to oneself to be wisdom. Consequently, not knowing a thing, but thinking we know everything, we do not turn over to others what we do not know how to do, and we therefore make mistakes when we do it ourselves. For these reasons, human beings should flee the excessive love of self, and always follow that which is better than oneself, not letting embarrassment with such a position get in his way. (731 D 6–732 B 4)

The 'selflessness' here recommended should not be confused with altruism.

[62] See Roberts (1987), 400–3, who argues against this implication. Roberts says that 'a soul "ruled by its opinion about the best" will thus be a soul controlled by reason, not only in the sense that it does what its reason thinks good (as many an unjust soul does), but also in the sense that reason has not been unduly influenced by bad appetites or desires of one kind or another'.

That it is 'excessive' self-love that is rejected is, I take it, a tacit recognition that embodied persons are inevitably self-lovers to some extent. We are, however, bidden to follow the deliverances of reason in all things over against the interests of our 'best friend'. What are these interests? In the context of the Platonic account of embodied personhood, can these be other than the idiosyncratic desires of the appetitive and spirited parts of the soul? Without the dividing of the embodied person, it is difficult to see how self-love is being contrasted with allegiance to truth. Honouring oneself before the truth amounts to identifying one's own good as other than and frequently in conflict with the good itself. That Plato consistently held that one's own good and the good are in fact identical is powerful evidence that he viewed embodied personhood as an image of the ideal. There is an exact coincidence of identification of oneself as a subject of reason and love of truth.[63]

I have hitherto argued in defence of the continued partitioning of the soul in *Laws*. One piece of evidence that has been adduced against this is that *tripartitioning* of the soul does not seem to be clearly operative in this work. And, so the argument goes, if tripartitioning is not present, then perhaps Plato's commitment to any sort of partitioning must be seen to have been reduced, if not to have disappeared altogether.[64] There is one passage in *Laws* in which Plato explicitly wonders whether 'spirit' or 'anger' ($\theta\nu\mu\delta s$) is some sort of 'state' ($\pi\delta\theta os$) or some sort of 'part' ($\mu\epsilon\rho os$, 863 B 2–3). I take it that his worry here is over whether $\theta\nu\mu\delta s$ is a *distinct* state or part of the soul. This is not the worry in *Republic*, where $\theta\nu\mu\delta s$ is the

---

[63] I would suggest that the identity of 'good' and 'good for me' is to be understood according to the virtuality of the Form of the Good as explained in Chapter 3. Since the good of each person is virtually identical with the nature of that Form, it is not possible for me to achieve my good by denying the good of anyone else. For example, if *A* commits an injustice against *B*, this could never be good for *A* since it is not good for *B*.

[64] Some scholars view the abandonment of a soul with three parts in *Laws* as a stage on the way to Aristotle's view of the soul as having two parts, although clearly 'parts' is not used in the same way by Aristotle. For Aristotle, the 'parts' of the soul are not different principles of action; there is only one principle of action, the human being. Thus, Fortenbaugh (1975) tends to speak of a 'dichotomy' rather than bipartition. See Rees (1957) and Görgemanns (1960), 122–3 (but see the qualification at 137), who argue for bipartitioning; and Saunders (1962), who argues that tripartitioning is retained. As Saunders (37) rightly points out, tripartition presupposes bipartition and bipartition is always capable of expansion into tripartition.

substance of a distinct part. The context of the *Laws* passage is essential. Here Plato is distinguishing types of legal offences, those that we would call felonies and those that we would call tortious. The former are injustices and the latter injurious. Instances of wrongdoing that arise from spirit, fear, pleasure and pain, envy, and appetite are injustices (863 E 5–8). Those that arise from an error of reason are only tortious. For this distinction, it does not matter if spirit is a separate part of the soul. If, as *Republic* holds, it is, this is irrelevant to the present distinction. So long as reason is not in charge, there is injustice, and this is entirely in line with what is said in Republic. It is perfectly consistent for Plato to hold that even if spirit is congenitally the ally of reason, actions done under its aegis are injustices.[65]

There is a passage late in *Laws* which is remarkably explicit regarding personhood, and which supports the division of the person that I maintain is present throughout this work. Plato is speaking in general about criminal punishment and adds a few remarks about the treatment of the dead:

We should, of course, trust whatever the legislator tells us, but especially his doctrine that the soul has an absolute superiority [τὸ πᾶν διαφέρουσαν] over the body, and that while one is alive, that which provides one's identity is nothing but the soul [ἐν αὑτῷ τε τῷ βίῳ τὸ παρεχόμενον ἡμῶν ἕκαστον τοῦτ᾽ εἶναι μηδὲν ἀλλ᾽ ἢ τὴν ψυχήν], whereas the body is just the semblance [ἰνδαλλόμενον] of each of us that we carry around.[66] This means we are quite right when we say that corpses are images [εἴδωλα] of the deceased. Our real selves [τὸν δὲ ὄντα ἡμῶν ἕκαστον ὄντως]—our immortal soul, as it is called—departs, as the ancestral law declares, to the gods to give an account of itself. To the wicked, this is a terrifying doctrine but a good man will welcome it. (959 A 4–B 7, trans. Saunders)

The priority of soul to body has already been argued for in the analysis of different kinds of motion in book 10 (896 B–C). In this passage the rather more specific point is made that each of us is identical with a soul. Even when embodied, one's identity is provided by the soul. But then in what sense is the human body a 'semblance' of the person? From the following

[65] Cf. *Tim.* 69 C 5–70 A 7, where the distinction between 'immortal' and 'mortal' no more negates tripartition than does the distinction made in the *Laws* passage.

[66] One might be tempted to suppose that 'identity' here is numerical. See England (1921), ii. 611, ad loc., who considers this interpretation before rightly rejecting it. The passage, though, indirectly raises the question of what accounts for one's identity when the human being is dead.

lines where it is said that the 'really real' version of each of us is a soul, the 'semblance' must be that which appears to be the real thing but is not. And this is consistent in general with the way that Plato treats appearances. This semblance is not the corpse, but the living entity, the embodied person. If this were not so—that is, if the 'body' that is the semblance were just the mass of flesh—it would not be different from the corpse. Thus, we can say precisely that a human being is a semblance of a real person. The real person is what departs from this life for divine judgement. Given what has been said previously, this real person would seem to be just the rational subject bearing the marks of its embodiment in a body and participation in bodily life. In short, there are no grounds for supposing that Plato has gone back on his commitment to embodied tripartition and to the identification of the person with the rational part of the soul. Far from it. He reaffirms the distinction in the most emphatic terms.

We have found nothing in *Laws* which would indicate a change from the *Republic*'s view of the moral psychology of the embodied person. Arguments to the contrary seem to me to rest on a misconception of what that view is. We should lift the curse of the homunculi from the discussion of whether Plato was right or wrong about the sort of thing that an embodied person is. Instead, we should focus on his unwavering assumption that the fundamental burden of embodied personhood is to be an image of the really real set adrift in a sea of images.

Concluding Remarks

For Plato, persons are not identical with individuals falling under the putative natural kind 'human being'. Alternatively, we could say that for Plato souls are not identical with individual composites of soul and body. But an embodied person (or an embodied soul) is not exactly the same thing as a disembodied person (or soul). So, it is a mistake to suppose that the human being is just the simple sum of person or soul and body. A person *with* a body is not a person *plus* a body. An embodied person is different from a disembodied person, roughly as images of the intelligible differ from their paradigms. It would be more accurate to characterize Plato's dualism as based upon the distinction between disembodied person and embodied person than upon the distinction between soul and body. Therefore, Plato's position avoids or at least changes the meaning of the question 'How is the soul related to the body?' The embodied person or soul is neither a *res cogitans* related to a *res extensa* nor even a 'captain' related to a bodily 'ship', to use Aristotle's metaphor. The embodied person has a body and is the subject of bodily states.

As Plato imagines it, embodiment does strange things to persons. It typically produces a sort of 'Stockholm Syndrome' of the body whereby persons become unaccountably attached to their prison and to their lives as prisoners. The Platonic exhortations to 'prepare for death' by philosophizing and to 'take flight from this world' are emblems of the strategy to wean persons away from their unhealthy attachment. Thus, I view as misguided suggestions that Plato's 'other-worldliness' can be safely detached from his accounts of ethics and human psychology.

The paradigm to which the embodied person stands as image is an ideal self or person. Of an embodied person, we can say that the ideal is to it as, say, the Form of Beauty is to Helen's beauty. Just as I cannot understand what *real* beauty is by giving an account of Helen's beauty, so I cannot understand what I am really by giving an account of my embodied self. Embodied persons and images of Forms have to be understood as equivocally intelligible in relation to their paradigms. The equivocal intelligibility of instances of Forms is analogous to the equivocal status of embodied persons as agents or subjects.

The fundamental difference between embodied persons and images of Forms—the place where the analogy breaks down—is that embodied persons, because they are, after all, persons, are capable of more or less identifying with their ideal selves whereas the images are not. A person, unlike an instance of a Form, can recognize what he is ideally and strive to identify with that ideal. However, an embodied person approaches that ideal asymptotically, as it were, because no embodied person can, by definition, eliminate his residual attachment to a body. For example, even the philosopher who identifies himself as wholeheartedly as a person can with the ideal of philosophical living still has desires that we may aptly term 'bodily'. The same person who thinks lofty thoughts desires to eat and sleep. That the same person can both think and have these desires makes evident the equivocal status of embodied personhood.

The tripartitioning of the soul by Plato is no more a multiplication of persons than the equivocal status of instances of Forms means that there are, say, many 'beauties' in Helen. An embodied person is a divided person or self, divided not into separate persons or homunculi, but into episodically or periodically identifiable agents or subjects. The division in the person is most dramatically evident in cases of incontinence and continence, when a person both desires to do something and thinks that he ought not do it. Whether he acts or refrains from acting, he is a divided self because he is a divided subject.

Three claims make the divided self nevertheless one self. First, the person self-reflexively identifies himself as the subject of an appetite and at the same time as the subject of the thought that the appetite ought to be resisted. Second, the self-reflexive subject doing this is a cognitive subject. Third, he is a self-reflexive cognitive subject even in his recognition of himself as the subject of an appetite. Thinking that one is 'giving in to' one's appetite, contrary to what one thinks ought to be done, does not alter the identity of the subject. Quite the opposite. The diminished intelligibility or dividedness of an embodied person is precisely locatable in the fact that one and the same person can be both the thinking subject of an appetite and the subject of the thought that the appetite ought to be resisted. Embodied persons are thinkers or reasoners even as they discover that they are the subjects of appetites or desires. For persons, even the basest or most trivial appetite is the object of a cognitive recognition. For example, to recognize that one is hungry involves formulating the proposition 'I am hungry' and assuming a propositional attitude towards it.

Owing to the fact that the embodied divided self is a rational subject or agent, its paradigm is naturally identifiable as a paradigm of rationality. The disembodied person is not the subject of appetites. So, he is not the subject of instrumental or practical thinking. The paradigm of rationality is thus non-practical or theoretical thinking. A disembodied person is a subject of what Plato identifies as the highest form of thinking, that is, knowing. The practical thinking that an embodied person engages in is a sort of image of theoretical thinking. It is, in fact, just imagistic theoretical thinking applied to embodied desires. Even the non-instrumental thinking of embodied subjects is or contains images. So, the embodied person is himself both an image and a subject of imagistic thinking. A disembodied knower is the paradigm for the embodied, thinking, and divided self.

I have argued that for Plato knowledge is essentially self-reflexive. One cannot know unless one is aware that one is in a state of knowing. Another aspect of the paradigmatic status of disembodied knowing is that all embodied modes of cognition are images of the paradigm. Most importantly, self-reflexive knowing is imaged in the acts of self-identification made by embodied persons. It is only because a person can identify himself as the subject of an appetitive desire at the same time as he identifies himself as one who desires not to act on that appetite that incontinence and continence are possible. This possibility practically defines embodied personhood as divided. If genuine or philosophical virtue is knowledge, then the absence of such knowledge in all or most embodied persons is a property of their divided selves. It also explains why most embodied persons are likely to attain only popular virtue at best.

We have seen throughout this study a certain ambivalence on Plato's part about the possibility of embodied persons having knowledge. I am inclined to the conclusion that Plato believed that embodied persons cannot have knowledge, though they must have *had* knowledge in a disembodied state. Owing to this fact and unlike the sceptic, whether Academic or not, Plato did not think that knowledge was irrelevant to our embodied lives. Far from it. Without our having had knowledge, we would not be correct in identifying ourselves as knowers. And we could not attain the cognitive states that image the ideal. Paradoxically, though we do not have knowledge while embodied, our lives are all about our being knowers.

If disembodied persons are nothing but knowers, do they all know the same things? And if they do, does this result in the elimination or occlusion of individuality? If, as I have argued, knowledge for Plato is non-propositional, and if the tendency of Plato's thought is to identify Forms reductively, then this would suggest an affirmative answer to the first question. A multitude of disembodied knowers, however, each knowing the same things, does not in principle seem to be a contradiction, just as a multitude of embodied knowers knowing the same thing, in a non-Platonic sense of 'knower', is not self-contradictory. But this still leaves us with the obvious question: if we are all destined to be disembodied knowers, what is the point of choosing one sort of life over another here below? Will not a Callicles or an Alcibiades now be doing exactly the same thing as Socrates in Platonic heaven?

One way Plato answers this question is with a doctrine of punitive reincarnation. Admittedly, the doctrine rests on nothing more than an argument from fittingness. It is, in a universe ruled by a good Demiurge, too grotesque to suppose that the wicked are ultimately no worse off than the just. But another way suggests itself, too. If there is no knowing without self-reflexivity—if one cannot know without knowing that one knows—then the status of one who did not self-reflexively know would be like a non-conscious repository of knowledge. He would be a non-person, roughly analogous to the way that someone in a chronic vegetative state might be characterized as a non-person, though he be alive none the less. But since no embodied person, even a philosopher, completely identifies with his rational self, on what basis can we say that some disembodied persons are knowers and some are, while disembodied, in perpetual limbo?

I recur to the idea of identification of one's embodied self with the ideal. Surely, this admits of degrees. Someone who lives a philosophical life would in Plato's view presumably embrace his destiny as someone who engages in nothing but the activity he desires here below. Someone who lives the opposite sort of life would abhor that activity. Perhaps at the extreme, someone who identifies himself completely as the subject of bodily appetites would not have enough of a self left to be the subject of disembodied knowledge. He would become the above-mentioned non-person. Thus, we could explain the connection between virtue and happiness via knowledge. The reason that virtue is knowledge and virtue is sufficient for happiness is that we are ideally knowers. Without a desire to be a knower, a person ultimately breaks the connection between what he is actually and what he is ideally. He destroys himself as surely as drinking poison destroys his body.

One may imagine the mechanism of this as something like the following. Consider someone who, owing to drugs, becomes progressively unable to focus or concentrate on any thought. Such a person perhaps gradually operates more according to dispositional beliefs than occurrent ones. He is on 'automatic pilot'. He becomes, in Frankfurt's phrase, a 'wanton'. That someone should impair or even lose his ability to think is hardly puzzling. As we have seen, Plato in *Republic* tends to treat moral deterioration like the deterioration caused by attacks on the body, whether self-inflicted or not. He does this because moral deterioration or improvement is a struggle within the embodied person. Someone who is not ruled by reason is someone who is ruled by the appetites occasioned by embodiment. Such a one incrementally identifies himself with that which is other than his ideal self. I suppose Plato believes that the consequence of such identification is a disembodied self that, so to speak, knows without knowing that it knows. And that is to say that it does not actually know at all.

What Plato says about embodied persons may well seem question-begging or at least inconclusive without a proof that the embodied person can attain disembodied status. Yet such a proof, as we have seen, depends very heavily on the phenomenology of embodied psychology, especially embodied cognition. Someone who unreservedly recognizes himself as ideally a thinker is probably the only plausible candidate for the sort of self-transformation Plato recommends. Such a one is least likely to regard attachments to the idiosyncratic as essential to happiness. Plato's ideal, in my view, is not accurately described as entailing the obliteration of the self. It does, however, entail an extraordinary transformation of the self. The rarity of the true philosophical temperament, as Plato understands that, is hardly in doubt.

Bibliography

ADAM, J. (1963), *The* Republic: *Edited with Critical Notes, Commentary, and Appendices* (Cambridge: Cambridge University Press).

ANNAS, J. (1975), 'On the Intermediates', *Archiv für Geschichte der Philosophie*, 57: 146–66.

—— (1981), *An Introduction to Plato's* Republic (Oxford: Clarendon Press).

—— (1985), 'Self-Knowledge in Early Plato', in D. J. O'Meara (ed.), *Platonic Investigations* (Studies in Philosophy and the History of Philosophy, 13; Washington, DC: Catholic University of America Press), 111–38.

—— (1999), *Platonic Ethics, Old and New* (Ithaca, NY: Cornell University Press).

APOLLONI, D. (1996), 'Plato's Affinity Argument for the Immortality of the Soul', *Journal of the History of Philosophy*, 34: 5–32.

ARCHER-HIND, R. D. (1888), *The* Timaeus *of Plato* (New York: Macmillan and Co.).

BAKER, L. R. (2000), *Persons and Bodies: A Constitution View* (Cambridge: Cambridge University Press).

BALTES, M. (1997), 'Is the Idea of the Good in Plato's *Republic* Beyond Being?', in M. Joyal (ed.), *Studies in Plato and the Platonic Tradition: Essays Presented to John Whittaker* (London: Ashgate Publishing Ltd.), 3–23.

BENSON, H. (1992), 'Why is There a Discussion of False Belief in the *Theaetetus*?', *Journal of the History of Philosophy*, 30: 171–99.

BETT, R. (1986), 'Immortality and the Nature of the Soul in the *Phaedrus*', *Phronesis*, 31: 1–26.

BOBONICH, C. (1994), 'Akrasia and Agency in Plato's *Laws* and *Republic*', *Archiv für Geschichte der Philosophie*, 76: 3–36.

BOSTOCK, D. (1986), *Plato's* Phaedo (Oxford: Clarendon Press).

—— (1988), *Plato's* Theaetetus (Oxford: Clarendon Press).

BRAINE, D. (1992), *The Human Person: Animal and Spirit* (Notre Dame: University of Notre Dame Press).

BREMMER, J. N. (1983), *The Early Greek Concept of the Soul* (Princeton: Princeton University Press).

BRENTLINGER, J. (1963), 'The Divided Line and Plato's Theory of Intermediates', *Phronesis*, 7: 146–66.

BRICKHOUSE, T. C., and SMITH, N. D. (1989), *Socrates on Trial* (Princeton: Princeton University Press).

BROADIE, S. (1977), 'Protagoras and Inconsistency: *Theaetetus* 171a6–c7', *Archiv für Geschichte der Philosophie*, 59: 19–36.

BURNET, J. (1911), *Phaedo* (Oxford: Clarendon Press).

—— (1924), *Plato's* Euthyphro, Apology of Socrates, *and* Crito (Oxford: Clarendon Press).

BURNYEAT, M. (1990), *The* Theaetetus *of Plato* (Indianapolis: Hackett Publishing Co.).

CARONE, G. (2000), 'Hedonism and the Pleasureless Life in Plato's *Philebus*', *Phronesis*, 45: 257–83.

CHEN, L. (1992), *Acquiring Knowledge of the Ideas* (Stuttgart: Franz Steiner).

COCKBURN, D. (ed.) (1991), *Human Beings* (Cambridge: Cambridge University Press).

COOPER, J. M. (1970), 'Plato on Sense-Perception and Knowledge (*Theaetetus* 184–6)', *Phronesis*, 15: 123–46.

—— (1977), 'Plato's Theory of Human Good in the *Philebus*', *Journal of Philosophy*, 74: 714–30.

—— (1985), 'Plato's Theory of Human Motivation', *History of Philosophy Quarterly*, 1: 3–21.

—— (1997), *Plato: Complete Works* (Indianapolis, Hackett).

COOPER, N. (1966), 'The Importance of Dianoia in Plato's Theory of Forms', *Classical Quarterly*, NS 16: 65–9.

—— (1995), 'Plato's Last Theory of Knowledge', *Apeiron*, 28: 75–89.

CORNFORD, F. M. (1934), *Plato's Theory of Knowledge* (London: Routledge and Kegan Paul).

—— (1937), *Plato's Cosmology* (London: Routledge and Kegan Paul).

CROMBIE, I. M. (1963), *An Examination of Plato's Doctrines*, i. *Plato on Knowledge and Reality* (London: Routledge and Kegan Paul).

DENYER, N. (1991), *Language, Thought and Falsehood in Ancient Greek Philosophy* (London: Routledge).

DE SOUSA, R. B. (1976), 'Rational Homunculi', in A. Rorty (ed.), *The Identity of Persons* (Berkeley: University of California Press), 217–38.

DEVEREUX, D. T. (1994), 'Separation and Immanence in Plato's Theory of Forms', *Oxford Studies in Ancient Philosophy*, 12: 63–90.

DODDS, E. R. (1959), *Plato: Gorgias* (Oxford: Clarendon Press).

EBERT, T. (1974), *Meinung und Wissen in der Philosophie Platons* (Berlin and New York: Walter de Gruyter).

ELTON, M. (1997), 'The Role of the Affinity Argument in the *Phaedo*', *Phronesis*, 42: 313–16.

ENGLAND, E. B. (1921), *The Laws of Plato* (2 vols.; Manchester: Manchester University Press).

FERBER, R. (1989), *Platons Idee des Guten*, 2nd edn. (Sankt Augustin: Akademia Verlag).

FINE, G. (1979*a*), 'False Belief in the *Theaetetus*', *Phronesis*, 24: 70–80.

—— (1979*b*), 'Knowledge and Logos in the *Theaetetus*', *Philosophical Review*, 88: 366–97.

—— (1984), 'Separation', *Oxford Studies in Ancient Philosophy*, 2: 31–87.

—— (1986), 'Immanence', *Oxford Studies in Ancient Philosophy*, 4: 71–97.

—— (1990), 'Knowledge and Belief in *Republic* V–VII', in S. Everson (ed.), *Companions to Ancient Thought*, i. *Epistemology* (Cambridge: Cambridge University Press), 85–115.

—— (ed.) (1999), *Plato*, i. *Metaphysics and Epistemology*; ii. *Ethics, Politics, Religion, and the Soul* (Oxford: Oxford University Press).

FORTENBAUGH, W. W. (1975), *Aristotle on Emotion* (London: Duckworth).

FRANKFURT, H. G. (1971). 'Freedom of the Will and the Concept of a Person', *Journal of Philosophy*, 68: 5–20; repr. in Watson (1989), 81–95.

FREDE, D. (1985), 'Rumpelstiltskin's Pleasures: True and False Pleasures in Plato's *Philebus*', *Phronesis*, 30: 151–80.

—— (1992), 'Disintegration and Restoration: Pleasure and Pain in Plato's *Philebus*', in R. Kraut (ed.), *The Cambridge Companion to Plato* (Cambridge: Cambridge University Press), 425–63.

—— (1996), 'The Hedonist's Conversion: The Role of Socrates in the *Philebus*', in C. Gill and M. M. McCabe (eds.), *Form and Argument in Late Plato* (Oxford: Clarendon Press), 213–48.

FREDE, M. (1987), 'Observation and Perception in Plato's Later Dialogues', in M. Frede, *Essays in Ancient Philosophy* (Minneapolis: University of Minnesota Press), 3–8.

GALLOP, D. (1965), 'Image and Reality in Plato's *Republic*', *Archiv für Geschichte der Philosophie*, 47: 113–31.

—— (1975), *Phaedo* (Oxford: Clarendon Press).

GEACH, P. T. (1969), *God and the Soul* (London: Routledge and Kegan Paul).

GERSON, L. P. (1987), 'A Note on Tripartition and Immortality in Plato', *Apeiron*, 20: 81–96.

—— (1990), *God and Greek Philosophy* (London: Routledge).

—— (1997*a*), 'Epistrophe Pros Heauton: History and Meaning', *Documenti e studi sulla tradizione filosofica medievale*, 8: 1–31.

—— (1997*b*), 'Socrates' Absolutist Prohibition of Wrongdoing', in Mark L. Mc-Pherran (ed.), *Wisdom, Ignorance and Virtue* (*Apeiron* suppl. 30; Edmonton: Academic Printing and Publishing), 1–11.

—— (1999), 'Knowledge and Being in the Recollection Argument', in Mark L. McPherran (ed.), *Recognition, Remembrance and Reality* (*Apeiron* suppl. 32; Edmonton: Academic Printing and Publishing), 1–15.

—— (2000), 'Plato *Absconditus*', in G. Press (ed.), *Who Speaks for Plato?* (Lanham, Md.: Rowman and Littlefield), 201–10.

GILL, C. (ed.), (1990), *The Person and the Human Mind: Issues in Ancient and Modern Philosophy* (Oxford: Clarendon Press).

—— (1991), 'Is There a Concept of Person in Greek Philosophy?', in S. Everson (ed.), *Companions to Ancient Thought*, ii. *Psychology* (New York: Cambridge University Press), 166–93.

—— (1996), *Personality in Greek Epic, Tragedy, and Philosophy: The Self in Dialogue* (Oxford: Clarendon Press).

GLIDDEN, D. (1985), 'Mimetic Ignorance, Platonic "Doxa", and "De Re" Belief', *History of Philosophy Quarterly*, 2: 355–74.

GLOY, K. (1986), 'Platons Theorie der Episteme Heautes im *Charmides* als Vorläufer der modernen Selbstbewußtseintheorien', *Kant-Studien*, 77: 137–64.

GOLDIN, O. M. (1993), 'Self, Sameness, and Soul in *Alcibiades I* and the *Timaeus*', *Freiburger Zeitschrift für Philosophie und Theologie*, 40 / 1–2: 5–19.

GONZALEZ, F. J. (1996), 'Propositions or Objects? A Critique of Gail Fine on Knowledge and Belief in *Republic V*', *Phronesis*, 41: 245–75.

—— (1998), 'Nonpropositional Knowledge in Plato', *Apeiron*, 31: 235–84.

GÖRGEMANNS, H. (1960), *Beiträge zur Interpretation von Platons Nomoi* (Munich: C. H. Beck'sche Verlagsbuchhandlung).

GOSLING, J. C. B. (1965), 'Similarity in *Phaedo* 73 seq.', *Phronesis*, 10: 151–61.

—— (1968), 'Doxa and Dunamis in Plato's *Republic*', *Phronesis*, 13: 119–30.

—— (1975), Philebus: *Translated with Notes and Commentary* (Oxford: Clarendon Press).

—— and TAYLOR, C. C. W. (1982), *The Greeks on Pleasure* (Oxford: Clarendon Press).

GOULD, J. (1955), *The Development of Plato's Ethics* (Cambridge: Cambridge University Press).

GRISWOLD, C. L. (1986), *Self-Knowledge in Plato's* Phaedrus (New Haven: Yale University Press).

GULLEY, N. (1962), *Plato's Theory of Knowledge* (London: Methuen).

HALL, R. (1963), *Plato and the Individual* (The Hague: Martinus Nijhoff).

HAMPTON, C. (1987), 'Pleasure, Truth and Being in Plato's *Philebus*: A Reply to Professor Frede's "Rumpelstiltskin's Pleasures"', *Phronesis*, 32: 253–62.

IRWIN, T. (1977), *Plato's Moral Theory: The Early and Middle Dialogues* (Oxford: Clarendon Press).

—— (1995), *Plato's Ethics* (New York: Oxford University Press).

JÄGER, G. (1967), *'Nus' in Platons Dialogen* (Göttingen: Vandenhoeck and Ruprecht).

JOSEPH, H. W. B. (1935), *Essays in Ancient and Modern Philosophy* (Oxford: Clarendon Press).

KAHN, C. (1981), 'Some Philosophical Uses of "To Be" in Plato', *Phronesis*, 26: 119–27.

—— (1987), 'Plato's Theory of Desire', *Review of Metaphysics*, 41: 77–103.

—— (1996), *Plato and the Socratic Dialogue* (Cambridge: Cambridge University Press).

—— (2001), *Pythagoras and the Pythagoreans: A Brief History* (Indianapolis: Hackett).

KANAYAMA, Y. (1987), 'Perceiving, Considering, and Attaining Being (*Theaetetus* 184–186)', *Oxford Studies in Ancient Philosophy*, 5: 29–81.

KARASMANIS, V. (1988), 'Plato's *Republic*: The Line and the Cave', *Apeiron*, 21: 147–70.

KEYT, D. (1963), 'The Fallacies in *Phaedo* 102a–107b', *Phronesis*, 8: 167–72.

KLOSKO, G. (1988), 'The Rule of Reason in Plato's Psychology', *History of Philosophy Quarterly*, 5: 341–56.

KOSMAN, L. A. (1976), 'Platonic Love', in W. H. Werkmeister (ed.), *Facets of Plato's Philosophy* (Assen: Van Gorcum), 53–69.

KRÄMER, H. J. (1969), 'Epekeina Tes Ousias: Zu Platon, *Politeia* 509b', *Archiv für Geschichte der Philosophie*, 51: 1–30.

KRAUT, R. (1991), 'Return to the Cave: *Republic* 519–21', *Proceedings of the Boston Area Colloquium in Ancient Philosophy*, 7: 43–62.

—— (ed.) (1992a), *The Cambridge Companion to Plato* (Cambridge: Cambridge University Press).

—— (1992b), 'The Defense of Justice in Plato's *Republic*', in Kraut (1992a), 311–37.

KREMER, K. (1981), 'Selbsterkenntnis als Gotteserkenntnis nach Plotin', *International Studies in Philosophy*, 13: 41–68.

LAFRANCE, Y. (1981), *La Théorie platonicienne de la doxa* (Montreal: Bellarmin).

LEAR, J. (1998), *Open Minded: Working out the Logic of the Soul* (Cambridge, Mass., and London: Harvard University Press).

LESSES, G. (1987), 'Weakness, Reason, and the Divided Soul in Plato's *Republic*', *History of Philosophy Quarterly*, 4: 147–61.

LEWIS, F. A. (1981), 'Knowledge and the Eyewitness: Plato *Theaetetus* 201 A–C', *Canadian Journal of Philosophy*, 11: 185–97.

LISKE, M.-T. (1988), 'Absolut Selbstreflexion oder wertkritisches Wissen: Thesen zu Platons *Charmides*', *Theologie und Philosophie*, 63: 161–81.

LLOYD, A. C. (1964), 'Nosce Teipsum and Conscientia', *Archiv für Geschichte der Philosophie*, 46: 188–200.

MCCABE, M. M. (1994), *Plato's Individuals* (Princeton: Princeton University Press).

MCDOWELL, J. (1973), *Plato:* Theaetetus (Oxford: Clarendon Press).

MACKENZIE, M. M. (1981), *Plato on Punishment* (Berkeley: University of California Press).

MARTENS, E. (1973), *Das selbstbezügliche Wissen in Platons Charmides* (Munich: Carl Hanser Verlag).

MASON, A. (1994), 'Immortality in the *Timaeus*', *Phronesis*, 39: 90–7.

MILLER, M. (1985), 'Platonic Provocations: Reflections on the Soul and the Good in the *Republic*', in D. J. O'Meara (ed.), *Platonic Investigations* (Studies in Philosophy and the History of Philosophy, 13; Washington, DC: The Catholic University Press of America), 163–93.

—— (1999), 'Figure, Ratio, Form: Plato's Five Mathematical Studies', in Mark L. McPherran (ed.), *Recognition, Remembrance and Reality* (Apeiron suppl. 32; Edmonton: Academic Printing and Publishing), 73–88.

MOLINE, J. (1978), 'Plato on the Complexity of Psyche', *Archiv für Geschichte der Philosophie*, 60: 1–26.

—— (1981), *Plato's Theory of Understanding* (Madison, Wis.: The University of Wisconsin Press).

NAILS, D. (1995), *Agora, Academy, and the Conduct of Philosophy* (Dordrecht and Boston: Kluwer Academic Publishers).

NEHAMAS, A. (1975), 'Plato on the Imperfection of the Sensible World', *American Philosophical Quarterly*, 12: 105–17.

—— (1984), 'Episteme and Logos in Plato's Later Thought', *Archiv für Geschichte der Philosophie*, 66: 11–36.

—— and WOODRUFF, P. (1995), *Plato:* Phaedrus (Indianapolis: Hackett Publishing Co.).

NUSSBAUM, M. C. (1986), *The Fragility of Goodness* (Cambridge: Cambridge University Press).

O'BRIEN, D. (1967), 'The Last Argument of Plato's *Phaedo*', *Classical Quarterly*, NS 17: 198–231.

—— (1968), 'The Last Argument of Plato's *Phaedo*', *Classical Quarterly*, NS 18: 95–106.

O'BRIEN, M. J. (1967), *The Socratic Paradoxes and the Greek Mind* (Chapel Hill: University of North Carolina Press).

OEHLER, K. (1962), *Die Lehre vom noetischen und dianoetischen Denken bei Platon und Aristoteles* (Munich: C. H. Beck'sche Verlagsbuchhandlung).

OWEN, G. E. L. (1953), 'The Place of the *Timaeus* in Plato's Dialogues', *Classical Quarterly*, NS 3: 79–95.

—— (1986), *Logic, Science and Dialectic: Collected Papers in Greek Philosophy*, ed. M. Nussbaum (Ithaca, NY: Cornell University Press).

PARFIT, D. (1984), *Reasons and Persons* (Oxford: Clarendon Press).

PATTERSON, R. (1985), *Image and Reality in Plato's Metaphysics* (Indianapolis: Hackett Publishing Co.).

PEACOCKE, A. R., and GILLETT, G. (eds.) (1987), *Persons and Personality: A Contemporary Inquiry* (Oxford: B. Blackwell).

PEGIS, A. C. (1934), *St. Thomas and the Problem of the Soul in the Thirteenth Century* (Toronto: St Michael's College).

PENNER, T. (1970), 'False Anticipatory Pleasures: *Philebus* 36a3–41a6', *Phronesis*, 15: 166–78.

—— (1971), 'Thought and Desire in Plato', in G. Vlastos (ed.), *Plato*, ii. *Ethics, Politics, Philosophy of Art and Religion* (Garden City, NY: Doubleday and Co.), 96–118.

—— (1973), 'The Unity of Virtue', *Philosophical Review*, 38: 35–68.

—— (1987), *The Ascent from Nominalism* (Dordrecht: D. Reidel).

—— (1990), 'Plato and Davidson: Parts of the Soul and Weakness of the Will', *Canadian Journal of Philosophy*, suppl. 16: 35–74.

—— (1991), 'Desire and Power in Socrates: The Argument of *Gorgias* 466a–468e that Orators and Tyrants Have No Power in the City', *Apeiron*, 24: 147–202.

—— (1996), 'Knowledge vs True Belief in the Socratic Psychology of Action', *Apeiron*, 29: 199–230.

—— (1997), 'Socrates on the Strength of Knowledge: "Protagoras" 351b–357e', *Archiv für Geschichte der Philosophie*, 79: 117–49.

PÉPIN, J. (1971), *Idées grecques sur l'homme et sur Dieu* (Paris: Société d'Édition 'Les Belles Lettres').

PERL, E. (1997), 'Sense-Perception and Intellect in Plato', *Revue de philosophie ancienne*, 15: 15–34.

—— (1998). 'The Demiurge and the Forms: A Return to the Ancient Interpretation of Plato's *Timaeus*', *Ancient Philosophy*, 18: 81–92.

PRADEAU, J.-F. (1999), *Alcibiade* (Paris: Flammarion).

PRESS, G. A. (ed.) (2000), *Who Speaks for Plato?* (Lanham, Md., Boulder, Colo., New York, and Oxford: Rowmann and Littlefield).

PRICE, A. W. (1989), *Love and Friendship in Plato and Aristotle* (Oxford: Clarendon Press).

—— (1995), *Mental Conflict* (London and New York: Routledge).

PRITCHARD, P. (1995), *Plato's Philosophy of Mathematics* (Sankt Augustin: Academia Verlag).

REES, D. A. (1957), 'Bipartition of the Soul in the Early Academy', *Journal of Hellenic Studies*, 77: 112–118.

REEVE, C. D. C. (1988), *Philosopher-Kings: The Argument of Plato's* Republic (Princeton: Princeton University Press).

ROBERTS, J. (1987), 'Plato on the Causes of Wrongdoing in the *Laws*', *Ancient Philosophy*, 7: 23–37.

ROBIN, L. (1985), *Phèdre* (Paris: Société d'Édition 'Les Belles Lettres').

ROBINSON, J. V. (1990), 'The Tripartite Soul in the *Timaeus*', *Phronesis*, 35: 103–10.

ROBINSON, R. (1953), *Plato's Earlier Dialectic*, 2nd edn. (Oxford: Clarendon Press).

—— (1971), 'Plato's Separation of Reason from Desire', *Phronesis*, 16: 38–48.

ROBINSON, T. M. (1995), *Plato's Psychology*, 2nd edn. (Toronto: University of Toronto Press).

RUTENBER, C. (1946), *The Doctrine of the Imitation of God in Plato* (New York: King's Crown Press).

SACHS, D. (1971), 'A Fallacy in Plato's *Republic?*', in G. Vlastos (ed.), *Plato*, ii. *Ethics, Politics and Philosophy of Art and Religion* (Garden City, NY: Doubleday and Co.), 35–51.

SANTAS, G. (1979), *Socrates: Philosophy in Plato's Early Dialogues* (Boston and London: Routledge and Kegan Paul).

—— (1999), 'The Form of the Good in Plato's *Republic*', in G. Fine (ed.), *Plato*, i. *Metaphysics and Epistemology* (Oxford: Oxford University Press), 247–74.

SAUNDERS, T. J. (1962), 'The Structure of the Soul and the State in Plato's *Laws*', *Eranos*, 60: 37–55.

—— (1968), 'The Socratic Paradoxes in Plato's *Laws*', *Hermes*, 96: 421–34.

—— (1991), *Plato's Penal Code* (Oxford: Clarendon Press).

SAYRE, K. (1969), *Plato's Analytic Method* (Chicago: University of Chicago Press).

SCOTT, D. (1995), *Recollection and Experience* (Cambridge: Cambridge University Press).

—— (2000), 'Plato's Critique of the Democratic Character', *Phronesis*, 45: 19–37.

SEDLEY, D. (1997), ' "Becoming Like God" in the *Timaeus* and Aristotle', in T. Robinson and L. Brisson (eds.), *Interpreting the* Timaeus–Critias (Sankt Augustin: Academia Verlag), 327–39.

SHINER, R. (1972), 'Soul in *Republic X*', *Apeiron*, 6: 23–30.

SMITH, N. D. (1996), 'Plato's Divided Line', *Ancient Philosophy*, 16: 25–46.

—— (2000), 'Plato on Knowledge as Power', *Journal of the History of Philosophy*, 38: 145–68.

SORABJI, R. (1982). 'Myths about Non-Propositional Thought', in M. C. Nussbaum and M. Schofield (eds.), *Language and Logos: Studies in Ancient Greek Philosophy Presented to G. E. L. Owen* (Cambridge: Cambridge University Press), 295–314.

SPRAGUE, E. (1999), *Persons and Their Minds: A Philosophical Investigation* (Boulder, Colo.: Westview Press).

SPRUTE, J. (1962), *Der Begriff der Doxa in der platonischen Philosophie* (Göttingen: Vandenhoeck and Ruprecht).

STALLEY, R. (1975), 'Plato's Argument for the Division of Reasoning and Appetitive Elements in the Soul', *Phronesis*, 20: 110–28.

STOKES, M. C. (1992), 'Plato and the Sightlovers of the *Republic*', *Apeiron*, 25: 103–32.

STRANG, C. (1986), 'Plato's Analogy of the Cave', *Oxford Studies in Ancient Philosophy*, 4: 19–34.

SZAIF, J. (1998), *Platons Begriff Der Wahrheit* (Freiburg and Munich: Verlag Karl Alber).

SZLEZÁK, T. (1976), 'Unsterblichkeit und Trichotomie der Seele im zehnten Buch der *Politeia*', *Phronesis*, 21: 31–58.

TAYLOR, A. E. (1928), *A Commentary on Plato's* Timaeus (Oxford: Clarendon Press).

TAYLOR, C. C. W. (1976), *Protagoras* (Oxford: Clarendon Press).

—— (1980), 'Plato, Hare, and Davidson on Akrasia', *Mind*, 89: 499–518.

—— (1983), 'The Argument in the *Phaedo* concerning the Thesis that the Soul is a Harmony', in J. Anton and A. Preus (eds.), *Essays in Ancient Greek Philosophy*, vol. ii (Albany: State University Press of New York), 217–31.

TUCKEY, T. G. (1951), *Plato's* Charmides (Cambridge: Cambridge University Press).

TUGENDHAT, E. (1986), *Self-Consciousness and Self-Determination* (Cambridge, Mass.: Harvard University Press).

TUOZZO, T. (1996), 'The General Account of Pleasure in Plato's *Philebus*', *Journal of the History of Philosophy*, 34: 495–513.

VLASTOS, G. (ed.) (1970–1), *Plato: A Collection of Critical Essays* (2 vols.; Garden City, NY: Anchor Books).

——(ed.) (1971), *The Philosophy of Socrates: A Collection of Critical Essays* (Garden City, NY: Anchor Books).

——(1973*a*), *Platonic Studies* (Princeton, NJ: Princeton University Press).

——(1973*b*), 'A Metaphysical Paradox', in Vlastos (1973*a*), 43–57.

——(1973*c*), 'Degrees of Reality in Plato', in Vlastos (1973*a*), 58–75.

——(1985), 'Socrates' Disavowal of Knowledge', *Philosophical Quarterly*, 35: 1–31.

——(1991), *Socrates, Ironist and Moral Philosopher* (Ithaca, NY: Cornell University Press).

——(1994), *Socratic Studies*, ed. M. Burnyeat (Cambridge: Cambridge University Press).

WATSON, G. (ed.) (1989), *Free Will* (Oxford and New York: Oxford University Press).

WELLMAN, R. (1964), 'The Question Posed at *Charmides* 165a–165c', *Phronesis*, 9: 107–13.

WHITE, F. C. (1977), 'The Many in *Republic* V', *Canadian Journal of Philosophy*, 7: 291–306.

——(1984), 'The Scope of Knowledge in *Republic* V', *Australasian Journal of Philosophy*, 62: 339–54.

WHITE, N. P. (1976), *Plato on Knowledge and Reality* (Indianapolis: Hackett Publishing Co.).

WILLIAMS, B. A. O. (1985), *Ethics and the Limits of Philosophy* (Cambridge, Mass.: Harvard University Press).

——(1990), *Moral Luck: Philosophical Papers, 1973–1980* (Cambridge and New York: Cambridge University Press).

WILLIAMS, C. J. F. (1969), 'On Dying', *Philosophy*, 44: 217–30.

——(1974), 'False Pleasures', *Philosophical Studies*, 26: 295–7.

WILSON, J. R. S. (1976), 'The Contents of the Cave', in R. A. Shiner and J. King-Farlow (eds.), *New Essays on Plato and the Presocratics* (*Canadian Journal of Philosophy*, suppl. 2; Guelph, Ont.: Canadian Association for Publishing in Philosophy), 117–27.

WOODS, M. (1987), 'Plato's Division of the Soul', *Proceedings of the British Academy*, 73: 23–47.

Aquinas, Thomas
Summa theologiae
  75, 4: 3

Aristotle
Categories
  3^{b}34–4^{a}9: 92 n. 42
De anima
  405^{b}10–17: 81 n. 33
  427^{a}28: 81 n. 33
  432^{a}22–^{b}7: 102 n. 4
Metaphysics
  987^{b}14–17: 183 n. 54
  1019^{a}2–4: 149 n. 2
  1050^{b}7: 149 n. 2
  1072^{b}14–15: 193 n. 80
  1077^{b}1–9: 149 n. 2
  1078^{b}30 ff.: 148
  1086^{b}4–11: 148 n. 2
Nicomachean Ethics
  1113^{a}2–7: 44 n. 47
  1113^{a}11: 104 n. 12
  1147^{b}9–12: 120 n. 39
  1147^{b}15–19: 43
Topics
  137^{b}3–13: 185 n. 58

Plato
Alcibiades I
  129 B 1–130 A 1: 22 n. 14
  130 C 1–3: 22
  131 A–E: 34 n. 29
  131 B 4–5: 30 n. 26

  132 D–133 C: 30
  133 B 9–10: 34 n. 28
  133 C 18–19: 30 n. 26
  133 C 21–3: 34 n. 30
Apology
  29 B 6–7: 19
  29 E 7–D 3: 18
  30 A 7–B 2: 18
  37 A 5: 122 n. 41, 245 n. 13
  38 A 5–6: 33
  40 C–41 D: 24
Charmides
  156 D 8–157 A 3: 21
  161 B 6: 35
  164 D 4: 30 n. 26, 35
  165 C 5–6: 35
  165 D 5: 35
  165 D 7: 35 n. 34
  165 E 4: 264 n. 48
  166 C 2–3: 35
  166 E 7: 36
  167 A 1–7: 34, 36
  167 C–169 C: 36
  169 D 3: 36
  169 E 4–5: 34
  170 A 2–4: 36
  170 C 9–D 2: 37
  170 D 5–9: 37
  171 D–175 E: 35 n. 33
Cratylus
  431–3: 67 n. 14
  439 A–B: 160 n. 13, 172 n. 36

Crito
  47 C 1–48 A 4: 18
  47 E 6–48 A 1: 20
  49 A 6–7: 19
Euthydemus
  279 A 1–281 E 2: 23 n. 15
Gorgias
  449 B–C: 133 n. 51
  461 D–462 A: 133 n. 51
  467 B 3–6: 41 n. 42
  468 B 7–8: 124 n. 42
  469 B 12: 19
  477 A 4–E 6: 18
  479 B–C: 20 n. 10
  481 C: 62
  488 A 3: 48 n. 53, 122 n. 41, 245 n. 13
  493 A ff.: 24
  493 A 1–C 3: 25
  504 B 4–5: 27
  504 D 9–E 4: 27
  508 C: 19
  511 C 9–512 B 2: 18
  512 A–B: 20 n. 10
  522 E 1–4: 26
  523 A ff.: 24
  525 A 1–6: 26 n. 19
  525 B 1–3: 26 n. 21
  526 C 1–2: 26 n. 19
  527 A 7: 26 n. 20
Laches
  199 C 1: 264 n. 48
Laws
  626 E: 267
  633 E: 267
  644 C 4: 268
  644 D 7–645 B 1: 266
  645 B 1–2: 267
  689 A 5–B 7: 270
  721 B 7–8: 22 n. 14
  731 C–D: 122 n. 41, 245 n. 13
  731 C 2–3: 268 n. 57
  731 C 2: 48 n. 53
  731 D 6–732 B 4: 272

  773 E 5 ff.: 22 n. 14
  863 B 2–3: 273
  863 D 10: 106 n. 15
  863 E 5–864 A 8: 271
  863 E 5–8: 274
  896 B–C: 274
  896 E 8–897 A 3: 239 n. 1
  899 D 7: 81 n. 33
  959 A 4–B 7: 240 n. 2, 274
  959 B 3–4: 22 n. 14
Letter VII
  335 A 2–7: 26 n. 20
  342 A–E: 81 n. 34
Lysis
  221 D–E: 248 n. 19
Meno
  77 C 1–2: 41 n. 42
  78 B 5: 124 n. 42
  81 A: 24
  86 A 8–B 2: 24
  97 A–98 A: 156 n. 9
  97 A 9–B 3: 222
  97 B–98 A: 44 n. 49
  97 E–98 B: 44
  98 A 1–8: 149
  98 A 3–4: 223 n. 51
Parmenides
  131 A–E: 56 n. 5
  132 A: 185 n. 58
  132 A 1–4: 67
  132 B 4 ff.: 74 n. 23
  132 D 3: 67, 249 n. 21
  132 D 7: 128 n. 47
  135 B–C: 196
  135 C 2: 196 n. 3
  135 C 8–D 1: 190 n. 72
Phaedo
  64 A 5–6: 53, 62
  64 B 9: 54 n. 4
  64 C 4–8: 56
  65 B 9: 57
  65 C 2: 57
  65 C 5–9: 57
  65 C 11–D 2: 57

Plato: *Phaedo* (cont.):

65 D: 69
65 D 4–7: 58
65 D 4: 54
66 A 1–3: 58
66 B 1–67 B 5: 57
66 E–67 B: 149
66 E 2–3: 119 n. 38
66 E 4–67 B 2: 58
67 C 2–3: 245 n. 11
67 C 3: 62
67 D 7–10: 53
69 A 6 ff.: 245 n. 11
69 B 6–7: 63, 144 n. 75, 214 n. 36
69 B 8–C 3: 245 n. 11
69 E 6–72 E 1: 51
70 D 2–5: 52
71 A 9–10: 63
71 A 12–B 2: 64
71 C 1–5: 64
71 C 6–7: 64
71 E 5: 64
71 E 13: 64
71 E 14–72 A 2: 64
72 A 6–8: 64
72 E 3–78 B 3: 52
72 E 5–6: 65
73 C 1–2: 65, 66
73 C 8: 66
73 D 3: 66
74 A 2–3: 66, 69
74 A 5–7: 68
74 A 9 ff.: 69
74 B 2–4: 150
74 B 2: 66
74 B 8–9: 70
74 C 1–2: 71
74 C 8–9: 73
75 A 5–B 2: 167
75 B–C: 206 n. 17
75 C 1–5: 72
75 E 1–6: 72
76 B 5–6: 73
76 B 8–9: 68, 150

76 C 1–4: 73
76 C 11: 22 n. 14
76 D 5–E 7: 52
76 E: 88
76 E 5–7: 72
77 B 1–C 5: 78
77 C 6–9: 78
78 B 4–84 B 4: 52, 79
78 C 1–4: 86
78 C 6–7: 86
78 D 5: 57
79 B 16–17: 79 n. 30
79 D 1–8: 52
79 D 1–7: 80
79 D 5–6: 58
79 D 6: 60
79 E 8–80 A 5: 86
80 C–D: 87
80 E–81 C: 87
81 A ff.: 78
81 B ff.: 128
81 C–82 A: 87
81 C 10: 87
82 A 10–B 8: 87
82 A 10–B 3: 144 n. 75, 214 n. 36
82 A 10–B 1: 63
82 D 9 ff.: 86
82 D 9–83 B 4: 80
82 E 6–7: 87
83 A 7: 112 n. 27
83 B 1: 57
83 D: 240 n. 4
83 D 5: 87
83 D 7–8: 87
83 D 7: 99, 107 n. 18
83 D 10: 87
84 A 8–B 1: 87
84 C 1–88 B 8: 52, 88
85 C 3–4: 59
85 E 3–86 E 5: 65, 89
86 D–E: 60
87 A 1–2: 89
87 D 7–88 B 8: 90
88 C 1–95 A 3: 52, 65

89 D 2–3: 63
92 B 5: 22 n. 14
92 C 11–E 3: 88, 89
92 E 4–93 A 10: 90
93 A 11–C 10: 90
93 B 4–7: 91
93 C 3–8: 91
93 D 1–94 B 3: 90
94 A 2–4: 91
94 B 4–95 A 3: 90
94 B 8–9: 91
95 A 4–102 A: 52
95 C 6: 22 n. 14
96 C 8–D 5: 92
97 B 8 ff.: 93
98 C–99 A: 164 n. 21
98 C 5: 103 n. 11
98 E 5: 104 n. 11
99 A–B: 93
99 D–100 A: 172 n. 36
100 B: 93
100 B 5: 57
100 C 5–6: 83
100 D 7–8: 56
102 A 10–107 B 10: 52
102 D 5–103 A 2: 94
102 D 6–103 B 5: 71 n. 21
102 D 6–E 2: 56
102 D 6–8: 75 n. 25
102 D 6–7: 185 n. 58
103 B 5: 56
103 B 10–105 C 7: 94
104 A 1–3: 176 n. 41
105 C 9–107 A 1: 94
107 C 1–D 5: 96
114 B 6–C 8: 63, 97
114 C 6–8: 97
115 C 4–D 1: 54 n. 3
Phaedrus
227 A ff.: 132
230 A: 132
230 E–234 C: 133
231 A 4–6: 133
231 C 5: 133 n. 54

231 E 1–2: 133 n. 53
235 B: 135
235 C–D: 133 n. 42
237 B–241 D: 134
237 C 3: 134
237 C 7: 133
237 D 1: 134
237 D 3: 134
237 D 4–5: 134
237 D 8: 134
238 B 7–C 4: 134
241 E–242 A: 135
242 C: 135
242 E–257 B: 135
244 A 5–7: 135
244 B–245 B: 135
245 C 2–4: 136
245 E 7–8: 136
246 A 5: 137
246 A 6–7: 137
246 C 5–246 A 2: 136
246 C 5–6: 2
247 C 7–8: 139 n. 65
248 D 2: 138 n. 62
249 B 3–5: 139
249 B 5: 2
249 B 7: 140
249 C 5: 140
249 C 7: 140
249 D 4: 140
249 D 6–7: 140
250 A 7: 141
250 E–252 C 2: 141 n. 70
250 E: 142
251 B 7–8: 139 n. 66
252 D ff.: 142 n. 72
253 A 6–B 1: 142 n. 73
253 B 8–C 2: 142 n. 73
253 C 7–257 A 2: 143
253 D ff.: 138 n. 64, 141
253 E–254 E: 143
253 E 5–6: 139 n. 66
254 E 5–255 A 1: 143
255 D 3–E 2: 146 n. 76

Plato: *Phaedrus* (*cont.*):

255 E 1–2: 135 n. 57
256 A: 143
256 C–D: 143
256 C 5–6: 143
256 E 5: 141 n. 71
257 B: 132
257 B 5: 170 n. 30
259 E–274 B: 144
261 A 8: 144
262 D 5–6: 144
265 A 9–11: 141
265 B 6–7: 144
271 C 10 ff.: 144
274 E ff.: 145
276 A 8–9: 145
276 C 7–9: 145

Philebus

11 B: 260 n. 40
11 B 4–C 3: 251 n. 25
20 D: 259 n. 39
20 D 7–10: 261
22 B 3–4: 251
22 C 7: 251
22 D 2: 251
32 B 2–4: 254
32 B 5: 255
32 D 2–34 A 5: 255 n. 29
33 B 6–7: 253 n. 28, 254
35 D: 259 n. 39
36 C–41 B: 256 n. 30
37 A 7–9: 256
37 A 11–B 3: 256
37 B 10: 256 n. 33
37 E 5–7: 259
37 E 12–38 A 2: 258
40 C 5: 260
40 C 8–10: 256
40 D 7–10: 258 n. 37
41 A 7–8: 259
41 B–42 C: 256 n. 30
42 C–44 D: 256 n. 30
44 A 9–10: 262 n. 44
44 D–50 E: 256 n. 30

47 C–D: 255 n. 29
51 A–B: 262
51 A 5–6: 258 n. 36
51 B 1–2: 262 n. 44
51 B 5–7: 255, 256
54 A–55 B: 261
54 C 9–11: 261
54 E: 261
55 C–59 C: 263
56 C: 263
57 B 1: 263
58 C 2–4: 264 n. 50
58 E 2–3: 264 n. 49
61 A: 259 n. 39
62 A–D: 264
62 A 2–3: 81 n. 34
65 A 1–5: 251
65 C 4–D 3: 251 n. 26
65 C 5: 260 n. 41, 267 n. 55
65 D 7–10: 251 n. 26
65 E 4–68 A 3: 251 n. 26
66 B 9: 264 n. 47
67 A 5–8: 253 n. 28

Protagoras

334 C–335 C: 133 n. 51
345 D 8: 48 n. 53, 122 n. 41
351 B–E: 42 n. 44
351 E 2–3: 42 n. 44
352 A 1–C 7: 40 n. 38
352 A 8–C 7: 40
352 E 8–353 A 2: 40 n. 39
353 E 6–354 A 1: 42 n. 44
355 A 5–B 2: 41
355 B 1–3: 269
355 B 3–C 1: 41
355 C 3–8: 41
355 D 1–3: 41
357 D 1: 40 n. 39
358 B 7–C 1: 44 n. 49
358 C 7: 48 n. 53, 122 n. 41, 245 n. 13
358 E 2–359 A 1: 48 n. 53

Republic

358 A 1 ff.: 124

365 C 3–4: 63, 144 n. 75, 214 n. 36
368 E–369 B: 100
382 A–B: 257 n. 35
412 E–413 A: 257 n. 35
414 B 4: 126
423 D 5: 112
430 E 6–9: 267
430 E 11–431 A 1: 109, 246 n. 14, 268
433 D 4–5: 113 n. 28
435 C 5: 239 n. 1
435 E 7: 118
436 A 8–B 3: 100
436 B 8–10: 101, 127 n. 46
437 B 1–C 6: 107 n. 18
438 E 3–4: 124 n. 42
439 A 1–D 2: 107 n. 18
439 B 8–11: 105
439 C 2–3: 101
439 C 5–7: 101
439 C 9–D 8: 268
439 C 9–D 2: 101
439 D 4–8: 102
439 E 2: 102 n. 4
439 E 6–440 A 2: 102
440 A 8–B 1: 110
442 B 11: 102 n. 4
442 C 5–6: 174 n. 38
442 C 5: 102 n. 4
442 D 1: 107
443 B 2: 103 n. 11
443 B 3: 103 n. 11
443 C 4–7: 113 n. 28
443 D 4: 112
443 D 7: 127 n. 46
443 E 1: 191
444 B–C: 125
444 B 3: 102 n. 4
445 A–B: 20 n. 10
445 A: 116
445 C 9–10: 116
454 A–B: 196 n. 3
472 D–E: 192 n. 79
476 A 9–D 6: 151

476 C 2–3: 151, 162
476 C 4–7: 191
476 D 6: 184
476 D 7–478 E 5: 151–3
476 E 7–477 A 1: 184 n. 56
477 A 2–4: 198 n. 6
477 A 7: 171 n. 33
477 B 9–10: 198
477 D–E: 198 n. 10
477 D 7–8: 199
477 E 6–7: 198
478 A 5–6: 92 n. 43
478 A 12–B 2: 162
478 B 1–2: 149
478 C 3–4: 198
478 C 10–11: 171 n. 33
478 D 5–6: 198
478 D 5: 102 n. 5
478 D 6: 171 n. 33
478 E 7–480 A 13: 153–4
479 A–C: 75 n. 26
479 A 9–B 1: 198
479 B 9–10: 198
479 D 3–6: 191 n. 77
479 D 3–5: 166 n. 23
479 D 5: 171 n. 33
484 C 6–D 3: 166 n. 23
490 B 4: 81 n. 33
498 E: 246 n. 15
499 B 5: 192 n. 78
500 C: 246 n. 15
500 C 5: 128, 129 n. 48
500 D 4: 192 n. 78
500 D 8: 144 n. 75, 214 n. 36
504 D 2: 126
505 A 2: 174
505 A 5–6: 174
505 D 11–E 1: 124 n. 42
506 C 2–3: 164
506 E 3–4: 164
507 B 5–7: 164
507 B 9–10: 165
508 D 2: 175
508 E 3–4: 175

Plato: *Republic (cont.)*:

509 B 6–7: 174
509 D: 180
509 D 8: 180 n. 51
510 A 5–6: 187
510 A 8–10: 164
510 A 9: 180
510 B 4–5: 181, 183
510 B 7: 181 n. 52
510 C 2–D 3: 182
510 C 3–5: 183
510 D 5–E 1: 181
510 C 6–D 1: 182
510 D 7–8: 185
511 A 1: 182, 185 n. 59
511 A 5: 181 n. 52
511 A 7–8: 184
511 B 2–C 2: 183
511 B 3 ff.: 181
511 B 4: 196 n. 3
511 B 6–7: 181 n. 52
511 C 4: 182
511 C 8–D 2: 182
511 C 8: 181 n. 52
511 D–E: 189 n. 70
511 D 4–5: 182
511 E 2–4: 182
514 A–517 B: 186
517 B: 188
518 C 5–10: 171 n. 33
518 D 3–519 A 6: 144 n. 75, 214 n. 36
518 D 4: 188 n. 67
519 C 8–521 B 10: 192 n. 78
520 C 3–6: 165, 166 n. 23
520 C 4–5: 191
521 C 5–8: 188
522 C 2: 264 n. 48
522 C 5 ff.: 188
523 C ff.: 75 n. 26
523 C: 206 n. 17
525 A–B: 191
525 A 1: 188 n. 67
525 B–C: 188 n. 67

525 B 5: 191
525 D 5: 188
526 A 6–7: 187
527 B 10: 184 n. 55
529 B: 191
529 B 7–C 1: 167 n. 26
529 C 7–D 6: 187
530 D 8: 264 n. 48
531 D–535 A: 189
532 B–C: 187 n. 62
532 C: 189
532 C 1–2: 187
532 C 6–8: 171 n. 33
533 A 1–12: 187
533 A 4–6: 185 n. 60
533 B–C: 187
533 C: 111 n. 25
533 C 1–3: 189
533 C 7–E 2: 181
533 C 8–D 1: 179 n. 46
533 C 8: 183, 189
533 D 3: 188 n. 67
533 D 4–7: 189
533 D 4: 264 n. 48
534 A–B: 187 n. 62
534 A 2–5: 189
534 B 2–3: 186
534 B 3–C 5: 160 n. 13
534 C 5–6: 164
534 C 5: 191
534 E 3: 264 n. 49
537 C 7: 190 n. 76
537 E: 189
539 D–540 A: 190
539 D 8–10: 190 n. 72
544 B ff.: 116
544 E 1: 114 n. 32
544 E 5: 114 n. 32
544 E 7–8: 114
545 B 4: 114 n. 32
548 D 4: 114 n. 32
549 B 3–4: 116
550 A 4–B 7: 112 n. 26
550 B 5–6: 111 n. 25, 116

550 B 6: 103 n. 11
553 B 7–D 7: 112 n. 26
553 C 4–8: 116
553 C 5: 107 n. 19
553 D 1–2: 116
554 A 2: 107 n. 19
554 B 2: 107 n. 19
554 D 1–575 A 7: 107 n. 18
554 D 9–10: 112 n. 27
561 B 4–5: 116
571 C 3–D 4: 107
571 D 1–5: 116
577 A 2: 114 n. 32
580 D 7–8: 118
580 D 8: 103 n. 11, 106 n. 16, 135
580 D 11: 127 n. 46
580 E 5–581 A 7: 107 n. 19
581 B–E: 247
581 B 9: 118 n. 38
581 C 6: 251
581 D 10–E 4: 119
582 A 5: 120
583–5: 257 n. 36
583 A: 263
583 A 1–3: 251
583 C 7–8: 257 n. 36
585 A 5: 258 n. 36
586 A–B: 261 n. 42
586 B 8: 258 n. 36
586 D 5–E 3: 107
586 E 4: 118 n. 38
588 B–590 A: 137 n. 60
589 A–590 A: 117
589 A 7: 130
589 C 6: 48 n. 53, 122 n. 41, 245 n. 13
590 B 7–8: 107 n. 19
596 B–C: 187 n. 64
598 A 7–8: 117
598 B 1–5: 172 n. 34
602 D 1–4: 172 n. 34
603 A 1: 127 n. 46
603 C 10–D 7: 107
605 A–B: 244 n. 9

608 C–612 A: 137
608 C 1 ff.: 122 n. 41
608 D 13–611 A 3: 125
609 C: 125
611 A 5–7: 126
611 A 10–612 A 6: 125
611 B 1–2: 126
611 B 9–612 A 6: 240 n. 2
611 B 10–612 A 6: 126–127
611 C 3: 128
611 D 6–7: 128
611 E 1 ff.: 81 n. 33
611 E 1–4: 128
619 C 7–D 1: 114 n. 33

Sophist
235 A–236 C: 245 n. 9
240 A 3: 198 n. 6
249 B 12–C 4: 199 n. 12
249 D 3–4: 199 n. 12
259 D–264 D: 216
263 D–264 B: 219 n. 47
264 B 1–2: 172 n. 35
266 C: 188 n. 66

Statesman
277 C: 172 n. 36

Symposium
193 C 5: 248 n. 18
193 D 2: 248 n. 19
205 A–206 A: 134
205 D 2–3: 134
205 D 5: 238 n. 72
205 E–206 A: 248 n. 19
207 D 1: 246 n. 15
235 A 3: 264 n. 48

Theaetetus
145 C–148 E: 195
146 E 9–10: 195
151 D–186 E: 195, 204
151 E–152 C: 201
151 E 8–152 A 2: 201
152 A 3–4: 205 n. 15
152 C–D: 201
152 C 5–6: 156 n. 8, 197, 198 n. 9, 199, 210

Plato: *Theaetetus (cont.)*:

152 C 8–10: 201
152 E 5–6: 198
156 E 7–157 C 3: 207
158 A 7: 207 n. 21
159 E 1–160 A 3: 205
159 E 7–160 A 3: 209
160 B 5–C 2: 204
160 B 8–C 2: 207 n. 21
160 C 4–5: 209
160 C 5–6: 198 n. 9
160 D 1–2: 204
162 D 1: 207 n. 21
166 D 4–E 4: 207 n. 21
167 C 7: 207 n. 21
172 B–177 C: 212
174 B: 197 n. 4
175 C: 197 n. 4
176 A: 213
176 B–D: 61
176 B–C: 246 n. 15
176 B 1–C 5: 213
177 B 8: 212 n. 32
178 B: 128 n. 47
184 B–186 E: 201
184 D 2–5: 207
185 C 9–D 4: 206
185 C 9: 210
185 E 1–2: 206
186 A–E: 198
186 A 4: 206
186 B: 211
186 B 2–9: 207
186 B 6–9: 206
186 B 6: 206 n. 19
186 C 7–10: 206, 210
186 C 7–8: 209
186 C 7: 209 n. 26, 224
186 D 2–5: 212
187 A–201 C: 195
187 E 1–188 C 7: 216
188 C 5–7: 216
188 C 8–189 B 9: 216
189 B 10–190 E 4: 216

189 E 6–190 A 6: 215
190 A 3–4: 215 n. 40
190 C 5: 215
190 E–195 B: 218
191 A 8–B 1: 225 n. 54
192 C 9–D 1: 218
194 A 8–B 6: 218
194 B 2–6: 219 n. 46
196 A–B: 219
196 A 6–7: 220 n. 48
196 D–199 C: 220
197 B–D: 215
197 B 8 ff.: 72
197 B 8–10: 220
199 B 7–C 1: 224
199 C–D: 220
200 E 4: 203
201 C–210 A: 195
201 C 9–D 3: 226
201 D 8–202 C 6: 227
202 B 8–C 5: 228
202 D 10–206 B 11: 228
203 D: 229 n. 60
205 E 3: 228
206 B: 229 n. 59
206 C–E: 231
206 C 1–5: 228 n. 57
206 E–208 B: 231
208 C–210 B: 231
209 D: 234
209 E–210 A: 234

Timaeus

27 D 6: 197 n. 5
29 D 7–30 C 1: 241
29 E 1–3: 249
30 C 2–D 1: 249 n. 22
35 A–B: 171 n. 33
41 A 7–8: 241
41 B: 240 n. 2
41 C–D: 125 n. 44, 240 n. 2
41 C 6–7: 249
41 C 7: 266 n. 53
41 D–E: 126, 171 n. 33
41 D 7: 245

42 D 1: 245 n. 10
44 B 6–7: 245 n. 12
46 C 7–E 6: 93
48 A 2: 108 n. 20, 242 n. 8
52 C 5–6: 198 n. 6
68 C 8–D 6: 137
69 C 5–70 A 7: 274 n. 65
69 C 5–6: 240, 240 n. 2
69 C 8–D 1: 125 n. 44
69 D 5–6: 125 n. 44
69 D 7: 240
69 E 1: 240 n. 2
70 A 2: 240 n. 2
70 A 3: 240
70 A 4–7: 241
70 A 5–7: 108 n. 20
70 B 5: 242
70 D 7: 240 n. 2
70 E 2: 240
70 E 4–5: 241 n. 6
71 A 3–B 5: 242
71 A 5–6: 245 n. 9

71 B 5–C 2: 242 n. 7
71 C 3–4: 244 n. 9
71 D 3–4: 242
85 D 2: 48 n. 53
85 E 1: 48 n. 53
86 D 7–E 1: 245, 268 n. 57
86 D 7–C 1: 122 n. 41
89 E 4–5: 239 n. 1
90 A: 125 n. 44
90 A 4: 240
90 B 1–C 7: 214 n. 37
90 B 1–C 6: 246–7
90 C 2–3: 22 n. 14
90 C 3: 243
90 C 6–D 7: 248
90 D: 81 n. 33
92 C 7: 249 n. 22

Plotinus
Enneads
    4.3.31–2: 9 n. 11

Index of Modern Authors

Ackrill, J. 68 n. 16

Adam, J. 126 n. 45, 174 n. 40, 183 n. 53

Annas, J. 6 n. 6, 22 n. 13, 23 n. 14, 33 nn. 26–7, 103 n. 8, 105 n. 14, 107 n. 17, 180 n. 49, 183 n. 53, 189 n. 71, 213 n. 35

Apolloni, D. 79, 86 n. 36

Archer-Hind, R. D. 242 n. 8

Baker, L. R. 1 n. 1, 7 n. 8

Baltes, M. 174 n. 39, 179 n. 47

Benson, H. 216 n. 41

Bett, R. 136 n. 59, 139 n. 65

Bobonich, C. 107 n. 17, 110 n. 23, 265 n. 51, 266 n. 52, 267 n. 55, 268 n. 56, 269 n. 58, 270, 271, 272

Bostock, D. 56 n. 5, 69 n. 17, 70 nn. 18–19, 71 n. 20, 74 n. 24, 86 n. 36, 195 n. 1, 203 n. 14, 205 n. 16, 206, 208 n. 23, 209 n. 26, 210, 211, 212 n. 30, 215 n. 40, 216 n. 43, 217 n. 44, 220 n. 49, 227 n. 56, 229 n. 60, 231, 234 nn. 66–7, 235 n. 68

Braine, D. 1 n. 1

Brentlinger, J. 183 n. 53, 185 n. 57

Brickhouse T. C. 24 n. 18

Broadie, S. 207 n. 22

Burnet, J. 20 n. 11, 62 n. 10

Burnyeat, M. 194, 195, 196, 197 n. 4, 198 n. 10, 199, 206 n. 19, 209 n. 25, 210, 212 n. 31, 217, 224 n. 53, 225, 228 n. 58, 229 n. 59, 231 n. 63, 233 n. 65, 234 n. 67, 235

Carone, G. 262 n. 43

Chen, L. 183 n. 53

Cockburn, D. 1 n. 1

Cooper, J. M. 6 n. 6, 102 n. 7, 103 n. 7, 206 n. 16, 211 n. 29

Cooper, N. 186 n. 61, 229 n. 61, 236 n. 69

Cornford, F. 50, 197 n. 4, 206 n. 18, 207, 213 n. 33, 220 nn. 48–9, 234 n. 66, 242 n. 7, 247, 248

Crombie, I. M. 208 n. 23

Denyer, N. 155 n. 6

Devereux, D. T. 148 n. 1

Dodds, E. R. 26 n. 20, 27

Ebert, T. 35 n. 32, 155 n. 6

Elton, M. 79 n. 29

England, E. B. 266 n. 53, 274 n. 66

Ferber, R. 174 n. 39

Fine, G. 136 n. 59, 139 n. 65, 148 n. 1, 150 n. 4, 161 n. 16, 162, 163, 164 n. 20, 165, 216 n. 41

Fortenbaugh, W. W. 107 n. 17, 267 n. 54, 273 n. 64

Frankfurt, H. G. 120 n. 40, 121, 122, 123, 129

Frede, D. 252 n. 27, 256 n. 32, 257

n. 34, 258 n. 36, 259 n. 38, 263
nn. 45–6
Frede, M. 208 n. 24

Gallop, D. 53 n. 2, 56 n. 5, 58, 62 n.
    10, 68 n. 16, 70 nn. 18–19, 71 n.
    21, 80, 86, 89 n. 37, 90 n. 38, 97,
    172 n. 36
Geach, P. T. 26 nn. 20–1
Gerson, L. P. 19 n. 5, 125 n. 43, 132
    n. 50, 137 n. 61, 250 n. 24
Gill, C. 1 n. 1, 5 n. 5, 8 n. 9, 107 n.
    17, 109 n. 21, 192 n. 78
Glidden, D. 169 n. 28
Gloy, K. 35 n. 32
Goldin, O. M. 22 n. 14
Gonzalez, F. J. 161 n. 14, 163 n. 19
Görgemanns, H. 271 n. 61, 273 n. 64
Gosling, J. C. B. 67 n. 14, 161 n. 16,
    255 n. 29, 256 n. 31, 259 n. 38
Griswold, C. L. 136 n. 59, 139 n. 67,
    140 n. 69, 142 n. 73, 146 n. 77
Gulley, N. 161 n. 15

Hall, R. 237 n. 71
Hampton, C. 259 n. 39

Irwin, T. 34 n. 31, 40 n. 38, 41 n. 40,
    103 n. 9, 107 n. 17, 117 n. 35,
    120 n. 40, 124 n. 42, 262 n. 43

Jäger, G. 189 n. 70
Joseph, H. W. B. 103 n. 9

Kahn, C. 6 n. 6, 36 n. 35, 38 n. 37, 40
    n. 38, 43 n. 46, 50 n. 1, 91 n. 41,
    103 n. 10, 107 n. 17, 114 n. 31,
    196 n. 3, 211 n. 29
Kanayama, Y. 208 n. 23, 210 n. 28
Karasmanis, V. 186
Keyt, D. 94 n. 44
Klosko, G. 107 n. 18, 115 n. 34
Kosman, L. A. 142 n. 73
Krämer, H. J. 177 n. 44, 179 n. 46

Kraut, R. 114 n. 33, 129 n. 48
Kremer, K. 30 n. 22

Lafrance, Y. 171 n. 32
Lear, J. 113 n. 28
Lesses, G. 107 n. 17
Lewis, F. A. 223 n. 51
Liske, M.-T. 35 n. 32
Lloyd, A. C. 32 n. 25
Locke, J. 17 n. 4

McCabe, M. M. 113 n. 30, 176 n. 42,
    201 n. 13
McDowell, J. 199 n. 11, 206 n. 16, 206
    nn. 18–19, 221 n. 50, 224 n. 53,
    228 n. 58, 229 n. 60, 233 n. 64
Mackenzie, M. M. 271 n. 61
Martens, E. 35 n. 32
Mason, A. 240 n. 2
Miller, M. 129 n. 48, 188 n. 68, 190 n.
    75
Moline, J. 107 nn. 17–18

Nails, D. 6 n. 6
Nehamas, A. 66 n. 13, 70 n. 19, 131 n.
    49, 227 n. 55
Nussbaum, M. C. 135 n. 57, 236 n.
    70, 237

O'Brien, D. 94 n. 44
O'Brien, M. J. 15 n. 2, 271 n. 61
Owen, G. E. L. 210 n. 27

Parfit, D. 113 n. 29
Patterson, R. 249 n. 21
Pegis, A. C. 3 n. 4
Penner, T. 34 n. 31, 40 n. 38, 41 nn.
    40–1, 42 n. 45, 44 n. 48, 48 n.
    54, 76 n. 27, 102 n. 6, 103, 110 n.
    24, 158 n. 10, 256 n. 33
Pépin, J. 22 n. 13
Perl, E. 173 n. 37, 250 n. 23
Pradeau, J.-F. 22 n. 13
Press, G. A. 6 n. 6

Price, A. W. 40 n. 38, 103 n. 8, 103 n.
    10, 105 n. 14, 112 n. 26, 140 n.
    68, 141 n. 71, 142 nn. 72–3
Pritchard, P. 66 n. 13, 70 n. 19, 180 n.
    51, 183 n. 53, 187 n. 63

Rees, D. A. 267 n. 54, 273 n. 64
Reeve, C. D. C. 162 n. 17
Roberts, J. 268 n. 57, 271 n. 61, 272 n.
    62
Robin, L. 138 n. 64
Robinson, J. V. 240 n. 2
Robinson, R. 101 n. 3, 189 n. 69, 189
    n. 71, 190 n. 73
Robinson, T. M. 21 n. 12, 245 n. 11

Sachs, D. 115 n. 34
Santas, G. 15 n. 2, 34 n. 31, 174 n. 39
Saunders, T. J. 266, 271 n. 61, 273 n.
    64, 274
Sayre, K. 208 n. 23, 229 n. 61
Scott, D. 107 n. 17, 118 n. 37, 207,
    223 n. 51
Sedley, D. 214 nn. 38–9, 240 n. 3, 246
    n. 15, 248 nn. 16–17, 248 n. 19
Shiner, R. 137 n. 61
Smith, N. D. 18 n. 5, 24 n. 18, 155 n.
    7, 169 n. 29, 180
Sorabji, R. 160 n. 13
Sprague, E. 1 n. 1, 21, 36

Sprute, J. 171 n. 32
Stalley, R. 101 n. 2
Stokes, M. C. 149 n. 3, 155 n. 6, 159
    n. 11, 161 n. 16, 168 n. 27
Strang, C. 187 n. 63, 188 n. 65
Szaif, J. 166 n. 24
Szlezák, T. 125 n. 43

Taylor, A. E. 242 n. 7, 245 n. 10
Taylor, C. C. W. 40 n. 38, 47 n. 52, 90
    n. 38, 91 n. 40, 256 n. 31
Tuckey, T. G. 35 n. 32
Tugendhat, E. 31 n. 23
Tuozzo, T. 258 n. 37

Vlastos, G. 19, 20 nn. 8–9, 23 n. 16,
    66 n. 13, 142 n. 73, 166 n. 25,
    171, 203 n. 14

Watson, G. 120 n. 40
Wellman, R. 35 n. 32
White, F. C. 162 n. 17, 163 n. 19
White, N. P. 216 n. 43, 224 n. 53, 236
    n. 69
Williams, B. A. O. 23 n. 17
Williams, C. J. F. 65 n. 12, 256 n. 33
Wilson, J. R. S. 187 n. 64
Woodruff, P. 131 n. 49
Woods, M. 101 n. 1

General Index

absolutism 20, 23, 24
acratic 47, 49, 102, 104, 105, 108, 110,
    111, 113, 117–20, 122, 143, 258,
    268, 269
afterlife 24, 54, 63, 89, 125, 263
agency 42–4, 47–9, 63, 65, 101, 104,
    106, 107, 109, 110–12, 114, 115,
    117, 121, 124, 130, 139, 141, 236,
    266–70, 272
agnosticism 24, 54
allegory 186–8
appetite 25, 36, 90, 91, 101–15,
    117–24, 127, 129, 130, 131, 134,
    138–41, 143, 146, 193, 242–4, 246,
    247, 259, 266, 267, 271, 272, 274
artefacts 180, 187–8
ascent 188, 191

Beauty 58, 76, 83, 128, 134, 140–6,
    151, 154, 159, 160, 165, 172, 184,
    251, 272
body 16–28, 34, 45, 51–60, 64, 65, 77,
    78, 85–91, 94, 95, 96, 99, 100,
    107, 125–30, 136, 140, 240–8,
    252, 255, 260, 274, 275

cave 164, 165, 173, 180, 183, 186–9,
    191, 192
cognition 14, 31, 32, 39, 49, 51, 59,
    60, 61, 65, 66, 68, 74–6, 80–3, 95,
    99, 110, 122, 123, 149, 151, 152,
    155, 156, 158, 160, 163, 164, 168,
    169, 171, 172, 174, 175, 177, 178,
    180–6, 188, 190, 193, 194, 199,
    200, 202, 203, 211, 217, 219, 221,
    222, 235, 242, 244, 252, 257, 264
cognitive states 39, 45, 46, 85, 155,
    191
colour 74, 75, 171, 172
conversion 188, 191, 262–4
corpse 46, 51, 52, 105, 108, 118, 119,
    275
crime 135, 203, 222, 223

death 16, 24, 26, 46, 51–6, 60, 65, 73,
    78, 90, 94, 125, 129, 140
deconstruction 28, 124, 131
Demiurge 240, 241, 244, 245, 249, 250
democracy 114, 116–18
desires 29, 30, 41–3, 47, 49, 55, 60, 87,
    88, 103, 104, 107, 110, 118–22,
    127, 128, 130, 131, 134, 139, 146,
    244, 250, 259, 261, 267–73
dialecticians 183, 185, 186, 189, 190
disembodied life 24–6, 45, 49, 50,
    54–66, 72–89, 96–8, 100, 115,
    124–31, 137–46, 150, 167, 179,
    194, 214, 236, 243, 244, 246, 253,
    263
divided line 164, 167, 180, 185–9
divine 24, 26, 27, 30, 86, 87, 89, 97,
    127, 128, 135, 136, 137, 140, 141,
    144, 187, 188, 214, 246, 247–54,
    266, 275
drink 91, 92, 101, 104, 111, 244

earth 97, 137

embodied life 24, 26, 29, 39, 45, 46,
    49, 50, 51, 54–6, 58–65, 73, 76–8,
    80, 84–8, 96–8, 109–17, 122–31,
    137–46, 151, 171, 178, 179, 186,
    192, 193, 194, 214, 220, 222, 237,
    238, 240, 243–7, 250–3, 259, 263,
    266, 271, 275

emotions 53, 106, 109, 138, 141, 243,
    247, 250, 267

encratics 105, 143, 144, 258

enslavement 143, 146

equality 70, 71, 73–5, 85, 92, 93, 96,
    167, 179

eschatology 26, 90

evil 15, 16, 17, 21, 63, 114, 122, 125,
    128, 213

eyewitness 203, 215, 222–5, 227

false belief 44, 162, 168, 215–25, 230,
    252, 253, 256, 262

falsity 41, 156, 255, 256–9

first principle 177, 179, 181, 182, 189

flux 201, 205

food 23, 43, 57, 92, 100, 101, 111, 161

friendship 133, 135, 146

geometry 35, 184

god 26, 28, 30, 51, 61, 85, 87, 126,
    128, 130, 137, 138, 142, 144,
    145, 178, 187, 188, 193, 199,
    213, 214, 240–2, 246, 248–50,
    266, 274

Good 28, 58, 129, 164, 165, 173–90,
    192, 193, 244, 273

government 114, 116, 117

Hades 24–6, 96

happiness 18, 20, 45, 60, 134, 239, 254

harmonious 27, 28, 112

health 18, 19, 21, 28

heaven 54, 114, 130, 137, 138, 140,
    236

hedonism 27, 40–2, 49, 254, 260–4

hedonist 41, 42, 49, 119, 254, 259,
    260–5

immaterialism 39, 53, 55, 76, 77,
    79, 80–9, 96, 102, 122, 123,
    129, 176, 180, 193, 194, 219,
    237, 244

immortality 24–6, 49, 50–66, 72, 76,
    77, 79, 85, 87, 90, 94–6, 97, 100,
    117, 124–6, 129–42, 184, 240,
    241, 246–8, 262–4

incontinence 40–2, 47, 62, 99, 103,
    104, 105, 108, 118, 120, 123, 245,
    246, 265

infallibility 82–4, 156, 158, 161, 163,
    164, 166, 186, 200, 202–7, 209,
    218, 221, 222

infinite regress 157, 216, 226, 235

injustice 20, 22, 26–8, 115, 125, 126,
    130, 252, 271, 273, 274

intellect 58, 171, 172, 251

interests 15–20, 23, 44, 45, 47, 62, 273

introspection 29, 30–3, 132

jury, 215, 222–7

justice, 20, 27, 76, 81, 116, 126, 128,
    130, 178, 253, 271, 272

Largeness 56, 67, 75, 93, 185

liver 241, 242, 244

love 36, 40, 107, 117, 127, 128, 132–5,
    137, 140–3, 146, 151, 154, 238,
    247, 272, 273

lover: see love

madness 15, 135, 137, 140, 141, 144

mathematicians 70, 182–6, 232

mathematics, 179, 188, 189, 221

mental state 31–3, 42, 47, 61, 82, 83,
    84, 161, 264

metaphysics 55, 56, 82, 99, 142, 195,
    225, 238, 249, 253

mind 26, 33–7, 43, 55, 57, 74, 75, 128,
    129, 134, 143, 169, 206, 207, 208,

210, 215, 225, 240, 242, 247, 250, 260, 263, 265, 271

morality 22–4, 33, 49, 60, 97, 113, 187, 213, 214, 229, 231, 267, 275

mortal 86, 87, 213, 239, 240, 241, 243, 246, 247–50, 267, 274

myth 25–7, 63, 90, 125, 134, 137, 139, 140, 144, 145

Oddness 168, 176

oligarchy 114, 116, 117

pain 15, 17, 21, 40, 53, 55, 105, 107, 146, 159, 222, 242, 252–7, 260, 261, 262, 265, 270, 271, 274

paradigms 48, 149, 167, 193, 220, 250

paradox, 15, 17, 20, 22, 27, 34, 62, 100, 123

partitioning of soul 99, 100, 102, 105, 108, 110, 127, 143, 265, 266, 267, 269, 270, 273

pleasure 19, 29, 40–4, 53, 116, 118–20, 134, 178, 179, 240, 245, 246, 251–67, 270–4

propositions 32, 37, 38, 45, 81, 82, 150, 160–3, 186, 189, 206, 211, 215, 217, 218

punishment 24, 26, 27, 130, 274

purification 62, 97, 128, 214, 245

racist 46–7

rational agents 43, 45, 47, 124

reasoning 43, 57, 97, 101–3, 106, 108, 110–12, 126, 127, 135, 158, 163, 217, 232, 243, 244, 269

recollection 38, 51, 65, 66, 68, 69, 72, 73, 76, 100, 140, 149, 167, 179, 185, 221

reincarnation 27, 50, 87, 95, 139, 140

relativism 201, 205, 207, 209, 213

representationalism 61, 81–5, 160, 179, 186, 193, 225, 257

salvation 96, 247

self-knowledge 15, 29, 31–6, 39, 132, 140, 145–7, 254

self-reflexivity 32, 35, 38, 39, 47, 51, 83, 84, 95, 96, 123, 130, 147, 193, 221, 222, 236, 237, 247

self-transformation 39, 115, 250

sense-perception 66, 69, 71–3, 127, 140, 167, 172, 195, 197, 198, 200–15, 226

sensible world 46, 55, 57, 74, 76, 89, 92, 120, 123, 149, 150, 163–5, 167, 172, 173, 176, 180, 184, 191, 192, 194, 195, 197, 198, 204, 210–14, 219, 225, 226, 231, 233

separation 26, 56–8, 64, 65, 78, 86, 148–50, 155, 162, 167, 176, 244, 248

sex 23, 100, 101, 106, 111, 133, 140, 141, 143

shame 15, 16, 106

Socratic paradoxes 15, 19, 53, 62, 263

sun 164, 165, 173, 174, 180, 181, 184, 187, 188

timocracy 114, 116

tripartition of soul 99, 100, 102, 103, 108, 109, 112, 113, 120, 127, 128, 132, 137, 139, 144, 239, 271, 273, 274, 275

true belief 44, 115, 149, 150, 151, 156, 157, 160, 162, 164, 166, 168, 190, 195, 199, 200, 203, 204, 208, 211, 212, 215–35, 245, 253

truth 56–8, 61, 82, 89, 103, 136, 139, 144–6, 156–60, 165, 174–82, 191, 193, 199, 201, 203–13, 222, 225, 232, 233, 246, 251, 256–8, 264, 272, 273

unjust actions, persons 15, 19, 20, 22, 26, 27, 75, 115, 117, 125, 128, 130, 131, 154, 213, 272

vice 25, 26, 105, 108, 111, 113, 119,
    122, 157, 177, 216, 226, 235, 268
virtue 20, 23, 24, 28, 33–5, 39, 51, 56,
    60, 63, 67, 72, 73, 80, 81, 87, 97,
    101, 102, 105, 114, 115, 121, 129,
    143, 144, 160, 178, 179, 188, 189,
    213, 214, 235, 242, 247, 256, 266,
    271, 272

volition 121, 122, 123, 130
wickedness 25–7, 87, 97, 213
wild animal 126, 139
wisdom 23, 34, 40, 58, 61, 80, 119,
    120, 127, 128, 174, 213, 238, 246,
    272
wrongdoing 19, 24, 27–9, 48, 122,
    124, 131, 140